ASPECTS *of*
the Eighteenth Century

ASPECTS *of*

⊰⊰⊰⊰⊰⊰⊰⊰⊰⊰⊰⊰⊰⊰⊰⊰⊰⊰⊰⊰⊰⊰⊰⊰⊰⊰⊰⊰⊰

In 1963 The Johns Hopkins University inaugurated an annual series of doctoral and postdoctoral seminars in the Humanities by devoting the year to studies of the eighteenth century. This volume is composed of the lectures delivered before that seminar by the distinguished extramural scholars who were invited to participate. In recognition of the complex and many-faceted nature of the eighteenth century, we intentionally neglected to focus on any single theme that might artificially bind the sessions together, and the chapters in this book display the rich variety of perspectives in which the culture of that age may be viewed.

On behalf of the Seminars I thank the contributors for having taken part in our meetings and for having made this volume possible.

E. R. W.

The Humanities Seminars
The Johns Hopkins University

the Eighteenth Century

➤➤➤➤➤➤➤➤➤➤➤➤➤➤➤➤➤➤➤➤➤➤➤➤➤➤➤➤

Edited by
EARL R. WASSERMAN

The Johns Hopkins Press
Baltimore, Maryland

Originally published, 1965
Second printing, 1967

This book was published with the assistance of
a grant from The Ford Foundation.

Contents

◄◄◄◄◄◄◄◄◄◄◄◄◄ ✿ ►►►►►►►►►►►►►

In Search of the Age of Reason

BY GEORGE BOAS

◄◄◄◄◄◄◄◄◄◄◄◄ ❋ ►►►►►►►►►►►►

Though it seems to be convenient to divide history into ages and periods and times, it is questionable whether the practice has not been abused. We have pretty nearly got rid of the Renaissance by splitting it up into the Early Renaissance, the High Renaissance, and the baroque, which breathed its last as the rococo. We have also found that there were proto-Renaissances occurring in what used to be the Middle Ages, the Carolingian Renaissance and the Renaissance of the twelfth century being the most important. Something similar has happened to the Romantic Period, which has been pushed forward into the twentieth century and backward at least to the time of Racine; whereas in my youth it was ushered in by the publication of the *Lyrical Ballads* (1798) and came to an end with the death of Scott (1832), which was also the date of the death of Goethe. This sort of thing was trouble enough, but added to the problem of chronological termini was that of determining the so-called spirit of such ages and movements. Nowadays we seldom use the term *Zeitgeist*, but we have little hesitation in using its equivalents. Thus terms like the Spirit of the Age, the Intellectual Climate, and the Time or Times have become common usage. As rough statistical generalizations denoting the modal interests of a chronological division, these words are harmless. But there is genuine harm when they are put to explanatory uses. There can be no denying the similarity of purpose among, for instance, the members of the group known as Encyclopedists, though no two of them agreed about everything. They agreed that education was a good, indeed the best, instrument for improving society, and d'Alembert agreed with Diderot that the manual and liberal arts were of equal importance. On most other points they disagreed. However to say that

1

they all shared the belief that education would give men certain blessings because the Age or the Times demanded these blessings — or because they were expressing the Spirit of the Times or were influenced by the intellectual climate — is sheer mythology if said seriously.[1] I can see how one can be influenced by an idea, either influenced in its favor or against it, but how one can be influenced by a time is too mysterious to be treated rationally.

Historians who are given to this sort of investigation have found that the eighteenth century was characterized by a strange variety of traits. It is a period which has been called rationalistic, sentimentalistic, optimistic and pessimistic, melancholy, necrophilic, contented with itself, and fond of nature. It has of course also been called the Enlightenment, the *siècle des lumières,* and the *Aufklärung.* But if the Spirit of the Times did not suffer from divided personality, these traits should turn out to be fairly general, and none of them do. And if its *Geist* is divided against itself, one had best find out how many *Geister* existed simultaneously. That is what my paper is hinting at, for to examine the matter in detail would require a book. Since one of the most popular labels for this century is the Age of Reason, I should like to see how far it is justified.

[1] Egon Friedell's *A Cultural History of the Modern Age,* trans. Charles Francis Atkinson (New York, 1931), will provide dozens of examples of explaining what individuals did as an effect of the spirit of their times. This is very much influenced by the type of philosophy which appeared in Spengler's *Decline of the West,* which in turn has Hegelian overtones. But it may be more profitable to cite one or two less prominent examples of this. See Lewis Mumford on the baroque in *The Culture of Cities* (New York, 1938), p. 77, where he writes, "The concept of the baroque, as it shaped itself in the seventeenth century, is particularly useful because it holds in itself the two contradictory elements of the age. First: the mathematical and mercantile and methodical side, expressed to perfection in its rigorous street plans, its formal city layouts, and its geometrically ordered landscape designs. And at the same time, in the painting and sculpture of the period, it embraces the sensuous, rebellious, anti-classical, anti-mechanical side, expressed in its clothes and its sexual life and its religious fanaticism and its crazy statescraft. Between the sixteenth and the nineteenth century these two elements existed together: sometimes acting separately, sometimes held in tension within a larger whole." The idea named in the verb "to express" is never clarified in this very interesting book, and the supposed conflict is common to all times. All that is said in ordinary terms is that the various types of interest existed contemporaneously. But one finds analogous expositions in books which lay down no formal principles of historical explanation. Wilfrid Mellers, for instance, in *The Sonata Principle* (London, 1957), after saying (p. xiii) that "No work of art can be 'explained' by reference to its historical connotations," immediately adds, "Every artist self-evidently 'reflects' the values and beliefs of his time; he has no choice in the matter, even though he may, like Swift, express them largely in negative terms. At the same time, any truly creative artist is also making those beliefs. It is true that we cannot fully understand Beethoven without understanding the impulses behind the French Revolution. It is equally true that we cannot fully understand the French Revolution without some insight into Beethoven's

But first we must take up the premise on which such practices seem to be built — the premise that a time is existentially different from the people who live in it. The time presumably causes people to think in a certain way, to express their thoughts in certain ways, and to value certain things more than others. But in the first place, how is one to discover what a time is without studying the men who lived in it? Take away Voltaire, Diderot, d'Alembert, d'Holbach, Helvétius, and their friends from the middle eighteenth century in France and what is left of the spirit of that time? Take away Johnson, Reynolds, Goldsmith, Garrick, Sheridan, Burke, Hogarth, and even Boswell from the latter half of the same century in England, and what would happen to the Age of George III?

Second, if something is to cause something else, it must be different from that something, and, if it is not, the effect is self-caused. At the risk of announcing truisms as if they were profundities, I should like to

---

music. We can see in his music those elements which are conditioned by his time (for they could not be otherwise) and yet are beyond the topical and local." Then (p. 7) after speaking of the rise of democratic ideas in Europe, he says, "The growth of eighteenth century sonata style is the musical expression of this new democracy. Indeed, the symphony orchestra itself reflected a new democratic ideal; Joseph von Holzmeister, in a speech delivered on the occasion of Haydn's admission to the Masonic Order, pointed out that Haydn had created a new order in the orchestra, 'for if every instrument did not consider the rights and properties of the other instruments, in addition to its own rights, if it did not often diminish its own volume in order not to do damage to the utterance of its companions, the end—which is beauty—would not be attained.' " Cf. Paul Henry Lang, *Music in Western Civilization* (New York, 1941), pp. 533, 570, 571. But we also come upon this sort of thing in histories of philosophy, where it is much more serious. I refer merely to J. H. Randall, Jr., *The Career of Philosophy* (New York, 1962), where we find that (p. 66), "Italian Aristotelianism was able to lead the European schools in the fifteenth and sixteenth centuries is due to . . . the settled commercial prosperity the Italian cities had now achieved"; that (p. 121) "when with the rise of industrialism social experience changed from an economy of thrift and scarcity to an economy of consumption, Protestant ethic shifted easily from its initial this-worldly asceticism to an ethic of pleasure and enjoyment and humanitarianism." But I have expatiated on this in my review of *The Career of Philosophy* that appeared in the *Journal of the History of Ideas*, XXIV (1963), 287–92. Though it is easy to read Hegel's philosophy of history into this type of exegesis, it comes more directly from Marx. For Hegel himself, as a reading of these sections of the *Phenomenology* that deal with the Enlightenment will show, was setting up an ideal conceptual model of a type of thinking which he implied might under certain conditions be exemplified in history. See Lanson's edition, pp. 383ff. May I add that one historian is outstanding in his rejection of this technique. I refer to Paul Hazard's *La Pensée européenne au XVIIIᵉ siècle* (Paris, 1946), where no attempt is made to fuse all the men of this period into one over-soul, though a great variety of individuals and interests are organized under specific headings, with due regard to their main preoccupations. Cf. James W. Johnson, "The Meaning of 'Augustan,' " *Journal of the History of Ideas*, XIX (1958), 507ff.

suggest that men are not made by the age in which they live but that, as far as cultural history is concerned, they make it. Our conception of their times comes from them, and there is no time, except on the calendar, save that found in and through them. We have not denied that groups of men may agree about certain matters. And if a group were found whose members agreed about everything within a given field, it might be said that they established an Age. But what one finds is that even when they do agree, they also disagree and that their disagreements are frequently about essential doctrinal matters. Samuel Johnson and David Hume, for instance, were both Tories. But Johnson not only disliked Hume personally, he disagreed with his ideas. He said at one time (Boswell's *Life of Johnson*, 1763, Everyman edition, I, 275), that "Hume and other sceptical innovators, are vain men, and will gratify themselves at any expence. Truth will not afford sufficient food for their vanity; so they have betaken themselves to error." And fourteen years later, when Boswell reported to him that Hume had no fear of death, he replied,

> It was not so, Sir. He had a vanity in being thought easy. It is more probable that he should assume an appearance of ease, than so very improbable a thing should be, as a man not afraid of going . . . into an unknown state, and not being uneasy at leaving all he knew. And you are to consider, that upon his own principle of annihilation he had no motive to speak the truth." (*Ibid.*, II, 114)

Burke was one of Johnson's best friends. He was called by him a "great man of nature" (*ibid.*, I, 320), an "extraordinary man" whose "stream of mind" was "perpetual" (*ibid.*, I, 619). This appreciation was reciprocated by Burke. Yet Johnson did not hesitate to disagree with Burke on the question of the American Revolution. We all know what Burke's sentiments were, but to his friend the Americans were "a race of convicts and ought to be thankful for any thing we allow them short of hanging" (*ibid.*, 1775, I, 526). Unfortunately his pamphlet *Taxation No Tyranny* is too long to be quoted and analyzed here, but anyone looking into it will see that his alliance with Burke did not lead to sharing his opinions *in toto*. In fact, as late as 1778 he shouted at Boswell, "I am willing to love all mankind, *except an American*," and, Boswell adds, "his inflammable corruption bursting into horrid fire, he 'breathed out threatenings and slaughter'; calling them, 'Rascals — Robbers — Pirates'; and exclaiming, he'd 'burn and destroy them' " (*ibid.*, II, 209). This sort of disagreement can be exemplified in any period.

In the third place, one sometimes forgets that philosophical positions, like political, religious, and even aesthetic positions, are taken because of a man's opposition to another position. If everyone had been a Tory, there would have been no Whigs, though there might have been splits within the Tory party caused by special questions. Two men might believe in monarchical government in England and yet violently disagree about the legitimacy of the rule of William III. Though Burke, again, was enchanted by the beauty of Marie-Antoinette and deplored her fate in one of the most fulsome pieces of oratory ever declaimed, he was not enchanted by absolute monarchy. His famous remarks about the French Revolution were made in opposition to a historical event and were based, to be sure, on a political philosophy that he had never before had occasion to articulate with such vehemence and eloquence. In short, it is as important to discover what a man is against as it is to discover what he is for. The preface to the *Lyrical Ballads* is admittedly a manifesto of one side of the Romantic aesthetics. But it is also a protest against traditional poetic diction and a protest which would not have made any sense had the poetic tradition not been fairly influential at the time of its publication. Its strength for that matter can be seen in the early poems of Byron, if any evidence of its survival is needed. Similarly, in seventeenth-century France, there were of course Cartesians, but there were also very outspoken anti-Cartesians, and what one group said was said in rebuttal to what the other proposed. Professor Henri Peyre has clearly demonstrated how unsystematic was that group of ideas which are called French classicism, and it requires a special purgation of inconsistencies to turn them into a doctrine. I do not deny that by selecting certain figures as typical, one can trace the history of the geometrical method in philosophy, just as by emphasizing certain of its aspects and supposed implications one can find it in Racine and even in Poussin. But neither Racine nor any other poet, Poussin nor any other painter, ever started out by drilling himself in the *Discours de la méthode*. Their Cartesianism is very dilute, as it was bound to be if it was to turn into an aesthetic doctrine. [2]

I think it will be found that in all the ages of which we have records, opinions and practices were responses to other opinions and practices when they were set forth in books and manifestoes. This is true even of the thirteenth century, hailed as the most unified of times. For though Aquinas, following Albertus Magnus, is nowadays thought of as its

[2] For a discussion of the influence of Cartesianism on the arts, see Emile Krantz, *Essai sur l'esthétique de Descartes* (Paris, 1882).

spokesman, there existed alongside of him the figure of Duns Scotus, and beside the two of them the equally influential figure of Bonaventura. It is just as important to unearth the clashes in opinion of these men as it is to insist upon their agreements. It would be absurd to deny that they were Catholics, but even an elementary history of medieval philosophy is forced to expound the differences among Catholic philosophers. There seems in fact always to be a Jefferson for every Hamilton, a Piccini for every Gluck, a Tennyson for every Browning, a Delacroix for every Ingres, as there was a Poussin to balance Rubens, a Roscellinus to balance William of Champeaux, and a Hippias to balance Socrates. I am not saying this because I believe in some historical law or a metaphysical principle of polarity. It need be nothing of the sort. The simple fact is that no one so far has appeared in human society whose opinions seem sound to all of his contemporaries, and, when opinions appear to be weak, someone is always there to say so. After all, even in the days of great papal authority there were heretics, and the heretics felt the need of speaking their minds, though they risked being burned alive and knew it. It took about 150 years for the Copernican Theory to be generally accepted, and the kinetic theory of heat, suggested by Bacon in the seventeenth century, was not accepted until the nineteenth. In scientific cases a theory makes its way by a man's dogged belief in it, by his attempting to refute one by one all of his opponents' refutations. In aesthetic matters the problem is more easily solved, for the factor of fatigue enters in.

Nor are there only two opposing groups in any period. Quite the contrary. Few men disagree with everything someone else has to say, and if Dr. Johnson disagreed with Voltaire's deism, he agreed with his attack on optimism. His refutation of Soame Jenyns is as strong as anything either in *Candide* or the poem on the Lisbon Earthquake. There was very little in Rousseau with which Diderot agreed, but he is in hearty agreement with Rousseau's individualism. So it went then as it goes now. Rather than absorb men into specimens of an ideology, would it not be better to admit that ideologies are composed of opinions that may or may not be held by any given man, regardless of the label which has been pasted on him by historians? For no man is all of a piece. The Horace Walpole of the *Castle of Otranto* does not seem to me to be the Horace Walpole of, for instance, the letters to Mme du Deffand, though I would not maintain that there was no similarity between them. One might compare the presentation which Macaulay makes of his character with that of F. L. Lucas[3] to realize how the complexities of human nature defeat classification. If one were to think of Walpole as merely the inventor of the Gothic novel, one would be hard put to it to understand why he took care of Tonton after the death of Mme du Deffand. But similarly, if one knew Rousseau only as the author of *La Nouvelle Héloïse*, one would never guess him to be the author also of the *Contrat social*. Who would guess that the Voltaire of the *Dictionnaire philosophique* had dedicated one of his tragedies to Pope Benedict XIV, as the *chef de la véritable religion?* If these suggestions were not plausible, little would be left for historians to do. What would be the grounds for all our reinterpretations if the men whose ideas we reinterpret were consistent?

In the fourth place, though certain catchwords become popular at certain times, it is clear that they are nothing more than catchwords and not the names of a pervasive interest. This appears with special clarity in such a book as Basil Willey's *Eighteenth Century Background*. It will be recalled that the catchword in this case is "nature," and, though Mr. Willey points out that an American scholar, otherwise unidentified, has distinguished many meanings of that term, yet he ventures to discuss nature as the prevailing interest of his period. The question immediately arises of whether there is such a thing as nature, which we all recognize, about which the eighteenth century had a number of opinions, or whether we are reading about the history of a word. And when the book is finished, one learns that he has been reading an amazing and erudite bit of historical semantics. For the word "nature," he says, meant the subject matter of science as opposed to the subject matter of theology and religion; it meant the state of nature as opposed to custom; it meant the true, i.e., the universal, as opposed to the false, the particular. In that form of meditation known as natural theology, the term meant whatever is described in natural science, mainly astronomy and physics, or what Mr. Willey neatly calls "Physico-theology." But here another assumption is introduced, and nature becomes good rather than evil, and the optimism of an Alexander Pope is inferred from natural theology. And it may not be superfluous to remind ourselves that before the book is ended, nature becomes the rural scene of Wordsworth, anticipated by such poets as Cowper, and is no longer the integrated system of moving bodies which formed the subject matter of the *Principia*

[3] See F. L. Lucas, *The Art of Living: Four Eighteenth Century Minds* (London, 1959), pp. 79ff., esp. pp. 104ff., which discuss Macaulay's comments on Walpole. Mr. Lucas has the advantage over many of his contemporaries in retaining his good sense even when dealing with men in whom it was conspicuously lacking.

Mathematica. The vernal woods, the lonely reapers, the primroses by the river's brim are not and cannot be made to be the Law of Gravitation.

Hence I say what Mr. Willey has given is not the history of an idea but the history of a word, of its changing denotations and connotations. And he has made an enviable job of it, too. But when one man says that the life according to nature is the life according to the dictates of the senses and another says that it is the life of reason, they are clearly not talking about the same thing, even though they declare that nature is the norm of good behavior. Two ideas are here expressed by the same term. The meaning of a term is not an idea which could possibly be true or false or even debated, except by men who insist that words have what they call real meanings as distinguished from those given by usage. The meaning of a term is a rule, an imperative, and, if you will, a state-ment of intention. When one uses "nature" in opposition to "art," or the natural in opposition to the supernatural, one undoubtedly has some idea in the back of one's mind which sets up an *argumentum ad hominem* to be utilized in ethical and aesthetic debates. For to those who believe that a life in accordance with nature is better than one which is dominated by custom, "nature" becomes a term denoting something factual and connoting something valuable. Thus if "nature" is defined as that set of harmonious laws decreed by God, no one will probably maintain that nature is inferior to, for example, art or custom. But if "nature" is defined as man's animal instincts, then fewer people will agree that it is better to follow nature than to elevate oneself above it. In attempting to de-scribe the character of a period in terms of general or pervasive ideas or of its modal desires and aversions, one always has to go behind the sacred words which are fashionable during the period being studied to try to discover what those words actually denoted. Their connotation can be studied later.

Let me now turn to that popular label of the eighteenth century, *The Age of Reason.* Rationalism, as a word, according to the *NED*, began by denoting a doctrine of theology and proliferated into meaning also a doctrine of women's clothing. From the reason embodied in God's laws exemplified in astrophysics to the reason embodied in costume is a long distance to travel. But when one realizes that both Voltaire and Joseph de Maistre found the source of all truth in the reason, one sees that another problem has arisen. To abbreviate matters, let us say that by the close of the eighteenth century in France the clash in opinion was not only rationalism versus sentimentalism, but the reason of the individ-ual versus the reason of the group, alias, tradition. De Maistre and

Bonald were convinced that all truth was rational, a conviction which was to be reinforced by Pius IX in his encyclical *Qui pluribus* (1846). But the rationality in question was that of the race as a whole expressed in language and, as I said, tradition. This, except for the religious element, was analogous to the doctrine of Reid, known as the philosophy of common sense. It can be shown, I think, to go back to the medieval belief in the natural light (*lumen naturale*), and it was therefore a revival rather than an innovation. Now neither Voltaire nor any of his associates, as far as I know, denied that if every man were rational, all men would agree, though the conclusion did not necessarily follow. But in the use of reason every man was independent of every other, nor was there any impulsion to seek agreement with something called tradition.

In this, however, the rationalistic individualist was more in accord with the sentimental individualist, like Rousseau and even Robespierre, than with the rationalistic traditionalist. And at the same time De Maistre was more in accord with Voltaire than he was with Rousseau or, for that matter, with Chateaubriand. Therefore, to label the eighteenth century the Age of Reason is either simply to say that the word "reason" was popular in certain circles as "nature" was or to overlook the ambiguities of the doctrine itself. For besides the two interpretations mentioned above, there was also the doctrine that opposed reason to the heart, or in Germany to the *Verstand*. The *Verstand* meant the processes used in reaching scientific conclusions; the *Vernunft*, though translated into English as "reason," denoted some higher and more glorious kind of insight.[4] Then there was that form of rationalism which denied the efficacy of faith or, indeed, of its need. If one may call doctrines of these sorts rationalism, then the eighteenth century is the Age of Reason only in the sense that the word was frequently used at that time.

If now one means by rationalism doctrines which depend on purely dialetical methods of reaching the truth, one has to go back to the seventeenth century to find them. It is men like Descartes and Spinoza and Leibniz who are the traditional rationalists, and the only thinkers of that sort in the eighteenth century are their disciples, the outstanding one being Wolff. By laying down supposedly self-evident or otherwise indubitable premises and deducing from them their consequences, one built a system of philosophy, psychology, ethics, and, in one case (that of Baumgarten), aesthetics, which was believed to be incontrovertible. This was reasoning *more geometrico* and, though it was a method pursued in some

[4] See A. O. Lovejoy, *The Reason, the Understanding, and Time* (Baltimore, 1961).

of the schools well into the eighteenth century,[5] it was precisely that method which the outstanding eighteenth-century philosophers rejected. The rejection was initiated by John Locke, who died in 1704; it was zealously adopted by his successors, Berkeley and Hume, and the one warrant for calling their philosophies empirical, as the histories do, is their belief, far from justified, that their first principles were garnered from experience. Even the Platonists of the eighteenth century in England thought they were basing their systems on experience, not on abstract rational principles. And when we come to France, we find that the two great names among the Encyclopedists and their friends were Bacon and Locke. It is true that the *Encyclopédie* dates from 1750, but even as early as Bayle, who died in 1706, we find a repudiation of the rationalistic method. Bayle was not more interested in logical inconsistency than he was in factual inconsistency, by which I mean inconsistency with the established facts of experience. His skepticism was aimed at authority as a source of truth and at uncriticized traditions. If, however, by reason we mean the use of our reasoning powers, then all ages are ages of reason, from that of Thales down to that of Sartre.

A moment's reflection will also justify calling this period the Age of Sentiment. In England we have men like Shaftesbury (died in 1713) and Hutcheson (died in 1746) whose ethical theories were founded on nothing more than feeling. And what is English hedonism if not a sentimental philosophy? The vogue of the word "sentimental" was such that we find the *NED* quoting Lady Bradshaugh writing to Richardson in 1749, "What in your opinion is the meaning of the word *sentimental*, so much in vogue among the polite. . . . I am frequently astonished to hear such a one is a *sentimental* man; we were a *sentimental* party; I have been taking a *sentimental* walk." And of course we all know about a famous sentimental journey that extended the use of the term until at least 1768. Nor must it be forgotten that the discipline known as aesthetics was elaborated by Baumgarten in 1739, and, if it was called *aesthetics*, it was because its inventor situated the basis for our judgments of beauty in our senses and feelings. It is unlikely that Carey in his *Namby-Pamby* (1725) would have written a parody of Philips's *Distrest Mother*, unless people were moved by it.[6] This was also the period, as we all know, when melancholy,

[5] I have in my library a MS that dates from the end of the eighteenth century and which was probably written by a pupil in a seminary in Angoulême. It consists of lectures which were presumably taken down, as the custom was, from dictation, and the thought is straight Cartesianism.

[6] E. F. Carritt, *A Calendar of British Taste* (London, n.d [1948?]), p. 166. Cf. the quotation from Steele which immediately follows.

tombstone poetry, weeping willows, the sublime and the awful were stylish, not the clarity and calm of a Boileau. [7] One could sustain the thesis that sentimentalism in all its forms was a reaction against the seventeenth-century cult of simplicity, logicality, and stoicism. But, I admit, this would be as unbalanced as its antithesis.

For I suspect, though I cannot prove, that for every sentimentalist in the eighteenth century there is an anti-sentimentalist. Think of Rousseau. A generation later his thesis in the fourth book of *Emile* passed into technical philosophy in the works of Immanuel Kant. But at the time Rousseau was writing, he found powerful antagonists among his compatriots, and he himself felt constrained to leave the circle of the Encyclopedists because of incompatibility of doctrine as well as of temperament. As for his love of solitude, we have the famous passage from Johnson, as given by Boswell, in which he thunders — or should I say fulminates? —"If man were a savage, living in the woods by himself, this might be true; but in civilized society we all depend upon each other, and our happiness is very much owing to the opinion of mankind" (*Life*, I, 272). And in 1766, when Boswell told him he had been seeing Rousseau "in his wild retreat," Johnson said,

> I think him the worst of men; a rascal, who ought to be hunted out of society, as he has been. Three or four nations have expelled him; and it is a shame that he is protected in this country. . . . Rousseau, Sir, is a very bad man. I would sooner sign a sentence for his transportation, than that of any felon who has gone to old Bailey these years. (*Ibid.*, I, 317)

As for melancholy, sublimity, the picturesque, the wild, we have Addison's delight, in his *Remarks on Italy*, [8] at seeing a plain after seeing the Alps. But we also have J. Forrester on Whitehall:

> That true politeness we can only call,
> Which looks like Jones's fabrick at Whitehall . . .
> It fills the mind with rational delight,
> And pleases on reflection, as at sight. [9]

[7] See F. Baldensperger, *Etudes d'histoire littéraire* (Paris, 1907), the essays on "Young et ses 'nuits' en France" (p. 54), for the vogue of this melancholy poem in France.
[8] Carritt, *A Calendar of British Taste*, p. 139.
[9] *Ibid.*, p. 210

Gray wrote to his mother in 1739 from Italy, "The country of Lombardy, hitherto, is one of the most beautiful imaginable; the roads broad and exactly straight, and on either hand vast plantations of trees, chiefly mulberries and olives."[10] Hume says about beauty, "In painting . . . a figure which is not justly balanced is disgraceful . . . the principal part of personal beauty is an air of health and vigour and such a construction of members as promises strength and activity."[11] Walpole wrote to West in 1739, "The last four [days] in crossing the Alps. Such uncouth rocks, and such uncomely inhabitants! My dear West, I hope I shall never see them again."[12] And need I mention that Warton wrote an *Ode to Health* in 1746 and Collins' one to simplicity? One could go on and make an impressive inventory of pieces ridiculing melancholy, the Gothic ruins, the awfulness of cascades and forests; but one could also make such an inventory of pieces in praise of them.

After all, this is the period of Chardin's paintings of children and domestic interiors, all quiet and simple, of Boucher's happy mythologies which turn Venus into a *cocotte* or a royal mistress, of Gabriel du Saint-Aubin and of L-L. Boilly who continued the tradition well into the nineteenth century. But the moment we see the eighteenth-century spirit objectified in such painters, we come upon the melancholy of Watteau and the wistfulness of some of Fragonard. We have the *Carceri* of Piranesi balanced by the sunny ruins of his friend, Hubert Robert. If in Spain Goya was painting his *Disasters of War* and his *Caprichos*, in Venice Guardi was painting his spirited and delightful scenes of fashionable life, while in England Reynolds was at work glorifying the ladies of the nobility and the stage. Goldoni was not only a contemporary of Carlo Gozzi and Metastasio, but also of Alfieri. The eighteenth century, along with its Voltaire, Diderot, and d'Holbach, also had its mystics, like Pasqualis Martinez, Swedenborg, Lavater, and Saint-Martin; its adventurers and rogues — Casanova, the Comte de Saint-Germain, and Cagliostro — who may have used their reason but were hardly rationalists; its Bernardin de Saint-Pierre, its Marquis de Sade, its Choderlos de Laclos, its Restif de la Bretonne, none of whom were on

---

[10] *Ibid.*, p. 218. Cf. Gray's ridicule of the poetry of melancholy in his famous letter to Walpole (1739), in *Elegant Epistles, being a Copious Collection of Familiar and Amusing Letters* (London, 1803).

[11] Carritt, *A Calendar of British Taste*, p. 218.

[12] *Ibid.*, p. 221.

the rationalistic side of the barriers.[13] Cowper's *The Task* came out in 1785, four years before the storming of the Bastille, Blake's *Songs of Innocence* four years later. David was the official painter of the Revolution. Could he be merged with the School of Greuze?

Another feature of the eighteenth century which is easily overlooked by students of literature is the contribution made at this time to natural science. Surely men like Réaumur, Lavoisier, Lagrange, Coulomb, Buffon, Volta, Spallanzani, Galvani, Haller, Cavendish, Herschel, Black, Priestley, Rumford, Jenner, Edwards the ornithologist, and Linnaeus are as important in determining the temper of a period as are poets, philosophers, and painters. Each of these men made discoveries which were far-reaching in their effects. As a group they annihilated what was left of alchemy, astrology, and traditional therapeutics, to select only the best known of their achievements. The eighteenth century saw the birth of modern biology, modern medicine, and modern chemistry, and it saw this because its scientists had rejected the rationalistic methods of the past in favor of observation and experimentation. And while all this was going on, phrenology, physiognomonics, and applications of what was known as animal magnetism were also popular.

Again, it was the eighteenth century during which an attempt was made to understand the historical origins of modern society, an attempt weakened by speculation, to be sure, but which in its independence of clerical authority laid the foundations for a philosophy of history. And no account of this period is complete without some mention of men like Vico, Herder, and Condorcet. Whatever may be said against the kind of evidence which they utilized, their naïveté, if you will, they did make one new assumption in common, that the past was not like the present. History to them was not just a repetition of universal and eternal human traits, but as times changed they believed that men's minds and ways of thinking and living changed too. Changes in history went deeper than modifications in clothing and speech. The laws which were formulated and the correlations which were made between geography and climate on the one hand and psychology on the other were faulty of course. But then the very fact that a search for law was made, as well as an attempt to

---

[13] A list of eighteenth-century rogues and adventurers would include at least Talvia, Schwerin, Saint-Germain, Casanova, Cagliostro, Trenck, and certainly the Chevalier d'Eon. For a partial bibliography, see Hazard, *La Pensée européenne au XVIIIᵉ siècle*, III, 102. Cf. Stefan Zweig, *Master Builders* (New York, 1939), Pt. 3, pp. 564ff. The eighteenth century also continued the magical traditions of the sixteenth and seventeenth centuries. See especially E. M. Butler, *Ritual Magic* (New York, 1959), pp. 225ff. and Kurt Seligmann, *The Mirror of Magic* (New York, 1948), pp. 453ff.

understand the varieties of human nature, was something to be remembered.

It is unfortunately true that these three figures were those mainly responsible for giving us the idea of ages and times, a gift of dubious value. The concept itself goes back, as everyone knows, to Hesiod. But the inhabitants of his ages disappeared at the ends of their periods, and new starts were made. The story of the Hesiodic ages and those like them has been told elsewhere and requires no repetition here. The Christian writers had at first only two ages, that before the Fall and that after, but later on the matter became more complicated. In St. Augustine[14] we find seven ages corresponding to the seven days of creation. But the differentia of each age was exclusively moral. In Vico, the three ages he called the mythological, the heroic, and the human differed in customs, language, jurisprudence, authority, reasoning, judgment, and general culture. By use of the comparative method Vico thought he could identify the occurrence of an age in any of the cultures which he knew, and it must be said that, though his evidence is both ambiguous and at times fictitious, Vico is no worse off in that respect than some of our own contemporaries, such as Spengler. He granted that in the later ages there were survivals from the earlier and hence was realistic enough to see that an age is made up of people and not of abstractions. In fact, of the three philosophers of history I have mentioned, he strikes me as the most sober. A reading of the *Scienza Nuova* should convince any fair-minded reader that in spite of certain fantastic details, his study of ancient jurisprudence had disciplined Vico's mind. But aside from this, two features stand out, the relative homogeneity of each age and the presence of its distinctive traits in all of its activities.

It is these two assumptions which gave birth to cultural history and which have led later scholars to look for unity rather than diversity, to neglect those traits which are inharmonious with their hypotheses as minor or exceptional, and above all to deal almost exclusively with the thoughts and doings of those whom they call representative men. And if Kant is right in thinking of the Enlightenment as "man's release from self-imposed tutelage," then the notion of the Enlightenment goes back to Vico. For Vico pointed out that as the human or third stage develops, it increases in its clarity of ideas. This is not happiness; it is simply illumination, understanding. Like Herder later, Vico speaks of human development under the metaphor of the biological growth. Having accepted

---

[14] For the legend of the ages in a medieval setting, see George Boas, *Essays on Primitivism and Related Ideas in the Middle Ages* (Baltimore, 1948), pp. 177ff.

this as fundamental, it was inevitable that he include senility and death in his narrative. In his 66th Axiom he says, "Men first feel needs, then look for the useful, then observe the fitting, then delight in pleasure, whereupon they become dissolute in luxury and finally turn to folly and waste their substance." This depressing picture of human history is not explained through any relation of man to God, as it would have been in St. Augustine. The one general principle which is clear is that history is human history and is a story of progress from bad to better only in the sense that clear ideas are better than nebulous ones, that true and general ideas are better than false and limited ones, and that the derivation from such ideas of philosophic laws is better than fables and myths. This is a straightforward assertion of the terminal or inherent value of knowledge. In short, for Vico knowledge in itself is better than ignorance, science is better than myth, regardless of pleasure or comfort.

If my interpretation of Vico is correct, one has here an idea of enlightenment which is closer to that of Kant than to that of Herder or the Encyclopedists. For Herder, it is true, something called Humanity was the goal of human history, and moreover it grew as a plant grows. Otherwise there were important differences between the two men. For reason in Herder's eyes is a tool which serves to liberate man from his linkage to the physical environment. Its full actualization was to be in the form of religion. Reason (*Vernunft*) was superior to understanding (*Verstand*), in spite of the fact that the latter proves the existence of God and the necessity of the former. Enlightenment, if I may paraphrase Herder, comes from the realization of all men's potencies, those which are expressed in the arts as well as in the sciences. Hence it should not be identified with the reason that was the special interest of the Encyclopedists. To Diderot and d'Alembert reason was the *Verstand*, scientific reasoning, based on facts furnished men by observation and closely related to the manual arts. It was, moreover, something which would provide human beings with the means of being happy, in the terrestrial sense of enjoying life. The moral improvement which it would induce through education was welfare, giving men food, clothing, physical and spiritual satisfaction. This was a much more *terre à terre* program than any envisioned by Herder. And when one examines the motives guiding these men, one sees that the freedom which enlightenment was to produce according to the Encyclopedists was freedom from ecclesiastical authority, whereas for Herder it was freedom from Mediterranean culture, as far as the Germans were concerned, and freedom for every nation to be itself. That nations had selves was not emphasized by the French, though variations in national character had long been a subject of remark.[15] Their cultural history and language went back to Rome; their religion to Saint Dionysius the Areopagite; their art to Latin Gaul. But it was difficult for Herder to take such a point of view. Germany as a nation did not exist in 1784; the popular mythology was not that of Hesiod and the other ancient mythographers; the dominant religion was Protestant and dated only from the sixteenth century; and the only monarch to whom they could all pretend to be loyal was either a local princeling or the Holy Roman Emperor. In practical terms what Herder was doing was what Fichte was to attempt later and with more success, namely to create in the minds of his readers a sense of their participation in a German soul that owed nothing to a Latin soul.

It is such novel problems which characterize a period as much as the ways in which they are solved. For example, in the fourth book of Rousseau's *Emile* we find the Savoyard Vicar maintaining that the results of natural science would deprive us of a belief in God, freedom, and immortality. His way out of this difficulty was to turn to feeling as a justification of such beliefs. He did not say that any feeling whatsoever was as good a witness to the truth as any other. But he did say that what he called the heart bore witness to these three truths. Now Europeans had for centuries been educated to believe in them. Their belief involved accepting certain assertions of fact which require no documentation here. They were promulgated by an institution that was protected by the state and had a monopoly on education. To deny their truth was to risk imprisonment and even death. But for our purposes it is enough to point out that the problems discussed were given to French thinkers by tradition, in exactly the same way as the problem of squaring the circle or that of the ultimate constitution of matter. They were not

---

[15] Though this in all probability goes back to the distinction between Greeks and barbarians, and reappears here and there in the Middle Ages and the Renaissance, it certainly was a preoccupation of some of the eighteenth-century writers. For this period, see especially Adrien Baillet, *Jugemens des savans, revus, corrigés, et augmentés par M. de la Monnoye* (Paris, 1722), Vol. I, Ch. vii, pp. 122ff. See also the Abbé Yart as quoted in Baldensperger, *Etudes d'histoire littéraire*, p. 60. But this type of thing continued into our own times. The young Vernon Lee, in her delightful *Studies in Eighteenth Century Italy* (2nd ed.; Chicago, 1908), p. 276f., in describing the court of Charles VI, mentions French elegance and levity, German coarseness and heaviness, oriental splendor and misery, and Italian pride and love of display. This was written in 1881 and retained in the edition of 1907. National characters were sometimes, at least in Italy, split up into local characters, as in France the Normand and the Auvergnat and Gascon were thought of as having special traits not generally French. So we have Pulcinella, Pantaleone, Meneghino, the *Dottore*, Brighella, and Truffaldino standing for certain cities. In the fixing of national types, cf. Hazard, *La Pensée européenne au XVIIIᵉ siècle*, II, 226 and 235.

suddenly invented by someone who had a fertile imagination. The rise of new problems is in itself a historical problem which so far has not been solved. But in this case the problem was to find acceptable answers to questions based on beliefs that the majority of men sustained. Rousseau was right in maintaining that if one accepted the principles of scientific method as then interpreted, one would come neither upon God nor an immortal soul nor a free will. These ideas did not follow from the indestructiblity of matter or universal determinism. He was probably wrong in thinking that feeling could supply premises that would be generally accepted, for it is too well known that men vary in what they feel to be true. But when feelings have been directed by religious instruction, they probably become general by the time men reach the age of putting them into words. Unfortunately we are too unwilling to assume that men were once children in the hands of teachers. We talk about them as adults with pure untrained and unindoctrinated minds. So in the eighteenth century, as in our own time, writers had a tendency to look for an aboriginal man who was common to all men. They all had a tendency to believe that variations in belief or even in customs, likes, and dislikes were accidents of a homogeneous substance called Humanity. If it occurred to any of the philosophers of the period that if you removed the accidents the substance would disappear, I have not come upon his books. Oddly enough they were willing to grant this in the case of material objects, but not in the case of men. Man before the Fall, man in a state of nature variously described, was the substance; man as he is here and now the problem.

It was not until the end of the century that the search for essential humanity took a new turn, though there were intimations of the development earlier. By the time of Bonald and de Maistre it appeared that reason was not the social cement which had been sought for so long, if one was thinking of the reason of individuals. It was now, as we have said, the reason of the race as found in tradition, expressed in language, which would give us the clue to truth. In short, mankind was thought of as a collective unity, and, since one could not put one's hands on it by the usual techniques of that period, one turned to something that was recorded and whose duration had been long enough to be impressive. That was Catholicism. No one item in it could be held in isolation from all the others. But as a whole it was truth itself. One must not, as de Maistre said, rely on the authority of evidence, but on the evidence of authority. Authority is not capricious; it expresses the rationally consistent knowledge of the race as a whole.

The notion that men were cells in the body politic was of course anticipated. The works of both Vico and Herder were based on that premise. It was, moreover, one of the most influential metaphors of our period. As early as 1750 Turgot had outlined a course of intellectual history in three stages which, except for the words he used, were identical with those that Comte was to promulgate in 1822 and thereafter.[16] Turgot's speech was not printed until 1808, but it was heard much earlier, and we may believe that coming from such a source, it was not without effect. In any event the habit of thinking of all culture as passing through progressive stages of growth could not have been as startling an idea as it might seem, inasmuch as some of its details had already been discussed. What was startling was the pervasiveness of change.

However one defines the Age of Reason, however revolutionary and anti-authoritarian one estimates its spirit to have been, it should be noted that neither the Roman Catholic nor the Anglican nor the Lutheran communions ceased their ministrations in 1750. Moreover, in England, men like Burke and Johnson and Goldsmith, as much earlier Pope and Addison, continued to believe in the religion and philosophy of their forefathers. In spite of Voltaire the Church was not crushed, and as soon as Napoleon became Emperor, the short-lived educational program of the *Idéologues* was ended. If rationalism in the sense of the analysis of ideas was the platform of the French Enlightenment, it proved a very shaky one indeed. At most it survived for about ten years.[17] In Germany the *Aufklaerung* of Herder and Jacobi, of Hamann, if he is to be considered an *Aufklaerer*, was really anti-intellectualistic. None of them would have advocated acting under the guidance of those principles bestowed upon us by natural science rather than by insight. Lessing's *Education of the Human Race* (1780), like Mendelssohn's *Phaidon* (1767), was soon swamped by the more mysterious writings of the early Romantics.

In short, we may as well say, however dogmatically, that when one is in search of an age, one ends with human beings. And if the history of philosophy contributes anything to the investigation, it is that two men may interpret the same idea in their own individual ways. We see this happening today in the case of Marxism, psychoanalysis, existentialism, and surrealism, to mention only four programs. All existentialists, for instance, may say that existence is prior to essence, but that does not

[16] See George Boas, *French Philosophies of the Romantic Period* (Baltimore, 1925), pp. 263ff., for the development of Turgot's schema.

[17] See F. Picavet, *Les Idéologues* (Paris, 1891), pp. 32ff., for the foundation and fortunes of the *Ecoles Normales* and *Centrales*.

turn Professor Tillich into Jean-Paul Sartre. Similarly, all psychoanalysts may say that unconscious determinants of overt behavior are more potent than conscious, but two of Freud's immediate associates, Jung and Adler, disagreed on how and why experiences are repressed. I conclude, then, with what the most naïve reader would have realized at the outset, namely that the eighteenth century, like all others, was made up of men, not of over-individual spirits, and that movements and ideas can be understood only as they are represented and manifested in men.

The Malleability of Man
in Eighteenth-Century Thought

BY J. A. PASSMORE

◄·◄◄◄◄◄◄◄◄◄◄◄ ☼ ►►►►►►►►►►►►

"Of all the men we meet with," John Locke wrote in his *Some Thoughts Concerning Education* (1690), "nine parts of ten are what they are, good or evil, useful or not, by their education. It is that which makes the great difference in mankind" (§ 1). The cautious limitations—"nine parts out of ten," "the *great* difference in mankind"—should certainly be noted. In treating the mind of the pupil as if it were "white paper, or wax, to be moulded and fashioned as one pleases" (§ 216), Locke's educational theory, he confesses, oversimplifies. "Each man's mind has some peculiarity," he goes so far as to admit, "as well as his face, that distinguishes him from all others; and there are possibly scarce two children, who can be conducted by exactly the same method" (§ 216). But although the child has an innate temperament, he has not an innate moral character. Born active or lethargic, vigorous or slow, gay or "pensive and grave" (§ 66), he is not born good or bad.

Approaching *Some Thoughts Concerning Education* from the standpoint of the first book of Locke's *An Essay Concerning Human Understanding*, one at first tends to assume that such phrases as "white paper, or wax" are particularly directed, as they were in the *Essay*, against innate ideas. No doubt they are in part; Locke would certainly have wished to deny that the knowledge the teacher communicates to the child is in any sense already present in the child's mind. But in his *Some Thoughts Concerning Education* he is only marginally interested in the communication of knowledge. "It is virtue," he writes, "direct virtue, which is the hard and valuable part to be aimed at in education" (§ 70)—and the child is to be made virtuous not by being taught moral principles but by habituation. "Pray remember, children are not to be taught by rules, which will be always slipping out of their memories. What you think necessary for them to do, settle in them by an indispensable practice" (§ 66). The crucial importance of Locke's *Some Thoughts Concerning Education,* or so I wish to suggest, lies not so much in its rejection of innate ideas as in its rejection of original sin.

That Locke was greatly concerned to reject the doctrine of original sin is sufficiently apparent from his theological writings. He reverts to an old heresy, condemned by the Council of Orange in 529, to the effect that, in the Council's words, "Only the death of the body, the wages of sin, was transmitted through one man to the whole human race, and not sin also, the death of the soul."[1] In *The Reasonableness of Christianity* (1695) Locke defends this heresy thus:

> Nobody can deny, but that the doctrine of the gospel is, that death came on all men by Adam's sin; only they differ about the signification of the word death: for some will have it to be a state of guilt, wherein not only he, but all his posterity was so involved, that every one descended of him deserved endless torment, in hell-fire. I shall say nothing more here, how far, in the apprehensions of men, this consists with the justice and goodness of God . . . but it seems a strange way of understanding a law, which requires the plainest and directest words that by death should be meant eternal life in misery.[2]

Locke's *The Reasonableness of Christianity* is based upon his reading of the Gospels. He was at once attacked by John Edwards in *Some Thoughts Concerning the Several Causes and Occasions of Atheism Especially in the Present Age* (1695). Edwards condemned Locke for ignoring the Epistles and argued that he could not possibly reconcile his interpretation of the Fall with Paul's teachings. Locke's *Paraphrases of the Epistles of St. Paul* (1705–7) took up Edwards' challenge. In a crucial passage of his Epistle to the Romans (5:12), Paul had written: "Wherefore, as by one man sin entered into the world, and death by sin; and so death passed upon all men, for that all have sinned." This obviously presented Locke with a problem; he overcomes it by suggesting that "all have sinned" must be taken to

---

[1] Canon II. Quoted from Henry Bettenson, *Documents of the Christian Church* (Oxford, 1943), p. 86.

[2] *The Works of John Locke,* (12th ed.; London, 1824), Vol. 6, p. 6.

mean that all have become mortal.[3] The very violence of this interpretation demonstrates the force of Locke's conviction that the doctrine of original sin was an evil to be rooted out.

So too, Pelagius had thought. In the year 400 A.D., when the monk Pelagius made his way to Rome, he was appalled by the immorality he there encountered. Like many another after him, he blamed the prevalence of immorality on the Augustinian interpretation of Christianity. The doctrine that man can act well only with the aid of divine grace sapped, he thought, man's moral energies. "Nothing good and nothing evil," he had argued with Augustine, "on account of which we are deemed either laudable or blameworthy, is born with us, but is done by us: for we are born not fully developed, but with a capacity for either conduct; we are formed naturally without either virtue or vice; and previous to the action of our own proper will, the only thing in man is what God has formed in him."[4]

That sounds very like Locke. But there is an important difference. Pelagius refers to "the action of our own proper will." In the subsequent history of Pelagianism and semi-Pelagianism, in its struggle with Augustinian Christianity, it is about the nature of this "proper will" and its relation to God's grace that controversy raged. The history of moral theology in the period between the twelfth and the seventeenth century can largely be written in terms of that controversy—of Pelagian reactions against the Augustinian emphasis on man's helplessness, and of the Augustinians' reactions against, in their judgment, the humanistic exaggerations of Pelagianism. Locke cuts through the whole controversy. A man can act freely, he admits, in the sense that he does not always pursue *immediate* pleasure or *immediate* pain. But this freedom is something he has to learn; he is no more born free, as Pelagius had thought, than he is born depraved. "It seems plain to me," Locke writes in *Concerning Education*, "that the principle of all virtue and excellency lies in a power of denying ourselves the satisfaction of our own desires, where reason does not authorize them. This power is to be got and improved by custom, made easy and familiar by an early practice" (§ 38). Notice the phrase, "*got* and improved": we become free, capable of resisting our desires, by habituation, we are not born free by nature. (For Locke, it is the man, not the will, that is free.)

So Locke rejects Pelagianism, for which man is born free, just as he

---

[3] *Works*, Vol. 7, p. 323.

[4] As translated by Peter Holmes from Augustine's *On the Grace of Christ and on Original Sin*, II, 14, in *The Works of Aurelius Augustine*, Vol. XII (London, 1874).

rejects Augustinianism, for which he is born depraved. Nor is he any happier with that other, stronger, anti-Augustinian thesis that man is born with a natural tendency toward goodness. One finds it in some measure in Cudworth, for whom "there is . . . a principle of common sympathy in everyone, that makes everyone to have another being besides his own private selfish particularity." Man is corrupt, in Cudworth's view, because he is not wholly governed by that principle of common sympathy —the working of God in man—by which he "looks upon himself as a member lovingly united to the whole system of all intellectual beings, as one animal, or as concerned in the good and welfare of all besides himself," [5] not because that principle does not exist within him. Richard Cumberland, similarly, had maintained that "there are in mankind, considered as animal-beings only, propensities of benevolence towards each other." [6] This was to become a standard eighteenth-century doctrine, but Locke will have none of it. In a marginal note to a copy of a tract by Thomas Burnet, he sums up succinctly: "Men have a natural tendency to what delights and from what pains them. This universal observation has established past doubt. But that the soul has such a tendency to what is morally good and from evil has not fallen under my observation, and therefore I cannot grant it." [7]

How then does man become a moral agent, and how does he fall into sin, if he has no natural tendency to goodness, none to depravity, and no inherent free will? In the case of sin, Pelagius had suggested that it was essentially a bad habit. "There is no other cause of the difficulty we find in doing well, but the long-continued customs of sin, which begin to grow upon us in childhood, and little by little corrupt us." [8] Montaigne, too, had seen in custom the source of vice: "I find that our greatest vices make their first habit in us, from out infancy, and that our chief government and education lieth in our nurse's hands." [9] What is striking in Locke's *Concerning Education* is that it makes such habituation by "government and education" the source of our virtues as well as our vices.

Locke does not simply mean, it should be observed, that by habituation the child can be taught to behave *as if* he were virtuous. So much any

[5] Brit. Mus. Add. MSS. 4983, 83 (quoted and discussed in J. A. Passmore, *Ralph Cudworth* [Cambridge, 1951], p. 72).

[6] *A Philosophical Enquiry into the Laws of Nature* [first published 1672], trans. John Towers (Dublin, 1750), p. 211.

[7] Quoted in A. Campbell Fraser's edition of Locke's *Essay*, p. 67n, from Noah Porter's "Marginalia Lockeana," *New Englander and Yale Review*, July, 1887.

[8] *A Letter to Demetrias*, Ch. 8, as quoted in Nigel Abercrombie, *The Origins of Jansenism* (Oxford, 1936), p. 22.

[9] *Of Custom*, trans. John Florio, Essay XXII.

Augustinian might have admitted. Locke thinks, rather, of habituation as creating in the child a stable moral character. He writes:

> Every man must sometime or other be trusted to himself and his own conduct; and he that is a good, a virtuous, and able man, must be made so within. And therefore what he is to receive from education, what is to sway and influence his life, must be something put into him betimes; habits woven into the very principles of his nature; not a counterfeit carriage, and dissembled outside, put on by fear, only to avoid the present anger of a father, who perhaps may disinherit him. [10]

Of course this, too, was not a wholly original doctrine. At first sight Locke is doing no more than reformulate the ideas contained in that familiar educational textbook, Plutarch's *De educatione puerorum*. [11] Plutarch —or whoever was the author of that work—had said that "just as seals leave their impression in soft wax, so are lessons impressed upon the minds of children while they are young" (§ 5); he had defined character as "habit long continued"; he had suggested—a doctrine with its roots in Aristotle [12]—"that if one were to call the virtues of character the virtues of habit, he would not seem to go far astray" (§ 4). But Plutarch had also written that "the first beginnings [of virtue] come from nature" (§ 4). For him, as for Cicero, [13] habit is only a second nature. For Locke, we might rather say, it is a *first* nature.

This, somewhat surprisingly, had also been suggested by Pascal. "Fathers fear," he wrote, "lest the natural affection of their children wear away. What then is this nature which is liable to be worn away? Custom is a second nature which kills the first. But what is nature? Why is custom not natural? I am much afraid that this nature is nothing else but a first custom, just as custom is a second nature." [14] But what Pascal fears—that what men call "natural" in fact derives from custom—is, from the point of view of Locke and his successors, greatly to be welcomed. If men have a fixed, determinate nature, education is so far limited; if they have *no* nature, then its possibilities are boundless.

---

[10] *Concerning Education*, §42. Contrast Leibniz: "The practices of virtue, as well as those of vice, may be the effect of a mere habit, one may acquire a taste for them; but when virtue is reasonable, when it is related to God . . . it is founded on knowledge." (Preface to his essays in *Theodicy* (1710), trans. E. M. Huggard, ed. Austin Farrer [London, 1952], p. 52.) For Locke, a *reasonable* virtue can be founded on habit.

[11] *Moralia*, Vol. 1.

[12] *Nichomachean Ethics*, Bk. II, Ch. 5, §6, where the virtues are defined as "habits or trained faculties."

[13] *De finibus*, Bk. V, Ch. 25, §74.

[14] *Pensées*, trans. H. F. Stewart (London, 1950), No. 376, p. 201.

There is an interesting relationship at this point between Locke's theory of education and certain seventeenth-century theories of the working of divine grace. The orthodox view had been that men cannot prepare themselves for grace without the help of grace.[15] But this seemed to leave men nothing they could do by their own efforts; it threatened, if taken seriously, to issue in antinomianism. Professor Perry Miller has shown how the doctrine, invoked against antinomianism in the New England colonies, that men could by their own efforts prepare for grace, proved to be fatal to Augustinianism.[16] Something very similar, I suspect, happened in Europe. Of more particular importance for our present theme is the special form the doctrine of preparation for grace took in the writings of the "Pyrrhonist" Pierre Charron, a writer much read in England and certainly read by Locke.[17] Charron writes thus: "Theology, even like mysticism, teaches us that to prepare the soul properly for God and his working . . . we must empty it, cleanse it, strip it, and denude it of all opinion, belief, inclination, make it like a white sheet of paper . . . so that God may live and operate in it."[18]

So we can put the matter in these terms: we are born, according to Locke, in that state to which, according to Charron, we ought to reduce ourselves, so that God can act upon us. We do not need to make the child a blank sheet of paper; he *is* a blank sheet of paper—not only in the intellectual sense, as Aristotle, and after him Gassendi, had argued, but also in a moral and theological sense. Education can work upon the soul of every child as God can work upon the soul of the man wholly prepared for grace; education is the secular equivalent of supervenient grace, in that it creates in us the will to be good. Locke was not brought up as a Calvinist for nothing.

From the point of view of the Augustinian tradition, however, Locke is attempting the impossible; for only God, no merely secular influence, can convert the empty soul into a vessel of morality. Consider the materials which, according to Locke, the educator has at his disposal. Ultimately no more than this: the human tendency (the only innate tendency) to avoid pain and pursue pleasure. That tendency makes it possible for the educator to inculcate habits by means of a system of rewards and

[15] Compare Aquinas, *Summa Theologica*, 12ae, Q. 109, Art. 6.

[16] "Preparation for Salvation in Seventeenth Century New England," *Journal of the History of Ideas*, Vol. IV, No. 3, pp. 253–86.

[17] As late as 1733 Pope speaks in the first of his *Moral Essays* of "Montaigne, or more sage Charron" (1. 87). Locke refers to Charron in the Bodley MSS. 3, 174 (see Carlo Viano, *John Locke* [Turin, 1960]).

[18] *Petit traité de sagesse* ([Paris, 1646], pp. 46–48) as translated in Louis I. Bredvold, *The Intellectual Milieu of John Dryden* (Ann Arbor, Mich., 1934), p. 35.

punishments. It is true that the pains include mental as well as physical "uneasiness," and it is also true that the rewards and punishments need not be physical. Indeed, Locke follows the general tradition of the Greek and Renaissance writers on education in seeking to restrict as far as possible the use of merely physical punishments and rewards; their use will encourage, he thinks, the child's tendency to take physical pains and pleasures more seriously than mental pains and pleasures. The educator, rather, will make use of praise and blame—of the pupil's concern, that is, for his own reputation. "Make his mind as sensible of credit and shame as may be: and when you have done that, you have put a principle into him, which will influence his actions, when you are not by . . . and which will be the proper stock, on which to graft afterwards the true principles of morality and religion" (§ 200).

How this works out in practice can be seen from Locke's account of the way in which the child is to be taught generosity. "As to having and possessing of things, teach them to part with what they have, easily and freely to their friends; and let them find by experience, that the most liberal has always most plenty, with esteem and commendation to boot, and they will quickly learn to practise it" (§ 110). This passage aroused Rousseau's ire: "That is to make the child superficially generous but really greedy. He [Locke] adds that 'children will thus form the habit of liberality.' Yes, a usurer's liberality, which expects cent. per cent."[19]

A traditional Augustinian would have been even more horrified. A morality founded on the search after pleasure, modified into the love of praise! Compare Pascal: "Admiration ruins all from childhood"; it was only another sign of human depravity that "the children of Port Royal who lack this spur of emulation and glory fall into indifference."[20] The orthodox doctrine of the theologians had been that men act well only when they act out of *caritas*—defined by Aquinas as "friendship for God." "Those things which she [the human soul] seems to account virtues," Augustine had written, "if they be not all referred unto God, are indeed rather vices than virtues . . . when they are desired only for their own account, and nothing else; yet even so they incur vainglory, and so lose their true goodness."[21] What would Augustine have said of "virtues" which are based on nothing more than the hope of earning future benefits and winning the commendation of others?

[19] *Emile*, trans. Barbara Foxley (London, 1911), pp. 67–68.
[20] *Pensées*, No. 142.
[21] *City of God*, Bk. XIX, Ch. XXV, translated by John Healey, revised by R. V. G. Tasker (London, 1945). Contrast Hume: "to love the glory of virtuous deeds is a sure proof of the love of virtue" ("Of the Dignity or Meanness of Human Nature," Essay X in *Essays, Moral and Political* [1741–42]).

In 1523 Ulrich Zwingli, by no means a purebred Augustinian, wrote a tract *Of the Upbringing and Education of Youth*. Young men must be taught, according to Zwingli, "that everything that we do has its origin in frailty, lust and temptation," that "whether we will or no we can do nothing but evil"; they must be forbidden "all desire for fame," persuaded that "ambition is a deadly poison" and told that whatever they do for God or state will as likely or not be "corrupted by the devil or self-pleasing."[22] But it is precisely the encouragement of "self-pleasing" which is vital to Locke's whole scheme of education; in Zwingli's eyes education is directed toward rooting out evil; in the eyes of Locke toward the encouragement of virtue—but the virtue Locke hopes to encourage is in large part identical with the vice which Zwingli hopes to root out.

The doctrine of the malleability of man, therefore, grew up hand-in-hand with the development of a utilitarian theory of ethics. If *caritas* is essential to morality, then morality cannot be inculcated by education. The Augustinian tradition had always admitted, of course, that there is an inferior sort of morality to which men might aspire without divine grace, although there were some qualms about how far even this was possible. "I do not so dissent from the common judgment," Calvin had written in his *Institutes of the Christian Religion*, "as to contend that there is no difference between the justice, moderation, and equity of Titus and Trajan and the madness, intemperance, and savagery of Caligula or Nero or Domitian . . . and—not to tarry over individual virtues and vices—between observance and contempt of right and of laws." But he goes on hastily to add that "what Augustine writes is nonetheless true: that all who are estranged from the religion of the one God, however admirable they may be regarded on account of their reputation for virtue, not only deserve no rewards but rather punishment because by the pollution of their hearts they defile God's good works" (§ 3). At best, their "virtues" are "dead images" of virtue.[23]

In that picture of the condition of Fallen Man devoid of grace, *The Leviathan*, Hobbes had put first among the motives that incline men to morality the "desire of ease, and sensual delight."[24] But Hobbes's state was scarcely an advertisement for human nature; if that was the best men

[22] Zwingli's tract is included in *The Library of Christian Classics*, Vol. **XXIV**. My quotations are from pp. 105, 106, 112, 113.
[23] Bk. III, Ch. XIV, §2, as translated by F. L. Battles in *The Library of Christian Classics*, XX, 769. Aquinas' view, as formulated in his *Summa*, 12ae, Q. 109, Art. 4 is not so very different.
[24] *Leviathan*, Pt. I, Ch. 11.

could by their own efforts achieve, it was easy to believe that man was hopelessly corrupt.

It is essential to Hobbes's view that although men can be governed, they cannot be reformed; they are not, in essentials, malleable. Pascal had probably read Hobbes, and accepts his general picture of human nature and of the roots of justice. [25] Arnauld, however, struck out of the official Port-Royal edition of the *Pensées* the section on justice. "It is false," he argued, "and very dangerous to say that there is no such thing as essential justice amongst mankind." [26] Nicole went much further:

> Entirely to reform the world, that is to say, to banish from it all vices and all the grosser disorders . . . one would only need, given the absence of charity, that men should possess an enlightened self interest. . . . However corrupted such a society might be within and to the eyes of God, there need be nothing lacking to it in the way of being well regulated . . . and what is even more wonderful is that although it would be entirely animated and moved by self love, self love would nowhere appear in it; and although it is entirely devoid of charity, one would see everywhere only the form and characteristics of charity. [27]

Such a society is, in Nicole's eyes as in the eyes of God, "corrupted"; but it is the society toward which Locke's educational ideals are wholly directed—a society governed by that "law of fashion" he described in the *Essay*. [28]

"The measure of what is everywhere called and esteemed virtue and vice," Locke had there written, "is this approbation or dislike, praise or blame, which, by a secret and tacit consent, establishes itself in the several societies, tribes, and clubs of men in the world; whereby several actions come to find credit or disgrace amongst them, according to the judgment,

[25] Gilbert Chinard, *En lisant Pascal* (Paris, 1948), Ch. IV.

[26] Quoted in J. S. Spink, *French Free-Thought from Gassendi to Voltaire* (London, 1960), p. 74, from a letter by Arnauld to Pascal's brother-in-law (*Oeuvres* [1775–83], I, 664).

[27] "De la charité et de l'amour propre," Ch. XI in *Essais de Morale* (1671–78), Vol. 3, 1707 edition, pp. 197–98. Nicole thinks of himself (p. 195) as following Augustine's "vanity so nearly imitates the works of charity, that there is almost no difference between their effects."

[28] Compare J. F. Herbart: "How to behave in a society, is what Locke's pupil will know best. The principal thing for him is conventionality. For fathers who destine their sons for the world, no book of education need be written after Locke." Introduction (p. 79) to Herbart's *Allgemeine Pädagogik aus dem Zweck der Erziehung abgeleitet*, trans. by H. M. and E. Felken as *The Science of Education* (Boston, 1892).

maxims, or fashion of that place."[29] It is true that this is not, ultimately, the law by which morality is determined; ultimately the law of God is the sole determinant of morality. But this distinction is less important than it at first seems, since "esteem and discredit, virtue and vice . . . in a great measure, everywhere correspond with the unchangeable rule of right and wrong, which the law of God hath established"[30]—just as, according to Nicole, men's behavior in a society based on self-love may in practice coincide with their behavior in a society based on *caritas*. And "he who imagines commendation and disgrace not to be strong motives to men to accommodate themselves to the opinions and rules of those with whom they converse, seems little skilled in the nature or history of mankind." These are the sanctions, rather than the fear of God or of the state, by which men chiefly "govern themselves."[31] So an Augustinian, too, might with melancholy have reflected.[32]

It is clear enough what was happening: men were lowering their sights for virtue as they had done for reason.[33] To an Augustinian, true reason made use of a direct intuition, since it was God's illumination of the soul, but a merely worldly reason could, in some measure, successfully govern men's conduct of life. But now, more and more, the successful governance of life, based not on divine illumination but on experience, came to be regarded as the sole concern of reason. The Augustinians had admitted that, governed by no higher principle than vanity, or self-love, or a concern for the public interest, men could display a semblance of virtue, although true virtue depended on *caritas*. But now true virtue had come to be identified with, to use the Platonic term, the merely "civic" virtue of the "well-adjusted citizen." The "virtue" which Locke proposes to teach is not identical with the virtue which Ralph Cudworth, for example,

[29] Essay, Bk. II, Ch. XXVIII, ed. A. C. Fraser, p. 477. Compare Nicole's difficulties in reconciling "la civilité" with Christianity ("De la civilité chrétienne," edition cited, II, 125–53).

[30] P. 478.

[31] P. 479.

[32] On the general attitude to self-esteem in the eighteenth century, see A. O. Lovejoy, *Reflections on Human Nature* (Baltimore, 1961).

[33] Thus the Marquis de Vauvenargues complains that moralists had "forgé une vertu incompatible avec la nature de l'homme, et ... après l'avoir ainsi feinte, ils aient prononcé froidement qu'il n'y avait aucune vertu." If we set our moral standards at a point more compatible with man's real nature, he argues, we shall no longer have to complain of his viciousness (*Réflexions et maximes* [1746], No. 296). Vauvenargues suggests (Maxime 219) that "l'homme est maintenant en disgrace chez tous ceux qui pensent." That is not quite correct; he was not in disgrace either with Locke or with Shaftesbury and his followers. But it is important to remember that the Augustinian view of man by no means died out with Locke.

denied to be teachable.[34] "We shall have to transform it [virtue] into the idea of doing good and vice into the idea of doing ill," according to the materialist Bordeu in Diderot's dialogue entitled *D'Alembert's Dream* (1769).[35] There could be no better description of what the eighteenth century had already done.

The disconcerting thing about Mandeville's *Fable of the Bees* (1714) was that it drew public attention to what was happening. It is often thought of as being directed against Shaftesbury. But although Mandeville was able to turn his argument very easily against Shaftesbury, he had not in fact read him when he first wrote the *Fable*.[36] On the other hand, he had read Locke's *Some Thoughts Concerning Education* very carefully, and had no doubt detected the moral tendencies within it. He may well, too, have read Nicole;[37] at any rate, we may think of him as denying, against Nicole, that a society based on self-love might be indistinguishable from a society based on *caritas*.

In his *Enquiry into the Original of Moral Virtue*,[38] Mandeville begins, like Locke, from the presumption that "untaught animals are only solicitous of pleasing themselves" (p. 41); he rests their capacity for being civilized on the observation that "none were either so savage as not to be charmed with praise, or so despicable as patiently to bear contempt" (p. 42); he observes that by this means they gradually come to be divided into the virtuous who "esteemed the improvements of the mind to be their fairest possessions" (p. 44) and the vicious, who "always hunting after immediate

[34] The distinction between "civic" and "philosophic" goodness employed by Plato in the *Republic* is in many ways parallel to the Augustinian distinction between "the image of virtue" and the virtue which involves enlightenment by God, and may well have suggested the Augustinian doctrine. For Cudworth, see his *Sermon Preached before the House of Commons* (1647) in *The True Intellectual Systems* (ed. 1820), IV, 298. "Men and books may propound some direction to us, that may set us in such a way of life and practice, as in which we shall at last find it [virtue] within ourselves . . . but they cannot teach it to us like a mechanic art or trade." Locke, as I pointed out previously, would strongly have rejected the view that the virtue acquirable by habit must be "merely external."

[35] First published in 1830; quoted from *Rameau's Nephew*, trans. J. Barzun and R. H. Bowen (New York, 1956), p. 168.

[36] See *The Fable of the Bees*, ed. F. B. Kaye (Oxford, 1924), Vol. I, p. lxxii.

[37] In his *En lisant Pascal*, Chinard says of Nicole and Domat that "en plus d'un sens, ils annoncent Bernard Mandeville" (p. 115). See also Kaye's introduction to his edition of Mandeville, Vol. 1, pp. lxxxvii–xciv.

[38] I.e. the prose essay which, added to *The Grumbling Hive* (1705) made up the first edition of *The Fable of the Bees*. Dugald Stewart noted the comparison with Locke: "The great object of Mandeville's *Enquiry into the Original of Moral Virtue*, is to show that all our moral sentiments are derived from *education* . . . a fundamental error which is common to the system of Mandeville and that of Locke" (*Collected Works*, ed. Sir W. Hamilton [1854–60], VI, 264–65, quoted in Kaye, Vol. 2, p. 442).

enjoyment, were wholly incapable of self-denial, and without regard to the good of others, had no higher aim than their private advantage" (p. 43). Mandeville professes to be describing the evolution of society, but there could be no better description of the distinction between the effects of a good and of a bad education as Locke conceives it. And Mandeville does not impugn its accuracy; he takes it to describe what actually happens. All that he denies, so far a true Augustinian, is that virtue, as a traditional moralist understands it, could arise out of an education conducted in such a spirit. I am not at all clear about the nature of Mandeville's own ethical views; the one thing certain, I think, is that he thought it wholly hypocritical to identify, even for practical purposes, a morality based on *caritas* and a morality based on self-love— Locke's "law of fashion" and divine law.

But that they largely coincided was a much more comfortable view. That doctrine served as a decorous screen for the eighteenth-century transvaluation of values, and Mandeville's determination to knock it down was not unnaturally regarded with disfavor. In general, he was dismissed; Butler's "self-love . . . does in general perfectly coincide with virtue"[39] came to be regarded, if by no means universally, as respectable Christian doctrine. (Contrast Pascal: "God alone is to be loved, self alone to be hated."[40]) Dr. Johnson said of Mandeville's *Fable*: "The fallacy of that book is, that Mandeville . . . reckons among vices everything that gives pleasure. He takes the narrowest view of morality, monastic morality."[41] So much for the Augustinians! Indeed, his eighteenth-century critics often proceed almost as if Mandeville had *invented* the view[42] that there cannot be virtue without self-denial. Yet as late as 1695 John Norris, erstwhile Cambridge Platonist, had in his *Letters Concerning the Love of God* put forward this position in its most unmitigated form.[43]

It is not surprising that Miss Pamela Andrews thought very well of *Some Thoughts Concerning Education;* its morality by no means disturbed that

---

[39] *Sermons* (1726), III, 12. In a way, of course, Butler is only saying what Nicole had said—but in how different a tone of voice! Butler's respectable followers include, for example, James Beattie in his *Elements of Moral Science* (1790). See his account of self-love in Pt. I, Ch. I, §4, pp. 242–44.

[40] *Pensées*, No. 617.

[41] Boswell's *Life of Johnson*, 1778, Everyman edition (London, 1906), Vol. 2, p. 210. On "monastic virtue," see *Fable*, I, 152–54.

[42] E.g., *Fable*, I, 156.

[43] Every human being, he argued, should, in Augustine's words, be "uti, non frui." Norris followed Malebranche very closely. Damaris Cudworth (Lady Masham) replied to Norris, on behalf of the Platonists, in her *Discourse Concerning the Love of God* (1696).

calculating young minx. She makes, it is interesting to observe, only one important criticism of Locke. Locke is, she thinks, too rigorous with children and that is because he does not pay sufficient attention to their "little *innate* passions."[44] Later in the century, when Henry Mackenzie introduces a discussion on education into his *The Man of the World* (1773), he so far follows Locke that he thinks of "the desire of honour" and "the fear of shame" as the major factors in "the incitement of virtue and the prevention of vice." But these now become full-blown innate instincts—"the two great movements of the soul, which the Moulder of our frames has placed in them"—rather than particular forms of the pursuit of pleasure and avoidance of pain.[45]

This was the general reaction; in fact the controversy between those who said that men's innate passions were good and those who said that they were evil went on quite as if Locke had never denied that there were any innate passions at all. Thus the common objection against Mandeville was that he had emphasized the wrong innate passions. "He hath left out of his system," Mr. Booth complains in Joseph Fielding's *Amelia* (1751), "the best passion which the mind can possess, and attempts to derive the effects or energies of that passion from the base impulses of pride or fear. Whereas it is as certain that love exists in the mind of man as that its opposite hatred does."[46] That *neither* of these "exist in the mind of man," was, of course, what Mandeville had actually argued.

Similarly, in *The History of Tom Jones* (1749), the question at issue between Thwackum and Square is whether virtue is natural to man, or whether by nature man is depraved; neither party so much as considers the suggestion that he has in this respect no nature at all.[47] Against them both, it is interesting to note, Fielding sets up the ideal of *goodness*—goodness of heart. This we can think of as the secular equivalent of *caritas*—friendship to man as distinct from friendship to God—and Fielding is suggesting that it is the root of all properly moral actions. Mr. Barnabas is an orthodox Augustinian when he tells Joseph Andrews that "he must divest himself of all human passions" and can achieve that

[44] Samuel Richardson, *Pamela* (1741), Vol. 2, letter XCI.

[45] Henry Mackenzie, *The Man of the World*, Ch. V. In general, as one might expect, Mackenzie places more emphasis on "the heart" and less on "judgment" than did Locke. But he does not follow the Rousseau-like praise of a "natural" as distinct from an "artificial" education exhibited in Henry Brooke's *Fool of Quality* (1766–70), a novel which John Wesley edited and Charles Kingsley greatly admired. See H. W. Thompson, *Henry Mackenzie* (Oxford, 1931), pp. 105–6.

[46] Bk. III, Ch. V.

[47] Bk. III, Ch. III.

end only "by grace"; but Fielding leaves us in no doubt concerning what he thinks of Mr. Barnabas. In the behavior he is prepared to allow his hero Tom Jones, there is implicit the antinomian suggestion that what is normally described as "morality" is not of the first importance for the goodhearted man. "How little one sort of amour has to do with the heart."[48] It is true that Tom Jones is, in the end, reformed into more respectable ways, but this has very much the air of a concession to conventional moralists. (Lady Wortley Montagu wondered that Fielding "does not perceive Tom Jones and Mr. Booth are sorry scoundrels."[49])

The attitude of eighteenth-century "sentimentalist" British philosophers is very like the attitude of the novelists. Shaftesbury, Hutcheson, Butler all agree against Locke that men are born with natural, disinterested affections (even if other now lesser-known moral theorists, alarmed at the idea that man might be good without God's help, continued to argue that men were selfish by nature and could act morally only with God's help— a help often defined, however, in terms of a system of rewards and punishments rather than of divine grace).[50] In Shaftesbury, the concern for public good is the most important of these affections and, like Fielding's "goodheartedness," in some measure functions in the same way as *caritas* in the Augustinian system. He writes:

> Whatsoever therefore is done which happens to be advantageous to the species, through an affection merely towards self-good, does not imply any more goodness in the creature than as the affection itself is good. Let him, in any particular, act ever so well; if at the bottom, it be that selfish affection alone which moves him; he is in himself still vicious. Nor can any creature be considered otherwise, when the passion towards self-good, though ever so moderate, is his real motive in the doing that, to which a natural affection for his kind ought by right to have inclined him.[51]

Hutcheson and Butler, however, are less rigorous; for Butler "self-love in its due degree is as just and morally good as any affection whatever."[52]

---

[48] Bk. XVIII, Ch. XII.

[49] Letter of July 23, 1755.

[50] In the preface to his edition of Benjamin Whichcote's *Sermons* (1698), Shaftesbury sees the great virtue of the Cambridge Platonists in their recognition that man possesses "a principle of good nature"; his ethics might be described as Cambridge Platonism without theology. The lesser-known moral theorists include John Clarke (*The Foundation of Morality* [1730]) and John Brown (*Essays on the Characteristics* [1751]).

[51] *An Inquiry Concerning Virtue and Merit* (1699), Bk. I, Pt. 2, §2, p. 25.

[52] Preface to *Sermons* (1726), §34.

Furthermore, Hutcheson, Butler, and their followers—a list which includes Hume and Adam Smith—were prepared to multiply considerably the number of independent innate "affections." By the time Thomas Reid came to write his *Essays on the Active Powers of the Human Mind* (1788), the number of innate "affections" of the human mind had grown to very considerable proportions. Writing as a good Lockian, Joseph Priestley, in his *An Examination of Dr. Reid's Inquiry* (1774), was moved to protest against "such a number of independent, arbitrary, instinctive principles, that the very enumeration of them is really tiresome."[53] But what Priestley really objects to is the doctrine, common to all the Scottish philosophers—and taken over from them by such twentieth-century "instinct" psychologists as Macdougall—that man is malleable only within the limits set by the fact that he possesses innate passions.

Hume may be regarded, in this respect, as a fairly typical representative of the Scottish point of view. On the whole, education comes off rather badly in Hume's *Treatise of Human Nature* (1739). Quite unlike Locke, Hume thinks of education mainly as a means of acquiring beliefs. "I am persuaded," he says, "that upon examination we shall find more than one half of those opinions, that prevail among mankind, to be owing to education."[54] It is, he says, "disclaimed by philosophy, as a fallacious ground of assent to any opinion."[55] Indeed, to the malign effects of education are to be ascribed the fact that people find it so difficult to accept any new ideas—especially those ideas Hume is putting before them.

On the moral side, however, education can be used to strengthen our regard for justice.

> For as parents easily observe, that a man is the more useful, both
> to himself and others, the greater degree of probity and honour he
> is endowed with; and that those principles have greater force,
> when custom and education assist interest and reflexion: for

[53] *The Theological and Miscellaneous Writings of Joseph Priestley* (1817–32), ed. J. T. Rutt, III, 27. The full title of Priestley's work is: *An Examination of Dr. Reid's Inquiry into the Human Mind on the Principles of Commonsense, Dr. Beattie's Essay on the Nature and Immutability of Truth, and Dr. Oswald's Appeal to Commonsense on Behalf of Religion.* It is often referred to as *An Examination of the Scotch Philosophers.* One can see what the Scottish view leads to in the list of springs of action in James Martineau, *Types of Ethical Theory,* (2nd ed.; Oxford, 1886) Vol. 2, Ch. V, p. 129ff.

[54] Ed. L. A. Selby-Bigge, Bk. I, Pt. III, §IX, p. 117.

[55] *Ibid.,* Bk. I, Pt. III, §x, p. 118. Cf. John Gay's reference to "what is generally called the prejudice of education" in his *Concerning the Fundamental Principles of Virtue and Morality,* first published as a preface to the 1731 translation by Edmund Law of William King's *The Origin of Evil.* My reference is to A. L. Selby-Bigge, *British Moralists* (Oxford, 1897), II, §887, p. 285.

these reasons they are induced to inculcate on their children, from their earliest infancy, the principles of probity, and teach them to regard the observance of those rules, by which society is maintained, as worthy and honourable, and their violation as base and infamous. By this means the sentiments of honour may take root in their tender minds, and acquire such firmness and solidity, that they may fall little short of those principles, which are the most essential to our natures, and the most deeply radicated in our internal constitution.[56]

Education, that is, although it may act as the secular equivalent of co-operative grace, is certainly not the equivalent of prevenient grace.

Hume contrasts, it should be observed, the principles inculcated by education with those which are "deeply radicated in our internal constitution." Such "radicated principles" cannot be reduced, Hume argues, to a desire for pleasure and an aversion from pain. Some of our passions, no doubt, arise from this source, but others—including "the desire of punishment to our enemies, and of happiness to our friends"—arise directly "from a natural impulse or instinct, which is perfectly unaccountable."[57] The attempt to reduce all the passions to different forms of the avoidance of pain or the pursuit of pleasure has its source, he self-righteously asserts, in "that love of simplicity which has been the source of much false reasoning in philosophy."[58] He is thinking particularly, I suspect, of John Gay's *Concerning the Fundamental Principles of Morality and Virtue*, in which Gay made the first serious, although very brief, attempt to work out an associationist-utilitarian theory of the passions.[59]

In his essay "Of the Dignity or Meanness of Human Nature,"[60] where he is considering competing theories of human nature, Hume tries to establish a *via media* between those which "exalt our species to the skies, and represent man as a kind of human demigod" and those which "insist upon the blind sides of human nature, and can discover nothing, except vanity, in which man surpasses the other animals, whom he affects so much to despise." He does not so much as discuss the doctrine that man

[56] Bk. III, Pt. II, §2, pp. 500–1. Compare Essay XVIII, "The Sceptic," in *Essays, Moral, Political and Literary* (1741–42), eds. T. H. Green and T. H. Grose (London, 1875).

[57] Bk. II, Pt. III, §IX, p. 439.

[58] *Enquiries Concerning the Human Understanding and Concerning the Principles of Morals*, ed. L. A. Selby-Bigge, Appendix II, p. 298.

[59] It appears from E. C. Mossner's *Life of Hume* (Austin, Tex., 1954) that Hume had read King in the 1731 edition as a young man and therefore, I presume, knew Gay's introductory essay. I did not know this when in my *Hume's Intentions* (Cambridge, 1952) I suggested that Hume was referring to Gay. But the roots of the matter are in Locke.

[60] Edition cited, Essay XI, p. 151.

has *no nature at all*. When, in a note to his *Enquiry Concerning Human Understanding* (§ 2), he asks "I should desire to know, what can be meant by asserting, that self-love, or resentment of injuries, or the passion between the sexes is not innate?",[61] the question is intended to be a rhetorical one—nothing, he thinks, *could* be meant by asserting that these passions are not innate.

He might well believe that he could take this for granted, for, as we have already seen, in the half-century which had passed since Locke wrote his *Some Thoughts Concerning Education*, the malleability doctrine had won few converts in England. John Gay's *Principles of Virtue and Morality* is one of the few exceptions in rejecting innate passions. Another exception, published just a year before Hume's *Enquiries*, is the anonymous *An Enquiry into the Origin of the Human Appetites and Affections Showing How Each Arises from Association*. It is interesting to observe that the author of that pamphlet[62] refers to Locke only as the author of the *Essay* and thinks of himself as being the first to say of the passions what, he seems to have thought, Locke had said only of ideas.

> All the writers who have hitherto obliged the world, either with set treatises, or occasional essays, upon ethics, have, to a man, taken for granted that the passions, or to speak more properly, the affections and dispositions of mind, consequent upon, and taking their rise from the passions, or *original sensations* of the soul were implanted there by the great Author of our beings.

And again: "The same arguments, which the great Mr. Locke made use of, in order to prove that there were no innate ideas, will, methinks, hold full as strong, and conclude with equal force against all implanted appetites whatever."[63]

It is not that *Some Thoughts Concerning Education* went unread. But it seems to have been read—as Pamela Andrews read it—as a manual on child-training, much as in the nineteen-twenties young mothers read similar manuals without realizing that they were being exposed either to Watson or to Freud, depending upon the manual they read. So rapidly,

---

[61] Edition cited, p. 22.

[62] Sometimes attributed to Gay, sometimes, as by Selby-Bigge, to Hartley. I do not accept either of these attributions. *The Dictionary of Anonymous and Pseudonymous English Literature* ascribes it on the evidence of the then librarian of Edinburgh University to James Long. Inquiries I made some years ago failed to reveal either on what evidence the librarian made his attribution or even who James Long was. The tract is republished in Samuel Parr, *Metaphysical Tracts by English Philosophers of the Eighteenth Century* (London, 1837).

[63] Parr, *Metaphysical Tracts*, Second Half, pp. 47–48.

for example, does it plunge into toilet-training—where Locke is a pioneer—to emerge only very many pages later into the discussion of morality, that its revolutionary implications easily went unnoticed. Not until Hartley and Condillac had carried Locke's ideas further than he himself had carried them was it at all generally realized—although the exceptions include Mandeville in England and Morelly in France—just how far Locke himself had gone. Both Gay and the author of *An Enquiry* were principally concerned, furthermore, to develop, by way of Locke, that variety of theological utilitarianism which was to culminate, under Gay's influence, in Abraham Tucker's *Light of Nature* (1768–77) and William Paley's *Principles of Moral and Political Philosophy* (1785). They were not specifically interested in malleability or in education.

But just one year after Hume had rhetorically asked what could be meant "by asserting, that self-love, or resentment of injuries, or the passions between the sexes is not innate," David Hartley took that question as a genuine one and answered it in painstaking detail—freely acknowledging his indebtedness to Locke and to Gay. Neither self-love, nor resentment of injuries, nor passions between the sexes is, according to Hartley, innate. Each of them derives from the working of association— the psychological mechanisms of habit[64]—upon our original tendencies to pursue the pleasant and to avoid the painful.

Hartley, indeed, denies that even the desire of happiness and aversion from misery are innate. "The young child learns to grasp and go up to the play-thing that pleases him, and to withdraw his hand from the fire that burns him, at first from the mechanism of his nature, and without any deliberate purpose of obtaining pleasure, and avoiding pain." The general desire for happiness is "factitious, i.e., generated by association." The burnt child, in other words, fears the fire, he does not fear pain as such. And such particular fears can continue to influence him in a way quite inconsistent with his having "an essential, original, perpetual desire of happiness, and endeavour to attain it."[65]

All we can properly say, then, is that the child, as John Gay had put it, is born with "the power of receiving sensitive pleasure or pain,"[66] not with a desire to avoid it. Desires arise only after reflection. Thus education

---

[64] "All that has been delivered by the ancients and moderns, concerning the power of habit, custom, example, education, authority . . . goes upon this doctrine [of association] as its foundation, and may be considered as the detail of it, in various circumstances" (*Observations on Man* [9th ed.; London, 1834], Pt. 1, Ch. I, §2, Prop. X).

[65] *Observations on Man*, Pt. I, Ch. III, §3, Prop. LXXXIX, p. 232.

[66] Quoted from the version of John Gay's *Concerning Virtue and Morality*, in L. A. Selby-Bigge, *British Moralists*, II, 276.

should direct itself to the formation of particular associations in particular cases. Hartley also argues:

> If beings of the same nature, but whose affections and passions are, at present, in different proportions to each other, be exposed for an indefinite time to the same impressions and associations, all their particular differences will, at last, be overruled, and they will become perfectly similar, or even equal. *They may also be made perfectly similar, in a finite time, by a proper adjustment of the impressions and associations.*[67]

What is true of our passions is also true of our judgments.

> Suppose two persons, A and B, to go together into a crowd, and there each of them to see a variety of persons whom he knew in different degrees, as well as many utter strangers. A would not have the same ideas and associations raised in him from viewing the several faces, dresses, etc., of the persons in the crowd, as B, partly from his having a different knowledge of, and acquaintance with them, partly from different predispositions to approve and disapprove. *But let A and B become equally acquainted with them, and acquire by education and association, the same predispositions of mind,* and then they will at last make the same judgment of each of the persons whom they see.[68]

So, it would seem, not only can children be educated to think and feel alike, but also men can be *re-educated* to the same effect, and in a finite time. This practical intention is never far from Hartley's mind.

> It is [he says] of the utmost consequence to morality and religion, that the affections and passions should be analyzed into their simple compounding parts, by reversing the steps of the associations which concur to form them. For thus we may learn how to cherish and improve good ones, check and root out such as are mischievous and immoral, and how suit our manner of life, in some tolerable measure, to our intellectual and religious wants.

Like Locke, he believes that our power of willing derives from this source. "The doctrine of association explains also the rise and progress of those voluntary and semi-voluntary powers, which we exert over our ideas,

[67] Pt. I, Ch. I, §2, Prop. XIV, cor. VI, p. 52 (my italics).
[68] Pt. I, Ch. III, §2, Prop. LXXXVI, p. 210 (my italics).

affections, and bodily motions and by doing this, teaches us how to regulate and improve these powers."[69] It is true that this possibility of making uniform the passions and the judgments is subject to a certain condition: it is "beings of the same nature" who can be educated, or re-educated, in this way. But this is not, to Hartley—even less than it was to Locke—an important distinction. It is bodily differences he has in mind, and these, he thinks, profoundly affect a few persons, but only a few.

In France, Etienne Condillac's *Treatise on the Sensations* (1754) runs partly parallel to Hartley. But Condillac makes use of the Lockian conception of habit, without reducing it to an associative mechanism. A weakness in Locke's *Essay* had been that it left quite uncertain the position of the "intellectual powers of the human mind." These, it has to be supposed, are innate. For Condillac, on the other hand, they are all habits. He speaks of "first, a habit of attending; second, a habit of recollecting; third, a habit of comparing; fourth, a habit of judging; fifth, a habit of imagining; and sixth, a habit of recognizing."[70] These habits replace the "innate powers" of attention, recollection, comparison, judgment, imagination, recognition. Condillac, too, argues that not even the aversion from pain is innate. Aversion from pain involves the recognition that a different state is possible, but at first we are only conscious of pain, not aware that "pain can cease and become something else, or that there can be no pain at all."[71]

Opposition to this conception of man as infinitely malleable came, in France, from two different sources. First, from the materialists. The Lockian view, they argued, grossly underestimated the importance of the innate characteristics of the human being, considered as an "active machine." In *L'Homme machine* (1747) La Mettrie distinguishes what he calls "the first excellence" (*premier mérite*) of man from his "second excellence." The first excellence is the natural constitution. "Whence comes," he asks, "skill, science and virtue if not from a disposition which makes us suitable to become skilful, wise and virtuous? And whence comes this disposition, if not by Nature? We have estimable qualities only from her; we owe her all that we are."[72] Only the "second excellences" derive from education—although without it, the finest natural constitution, he

[69] Pt. I, Ch. I, §2, Prop. XIV, cor. V, p. 52.
[70] Pt. I, Ch. II, §39.
[71] Pt. I, Ch. II, §3.
[72] Ed. A. Vartanian (Princeton, 1960), p. 166. See also P. J. G. Cabinis, *Rapport du physique et du moral* (1802): Condillac and Helvétius, according to Cabinis, could never have argued for the equality of men had they possessed a better knowledge of "l'économie animale" (*Oeuvres philosophiques* [Paris, 1956], p. 141).

grants, would be wasted. But also, and this is the point he rather insists upon, "what would be the fruit of the most excellent school, without a matrix open to the entry or to the conception of ideas?" Some people, he says in his *Discours sur le bonheur* (1748), might be reformed by education, but very few. In general, "it is easier for the good to become wicked, than for the latter to improve."[73]

The second type of reaction comes from Rousseau. Historians of educational thought have sometimes insisted upon Rousseau's indebtedness to Locke.[74] And no doubt the educational practices Rousseau advocated in *Emile* (1762) are in part derived from *Some Thoughts Concerning Education*—although many of them are the commonplaces of humanistic education, which Locke in turn had derived from Plutarch or from Comenius. But the general tenor of *Emile* is in complete opposition to Locke. I have already quoted Rousseau's adverse comment on Locke's analysis of liberality. Let me add these quotations from *Emile*: "The only habit the child should be allowed to contract is that of having no habits" (p. 30); "The main thing is that the child shall do nothing because you are watching him or listening to him; in a word, nothing because of other people, but only what nature asks of him" (pp. 56–57); "Fathers and teachers who want to make the child, not a child but a man of learning, think it never too soon to scold, correct, reprove, threaten, bribe, teach, and reason. Do better than they; be reasonable, and do not reason with your pupil" (p. 58).[75] The last is of course in direct opposition to Locke's remark that "it will perhaps be wondered, that I mention reasoning with children; and yet I cannot but think that the true way of dealing with them" (§ 81).

Locke would certainly have approved Rousseau's flat assertion that "there is no original sin in the human heart, the how and why of the entrance of every vice can be traced," but not at all the statement which precedes it: that "the first impulses of nature are always right" (p. 56).

---

[73] Quoted in Lester G. Crocker, *An Age of Crisis* (Baltimore, 1959), p. 208, from La Mettrie, *Oeuvres philosophiques*, II, 118–77.

[74] For example, J. W. Adamson, *A Short History of Education* (Cambridge, 1919), pp. 209–11. One can certainly find passages in Locke which Rousseau might have written, especially when Locke is insisting upon the importance of ensuring that children "are not hindered from being children, or from playing or doing as children" (§69). But Locke is suggesting, only, that habituation is easier when it accords with the temperament of the child and his rate of growth. I cannot at all agree with Paul Hazard that Locke "seeks above all to elicit and develop . . . the spontaneity of Nature" (*The European Mind* [London, 1953], trans. J. Lewis May from *La Crise de la conscience européenne* [Paris, 1935], p. 402).

[75] Page references are to the translation by Barbara Foxley (London, 1911).

For Rousseau, the function of education, at least in its early years, is entirely negative: "it consists, not in teaching virtue or truth, but in preserving the heart from vice and from the spirit of error" (p. 57). And this is because the child is not morally malleable; he cannot be moralized by education, but only by the flowering of his own natural impulses—his innate feelings of "self-love, fear, pain, the dread of death, the desire for comfort" (p. 253). From Rousseau it is a short step to the most un-Lockian Pestalozzi.

Thus Helvétius, setting out to expound, defend, and develop the Lockian conception of the malleability of man, found it necessary to direct his fire against two classes of "enlightened" opponents. "Quintillian, Locke and I say," he wrote, "that the inequality of minds is the effect of a known cause, and that cause is the difference in education."[76] (His French disciples turn Locke's "nine parts out of ten" into "ten parts out of ten.") In contrast, to ascribe the inequality of men, as La Mettrie had done, to a difference in their "constitution" is, Helvétius suggests, to appeal to an *unknown* cause—an "occult quality"—as distinct from the *known* cause of education. Furthermore, this view has fatal moral consequences: "if our constitution makes us, almost entirely, what we are, what right have we to blame teachers for their ignorance or masters for their stupidity?"[77] Pelagius had urged a very similar objection against the Augustinians: if we can be moral only by God's grace why attempt to be moral? The new dispute between the claims of nature and the claims of nurture had by the eighteenth century replaced the old dispute about grace and free will, but in important respects the points at issue remained unchanged.

In Rousseau's *Emile*, so Helvétius not unjustly complains, he can find no consistent doctrine; at times Rousseau seems to be saying that men's native constitution is all-important, at times that their innate impulses are all-important, at times, even, that their education is all-important.[78] To the last view, of course, Helvétius has no objection; to the first he has, he thinks, already replied; in answering Rousseau on the second point, Helvétius is led, interestingly enough, into a position very like that of Hobbes. Of the "natural man," he writes: "His hands are always filthy with blood. Accustomed to murder, he must be deaf to the cry of pity."[79]

[76] Translated from *De l'homme et de l'éducation* (1772), Sec. II, Ch. I (*Oeuvres d'Helvétius* [Paris, 1794], III, 100). Much the same views are developed, but in less detail, in *De l'esprit* (1758), Helvétius' most influential work.

[77] Sec. I, Ch. II, p. 14.

[78] Helvétius' principal criticisms of Rousseau are contained in Sec. V. of *De l'homme.*

[79] Sec. V, Ch. IV, p. 73.

The "natural man" in such contexts is the uneducated man. Helvétius still subscribes to the Lockian doctrine that by nature men have no impulses except a tendency to pursue pleasure and avoid pain, but these tendencies, he argues, inevitably give rise in natural, uneducated man to a love of power.[80]

Thus education, as he conceives it, is the sole source of virtue. It is true that education can go wrong; much of *De l'homme* is an attack upon Jesuit-controlled education. More and more, indeed, Helvétius comes to think of the state as the origin of all goodness; education becomes one method, but only one, by which the state operates upon the citizens. "Laws," he writes, "are the soul of empires, the instruments of public welfare. These instruments are still imperfect, but they can be from day to day made more perfect."[81]

Now we are far from the moral and political atmosphere of Locke; with Helvétius[82] we are moving toward—or, should we say, remembering Plato, back to—the conception of society as the great moralizing agent, with education as its instrument. But not all enthusiasts for malleability were willing to accept this consequence. Joseph Priestley knew and feared, as a Dissenter, the power of the state. No one could be a more enthusiastic supporter than he was of the principles of Locke and Hartley. When as a young man of twenty his eye had lighted on Hartley's *Observations on Man*, he was at once and permanently converted to its principles. Nobody could have believed more passionately than he did in the malleability, and consequent perfectibility, of man. But just for that reason when John Brown proposed in 1763, for reasons very similar to Helvétius', the setting up of a state system of education, Priestley's opposition to it was violent.

"The chief and essential remedy of licentiousness and faction," Brown had written, "the fundamental means of the lasting and secure establishment of civil liberty, can only be in a general and prescribed improvement

[80] Sec. IV, Ch. IV, p. 291.
[81] Sec. VII, Ch. XII, p. 235.
[82] As earlier with Morelly's *Essai sur l'esprit humain, ou principes naturels de l'éducation* (1743) and *Code de la nature* (1755). Morelly took his basic ideas from Locke, and developed out of them a despotic society, although one based, unlike a tyranny, on what Morelly took to be the rule of the majority. For rather different interpretations of Morelly, see Gilbert Chinard's edition of *Code de la nature* (Paris, 1950) and R. N. C. Coe, *Morelly. Ein Rationalist auf dem Wege zum Sozialismus* (Berlin, 1961). The *Code de la nature* was at one time ascribed to Diderot: its revolutionary possibilities were brought out in its use by Babeuf in the conspiracy of 1796. It is an important document in the development of "totalitarian democracy." But its theoretical foundations are difficult to state at all precisely. See J. L. Talmon, *The Origins of Totalitarian Democracy* (London, 1952).

of the laws of education, to which all the members of the community should legally submit."[83] The effect would be, Priestley thought, to produce a quite undesirable uniformity in society; immeasurably to strengthen, in fact, the power of the ruling group. "The only method of preserving the balance, which at present subsists among the several political and religious parties in Great Britain," he argued, "is for each party to provide for the education of their own children."[84] "Education," he went on, "is a branch of civil liberty which ought by no means to be surrendered into the hands of the civil magistrate, and the best interests of society require that the right of conducting it be inviolably preserved to individuals."[85]

This became the great point of difference between French and English Lockians. For the French Lockians, it seemed to follow directly from the principle of the malleability of man that it was the state's duty to mould him into shape. No doubt, they were critical of the *actual* state, but even the actual state, they thought, was better than private interests. De la Chalotais' *Essai d'éducation rationel* (1763) based itself on the educational principles of Locke, but claimed "for the Nation an education dependent upon the State alone because education belongs essentially to the State," and this on the ground that "the teaching of morality belongs, and always has belonged, to the state."[86] The sharply contrasted attitude of the English followers of Locke is evident in William Godwin. Although in the first edition of his *Political Justice* (1793), he wholly adopted the Lockian theory of malleability—"the actions and dispositions of men are not the offspring of any original bias that they bring into the world in favour of one sentiment or character rather than another, but flow entirely from the operation of circumstances and events acting upon a faculty of receiving sensible impressions"[87]—he was a bitter enemy of all government, and argued that "public education has always expended its energies in the support of prejudice."[88] Mill's *On Liberty* (1859) carried Priestley's attitude into the nineteenth century.

[83] *Thoughts on Civil Liberty, Licentiousness & Faction* (1765), p. 156.
[84] *An Essay on the First Principles of Government* (1768), second edition (1771), p. 108.
[85] *Ibid*, p. 109.
[86] *Essai*, p. 17; p. 132 as quoted in Adamson, *A Short History of Education*, pp. 213–15.
[87] Bk I, Ch. IV, 3rd edition, 1797, p. 26. See on this question Basil Willey, *The Eighteenth Century Background* (London, 1940), Ch. XI. Godwin later came to feel that he had laid too much stress on the unimportance of innate differences.
[88] Bk. VI, Ch. VIII, edition cited, II, 299. "It teaches its pupils, not the fortitude that shall bring every proposition to the test of examination, but the art of vindicating such tenets as may chance to be established."

A general State education is a mere contrivance for moulding
people to be exactly like one another; and as the mould in which it
casts them is that which pleases the predominant power in the
government . . . in proportion as it is efficient and successful, it
establishes a despotism over the mind, leading by natural tendency
to one over the body.[89]

Thus, whereas in France the doctrine that education is all-powerful led
to a demand that it be entrusted to the state, in England it had precisely
the contrary effect. But the choice of educational agent did not lie for
Priestley, Godwin, and Mill, as it had for Helvétius and de la Chalotais,
between state and Jesuit; they identified the state with the Anglican
Church, and they wrote as dissenters. As John Bright put it in his speech
on proposals for a system of state education:

they [the Dissenters] have come to the conclusion that it is dangerous to them as members of Dissenting bodies, and dangerous
also to the civil liberty of the people, that the State should interfere
with education, since the government, it appears, is not able to
interfere without giving increased power to the clergy of an
already dominant Church.[90]

It was in the nineteenth century and the early twentieth century that
the doctrine of the malleability of man, and his perfection by, in a broad
sense, education reached the peak of its influence. As in Godwin, education is now taken to include, in the words of James Mill, "every thing,
which acts upon the being as it comes from the hand of nature, in such a
manner as to modify the mind, to render the train of feelings different
from what it would otherwise have been."[91] But in principle James Mill
does no more than follow Locke. "Custom; and Pain and Pleasure," he
writes, "these are the grand instruments or powers, by the use of which,
the purposes of education are to be attained."[92]

With this was associated, as it had not been in Locke, a doctrine of
perfectibility. "In psychology," wrote John Stuart Mill of his father, "his

[89] In *Utilitarianism, Liberty and Representative Government* (London, 1910), p. 161.

[90] *Speeches by John Bright*, ed. J. H. T. Rogers (London, 1868), II, 500. Matthew
Arnold's *The Popular Education of France* (1861) set out to break down resistance to the
idea of a state supported educational system, but Arnold admits the extent of the
opposition he has to contend against.

[91] Article on "Education," first published in the Supplement to the fifth edition of
the *Encyclopaedia Britannica*. It was written about 1818. My reference is to *James and
John Stuart Mill on Education*, ed. F. A. Cavenagh (Cambridge, 1931), p. 28.

[92] *Ibid.*, p. 17.

fundamental doctrine was the formation of all human character by circumstances, through the universal Principle of Association, and the consequent unlimited possibility of improving the moral and intellectual condition of mankind by education."[93] Robert Owen's significantly subtitled *New View of Society* or *Essays on the Formation of Character* (1813) is no less enthusiastic about the prospects of reforming human beings by educational means.

There is obviously a gap here; it is one thing to say that men are made by circumstances, quite another to say that circumstances are, or could be, such as to perfect them. Marx's question: "Who shall educate the educators?" had, indeed, been anticipated by Rousseau. "How can a child be well educated," he asks in *Emile*, "by one who has not been well educated himself? Can such a one be found? I know not."[94] Plato's philosopher-king, Bentham's legislator, are fictions invented to fill this gap; Hartley[95] and Priestley looked with confidence to the guiding hand of Providence; Helvétius dedicated *De l'homme* to Frederick, and Catherine, the Great—benevolent despots both.

Now, of course, the eighteenth-century dream has become the twentieth-century nightmare; we see no cause for optimism, far from it, in the belief that man is infinitely malleable. The eighteenth century was the century in which issues were reshaped; in which men began to argue whether nature or nurture, rather than whether God's grace or man's free will, is the fundamental moral agent. But in a sense the old issues remain. How can men be remade? Only by forces outside of them, or only by their own efforts, or by both in combination? The first supposition leads to tyranny; the second seems greatly to overestimate the extent and the potentialities of natural endowment. The third is, on the face of it, the most sensible alternative, the only one which accords with our everyday experience. But human beings are never for long content to be sensible.

---

[93] *Autobiography* (3rd ed.; London, 1874), p. 108. This view was attacked by Herbert Spencer in *On Education* (1861), ed. F. A. Cavenagh (Cambridge, 1932), pp. 116–17. Spencer rejects the view that man is born good, takes the view that he is born evil to be nearer the truth, and denies that he can be perfected by education.

[94] Edition cited, p. 17.

[95] But with certain qualms in Hartley's case. The doctrine of association, in its relation to education, "cannot fail both to instruct *and alarm* all such as have any degree of interested concern for themselves, or of a benevolent one for others" (Pt. 1, Ch. I, §2, Prop. XIV, cor. V, p. 52).

Herder and the Enlightenment

BY ISAIAH BERLIN

⊰⊰⊰⊰⊰⊰⊰⊰⊰⊰⊰ ☼ ⊱⊱⊱⊱⊱⊱⊱⊱⊱⊱⊱

"We live in a world we ourselves create." [1]

According to the traditional view, Herder's fame rests on the fact that he is the father of related notions of nationalism, historicism, and the *Volksgeist*, one of the leaders of the romantic revolt against classicism, rationalism, and faith in the omnipotence of scientific method—in short, the most formidable of the adversaries of the French *philosophes* and their German disciples. Whereas they—or at least the best known among them, d'Alembert, Helvétius, Holbach, and, with qualifications, Voltaire and Diderot, Wolff and Reimarus—believed that reality was ordered in terms of universal, timeless, objective, unalterable laws which rational investigation could discover, Herder maintained that every activity, situation, historical period, or civilization possessed a unique character of its own; so that the attempt to reduce such phenomena to combinations of uniform elements, and to describe or analyze them in terms of universal rules, tended to obliterate precisely those crucial differences which constituted the specific quality of the object under study, whether in nature or in history. To the notions of universal laws, absolute principles, final truths, idealized, eternal models and standards in ethics or aesthetics, physics or mathematics, he opposed a radical distinction between the method appropriate to the study of physical nature and that called for by the changing and developing spirit of man. He is credited with having revived the notion of social patterns, social growth, the vital importance of

[1] Unless otherwise indicated, all references are to J. G. Herder, *Sämtliche Werke*, ed. B. Suphan (Berlin, 1877–1913). The quotation is from *Uebers Erkennen und Empfinden in der Menschlichen Seele*, VIII, 252.

considering qualitative as well as quantitative factors—the impalpable and the imponderable, which the concepts of natural science ignore or deny. Preoccupied with the mysteries of the creative process, whether in individuals or groups, he launched (so we are told) a general attack on rationalism with its tendency to generalize, abstract, assimilate the dissimilar, unify the disparate, and, above all, on its avowed purpose to create a corpus of systematic knowledge which in principle would be capable of answering all intelligible questions—the idea of a unified science of all there is. And in the course of this propaganda against rationalism, scientific method, and the universal authority of intelligible laws, he is held to have stimulated the growth of particularism, literary, religious, and political irrationalism, and thereby transformed human thought and action in the generation that followed.

This account, which is to be found in the best known monographs on Herder's thought, is oversimple but broadly true. He was a sharp and remorseless critic of the Encyclopedists. His views did have a profound and revolutionary effect upon later thought and practice. He has been praised by some as the champion of faith against reason, poetical and historical imagination against the mechanical application of rules, insight against logic, life against death; by others he has been classed with confused, or retrograde, or irrationalist thinkers who misunderstood what they had learned from the Enlightenment, and fed the stream of German chauvinism and obscurantism; still others have sought to find common ground between him and Comte, or Darwin, or Wagner, or modern sociologists. It is not my purpose in this paper to pronounce directly upon these questions, although I am inclined to think that the extent of his acquaintance with, and fidelity to, the natural sciences of his day have often been underestimated. He was fascinated and influenced by the findings of the sciences no less than Goethe, and, like him, thought that false general inferences were often drawn from them. But it is not this that I propose to discuss. I wish to confine myself, so far as possible (and at times it is not) to what is truly original in Herder's views, and by no means to all of this: in particular I shall try to examine three cardinal ideas in the rich welter of his thought, ideas which have had great influence for two centuries and are novel, important, and interesting in themselves. These ideas, which go against the main stream of the thought of his time, I have called Populism, Expressionism, and Pluralism.[2]

---

[2] I shall necessarily have to omit much else that is relevant and interesting: for example, Herder's dominant influence on romanticism, vitalism, existentialism, and, above all, on social psychology, which he in effect founded; as well as the use made of

I

Let me begin by conceding the most obvious of Herder's debts to other thinkers:[3]

a) Herder's thesis that the proper subject of the historical sciences is the life of communities and not the exploits of individuals—statesmen, soldiers, kings and dynasties, adventurers, and other prominent figures— had been stated by Hume and Montesquieu, by Schlözer and Gatterer, and with incomparable imagination and originality by Vico. There is, so far as I know, no conclusive evidence that Herder had read Vico's *Scienza nuova* until at least twenty years after his own historical views had been fully formed; but if he had not read Vico he had heard of him, and probably read Wegelin, and Cesarotti's Homeric commentaries. At any rate, the notion of cultural history was far from new in his day, as the ironical title of his early *Yet Another Philosophy of History* was meant to emphasize. The case for it had been presented effectively by his arch-enemy Voltaire in the celebrated *Essai sur les moeurs* and elsewhere.

b) The notion that the variety of civilizations is, to a large degree, determined by differences of physical and geographical factors—referred to by the general name of "climate"—had become, since Montesquieu, a commonplace. It occurs, before Montesquieu, in the thought of Saint-Evremond, the Abbé Du Bos, and their followers.

c) The dangers of cultural arrogance—the tendency to judge ancient societies in terms of modern values—had been made a central issue by his older contemporary Lessing (even though Lessing may well have been influenced by Herder). Nor had anyone written more pungently than Voltaire against the European habit of dismissing as inferior remote civilizations, such as that of China which he had extolled in order to ex-

---

his imprecise, often inconsistent, but always many-faceted and stimulating thought, by such writers as the Schlegels and Jakob Grimm (especially in their philological excursions), Savigny (who derived from him the notion of organic national growth), Görres (whose nationalism is rooted in, even if it distorts, Herder's vision), Hegel (whose concepts of becoming, and of the growth and personality of impersonal institutions, derived directly from Herder's pages), as well as historical geographers, social anthropologists, philosophers of language and of history, and historical writers in the nineteenth and twentieth centuries. My principal reason for choosing the three ideas on which I intend to concentrate is that they are conceptions of the first order of originality and historical importance, the origins and properties of which have not received sufficient notice. My purpose is to do justice to his originality rather than his influence.

[3] The best discussion of this topic known to me occurs in Professor Max Rouché's excellent introduction to his edition and French translation of Herder's *Auch Eine Philosophie der Geschichte* (Aubier, Editions Montaigne, n.d.).

pose the ridiculous vanity, exclusiveness, and fanaticism of the "barbarous" Judeo-Christian outlook that recognized no values beside its own. The fact that Herder turned this weapon against Voltaire himself, and accused him of a narrowly *dix-huitième* and Parisian point of view, does not alter the fact that the head and source of all opposition to Europocentrism was the Patriarch himself. Voltaire had praised ancient Egypt, and Winckelmann the Greeks; Boulainvilliers had spoken of the superiority of the Northern nations, and so had Mallet in his celebrated history of Denmark; Hurd, Millar, and, after them Justus Möser, sang the praises of medieval Europe at the very height of the contemptuous dismissal of the Dark Ages by Voltaire and the *Encyclopédie*. They were, it is true, a minority, and while Möser's views may have been influenced by Herder, they were not created by him.

d) The dangers of taking profound differences of culture too lightly— that notorious lack of historical sense that made Racine and Corneille represent classical or exotic oriental personages in the clothes and with the manners of the courtiers of Louis XIV—had been commented on by Du Bos and successfully satirized by Saint-Evremond. At the other end of the scale, some of the German pietists, Zinzendorff and Arnold among others, had laid great stress on the proposition that every religion had a unique insight peculiar to itself, and based on this belief a passionate and unpopular plea for toleration of deviations from Lutheran orthodoxy and even of heresies and unbelief.

e) The notion of the spirit of a nation or a culture had been central not only to Vico and Montesquieu, but to the famous Karl Friedrich von Moser, whom Herder read and knew, to the Swiss scholars Bodmer and Breitinger, to Hamann and to Zimmermann. Bolingbroke had spoken of the division of men into nationalities as being deeply rooted in Nature herself. By the middle of the century there were plenty of Celtomaniacs and Gothomaniacs—notably Irishmen and Scotsmen who, even without the aid of Ossian, praised the virtues of Gaelic or Germanic tribes, and were representing them as being morally and socially superior to ancient Greeks or Romans, still more to the decadent civilization of modern Latin and Mediterranean peoples. Rousseau's celebrated letter to the Poles, advising them to resist forcible assimilation by Russia—to do this by deliberately exaggerating their national customs and characteristics, unacceptable as this was to the cosmopolitanism of his time, exhibits the same spirit.

f) The notion of society as an organism was by this time very old indeed. The use of organic metaphors is at least as old as Aristotle; nobody had used them more lavishly than medieval writers; they are the heart and center of John of Salisbury's political tracts, and are a weapon consciously used by Hooker and Pascal against the new scientific-mechanical conceptions. There was certainly nothing novel in this notion; it represents, on the contrary, if anything, a deliberate return to older views of social life. This is no less true of Burke, who was equally prone to the use of analogies drawn from the new biological sciences; I know of no evidence that Burke had read or heard of Justus Möser's or Herder's ideas.

g) Differences of ideals—of what made men happy—had been noticed vividly by Adam Ferguson in his highly original essay on the "History of Civil Society," which Herder had read. [4]

h) As for the general explanation of events in naturalistic terms, whether geophysical or biological, this was the normal approach of the followers of Locke, Helvétius and the Encyclopedists, and indeed of the entire Enlightenment. Unlike his teacher Hamann, Herder was decisively affected by it; he gave it a vitalistic but not the mystical or theosophical interpretation favoured by Hemsterhuis, Lavater, and other "intuitivists."

i) The ancient notion of a single great cosmic force of Nature, embodied in finite, dynamic centers, had been given new life by Leibniz and was common to all his disciples.

j) In the same manner the idea of a divine plan realized in human history had passed in uninterrupted succession from the Old Testament and its Jewish interpreters to the Christian Fathers and then to the classical formulation of Bossuet.

k) The parallels between primitive peoples remote from one another in time and space—Homeric Greeks and early Romans on the one hand, and Red Indians or Germanic tribes on the other—had been put forward by Fortenelle and by the French Jesuit Père Laffitteau; the protagonists of this approach in the early years of the century, especially English writers such as Blackwell and the Wartons, owed much to these forerunners. It had become part and parcel of Homeric scholarship, which flourished both in England and under the impulsion of Vico in Italy. Certainly Cesarotti had perceived the wider implications of this kind of approach to literature for comparative philology and anthropology; and when the *Encyclopédie* dismissed Homer in the course of a general article devoted to the Greeks as "a Greek philosopher, theologian and poet" unlikely to be read much in the future, this was a characteristically partisan *boutade*, in

---

[4] The late Mr. Harold Laski's description of Ferguson as "a pinchbeck Montesquieu" throws light only on the quality of Mr. Laski's critical judgment, in this intance probably a mere echo of Leslie Stephen.

the spirit of Descartes and Pierre Bayle, against reverence for the past and dreary scholarship. Nor was the Bible itself, which Vico had not dared to touch, left unmolested. Philological and historical criticism of the text, which had begun with Spinoza and Père Simon in the previous century, had been carried on cautiously—despite some opposition from Christian orthodoxy, both Catholic and Protestant—with strict regard to the rules of secular scholarship. Astruc in France, Lowth in England, and after them Michaelis in Germany (and Denmark), treated the Bible as a piece of oriental antiquity composed at various dates. Everyone knows of Gibbon's debt to Mosheim's coldly secular treatment of early Christian ecclesiastical history. Herder, who was in no sense a trained researcher, had plenty to lean upon.

l) The same is true of Herder's linguistic patriotism. The defense of the German language had been vigorously taken up by Opitz at the turn of the sixteenth century, and had since then formed part of the conscious program of theologians, men of letters, and philosophers. Menke, Horneck, Moscherosch, Logau, and Uden are names that may not mean a great deal to English readers today; but in the two centuries that followed the Reformation they fought with stubbornness and success under Luther's banner against both Latin and French; and more famous men, Puffendorff and Leibniz, Thomasius and Wolff, Hamann and Lessing were also engaged in the same campaign that had begun long before. Once again, Herder began with something that had by that time become established as a traditional German attitude.

m) As for the famous reversal of values—the triumph of the concrete over the abstract; the sharp turn toward the immediate, the given, the experienced and, above all, away from abstractions, theories, generalizations, and stylized patterns; and the restoration of quality to its old status above quantity, and of the secondary qualities of the senses to their primacy over the primary qualities of physics—it is in this cause that Hamann made his name. It formed the basis of Lavater's "physiognomical" researches; it was at least as old as Shaftesbury; it is pertinent to the works of the young Burke.

n) The reaction against the reorganization of knowledge and society by the application of rationalist and scientific principles was in full swing by the time Herder came upon the scene. Rousseau had struck against it in 1750 with his First Discourse. Seven years later his moralizing and reactionary letter to d'Alembert denouncing the stage had marked a total break with the party of the *philosophes,* as both sides swiftly recognized. In Germany this mood was strongly reinforced by the inward-looking tradition of the Pietist movement. The human solidarity and mutual respect of these small groups, inspired by their burning Protestant faith; their belief in the unadorned truth, in the power of goodness, in the inner light; their contempt for outward forms; their rigid sense of duty and discipline; their perpetual self-examination; their obsession with the presence of evil, which at times took hysterical or sadistic forms and generated a good deal of unctuous hypocrisy; and above all their preoccupation with the life of the spirit which alone liberated men from the bonds of the flesh and of nature—all these strains are very strong in those who were brought up in this stern atmosphere, and particularly in Prussians like Hamann, Herder, and Kant. Although a great intellectual gulf divides Kant from Herder, they share a common element: a craving for spiritual self-determination as against half-conscious drifting along the streams of uncriticized dogma (whether theological or scientific), for moral independence (whether of individuals or groups), and above all for moral salvation.

If Herder had done no more than create a genuine synthesis out of these attitudes and doctrines, and built with them, if not a system, at any rate a coherent *Weltanschauung* destined to have a decisive influence on the literature and thought of his country, this alone would have been a high enough achievement to earn for him a unique place in the history of civilization. Invention is not everything. If one were called upon to show what is strictly original in the individual doctrines of Locke or Rousseau, Bentham or Marx, Aquinas, and even Hegel, one could, without much difficulty, trace virtually all their doctrines to antecedent "sources." Yet this does not derogate from the originality and genius of these thinkers. "Small change for a *Napoléon d'or* is not a Napoleon." It is not, however, my purpose to evaluate the work of Herder as a whole, but only to consider certain authentically *sui generis* doctrines which he launched; to discuss them not only for the sake of historical justice, but also as views that are peculiarly relevant and interesting in our own time. Herder's final claim need not rest upon what was, if I am right, most original in his thought. For his vast general influence has sometimes, paradoxically, served to overshadow that which he, virtually alone, launched upon the world.

II

Let me return to the three topics of this study, namely:

1. *Populism:* the belief in the value of belonging to a group or a culture, which for Herder at least, is not political, and is indeed, to some degree,

anti-political; it is therefore different from and even opposed to nationalism.

2. *Expressionism:* [5] the doctrine that human activity in general, and art in particular, express the entire personality of the individual or the group, and are intelligible only to the degree to which they do so. Still more specifically, expressionism claims that all the works of men are above all voices speaking, are not objects detached from their makers, are part of a living process of communication between persons and not independently existing entities, beautiful or ugly, interesting or boring, upon which external observers may direct the cool and dispassionate gaze with which scientists—or anyone not given to pantheism or mysticism—look on objects in nature. This is connected with the further notions that all forms of human self-expression are in some sense artistic, and that self-expression is part of the essence of human beings as such; which in turn entail such distinctions as those between integral and divided or committed and uncommitted (that is, unfulfilled) lives; and thence lead to the concept of various hindrances, human and non-human, to the self-realization which is the richest and most harmonious form of self-expression that all creatures, whether or not they are aware of it, live for.

3. *Pluralism:* the belief not merely in the multiplicity but in the incommensurability of the values of different cultures and societies and, in addition, in the incompatibility of equally valid ideals, together with the implied revolutionary corollary that the classical notions of an ideal man and of an ideal society are intrinsically incoherent and meaningless.

Each of these three theses is relatively novel; all are incompatible with the central moral, historical, and aesthetic doctrines of the Enlightenment. They are not independent of each other. Everything in the illimitable, varied, and exceedingly rich panorama which Herder's works present is interwoven. Indeed, the notion of unity in difference, still more that of differences in unity, the tension of the One and the Many, is his obsessive *idée maîtresse.* Hence the recurrence through all his discussions of a constant theme: the "organic" oneness of personality with the form of life that it leads, the empirical and metaphysical unity of the physical and the mental, of intellect, will, and emotion—distinctions and classifications that he regarded as, at best, superficial, at worst, as profoundly misleading; hence the stress on the oneness of thought and feeling, of theory and practice, of the public and the private, or, in other words, on the heroic

---

[5] I use this term in its wider, most generic sense, with no specific reference to the Expressionist painters, writers, and composers of the early decades of the twentieth century.

effort to see the universe as a single process. The celebrated words with which he opens his most famous and ambitious work, *Ideas towards a Philosophy of History*—"the earth is a star among stars"—are very characteristic. There follow chapters on geology, climate, mineral, vegetable and animal life, and lessons in physical geography, until, at last, early man is reached; there is a corresponding attempt to link all the arts and all the sciences, to represent religious, artistic, social, political, economical, biological, philosophical experience as facets of one activity. And since the pattern is one, fact and value are not divided (*pace* Hume and Kant, with whose works Herder was only too familiar). To understand a thing was, for him, to see how it could be viewed as it was viewed, assessed as it was assessed, valued as it was valued, in a given context, by a particular culture or tradition. To grasp what a belief, a piece of ritual, a myth, a poem, or a linguistic usage meant to a Homeric Greek, a Livonian peasant, an ancient Hebrew, an American Indian, that is, what part it played in his life, was for Herder to be able not merely to give a scientific or common-sense explanation but to give a reason or justification of the activity in question, or at least to go a long way toward this. For to explain human experiences or attitudes is to be able to transpose oneself by sympathetic imagination into the situation of the human beings who are to be "explained"; and this amounts to understanding and communicating the coherence of a particular way of life, feeling, action: and thereby the validity of the given act or action, the part it plays in the life and outlook which is "natural" in the situation. Explanation and justification, reference to causes and to purposes, to the visible and the invisible, statements of fact and their assessment in terms of the historical standards of value relevant to them, melt into one another, and seem to Herder to be a single type, and not several types of thinking. Herder is one of the originators of the secular doctrine of the unity of fact and value, theory and practice, "is" and "ought," intellectual judgment and emotional commitment, thought and action.

The sharpest critics of Herder have always conceded the power and breadth of his imagination. He did have an astonishing capacity for conceiving a great variety of actual and possible societies in the past and the present, and an unexampled warmth of sympathy for them all. He was inspired by the possibility of reconstructing forms of life as such, and he delighted in bringing out their individual shape, the fullness of human experience embodied in them; the odder, the more extraordinary a culture or an individual, the better pleased he was. He can hardly condemn anything that displays color or uniqueness; Indians, Americans, and Persians, Greece and Palestine, Arminius and Machiavelli, Shakespeare and Savonarola, seem to him equally fascinating. He deeply hates the forces that make for uniformity, assimilation, whether in life or in the books of historians, of one culture or way of life to another. He conscientiously looks for uniformities, but what fascinates him is the exception. He condemns the erection of walls between one genus and another; but he seeks for the greatest possible number of distinctions of species within a genus, and of individuals within the species. Hamann had preached to him the need to preserve sensitiveness to specific historical and cultural phenomena, to avoid becoming deadened by the passion for classification and generalization demanded by networks of tidy concepts, a fatal tendency which he attributed to the natural sciences and to their slaves, the Frenchmen who wished to transform everything by the application of scientific method. Like Hamann, Herder preserved his childlike impressionability—his capacity to react spontaneously to the jagged, irregular, not always describable data provided by the senses, by imagination, by religious revelation, by history, by art. He did not hasten to refer them to their appropriate cases in the museum of concepts; he was penetrated through and through by the spirit of empiricism, of the sacredness of facts. Not so much as Hamann, but more than even Lessing and Diderot, and incomparably more than such official materialists and "sensualists" as Condillac or Helvétius, Herder avoided the temptation to reduce the heterogeneous flow of experience to homogeneous units, to label them and fit them into theoretical frameworks in order to be able to predict and control them. The notorious luxuriance and formlessness of his ideas is due at least as much to his sense of the complexity of the facts themselves as to a naturally rhapsodical and turbid mind. As a writer he is exuberant and disordered, but not obscure or vague. Even at his most rapt he is not somnambulistic or self-intoxicated; he does not, even in his most lyrical moments, fly from the facts to an ideal heaven above, like the German metaphysical poets of his time, Gleim or Uz or Klopstock or even Goethe on occasions. Great scientists and philosophers have often made their impact by violently exaggerating their original insights. But Herder cannot let go of what he sees, feels, hears, learns. His sense of the texture of reality is concrete, while his analytical powers are feeble. The three original theses which form the subject of this study display this and have consequently often been a source of irritation to tidier, clearer, logically more gifted thinkers.

III

Let me begin with Herder's Populism, or the idea of what it is to belong to a group. Everyone seems agreed that "Herder began as a typical, almost routine defender of the great ideals of eighteenth-century enlightenment, that is, as a humanitarian, a cosmopolitan, and a pacifist. Later, so it seems to be assumed, he evolved toward more reactionary views: the abandonment of reason and intellect, intuitionism, nationalism, Gallophobia, faith, and belief in tradition. Was this, after all, not the evolution in some degree of other thinkers of his and the succeeding generation in Germany? Almost without exception, they began by welcoming the French Revolution rapturously, planting trees of liberty, and denouncing as obsolete and brutally oppressive the rule of the three hundred German princes, until, horrified by the Terror and wounded by the military humiliation of Germany before the armies of Revolutionary France and, still more, those of Napoleon, they turned into patriots, reactionaries, and romantic irrationalists. Was not this the path pursued by Fichte (above all Fichte), Goerres, Novalis and the Schlegels, Schleiermacher and Tieck, Gentz and Schelling, and to some degree even by Hegel and Schiller? Were not Goethe and Humboldt (and Georg Forster, though he died before the reaction set in) almost alone in their unswerving fidelity to reason, toleration, and the unity of mankind, and in their loathing of nationalism and all forms of collective emotional afflatus? It it not reasonable to assume that this process of retreat from reason took place in Herder too? True, he died before the most crushing defeats had been inflicted by Napoleon on the German armies and princes; yet was it not the case that Herder began as a cosmopolitan and ended as a nationalist? Here too, then, so it would seem, wounded national pride, and perhaps age and the cooling of youthful utopianism, had had their inescapable effect. Yet this view seems to me untenable. Whatever may have been the evolution of Fichte or Friedrich Schlegel, Herder's form of nationalism remained unaltered throughout his life. His national feeling was not political and never became so, nor yet did he abandon or modify the peculiar brand of universalism with which he had begun, whether or not the two tendencies were consistent (the least of his concerns) throughout his long and voluminous intellectual activity.

As early as 1765, in an address composed in Riga, where at the age of twenty-one he occupied the post of a Lutheran preacher in that officially Russian city, in answer to the question "Have we still a republic and a fatherland like the Ancients?," [6] Herder declared that this was no longer the case. In Greece the strength and the glory of the *polis* were the supreme goals of all free men. Religion, morals, tradition, every aspect of human activity stemmed from and were directed to maintaining the city, and any danger to it was a danger to all that these men were and lived by; if it fell, everything fell with it. But then, he went on to say, Christianity came and the horizons of mankind became immeasurably wider. Christianity, he explained, is a universal religion: it embraces all men and all peoples; it transcends all local and temporary loyalties in the worship of what is universal and eternal. [7]

This thesis was highly characteristic of the Christian humanism of the German *Aufklärung*, and, despite all that has been said to the contrary, Herder never abandoned this point of view. His central belief was expressed toward the end of his life in words similar to those of his early writings: "To brag of one's country is the stupidest form of boastfulness. A nation is a wild garden full of bad plants and good, vices and follies mingle with virtues and merit. What Don Quixote will break a lance for this Dulcinea?" [8] Patriotism was one thing, nationalism another: "An innocent attachment to family, language, one's own city, one's own country, its traditions, are not to be condemned." But he goes on to say that "aggressive nationalism" is detestable in all its manifestations, and wars are mere crimes. This is so because "All large wars are essentially civil wars, since men are brothers, and wars are a form of abominable fratricide." [9] A year later he adds: "We must have nobler heroes than Achilles, loftier patriots than Horatius Cocles." [10] And many years later, in 1794, he repeats this: "One fatherland ranged against another in bloody battle is the worst barbarism in the human vocabulary." These views can scarcely be due merely to the fact, by which they are sometimes explained, that political nationalism would have been too unrealistic an outlook in a feeble and divided country governed by several hundred hereditary despots; so that even to look for it there demonstrates a lack of historical sense. For the Italians, who were no less divided and politically impotent, had developed a distinct craving for political unification which dated back at least to Machiavelli, even though the prevailing social and political conditions in Italy were not so very unlike those of eighteenth-century Germany.

[6] I, 13–28.
[7] *Ibid.*
[8] XVII, 211.
[9] XVII, 319.
[10] XVIII, 86.

Herder's attitude is clearly the normal enlightened attitude of his time; the point, however, is that he did not abandon it. He believed in kinship, social solidarity, *Volkstum*, nationhood, but to the end of his life he detested and denounced every form of centralization, coercion, and conquest, which were embodied and symbolized both for him, and for his teacher Hamann, in the accursed state. Nature creates nations, not states.[11] "The State is an instrument of happiness for a group,"[12] not for men as such. There is nothing against which he thunders more eloquently than imperialism—the crushing of one community by another, the elimination of local cultures trampled under the jackboot of some conqueror. He vies with Justus Möser in his tenderness toward long-lived traditions and institutions embodied in particular forms of life that have created unity and continuity in a human community. He cares nothing for *virtù* in the Renaissance sense of the term. Alexander the Great is not a hero for him. The basis of the state is conquest, the history of states is the history of violence, a bloodstained story of aggression. The state is Ixion's wheel and calls for meaningless self-immolation. "Why should hundreds suffer hunger and cold to satisfy the whim of a crowned madman, or the dreams bred by the fancy of a *philosophe?*" This may be directed specifically at Frederick the Great and his French advisers, but the import of it is universal. All rule of men over fellow men is unnatural. True human relations are those of father and son, husband and wife, sons, brothers, friends, men; these terms express natural relations which make people happy. All that the state has given us is contradictions and conquests[13] and, perhaps worst of all, dehumanization ("What pleasure is there in being a blind cog in a machine?"[14]). God has divided the world by mountains and oceans in order to prevent some fearful Nimrod from conquering the whole. The *Ideen* anticipate socialist historians in representing the history of conquerors as the history of man-hunters. Despite his vow to look with a sympathetic, or at least impartial, eye upon all cultures and all nations, he cannot bring himself to forgive Rome for crushing the cultures of the peoples it has conquered, not even that of Carthage. There may be merit in efficiency and unity, but it is for him more than offset

[11] XIII, 340, 375. Millions of people on the globe live without states. Father and mother, man and wife, child and brother, friend and man—these are natural relationships through which we become happy; what the *state* can give us is an artificial construction; unfortunately it can also do something much more far-reaching to us—rob us of ourselves (XIII, 340–41).

[12] XIII, 333ff.

[13] *Ibid.*

[14] *Ibid.*

by the tragedy of the destruction; that is, by the evil of the barbarous disregard of so many spontaneous, natural forms of human self-expression: "Whom nature separated by language, customs, character, let no man artificially join together by chemistry,"[15] This is what the Romans tried to do and how the whole Roman Empire was held together. And its "Holy" successor was no better, but was rather an unnatural monster— an absurd clamping together of disparate cultures—"a lion's head with a dragon's tail, an eagle's wing, a bear's paw, ["glued together"] in one unpatriotic symbol of a state."[16] The Jews, "parasitic money-lenders" now, [16a] were at least not self-worshippers; and they are praised for not having made Palestine the source and center of the world, for not having idealized their ancestors, and for not deriving their genealogy from gods and demigods (it is this last that has enabled them to survive the Diaspora[16b]). Empires, especially multinational ones ("a wild mingling of various tribes and peoples under one sceptre"), rest on force; they have feet of clay and must collapse. Theocracies that are founded upon some non-political principle, a spiritual or religious force—China or Egypt, for example, to take only non-Christian faiths—have proved correspondingly more durable. The sword of the spirit is better than mere brute force: not even the acutest poverty, the deepest squalor, still less ambition and love of power, entitle men to have recourse to violence. Like Möser, Herder laments the fact that the Germans are poor, hungry, and despised; that Luther's widow had to beg for help from the King of Denmark; that Kepler died of hunger; that men of German speech have been scattered and exiled to England, Russia, and Transylvania; that gifted artists and inventors are compelled to leave their country and lavish their gifts upon

---

[15] XVIII, 206.

[16] XIII, 385.

[16a] XIV, 65.

[16b] "Herder was fascinated by the survival of the Jews; he looked upon them as a 'most excellent example' of a *volk* with its own distinct character" (X, 139). "Moses bound the heart of his people to their native soil" (XII, 115). Land, common language, tradition, sense of kinship, common tradition, common law as a freely accepted "covenant"—all these interwoven factors, together with the bond created by their sacred literature, enabled the Jews to retain their identity in dispersion—but especially the fact that their eyes remained focused upon their original geographical home (XII, 115; VIII, 355; and XVII, 312)—historical continuity, not race, is what counts (XII, 107). This is what creates historical individuality (XII, 123, and XXXII, 207). On this entire subject, and especially the view of the "Jewish problem," not as religious, but political, needing what later came to be known as a Zionist solution, see the very interesting article by Professor F. M. Barnard, "Herder and Israel," contributed to *Jewish Social Studies*, which the author has kindly allowed me to read before publication.

foreigners; that Hessians are sold and bought like "Negro slaves" while their families starve and perish. Nevertheless, conquest is not the answer. The German mission is to be a nation of thinkers and educators. This is their true glory.[17] Sacrifice—self-sacrifice—not the domination of one man over another, is the proper end of man. Herder sets his face against everything that is predatory, against the use of force in any cause but that of self-defense. The Crusades, no matter how Christian in inspiration, are hateful to him, since they conquered and crushed other human communities. Yet consent for him is a false basis of society, for consent is ultimately a form of yielding, however rational or voluntary, to strength, whereas human relations must rest upon respect, affection, kinship, equality, not fear or prudence and utilitarian calculation. It is when religions forget the ends of man and turn into empty, mechanical cults, that they develop into a source of unintelligible mystification and their ceremonies decay into a recital of dead formulas, while the priests, who no longer understand their own faith, become instruments of other forces—in particular of the state and the men who control it. For him, as for Nietzsche, the state is the coldest of all cold monsters. Nothing in the whole of human history is more hateful to him than the churches and priests who are the instruments of political power; of these he speaks with the same voice as Voltaire or d'Holbach; while "The State" (he says in words that could have been Rousseau's) "robs men of what is most important—themselves."[18] The state becomes a drug with the help of which men seek to forget themselves, a self-generated method of escaping from the need to live, create, and choose. Furthermore, the sheer exercise of bureaucratic activity is a form of self-intoxication, and he speaks of it as a kind of opium by which men are transformed into mechanical functionaries. Profound differences, both personal and literary, came to divide Herder from Goethe and Schiller, but when in their jointly written *Xenien* they say

Deutschland? aber wo liegt's, Ich weiss das Land nicht zu finden.
Wo das Gelehrte beginnt, hört das Politische auf.

("Das Deutsche Reich")

or

[17] The most eloquent statement of Herder's conception of the German's earthly miseries and spiritual task is to be found in his epistle in verse, *German National Glory*, written in 1792, but published posthumously in 1812 (XVIII, 214–16) when the mood of many of his countrymen, whipped into a frenzy of nationalism by Jahn, Arndt, Körner, and Görres, was wholly different.

[18] XIII, 341.

Zur Nation euch zu bilden, Ihr hoffet es, Deutsche vergebens;
Bildet, Ihr Könnt es, dafür, freier zu Menschen euch aus,
("Deutscher National Charakter")

they speak for Herder too. The state is the substitution of machinery for life—a prospect, and a reality, that frightened him no less than it did Rousseau.

What then is the right life for men? They should live in natural units, that is, in societies united by a common culture. Nature creates nations, not states,[19] and does not make some nations intrinsically superior to others.[20] There is no *Favoritvolk*.[21] A nation is made what it is by "climate," education, relations with its neighbors, and other changeable and empirical factors, and not by an impalpable inner essence or an unalterable factor such as race or color. All this, said late in his life, is the pure milk of the doctrine of the Enlightenment. Herder protests, not without a certain malicious satisfaction (as Hamann also did, with equally ironical pleasure) that the great liberal Kant in his *Anthropologie* emphasized race and color too much. He is equally indignant about Kant's proposition that men need a master; he replies that "animals need a master, not men";[22] and he denounces Kant's philosophy of history, according to which it is the vices of mankind—desire for power and mastery over the scarce resources of the earth—that stimulate competition, struggle, and thereby progress, with the corollary that the sufferings of the individual are indispensable to the improvement of the species (a doctrine that was destined to reach its richest development in Hegel, and in another form in Spencer's evolutionary doctrine and the vagaries of social Darwinism). Herder repudiates these doctrines in the pure spirit of liberal, individualist, Weimar cosmopolitanism. Indeed, the perception that cruel and sinister implications are contained in any doctrine that preaches the sacrifice of individuals on the altar of vast abstractions—the human species, society, civilization, progress (later thinkers were to say, race, state, class, and a chosen élite)—has its true beginnings here. Kant's unconcealed lack of sympathy for Herder's sweeping and imprecise generalizations, and his complaints that these were never supported either by adequate evidence or rigorous argument, may in part

---

[19] XIII, 340, 375.

[20] XVII, 212.

[21] XVIII, 247, 248. "There must be no order of rank;...the negro is as much entitled to think the white man degenerate, as the white man is to think of the negro as a black beast." I owe this quotation to Barnard, *op. cit.*

[22] XIII, 383.

account for Herder's deliberate choice of the famous champion of the inexorable voice of duty, the moral equality of men, and the infinite value of the individual, as the butt of his own passionate anti-racialism and anti-imperialism and of his defense of the right of all men and nations to develop along their own, self-chosen, lines. Variety does not, for Herder, entail conflict. He does not see why one community absorbed in the development of its own native talent should not respect a similar activity on the part of others. The Kant of the *Grundlegung* or of *Zum ewigen Frieden* might have agreed; but the Kant of the *Anthropologie* and the other essays on universal history evidently did not. Kant's reputed consistency is largely mythical.

IV

What determines the units in which it is "natural" for men to live? Herder implicitly rejects Aristotle's (and Rousseau's) doctrine that a "natural" or satisfactory human society is constituted only of small human groups in which men can know each other face to face and where (in Aristotle's phrase) one herald can be heard by all. Societies are created by climate, geography, physical and biological needs, and similar factors; they are made one by common traditions and common memories, of which the principal link and vehicle—indeed, more than vehicle, the very incarnation—is language. "Has a nation anything more precious than the language of its fathers? In it dwell its entire world of tradition, history, religion, principles of existence; its whole heart and soul."[23] It is so because men necessarily think in symbols, since to think is to use symbols; and their feelings and attitudes of life are incorporated in symbolic forms—worship, poetry, ritual. This is so whether what they seek are pleasures or necessities—the dance, the hunt, primitive forms of social solidarity expressed and preserved by myth and formalized representation, in fact, the entire network of belief and behavior that binds men to one another, can be explained only in terms of common, public symbolism, in particular by language. Herder had derived from Hamann his notion that words and ideas are one. Men do not think, as it were, in thoughts and ideas and then look for words in which to "clothe" them, as one looks for a glove to fit a fully formed hand. Hamann taught that to think was to use symbols, and that to deny this was not so much false as unintelligible, because without symbolism one was led fallaciously to divide

[23] XVII, 58.

the aspects of a single experience into separate entities—the fatal doctrine of Descartes, who spoke of mind and body, thought and its object, matter and mind, as though they were independent existents. Such distinctions as we draw between thought and feeling (and their "objects"), physical sensation and intellectual or moral or aesthetic awareness are, according to Hamann (where one can understand him), an attempt to draw attention now to this, now that facet of a single experience; a tendency which, pushed too far, tends to separate and abstract one facet from another, and, pushed further still, to invent imaginary abstract objects—or idealized entities—to transform reality into a collection of artificial figments. This springs from a craving for tidy scientific classification, but it distorts the facts, congeals the continuous flow of the living sense of Nature and of God into dead fragments, and kills the sources of the true sense of reality—the imagination, the sense of divine revelation, which men, unspoiled by the logic and metaphysics of rationalism, always have. Hamann was a Christian touched by mysticism: he looked upon the world, upon nature and history, as the speech of God to man; God's words were hieroglyphs, often tormentingly dark, or they were allegories, or they were symbols which opened doors to the vision of the truth which, if only men saw and heard aright, answered the questions of their heads and hearts.[24] Hamann was not himself a visionary. He had had no special revelation; but when, in the midst of an acute spiritual crisis, he turned to the Bible, he was overwhelmed by the realization that the history of the Jews embodied a universal, trans-historical truth: for it symbolized his own—and every man's—painful quest for God. Men were made in God's image, but as Hamann's Pietist ancestors had taught, man was sinful and weak, he stumbled and fell and rose again as he sought to hear the voice of his father and master, the Christ within and without him, who alone could make him whole. Man was healed only by surrendering himself to the unity of life, by allowing his entire being—spirit and flesh, mind, will, and above all senses—to take in that which God was saying to him directly, and also signified by means of the working of Nature and by the pattern of human history. Nature and history were symbols—cryptograms—of the Logos, for those who were not perverted by metaphysical subtleties, to read. Sin was denial of divine grace and of what God had given man: passions, desires, love, a sense of joy in every manifestation of life, of sensuous nature, of creation and procreation in all forms. The

[24] The sources of this view in Christian mysticism and Neoplatonism, and its form in other philosophical systems—for instance, that of Berkeley—have not been sufficiently investigated.

existence of this reality could not, indeed, be proved; Hume was right; no facts or events can be demonstrated to exist by reason; yet we accept them because we cannot help it, because it is animal faith in the external world which alone makes it possible for us to think or act at all. God, the world of the senses, the meanings of words—all are directly given and intimately present to any man if only he will let himself see, hear, be.

Herder remained free from mysticism. It was Hamann's rejection of rationalist analyses, and his unabashed sensualism and empiricism as well as his simple Christian faith that influenced Herder, and not the peculiar mystical nominalism which led Hamann to seek to understand God's hidden purposes in the occult significance of the individual Hebrew or Greek words of Holy Writ. Hamann's doctrine of language—that language alone was the central organ of all understanding and all purposive action, that men's fundamental activity was to speak to others (to men or God or themselves), and that only through language could individuals, or groups, and the meanings that they embodied in poetry or ritual, or in the network of human institutions and ways of life, be understood—this great revelation became an article of faith for Herder. To understand men was to understand what they meant, intended, or wished to communicate. Creation is communication. During the great debate in the eighteenth century about the origins of human speech he acquired a European reputation by saying that language was neither a sudden gift by God, as Süssmilch and other orthodox Christian writers maintained, nor a deliberate invention of particular men at a specific moment of time, like the wheel or the compass, a tool for the improvement of life, as the French scientists—Maupertuis and Condillac—came near to saying, and Monboddo explicitly maintained. Language was a natural growth, no more and no less mysterious than any other form of natural development which, if one believed in a creative God, was divine, inasmuch as God had given man a nature capable of generating symbols, the power of communication, and intentionality. At other times—recalled, perhaps by Hamann, to his beliefs as a Lutheran clergyman—indeed the clerical head of the Grand Duchy in Weimar—Herder recanted and conceded that language was indeed planted in, or taught to, man by God, by a specific creative act. But he could not rest in this belief. How could creatures not spiritually developed enough to use language come suddenly to be capable of doing so? And what is it to be spiritually developed, if not to be capable of thought (i.e., the use of symbols, whether images or gestures or words)? Defying the strict Lutherans, toward the end of his life Herder returned openly to the belief that language was an intrinsic part of the natural process of the growth of consciousness, indeed, of human solidarity, which rests on communication between men; for to be fully human is to think, and to think is to communicate; society and man are equally inconceivable without one another. Hence, "Mere intelligence without the expression of language is on earth a mere Utopia."[25] Herder means that it is inconceivable rather than improbable. Words, by connecting passions with things, the present with the past, and by making possible memory and imagination, create family, society, literature, history. He declares that to speak and think in words is to "swim in an inherited stream of images and words; we must accept these media on trust: we cannot create them." The notion of a wholly solitary—not an artificially self-isolated—man is to him as unintelligible as to Aristotle or to some linguistic philosophers of our own time. Mere contemplation yields no truth; it is only life, that is, action with or against others, that does so. For Herder man is shaped by, and must be defined in terms of, his association with others. We can purify and reform a language, but we cannot create one out of nothing; for to create a language is to think, and to think is to use language. This circle cannot be broken. The relation of particular words or groups of words to specific things is not logically or metaphysically necessary, but causal or conventional. Particular words are used in communicating particular experiences, either as a result of natural influences—environmental factors—collectively called "climate," after Montesquieu; or of psychological ones; or of mere chance; or of the decisions of human beings who, acquiring some terms by "natural" means (in some preconscious state) invent others as they please, arbitrarily. That is why the doctrine of real essences—the Wolffian plan of discovering the truth by the analysis of concepts—is a chimaera. We have no insight into "essences." Locke was right: only experience can tell us if the expression X in a particular text means the same as the expression Y. The dogmatic certainty of fanatical sectarians about what this or that sacred writing must mean is therefore irrational and groundless. Knowledge of philology—the historical development of languages—alone yields the story of changing uses and meanings. Herder is anti-mechanistic: but he is an empiricist, in direct descent from Occam and the English naturalists. Only assiduous historical research, sympathetic insight into the purpose of the speaker, a grasp of the machinery of communication whereby human beings understand each other, whether directly or across the centuries, can bridge the chasms between different, yet never wholly divorced, civilizations. "Language expresses the collective experience of the group."[26]

[25] XII, 357.
[26] XI, 225. See also XVII, 59; XVIII, 346; XXX, 8.

Has a nation anything more precious? From a study of native literatures we have learned to know ages and peoples more deeply than along the sad and frustrating path of political and military history. In the latter we seldom see more than the manner in which a people was ruled, how it let itself be slaughtered; in the former we learn how it thought, what it wished and craved for, how it took its pleasures, how it was led by its teachers or its inclinations.[27]

Hence Herder's stress on the importance of genetic studies and the history of language, and hence, too, the great impulsion that he gave to studies of comparative linguistics, comparative anthropology and ethnology, and above all to the great philological movement that became the pride of German scholarship toward the end of his life and in the century that followed. His own efforts in this direction were no less suggestive or speculative than those of Vico. After declaring, in language borrowed from Lavater, that "the physiognomy of language is all important," he insisted, for example, that the languages which preserved genders (e.g., Russian, with which he came into contact during his Riga years) implied a vision of a world different from the world of those whose languages are "sexless"; so too did particular uses of pronouns. He insisted that verbs— connected with action—came before nouns connected with contemplative objects; that active nations employ different linguistic modes from passive ones; that the nuances of language are pointers to differing forms of experience (*Weltanschauungen*). Logic for him is only an abstraction from languages living or dead. There is no logical structure "presupposed" *a priori* by all forms of rational thought; in his *Sprachphilosophie*, logic is an approximation to what is common in isomorphic languages, which themselves point to a high degree of similarity in the experiences of their users. Anthropology, not metaphysics or logic, whether Aristotelian or Leibnizian or Kantian, is for Herder the key to the understanding of human beings and of their world. It is the history of language that most clearly and continuously reveals such phenomena as social growth—the cycles of infancy, youth, maturity, decay—that are common to individuals and nations. The relation of language to thought, although in a sense they are one, is an ambivalent one. At any rate, the art of writing, the incorporation of thought in permanent forms, while it creates the possibility of a continuity of social self-awareness, and makes accessible his own and other worlds to an individual, also arrests and kills. What has been put down in writing is incapable of that living process of constant adaptation and change, of the constant expression of the unanalyzable

[27] XVIII, 137.

and unseizable flow of actual experience, which language, if it is to communicate fully, must possess. Language alone makes experience possible, but it also freezes it. Hamann spoke of the valley of dry bones which only "a prophet" (that is, Socrates, St. Paul, Luther, and perhaps himself) could cover with flesh. Herder speaks of corpses—forms of linguistic petrifaction—against which, in due course, men revolt. The history of linguistic revolutions is the history of the succession of cultures, the true revolutions in the history of the human race. Was there once a language common to all men? He does not wish to assert this. On the one hand, he clings to the notion of one world, one basic human personality, the "organic" interrelation of everything; he insists on the folly and danger of abstraction, of fragmentation, of splitting the human personality into separate faculties, as not only Wolff but Kant, too, had done in their psychologies and in their strict division of body from soul, nature from spirit, the empirical from the *a priori*, the historical from the eternal. Yet he is a Christian, too, and he is committed to the doctrine of natural kinds. Man is unique; Lord Monboddo and the naturalists must be mistaken. That, no doubt, is why language had to be a direct gift of God, and not the product of a gradual process of emergence of rational beings out of some prerational state of nature—from the animal kingdom and subhuman forms of sentience, or even from insentience.[28] The contradiction is never reconciled. The only identification that Herder never abandons is that of thought and action, language and activity. Poetry, particularly early epic poetry, is for him pure activity. He was taken in by Ossian, like many of his contemporaries. It is probably from these poems rather than from Homer—although he speaks of the Homeric poems as improvisations, not a "dead artefact"— that he derives his notion of poetry as activity. Poetry, particularly among early peoples, is, he maintains, magical in character; it is not cool description of nature or of anything else: it is a spur to action—to heroes, hunters, lovers; it stimulates and directs. It is not to be savored by the scholar in his armchair, but is intelligible only to those who have placed themselves in situations similar to the conditions in which such words sprang into existence. During his voyage from Riga to Nantes, he observed the sailors during rough seas. These dour men under a savage discipline who lived in terror of, and in constant intimate contact with, the elements which they sought to dominate, resurrected for him the dark world of Skalds and Vikings and the Eddas, a world scarcely open to tranquil philologists in their studies, or to detached literary epicureans who turn over the pages

[28] Mr. G. A. Wells in his *Herder and After* (The Hague, 1959) advances this view, which seems to me very illuminating.

idly, without the power to re-create the world of which these works are the vision and the voice. Words, rhythms, actions are aspects of a single experience. These are commonplaces today, but (despite Vico) they were far from being such in Herder's time.

All authentic expressions of experience are valid. They differ because lives differ: perhaps because the earth's axis is inclined by twenty-four degrees. This generates different geophysical "climates," different experiences, different societies. Anything that seems to Herder authentic delights him. He has his preferences: he prefers the Greeks, the Germans, and the Hebrews, to the Romans, the ancient Egyptians, or the Frenchmen of his own time or of the previous century. But, at least in theory, he is prepared to defend them all and to penetrate—"feel himself" (*Einfühlen* is his invention)—into their essence, grasp what it must be like to live, contemplate goals, act and react, think, imagine, in the unique ways dictated by their circumstances, and so grasp the patterns of life in terms of which alone such groups are to be defined. The central concept here is that of natural growth. Everything that is natural is valuable. The notion (for example, the Marquis de Sade's) that vices or decadence or aggression are as natural as the rich and harmonious development of all human potentialities is not allowed for. In this respect Herder is a true child of the Enlightenment at its most naïve as well as at its most imaginative and penetrating. The late Professor Arthur Lovejoy was surely right when he included Herder among the thinkers (perhaps the majority in the West) who identified the "must" of natural laws that caused things to be as they are and governed the world inexorably, with the "ought" of the normative rules, derived, apparently, from the self-same nature, obedience to which alone conducts men toward happiness and virtue and wisdom. But this consensus has its limits. Herder sharply differs from the central thought of the French Enlightenment, and that not only in the respects that all his commentators have noted. What is usually stressed is, in the first place, his relativism, his admiration of every authentic culture for being what it is, his insistence that outlooks and civilizations must be understood from within, in terms of their own stages of development, purposes, and outlooks; and in the second place his sharp repudiation of that central strain in Cartesian rationalism which regards only what is universal, eternal, unalterable, governed by rigorously logical relationships—only the subject matter of mathematics, logic, physics and the other natural sciences—as true knowledge. But Herder rebelled against the *Aufklärung* in an even profounder way, by rejecting the very notion of impassable barriers in nature or experience—barriers between types of

consciousness or faculties or ideas or natural objects. What repels him
equally in such deeply disparate thinkers as Descartes and Kant and the
French *philosophes* is their common insistence on rigid divisions between
"faculties" and types of experience, which they seem to him to have introduced merely to make it possible to classify and generalize. He admires
Leibniz more than Kant: he recognizes the logical gulf between mathematical truths and those of fact, but he regards the former (probably
following Hume) as tautologies, statements unconcerned with nature.[29]
He is a thoroughgoing empiricist in matters of epistemology. Kant's
transcendental categories, which claim to determine experience *a priori*,
seem to him a monstrous conflation of analytic and synthetic: he rejects the
"synthetic *a priori*" as a hideous confusion.[30] Reality for him admits of no
a priori laws; Kant's attempt to distinguish contingent from necessary
judgments about experience seems to him to be far more misleading than
the distinction between intuited necessities and observed contingencies
out of which Spinoza and Leibniz built their systems. Walls erected
between kinds of truth about the nature of reality—like rigid distinctions
drawn between words and concepts—distort judgment not only in
epistemology and logic, but in politics and ethics and the arts, and
indeed all regions of experience. All activities, he insists, express the whole
and undivided man whom Descartes and Kant, in their several ways,
have done their best to carve up into compartments—denominated
faculties—such as "reason," "imagination," "intuition," "feeling,"
"will."[31] The attack on Kant in the *Metakritic* of 1799 merely summarizes
a lifelong attitude. The black-and-white terms these neo-scholastics use to
describe man—an inexhaustibly complex organization—seem to Herder
willfully absolute and arbitrary. Instead, for example, of asking themselves
how free men are, free from or for what, and where and when, and in
what respects, or what renders them more or less free, these thinkers
dogmatically pronounce man to be free, wholly free in some absolute
sense, as against animals who are wholly mechanical, or at least wholly
lack freedom. They speak of man as distinguished by his possession of
reason (not as being more or less rational), and define him in terms of
selected properties that one must either possess wholly or not possess at all;
they describe him in terms of sharp, artificial dichotomies that arbitrarily
break up the interwoven, continuous, at times irregular, fluid, shapeless,
often unanalyzable but always perceptible, dynamic, teeming, boundless,

[29] XXI, 36.
[30] XXI, 38.
[31] XXI, 18.

eternal multiplicity of nature; and so provide distorting lenses both to philosophers and historians. Attempts to bring manifestations so complex and so various under some general law, whether by philosophers seeking knowledge or by statesmen seeking to organize and govern, seemed to Herder no better than a search for the lowest common denominator—for what is least characteristic and important in the lives of men—and, therefore, as leading to shallowness in theory and to a tendency to impose a crippling uniformity in practice. All regionalists, all defenders of the local against the universal, all champions of deeply rooted forms of life, both reactionary and progressive, both genuine humanists and obscurantist opponents of scientific advance, owe something, whether they know it or not, to the doctrines that Herder (with a far wider and more magnificent sweep than Möser or Burke or Ferguson) introduced into European thought. Vico might have achieved something of this. But he was (and is) not read; as Savigny remarked, he came into his own too late to have a decisive influence.

However much lip service Herder may have paid to "natural kinds," in general he conceived of nature as a unity in which the *Kräfte*—the mysterious, dynamic, purpose-seeking forces, the interplay of which constitutes all movement and growth—flow into each other, clash, combine, coalesce. These forces are not causal and mechanical as in Descartes; nor insulated from each other as in the *Monadology* of Leibniz. For Herder reality is a kind of symbiosis of these *Kräfte* (whose character remains obscure) with an environment that is conceived in somewhat static terms; if the environment is altered too abruptly, the result is some kind of collapse. Herder found more and more evidence for this. Transplanted flowers decay in unsympathetic climates; so do human beings. Greenlanders do not thrive in Denmark. Africans are miserable and decay in Europe. Europeans become debilitated in America. Conquest crushes, and emigration sometimes leads to enfeeblement—lack of vital force, the flattening out of human beings, and a sad uniformity. The *Ideen* is full of such examples. Like Fourier after him, Herder believed in the complete realizability of all potentialities ("All that can be, will come into being"), since everything fits somewhere. Only artificiality is destructive, in life as in art. Marriages of convenience, coldly entered into, ruin children, and are worse for them than pure animality. The patriarchs at times exercised severe and cruel authority: but at least this is more "natural"—and therefore less harmful—than the artificial reasonings of philosophers. Herder harbors a Rousseau-like suspicion of "reasoning." He does not think that Voltaire's desiccated maxims or Wolff's syllogisms are better for children than the stern but natural behavior of primitive men. Anything is better than that which imposes the ideal of one culture on another and which arranges, adjusts, makes for uniform "physiognomies," as opposed to that which is "natural," in a state of "creative disorder," the sole state where individuality lives and grows. Hence his condemnation of all theories which over-categorize men—into racial types, for example— and thereby divide them from each other. He condemns the anthropologies which treat men in general and leave the individual drained of too many differentiating characteristics. Even tradition, which otherwise acts as a preservative of the most vital characteristics of human groups, can be a danger when it becomes too mechanical and acts as a narcotic, as it seems to him to have done in Asia, which it put to sleep by eliminating too many of the other ingredients of a healthy life, too many other *Kräfte* that are indispensable to life and activity. This thought is unrelated to any articulated rule or method, it is unstructured, perhaps it is altogether incapable of precise formulation; but as always with Herder, it is suggestive and has a clear general direction. "If a savage loves his family as part of himself, and treats the interests of the tribe as his own, he is more genuine and real than mere specious phantoms [i.e., his *bêtes noires*—the hollow 'cosmopolitan' lovers of humanity in the abstract] who burn with love for other ghosts." "The savage who loves himself, his wife and his child, and his tribe, can find room in his hut for a stranger: the saturated heart of the idle cosmopolitan is a home for no one." [32] He repeats throughout the *Ideen* that originality, freedom of choice and creation, is the divine element in man. When a savage speaks with vigor and precision he is superior to "the civilized man who stands on a pedestal built by others." There is much talk in the *Ideen* about men who live on other men's accounts: they are viewed as "dead cosmopolitans," men whose feelings have been drained away, dehumanized creatures, victims of nature or history, moral or physical cripples, parasites, fettered slaves.

How do men come to lose their humanity? By living on others and by the labor and ideas of others. Herder, in opposition to the primitivists, welcomed invention—the arts and sciences are fruits of the creative powers of man, and through them he rises to the full height of his purposive nature. Inventions as such do not corrupt (in this Herder differs sharply from Rousseau [33]); only if one lives on the inventions of others does one become mechanical and devitalized. Here, as in the writings of Mably

[32] XIII, 339.
[33] In the First Discourse

and Rousseau and Karl Friedrich von Moser[34] begins that lament, still more characteristic of the following century, and perhaps still more often heard in our own, for the youth that is gone for ever—for the lost virtues of an earlier, more vigorous epoch in the life of mankind. Herder, no less than Mill or Carlyle or Ruskin, speaks with gloom about the triviality and lifelessness of modern men and modern art, in contrast with the full-blooded, doughty, independent human beings of the morning hours of humanity—the creators of the great epics and songs, of an anonymous but more robust age. Before Henri de Saint-Simon he draws a contrast between the creative and the relatively sterile epochs in the history of culture. Herder has his optimistic moments, when he supposes that a renewal is possible: that if man can only "cease to be in contradiction with himself" and "return to himself," and if peoples can only find themselves" and "learn not to think in other people's thoughts,"[35] they can recover and revive and create new works of art, in modern terms, as noble and expressive of their true nature as anything that men have created in the past. There is only one course against which Herder sets his face absolutely: that is any attempt to return to the past. Here there is no salvation. To sigh after the Greeks and wish to return to them, of which he suspects Winckelmann, is absurd and impossible: his idealization of the Greeks as the originators of art which among them attained to a sublime height never reached by, say, the Egyptians, is wholly unhistorical and nothing but a "terrible delusion."[36]

The dangers to free development are many. In the first place, there is the centralized state; it can rob us of something essential: it can rob us of ourselves. There are foreign cultures that "devour German folk song like a cancer"—folk song that is an answer to cravings, to collective desires that seek to embody common experiences in symbolic forms not dreamed of in Voltaire's philosophy. There is the more specific danger of foreign languages: "I am able to stammer with immense effort in the words of a foreign language; its spirit will evade me." Yet "to this we devote the best years of our life!"[37] But we are not Greeks; we are not Romans; and we cannot become such. To wish to return is to be dominated by a false

---

[34] Especially in Moser's *Von Dem Deutschen Nationalgeist*, published in 1765–66, which speaks of the Germans as despised, disregarded, mocked, and preyed upon by everyone.

[35] Such phrases are almost verbally exact echoes of Hamann's sentences, dealing with what much later came to be called the problem of "alienation."

[36] Johann Gottfried Herder, *Werke in Zwei Bänden*, ed. Karl Gustav Gerold (München, 1953), II, 117, 128. Also see pp. 658 and 663.

[37] IV, 388.

vision, a crippling illusion as fatal as any for which it attempts to be the cure. What then must we do? We must seek to be ourselves. "Let us be characteristic of our nation, language, scene, and posterity will decide whether or not we are classical." Perhaps Klopstock's *Messias* was less successful than it might have been because it was not "national" enough.[38] It is here that Herder utters his most ardently nationalist sentiments: "I cry to my German brothers . . . the remnants of all genuine folk songs are rolling into the abyss of oblivion . . . the night of so-called culture is devouring all about it like a cancer."[39] "We speak the words of strangers and they wean us from our own thought. . . ."[40] He sees no merit in "peasants in wigs," much as Hamann talks of "false noses." He appeals to the Germans to know themselves, to understand their place and respect their role in the cosmos, in time and in space.

V

Is this nationalism? In an obvious sense it is. It is anti-French—the voyage to Nantes and Paris (like the later journey to Rome) depressed Herder acutely. He only understood the written languages: he could not understand what the French and the Italians said to him. He suffered that mixture of envy, humiliation, admiration, resentment, and defiant pride which backward peoples feel toward advanced ones, members of one social class toward those who belong to a higher rung in the hierarchy. Wounded national feeling—this scarcely needs saying—breeds national-ism, but it is important to realize that Herder's nationalism was never political. If he denounces individualism, he equally detests the state, which coerces and mutilates the free human personality. His social vision is antagonistic to government, power, domination. We cannot return to the Greek *polis*. Louis XIV and Frederick the Great (like Caesar and Charlemagne before them) represent a detestable ideal. Herder does not ask for power and does not wish to assert the superiority of his own class or culture or nation. He wishes to create a society in which men, whoever they are, can live full lives, attain to free self-expression, "be someone"; and he thinks that the less government they have the better. This may, indeed, have been the first stage of a development destined in its later stages to become nationalistic and chauvinistic in the full, aggressive

[38] Professor Rouché is understandably surprised by the spectacle of a Christian clergyman complaining that the central theme of the Christian religion is perhaps too foreign a topic for a German poem.

[39] XXV, 11.

[40] IV, 389.

sense. Whether or not this is historically and sociologically true, it is clear that Herder did not himself harbor these sentiments. Even though he seems to have coined the word "Nationalismus," his conception of a good society is closer to the anarchism of Thoreau or Proudhon or Kropotkin, and to the conception of a culture (*Bildung*) of which such liberals as Goethe and Humboldt were proponents, than to the ideals of Fichte or Hegel or political socialists. For him the *Nation* is not a political entity. He is repelled by the claims of contemporary Celtomaniacs and Teutomaniacs who rhapsodized over the ancient Gaels or Northmen. He celebrates German beginnings, German civilization, because it is his own, not because it ranks higher than that of others on some cosmic scale. "In the works of the imagination and feeling the entire soul of a nation reveals itself most clearly."[41] This was developed by Sismondi, Michelet, and Mazzini, into a full-scale political-cultural doctrine; but Herder stands even closer to the outlook of Ruskin or Lamennais or William Morris, to populists and Christian socialists, and to all of those who, in the present day, are opposed to hierarchies of status or power, or to the influence of manipulators of any kind (advertisers and "hidden persuaders"). He stands with those who protest against mechanization and vulgarization rather than with the nationalists of the last hundred years, whether moderate or violent. He favors autarky, but only in personal life; that is, in artistic creation and the rights of natural self-expression. All his invocations of the *Nationalgeist* (an expression probably coined by Karl Friedrich von Moser), and of its many aliases—the *Geist des Volkes*, *Seele des Volkes*, *Geist der Nation*, *Genius des Volkes* and the more empirical *Nationalcharakter*[42]—are intended to stress what is ours, not theirs, even though theirs may intrinsically be more valuable, viewed on some vaster scale. Socrates is for him neither the timeless cosmopolitan sage of the Enlightenment, nor Hamann's destroyer of pretentious claims to knowledge whose irony and self-confessed ignorance opened the path to faith and salvation. Socrates is, above all, an Athenian of the fifth century; and that age is over. Aristotle may be more gifted than Leibniz. But Leibniz is ours and so is Shakespeare; other great geniuses, Homer and Moses, are not. Individuality is all; artificial combinations lead to false ideas and ruinous practice.[42a] "Let us follow our own path . . . let men speak well

[41] XVIII, 58.

[42] I, 263; II, 160; III, 30; V, 185, 217; VIII, 392; XIII, 364; XIV, 38, 84; XXV, 10, and *passim*.

[42a] VIII, 207, 314, 315; XIV, 227; XV, 321; XVIII, 248 (I owe these and several other references to Professor F. M. Barnard).

or ill of our nation, our literature, our language: they are ours, they are ourselves, and let that be enough."[43] Better Germans, whatever they are, than sham Greeks, Frenchmen, Englishmen.[43a] But when he says, "Awake, German nation! Don't let them ravish your Palladium!,"[44] when he declares that fearful storms are coming and warns men not to lie asleep like Jonah in the tempest, and when he tells men to take warning from the terrible example of partitioned Poland,[45] and says, "Poor torn, crushed Germany, be hopeful!" and "Germans, speak German! Spew out the Seine's ugly slime!,"[46] it is conceivable that this may have fed the sinister nationalism of Görres or Jahn or Arndt or Treitschke and their monstrous modern successors. But Herder's own sentences refer to purely cultural self-determination; he hates *"policirte Nationen."* Nationality for him is a purely and strictly cultural entity; he believes that people can and should defend their cultural heritage: they need never give in. He almost blames the Jews, despite his passionate addiction to their antiquities, for not preserving a sufficient sense of collective honor and making no effort to return to their home in Palestine, which is the sole place where they can blossom again into a *Nation.* He is interested, not in nationality, but in cultures, in worlds, in the total experience of peoples; and the aspect of this experience that he celebrates are personal relationships, friendship and enmity, attitudes to nature, war and peace, art and science, ways in which truth, freedom, and happiness are pursued, and in particular the relations of the great civilizing leaders to the ungrateful mob. He fears organization as such, and, like the early English Romantics, Young, Henry and Joseph Warton, he wants to preserve what is irregular and unique in life and in art—that which no system can wholly contain. His attack on political centralization and intellectual polarization springs from the same source. When he imagines the world as a garden which can contain many flowers, and when he speaks of the possible and desirable harmony between all the national cultures, he is not simply ignoring the aggressive potentialities of nation states or blandly assuming that there is no reason for conflict between various nationalisms. Rather, he is deeply hostile to the growth of political, economic, military centralization, but sees no reason why culturally autonomous communities need clash. It may, of course, be unrealistic and unhistorical to suppose that one kind of

---

[43] Quoted by H. Lévy Bruhl, *L'Allemagne depuis Leibniz* (Paris, n.d.), pp. 168–69.
[43a] I, 366, 367.
[44] XVII, 309.
[45] XXIX, 210.
[46] XXVII, 129.

autarchy need not lead to other and more dangerous kinds. But it is not the same kind of unrealism as that with which he, and the Enlightenment generally, are usually charged. His faith is not in nationalism, collectivism, Teutomania, or romantic state worship, but in something that is, if anything, incompatible with these ideals. He is the earliest and greatest champion of those mysterious *Kräfte* which are "living and organic." There is, in the end, only one great creative *Kraft:* "what is alive in creation is, in all forms, shapes, channels, one spirit, one single flame."[47] This is scarcely an empirical or scientific notion. He sings paeans to the *Seele des Volkes* which is the social incarnation of this Leibnizian *vis viva,* "unique, wonderful, inexplicable, ineradicable, and as old as the *Nation.*"[48] Its most vivid expression is, of course, not the state, but "the physiognomy of its speech."[49] The point that I wish to stress is that the true heir of this doctrine is not power politics but what came to be called populism. It is this that acquired such momentum among the oppressed peoples of Eastern Europe, and later spread in Asia and Africa. It inspired not *étatistes,* but believers in "grass roots"—Russian Slavophils, *Narodniks,* Christian Socialists, and all those admirers of folk art and of popular traditions whose enthusiasm assumed both serious and ridiculous shapes still not unfamiliar today. It may often have taken reactionary forms and fed the stream of aggressive nationalism; but the form in which Herder held it was democratic and peaceful, not only anti-dynastic and anti-élitist, but deeply anti-political,[50] directed against organized power, whether of nations, classes, races, or parties. I have called it populism: this movement, whether in Europe or outside it, is the nearest approximation to Herder's ideal. It is, as a rule, pluralistic, looks on government as an evil, and to this day, animates folk enthusiasts and cultural fanatics, egalitarians and agitators for local autonomy, champions of arts and crafts and of simple life, and innocent utopians of all brands. It is based on belief in loose textures, voluntary associations, natural ties, and is bitterly opposed to armies, bureaucracies, "closed" societies of any sort.

Historically, populism has, of course, become closely interwoven with real nationalism, and it has, indeed, often provided the soil in which blind xenophobia and irrationalism grew to monstrous heights; and this is no more accidental than the alliances of nationalism with democracy or

[47] VIII, 178.
[48] XIV, 38.
[49] XIII, 364.
[50] "As you know, I do not concern myself with political matters," he wrote to Goethe from Paris, late in the century, and spoke the truth.

romanticism or liberalism at various points in the nineteenth century. Nevertheless, it is a historical and moral error to identify the ideology of one period with its consequences at some other, or with its transformation in another context and in combination with other factors. The progeny of Herder in, let us say, England or America are to be found principally among those amateurs who became absorbed in the antiquities and forms of life (ancient and modern) of cultures other than their own, in Asia and Africa or the "backward" provinces of Europe or America, among professional amateurs and collectors of ancient song and poetry, among enthusiastic and sometimes sentimental devotees of more primitive forms of life in the Balkans or among the Arabs; nostalgic travellers and exiles like Richard Burton, Doughty, Lafcadio Hearn, the English companions of Gandhi or Ibn Saud, as well as serious students and philosophers of language and society.

Perhaps Herder's most characteristic descendants were to be found in Russia, in which he took so abiding an interest. In that country his ideas entered the thought of those critics and creative artists who not merely developed national and pseudonational forms of their own native art but became passionate champions of all "natural," "spontaneous," traditional forms of art and self-expression wherever they manifested themselves. These admirers of ethnic color and variety as such, Mussorgski, Stassov, and the musicians and painters whom they inspired, so far from supporting authority and repression, stood politically on the left, and felt sympathy for all forms of cultural self-expression, especially on the part of persecuted minorities—Georgians, Poles, Jews, Finns, but also Spaniards, Hungarians, and other "unreconstructed" nations. They denounced, however unjustly and intemperately, such "organ grinders" as Rossini and Verdi, or neoclassical schools of painting, for alleged cosmopolitanism, for commercialism, for a tendency to destroy regional or national differences in favor of flat and mechanical forms of life, in short, for rootlessness (a term which afterward became so sinister and ominous in the mouths of obscurantists and fascists), heartlessness, oppression, and dehumanization. All this is typically Herderian.

Something of this kind, too, may have entered Mazzini's ideal of the Young Italy which was to live in harmony and mutual understanding with Young Germany—and the "Young" of all nations—once they had thrown away the shackles of oppressive imperialism, of dynastic autocracies, of the denial of the rights of all "natural" human units, and attained to free self-determination. Such views may have been thoroughly utopian. But if they were nationalistic, they were so in a sense very different from the later—and pejorative—sense of the word. Populism may have been in part responsible for isolationism, provincialism, suspicion of everything smooth, metropolitan, elegant and socially superior, hatred of the *beau monde* in all its forms; but with this went hostility to centralization, dogmatism, militarism, and self-assertiveness, or, in other words, all that is commonly associated with the full-grown nationalism of the nineteenth century, as well as with deep antipathy to mobs (Herder carefully distinguishes the *Pöbel auf die Gassen* ["the rabble"] from *Das Volk* [i.e., "the body of the nation"], however this is done),[51] and with a hatred of violence and conquest as strong as any to be found among the other great Weimar humanists, Goethe, Wieland, and Schiller. The faithful followers of Herder may often have been—and can still be—confused, sentimental, impractical, ineffective, and sometimes ridiculous, but not managerial, calculating, or brutal. No one made more of this profound contrast than Herder himself.

In this connection it is worth considering Herder's attitude to three great eighteenth-century myths which fed the stream of nineteenth-century nationalism. The first is that of the superiority of a particular tribal culture. His denunciation of patriotic boastfulness—the *Favoritvolk* doctrine—has already been referred to. One of the most quoted sentences from *Yet Another Philosophy of History* tells us that "Every nation has its own inner center of happiness, as every sphere its own center of gravity."[52] This is what the historian, the critic, the philosopher must grasp, and nothing is more fatal than the attempted assimilation of the *Mittelpunkt* of one culture with those of others. "One must enter the time, the place, the entire history[53] [of a people]"; one must "feel oneself [*sich Einfühlen*] into everything."[54] "This is what contemporary historians [he is referring to Schlözer] conspicuously fail to do."[55] The reader of the Hebrew scriptures must be "a shepherd with shepherds, a peasant in the midst of an agricultural people, an oriental with the primitive dwellers in the East,"[56] whereas the *Aufklärer*—Gottsched, Lessing, and Mendelssohn—tended to grade, to give ethical marks for excellence. Herder, in this (what he would regard as a Spinozan) mood, warns, at any rate in *Auch Eine Philosophie* of 1774, against moral evaluation (prone though he was to it himself then and later), and urges the critic above all to understand. If one must con-

[51] XXV, 323.
[52] V, 509.
[53] V, 502.
[54] V, 502.
[55] V, 436–38.
[56] X, 14.

demn and praise, this should be done only after an exercise of sympathetic insight—of one's capacity for *Einfühlung* ("empathy"). This work contains the most eloquent description of the newly discovered sense of history, with its uncanny resemblance to that of Vico, whom, so far as we can tell, Herder did not read until twenty years later:

> How unspeakably difficult it is to convey the particular quality of an individual human being [*Eigenheit*] and how impossible it is to say precisely what distinguishes an individual, his way of feeling and living; how different and how individual [*anders und eigen*] everything becomes once his eyes see it, once his soul grasps—his heart feels—it. How much depth there is in the character of a single people, which, no matter how often observed (and gazed at with curiosity and wonder), nevertheless escapes the word which attempts to capture it, and, even with the word to catch it, is seldom so recognizable as to be universally understood and felt. If this is so, what happens when one tries to master an entire ocean of peoples, times, cultures, countries, with one glance, one sentiment, by means of one single word! Words, pale shadow-play! An entire living picture of ways of life, or habits, wants, characteristics of land and sky, must be added, or provided in advance; one must start by feeling sympathy with a nation if one is to feel a single one of its inclinations or acts, or all of them together.[57]

Greece, he continues, was not Athens. It was inhabited, and ruled by Athenians, Boeotians, Spartans, Corinthians. Egyptians were traders no less than Phoenicians. Macedon was conqueror like Rome. Aristotle had as good a speculative mind as Leibniz. Yet (Herder repeats in and out of context) they were Egyptians, Romans, Greeks, Macedonians, and *not* inhabitants of our world. Leibniz is ours; Plato is not. Similarity is not identity; one must see both the wood and the trees, although only God can do this completely. All history is an unending conflict between the general idea and the particular; all general ideas are abstractions, dangerous, misleading, and unavoidable. One must seek to see the whole, however unattainable this goal may be. Exceptions and deviations will amaze only those who insist upon forcing an idealized image on the manifold of reality. Hume and Voltaire, Robertson and Schlözer, are denounced for using the measuring rod of their own time. All civilizations are incommensurable.[58] The critic must, so far as he is able, surrender to his author

[57] V, 502.
[58] V, 509.

and seek to see with the author's eyes. Herder disagrees with Diderot's justly celebrated theory of the actor who is inwardly detached from it when he plays a role.[58a] Genuine translation from one language—that is, way of life—into another is, of course, impossible; no real idiom is literally translatable: the olives sacred to Minerva that grew round the Academy cannot be taken beyond the frontiers of Athens. "Even when Sparta ravaged Athens, the goddess protected her grove. So no one can take the beauties of our language from us: beauties woven into its texture, glimmering like Phryne's bosom beneath her silken veil."[59] To translate is—for better or for worse—to create; the translation must be an *Original Arbeit* by a *Schöpferisches Genie;*[60] and, of course, because the creator is what he is, and not someone or something else, a great deal is, and must be, lost. Egypt must not be judged by Greek criteria, or by Shaftesbury's modern ones; the school boy is not joyless because he takes no pleasure in the avocations of a grown man, nor were the Middle Ages worthless because they do not please Voltaire: there is more in the great ferment of the Dark Ages than the absurdities of Ripuarian or Salic laws. The Middle Ages are not a corridor to the Renaissance, nor is paganism an ante room of Christianity. One culture is never a mere means to another; even if there is a sense in which mankind as a whole is advancing, each of the stages is an end in itself: men are never means to ends beyond themselves. No less than his opponent Kant, he fervently preaches the doctrine that only persons and societies, and almost all of these, are good in themselves— indeed they are all that is good, wholly good, in the world that we know. These maxims, which now (at least in the West) seem so platitudinous, were antinomian heresies in the middle of the eighteenth century in Paris and in its intellectual dependencies.

So much for the myth of the Dominant Model. Still bolder was Herder's rejection of the historical myths of the century:[61] of the French myth of classical culture created by the Gallo-Romans, in which lay the true soul of France, and which the barbarians destroyed, and equally of the counter-myth of the superiority of the Frankish conquerors, to which support had been given by Montesquieu, Mallet, and Boulainvilliers. Similarly Herder has no truck with the Renaissance myth of the sunlit pagan world killed by the gloomy, pleasure-destroying Christian religion; he uses harsh

---

[58a] "Nous sentons, nous; ils observent..." (*Oeuvres*, ed. Asisézat et Tourneux, VIII, 170–71), which holds for all artists.

[59] II, 44.

[60] I, 173; I, 178.

[61] M. Rouché (*op. cit.*) deals with this far more faithfully than Herder's better-known German commentators.

words about the monks who suppressed the old German songs; but this does not lead him to a general denunciation of the Middle Ages: it is not the dark haunt of the "demons, slaves, diabolical priests and tyrants" represented by Voltaire, Gibbon, Hume, and later still, Heine and all the neopagans. But neither does he uphold the growing German-Protestant legend of the uncorrupted, fearless, Cheruscan warrior Hermann canonized by Klopstock as Arminius, and then, in the shape of the young Siegfried, placed by Wagner in the German nationalist pantheon. These fantasies offer no avenue of escape. All attempts to flee, whether to modern Paris or the dark German woods, are condemned by Herder as being equally deluded. Those who, for whatever reason, will not face reality are doomed.

The third great myth of the eighteenth century was that of steady progress, if not inevitable, at least virtually certain; with consequent disparagement of the benighted past, which entailed the view of all earlier centuries as so many steps toward the superior life of the present and the still more wonderful life of the future. Herder rejects this completely. "Each [culture] is a harmonious lyre—one must merely have the ear to hear its melodies." Those who seek to understand must learn to grasp the respects in which Abraham or Leonidas or Caesar are not men of our time—to see change as it occurs, not in juxtaposed segments which can be detached, compared, and awarded marks for merit, for the degree to which they approach our standards of enlightenment. Is there, then, no progress? Are all cultures equally valuable? This is not Herder's view. There is *Fortgang*, but this is not the same as the notion of progress enunciated by, say, Turgot or Condorcet, or, in particular by Voltaire (for example, in *La Philosophie d'histoire par feu l'Abbé Bazin*), against whom, together with the Swiss philosopher of history Iselin, Herder's thunderbolts are specifically directed. *Fortgang* ("advance") is the development of human beings as integrated wholes and, more particularly, their development as groups—tribes, cultures, and communities determined by language and custom, creating out of the "totality of their collective experience,"[62] and expressing themselves in works of art that are consequently intelligible to common men, and in sciences and crafts and forms of social and political and cultural life that fulfill the cravings (conscious and unconscious) and develop the faculties of a given society in its interplay with its alterable, but not greatly alterable, natural environment.

[62] XI, 225; XVII, 59; XVIII, 346; XXX, 8.

"To bind and interrogate this Proteus, which is usually called national character and which shows itself certainly not less in the writings than in the usages and actions of a nation—that is a high and beautiful philosophy. It is practiced most surely in poetry; for in the works of imagination and feeling the entire soul of nations reveals itself most freely." [63] This is what the classical Greeks succeeded in doing so marvellously. Despite all Hamann's anathemas, Herder cannot refrain from expressing his passionate admiration for the culture of Athens—a feeling that he shared with Goethe and Hegel, Hölderlin and Schiller and, indeed, with the majority of the civilized Germans of his time, romantic and anti-romantic alike. Herder thinks the Greek achievement is in part due to the beauty of nature in Greece, a beauty which inspired principles that those fortunate inhabitants (mistakenly but excusably) regarded as objective and universally valid. But there must be no *Favoritvolk;* he hastens to add to the list Kashmiris and Persians, Bokharans and Circassians, who also lived in beautiful natural surroundings, grew handsome themselves and produced beautiful cultures (unlike the Hebrews whose merits are not aesthetic). The Greeks advanced; they developed their own faculties harmoniously and triumphantly, because nature was propitious and because no great natural accidents arrested this development. But they are not a hallway to the Romans, whose civilization must be judged in terms of its own internal criteria, its own *Schwerpunkt* ("center of gravity"). *Fortgang* is the internal development of a culture in its own *habitat*, toward its own goals; but because there are some qualities that are universal in man, one culture can study, understand, and admire another, even though it cannot return to it and will only make itself foolish if it tries. At times Herder speaks like Bossuet: as if history were not an episodic story but a vast drama; as if the finger of God guided the destinies of humanity in some teleological fashion, a play in which each great cultural epoch was an act. He does not develop this notion, which led Bossuet to see each act as in some degree a link between its predecessor and it successor. More often he speaks as if history were indeed a drama, but one without a *dénouement:* as if it were like a cosmic symphony of which each movement is significant in itself, and of which, in any case, we cannot hear the whole, for God alone does so. The later movements are not necessarily closer to, or a prefiguring of, some ultimate goal and, therefore, superior to the earlier movements. There is for Herder no great single world-tree, no *Ygdrasil*. Life is not a jigsaw puzzle of which the fragments must fit into

[63] XVIII, 57–58.

some single pattern in terms of which alone they are all intelligible, so that what seems, taken in isolation, irrational or ugly, is seen to be an indispensable ingredient in the great harmonious whole—the world Spirit come to full self-consciousness of itself, in Hegel's famous image. Herder believes in the development of each movement of the symphony (each act of the drama) in terms of its own ends, its own values, which are none the worse or less morally valuable because they will pass or be destroyed and be succeeded by others. There is a general purpose to be achieved by human life on earth, which he calls *Humanität*. This is a notoriously vague term, in Herder and the *Aufklärung* generally, connoting harmonious development of all immortal souls toward universally valid goals: reason, freedom, health, finer perceptions, dominion over the earth, the harmonious realization of all that God has implanted in His noblest work and made in His own image.[64] This is a characteristically general and optimistic formula of the humanist enlightenment, which Herder adopts, but which he does not seem to have used widely (for it has no precise connotation) as a universal criterion either of explanation or of value. He wants above all to be comprehensive and fair. He dislikes Gothic architecture despite the eloquence which made so deep an impression on Goethe in Strasburg; he is repelled by chivalry, by medieval values in general, but he defends them against Voltaire, against caricatures. He placed no great value, particularly toward the end of his life, upon primitivism as such, and in this respect differed from its true admirers in the eighteenth century. Yet colonial subjugation of native populations is always represented as being morally odious and as a crime against *Humanität*. If paganism requires to be defended against Christian attack, and Homer against Klotz and the *Encyclopédie*, so must Christianity be defended against d'Holbach, Voltaire, and the Sinophiles, and the Chinese and Mongols in their turn against the arrogance of Europeans. The shamans of central Asia, he insists, are not just deceivers; nor are myths simply false statements about reality invented by wicked priests to bamboozle and acquire power over the masses, as Bayle and Voltaire had made the world believe; nor are the inventions of poets merely intended to give pleasure or to instruct. Here he stands with Vico, long before he read him (if ever he did). Shamans express in the form of myth and superstition objects of men's natural wishes—a vision of the world from which poetry naturally springs and which it expresses. Whole worlds are created by such poetry, worlds worthy of man and his creative powers, worlds not

[64] See the remarks on *Humanität* in XIII, 154.

commensurable with other worlds, but all equally worthy of our interest and in need of our insight, because they are worlds made by men; by contemplating them we may succeed in grasping what we, in our turn, can be and create. We do this not by learning the lessons of the past (he sometimes says that the past repeats itself, but his central doctrine, in opposition to Hume or Voltaire, is that each page is unique), but rather because the vision of past creation inspires us to find our own center of gravity, our own *Mittelpunkt* or *Schwerpunkt* or that of the group—nation, region, community—to which we belong. Without such belonging there is no true creation and no true realization of human goals. Hence to foist a set of alien values on another *Nation* (as missionaries are doing, for example, in India) is both ineffective and harmful.[64a] Worst of all are those who have no group, because they are exiled or self-exiled, physically or spiritually (for Herder the two are not very different), and are doomed to sterility. Such disintegration seemed to him to threaten the Germans in his own day. Indignantly some of his modern critics point out that he condemned France—the France of the eighteenth and nineteenth centuries!—as being an exhausted society. But whatever his failings as a prophet (and he speaks with many voices, some of them far from distinct and often uttering contradictory sentiments), as a social psychologist he rose above his generation; more clearly than any other writer, he conceived and cast light upon the crucially important social function of "belonging"—on what it is to belong to a group, a culture, a movement, a form of life. It was a most original achievement.

VI

"It is the composer's duty, as a member of society, to speak to and for his fellow human-beings."

"I believe in roots, in associations, in backgrounds, in personal relationships . . . My music has its roots in where I live and work."

BENJAMIN BRITTEN, on receiving the first Aspen Award, 1964

The notion of belonging is at the heart of all Herder's ideas. His doctrine of the unity of theory and practice, like that of his populism, is intelligible only in terms of it. To belong is not a passive condition, but active co-operation, social labor. "Complete truth is always only the

[64a] VII, 210, 303.

Deed."[65] Whether one reads the last books of his *Ideas about the Philosophy of History of Mankind*, the earlier treatise *On Hebrew Poetry*, the essays on Shakespeare, Ossian, Homer and the critical "Groves," or the late *Adrastea* and *Kalligone*, one finds that what dominates them all is the notion that there are central patterns in terms of which each genuine culture—and the human beings who constitute it—can, and indeed must, be identified. For Herder, to be a member of a group is to think and act in a certain way, in the light of particular goals, values, pictures of the world: and to think and act so is to belong to a group. The notions are literally identical. To be a German is to be part of a unique stream of which language is the dominant element, but still only one element among others. He conveys the notion that the ways in which a people— say, the Germans—speak or move, eat or drink, their handwriting, their laws, their music, their social outlook, their dance forms, their theology, have patterns and qualities in common which they do not share, or share to a notably lesser degree, with the similar activities of some other group— the French, the Icelanders, the Arabs, the ancient Greeks. Each of these activities belongs to a cluster which must be grasped as a whole: they illuminate each other. Anyone who studies the speech rhythms of the history of the architecture or the physical characteristics of the Germans will thereby achieve a deeper understanding of German legislation, music, dress. There is a property, not capable of being abstracted and articulated—that which is German in the Germans—which all these diverse activities uniquely evince. Activities like hunting, painting, worship, common to many groups in widely differing times and places, will resemble each other because they belong to the same genus. But the specific quality, which each type of activity will show forth, will have more in common with generically different activities of the same culture[65a] than with specifically similar activities of another culture. Or, at the very least, that which the various activities of the same culture will have in common—the common pervasive pattern in virtue of which they are seen to be elements in one and the same culture—is more important, since it accounts for the characteristics of these activities at a deeper level, than their more superficial resemblances to the corresponding activities of other cultures and other human groups. In other words, what German epic poetry has in common with German family life or German legislation or German grammar determines the patterns of these activities—runs through them

[65] "Die vollstaendige Wahrheit ist immer nur That," he wrote in 1774, long before Fichte or Hegel (*Uebers Erkennen und Empfinden in der Menschlichen Seele*, VIII).
[65a] This notion is to be found in Hamann.

more deeply—than that which German poetry has in common with Hindu or Hebrew poetry. This common property is not occult; no special non-empirical faculty is needed to detect it: it is a natural attribute and open to empirical investigation. Despite his theology, his belief in the primacy of religion, and his use of such metaphysical notions as the collective "soul" and "spirit," despite the mysterious *Kräfte*, despite occasional lapses into belief in the dogma of natural kinds, Herder was far more of an empiricist from the beginning to the end of his life than Leibniz, Kant, or even Helvétius. This was obscured by the fact that the following generation of German metaphysicians who he influenced dealt freely in transcendent formulas. Yet in his own day he was at times suspected by the stricter among his fellow churchmen of inclining dangerously toward materialistic heresies. The heart of his empiricism lay in the importance that he attributed to the discovery of patterns in history and nature. It is this directly perceptible, but literally unanalyzable, pattern quality in virtue of which what Germans think or do or say is unmistakably German, it is this that makes us attribute the doer and the deed, the thinker and the thought, to a specific German culture at a specific stage of its development. To fit into such a pattern is to belong: it is for this and no other reason that a German exiled from the milieu of his fellow Germans, perhaps a Saxon or a Prussian forced to live elsewhere, will not feel at home there; and whoever does not feel at home cannot create naturally, freely, generously, unself-consciously, in the manner that Schiller called "naïve," and that Herder, whether he admits it or not, most admires and believes in. All his talk about the national character, the national genius, the *Volksseele*, the spirit of the people and so forth, comes in the end to this alone. This notion of what it is to belong to a family, a sect, a place, a period, a style is the foundation of his populism, and of all the later conscious programs for self-integration or re-integration among men who felt scattered, exiled, or alienated. The language in which he speaks of his unfortunate fellow countrymen, driven through poverty or the despotic whims of their masters to Russia or Transylvania or America to become "blacks and slaves," is not simply a lament for the material and moral miseries of exile, but is based on the view that to cut men off from the "living center"—from the network to which they naturally belong—or to force them to sit over the rivers of some remote Babylon, and to prostitute their creative faculties for the benefit of strangers, is to degrade, dehumanize, destroy them. No writer has stressed more vividly the damage done to human beings by being torn from the only conditions in which their history has made it possible for them to live full lives. He insists over and over again that no one milieu is necessarily superior to any other. He assumes only that to be fully human, that is, fully creative, one must belong somewhere, to some group or some historical stream which cannot be defined save in the genetic terms of tradition and milieu and culture, themselves generated by natural forces—the *Klima* (i.e., external world) and physical structure and biological needs which, in interplay with every individual's mind and will create the dynamic, collective process called society. This theory entails no mythology. For Herder all groups are ultimately collections of individuals; his use of "organic" and "organism" is still wholly metaphorical and not, as in later, more metaphysical thinkers, only half metaphorical. There is no evidence that he conceived of groups as metaphysical "super-individual" entities or values. For Herder there is no mystique of history, or of a species to which individuals were to be sacrificed, still less a mystique of the superior wisdom of the race, or of a particular nation or even of humanity as a whole. Nevertheless, to understand men is to understand them genetically, in terms of their history, of the one complex of spiritual and physical "forces" in which they feel free and at home. This notion of being at home (and the corresponding notion of homelessness) which lies at the heart of his reflections on the emptiness of cosmopolitanism, on the damage done to men by social barriers, oppression by strangers, division, specialization—like the allied concepts of exploitation, and of the alienation of men from each other and in the end from their own true selves— derives from his one central conception. Those who have grasped the notion that men are made miserable not only by poverty, disease, stupidity, or the effects of ignorance, but also because they are misfits or outsiders or not spoken to, that liberty and equality are nothing without fraternity; that only those societies are truly human which may follow a leader but obey no master,[66] are in possession of one of Herder's *idées maîtresses*. His writings radically transformed the notion of relations of men to each other. The proposition that man is by nature sociable had been uttered by Aristotle and repeated by Cicero, Aquinas, Hooker, Grotius, Locke, and innumerable others. The depth and breadth of Herder's writings on human association and its vicissitudes, the wealth of concrete historical and psychological observation with which he developed the concept of what it is for men to belong to a community, made

---

[66] "The man who needs a master is an animal; as soon as he becomes human, he no longer needs any master at all" (XIII, 383). This is specifically directed against Kant, who in his *Idea for a Universal History from a Cosmopolitan Point of View* appeared to maintain the opposite ([Prussian Academy edition], VIII, 23).

such formulas seem to be thin abstractions and drove them permanently out of circulation. No serious social theorist after Herder dared advance generalizations of this type in lieu of thought. His vision of society has dominated Western thought; the extent of its influence has not always been recognized because it entered too deeply into the texture of ordinary thinking. His immense impact, of which Goethe spoke and to which J. S. Mill bore witness, is due principally to his central thesis—his account of what it is to live and act together—from which the rest of his thought flows, and to which it constantly returns. This idea is at the heart of all populism. And it has entered every subsequent attempt to arrive at truth about society.

VII

So much for Herder's specific contribution to the understanding of men and their history. There are two implications of his conception of men that have received little attention from his interpreters. These are firstly, his doctrine of the indivisibility of the human personality and, as a corollary of this, his conception of the artist and his expressive role in society; and secondly, his pluralism and the doctrine of the incompatibility of ultimate human ends. Herder was, as everyone knows, much occupied with aesthetic questions and tried to seek out all manifestations of art in their richest and fullest forms. He tended to find them in the creations of the early ages of man. For Herder art is the expression of men in society in their fullness. To say that art is expression is to say that it is a voice speaking rather than the production of an object—a poem, a painting, a golden bowl, a symphony, all of which possess their own properties, like objects of nature, independently of the men who created them, and of why or when or for whom.[67] By the very appropriately called *Stimmen der Völker in Liedern* and by explicit argument, Herder seeks to demonstrate that all that a man does and says and creates must convey, whether he intends it to do so or not, his entire personality; and, since a man is not conceivable outside a group to which, if he is reasonably fortunate, he continues to belong (he retains its characteristics in a mutilated state, even if he has been torn from it) conveys also the "collective individuality"[68]—a culture conceived as a constant flow of thought,

[67] A doctrine maintained, so it seemed to Herder, by such despotic arbiters of artistic beauty as the Abbés Du Bos and Batteux.
[68] V, 502.

feeling, action, and expression. Hence, he is bitterly opposed to the view, influential in his day as in ours, that the purpose of the artist is to create an object whose merits are independent of the creator's personal character or his intentions, conscious or unconscious, or his social situation. This is an aesthetic doctrine that reigned long before the doctrine of art for art's sake had been explicitly formulated. The craftsman who makes a golden bowl is entitled, according to this view, to say that it is no business of those who acquire or admire his creation to inquire whether he is himself sincere or calculating, pious or an atheist, a faithful husband, politically sound, a sympathetic boon companion or morally pure. Herder the true father of the doctrine that it is the artist's mission, above others, is to testify in his works to the truth of his own inner experience; from which it follows that any conscious falsification of this experience, from whatever motive—indeed any attempt merely to satisfy the taste of his customers, to titillate their senses, or even to offer them instruction by means that have little to do with his own life or convictions, or to use techniques and skills as a detached exercise, to practice virtuosity for its own sake or for the sake of the pleasure it brings—is a betrayal of his calling. This was implicit in the artistic movement which came to be called *Sturm und Drang*, of which Herder was one of the leaders. To view oneself as a professional who in his works of art plays a role or performs with a specialized part of himself, while the rest of him is left free to observe the performance; to maintain that one's behavior as a man—as a father, merchant, as a political terrorist—can be wholly detached from one's professional function as an artist, this view, to which Voltaire, if he had considered it, could scarcely have offered any objection, is, for all the writers of the *Sturm und Drang*, a fatal misapprehension and distortion of the nature of man and his relations with other men. Since man is in fact one and not many (and those who are genuinely divided personalities are literally no longer sane), it follows that whether a man be an artist, a politician, a lawyer, a soldier, anything that he does expresses all that he is. Some among the *Stürmer* remained individualistic—Heinse, for example, or Klinger. But Herder is uncompromisingly hostile to such egomania. The individual, for him, is inescapably a member of some group; consequently all that he does must express, consciously or unconsciously, the aspirations of his group. Hence, if he is critical of his own life (and all self-consciousness is embryonic assessment and therefore critical), such criticism, like all true criticism, is inevitably to a high degree social criticism, because it is the nature of human beings to be aware socially: expression is communication. Herder feels that all history shows this to be so. To divide (and not merely to distinguish as facets or aspects of one substance) body and soul, science and craft or art, the individual and society, description and evaluation, philosophical, scientific, or historical judgment, and empirical and metaphysical statements, as if these were independent of one another, is for Herder false, superficial, and misleading. The body is the image, the expression, of the soul, not its tomb or instrument or enemy. There are no "iron planks between body and soul";[69] everything can pass into everything else by the insensible transitions of which Leibniz had spoken in his *New Essays*. "Once upon a time men were all things: poets, thinkers, legislators, land surveyors, musicians, warriors."[70] In those days there was unity of theory and practice, of man and citizen, a unity that the division of labor destroyed; after that "Men became half thinkers, half feelers." There is, he remarks, something amiss about moralists who do not act, epic poets who are unheroic, orators who are not statesmen, and aestheticians who cannot create anything. Once doctrines are accepted uncritically—as dogmatic, unalterable, eternal truths—they become dead formulas, or else their meaning is fearfully distorted. Such ossification and decay lead to nonsense in thought and monstrous behavior in practice.[71]

This doctrine was destined to have a great flowering, not merely in the application of the concept of alienation in the writings of the young Marx and his friends in their left-Hegelian phase, and among those who have used these ideas in our own time, but more particularly among pre-Marxist Russian radicals and revolutionaries. No body of men ever believed so devoutly and passionately in the unity of men as the Russian intelligentsia of the last century. These men—at first dissident members of the nobility and gentry, later members of all classes—were united by a burning faith in the right and duty of all men to realize their creative potentialities (physical and spiritual, intellectual and artistic) in the light of the reason and the moral insight with which all men are endowed. What the eighteenth-century French *philosophes* and the German Romantics preached, these men sought to practice. Light to them came from the West. And since the number of literate—let alone well-educated men—in Russia was infinitesimal compared to the number who lived in ignorance, misery, hopeless starvation, and poverty, it was plainly the first duty of any decent man to give all he could to the effort to lift his

---

[69] VIII, 256–62.

[70] *Ibid.* The celebrated statement in the introduction to Karl Marx's *German Ideology* is a direct echo of this doctrine.

[71] XIII, 195.

brothers to a level where they could lead a human existence. From this sprang the conception of the intelligentsia as a sacred order called upon by history to dedicate their lives to the discovery and use of all possible means—intellectual and moral, artistic and technological, scientific and educational—in a single-minded effort to discover the truth, realize it in their lives, and with its aid to rescue the "hungry and the naked" and make it possible for them to live freely and to be men once more. Man is one and undivided; whatever he is and does flows from a single center; but also he is as he is within a social web of which he is a constituent; to ignore is to falsify the nature of man. The famous doctrine that the artist, and above all the writer, has a social obligation to express the nature of the milieu in which he lives, and that he has no right to isolate himself artificially, under the cover of some theory about the need for moral neutrality, or the purity of art, or the need for specialization, or some specifically aesthetic function—a priestly task that is to be kept pure and uncontaminated especially by politics—this entire conception, over which such ferocious battles were fought in the following century, stems from Herder's doctrine of the unity of man.

"Everything that a man undertakes, whether it be produced in action or word or anything else, must spring from his whole united powers; all separation of powers is to be repudiated."[72] These words of Hamann's, so much admired by Goethe, formed Herder, and became (through Schiller and Friedrich Schlegel) the creed of the Russian radical critics. Whatever a man does, if he is as he should be, will express his entire nature. The worst sin is to mutilate oneself, to suppress this or that side of oneself, in the service of some false aesthetic or political or religious ideal. This is the heart of the revolt against the "pruned" French garden of the eighteenth century. Blake is a passionate spokesman of this faith no less than Hamann or Herder or Schleiermacher. To understand any creator— any poet or, for that matter, any human being who is not half dead—is to understand his age and nation, his way of life, the society which (like nature in Shaftesbury) "thinks in him." Herder says over and over again that the true artist (in the widest sense) creates only out of the fullness or the experience of his whole society, especially out of its memories and antiquities which shape its "collective individuality"; and he proceeds to speak of Chaucer, Shakespeare, Spenser, as being steeped in their national folklore. About this he is doubtless mistaken, but the direction of his

---

[72] Quoted from Goethe's *Dichtung und Wahrheit*, Bk. 6. Ch. 12 by Professor Roy Pascal, in *The German Sturm und Drang* (London, 1953), who gives an admirable account, the best in English, of this entire movement.

thought is clear enough. Poetry—all literature and all art—is the direct expression of uninhibited life. The expression of it may be disciplined, but the life must not be. As early poetry was magical, a spur to "heroes, hunters, lovers," men of action, a continuation of experience, so, *mutatis mutandis*, it must be now also. Society may have sadly disintegrated since those days, and Herder concedes that the rhapsodical Klopstock may now be able to express only his own individual, rather than the communal, life; but express he must whatever is in him, and his words will illuminate the experience of his society to his fellow men. "A poet is a creator of a people; he gives it a world to contemplate, he holds its soul in his hand."[73] He is, of course, equally created by it.[74] A man lives in a world of which, in some sense, together with others, he is the maker. "We live in a world we ourselves create."[75] These words of Herder's were destined to be inflated into extravagant metaphysical shapes by Fichte, Schelling, Hegel, and the Idealist Movement in philosophy; but they are equally at the source of the profounder sociological insights of Marx and the revolution in the historical outlook that he initiated.[76]

Herder may be regarded as being among the originators of the doctrine of artistic commitment—perhaps with Hamann, the earliest thinker consciously to speak (as one would expect of the founder of populism) in terms of the totally *engagé* writer, to see the artist as *ipso facto* committed and not permitted to divide himself into compartments, to separate body from spirit, the secular from the sacred, and above all life from art. He believed from the beginning to the end of his life that all men are in some degree artists, and that all artists are, first and last, men—fathers, sons, friends, citizens, fellow worshippers, men united by common action. Hence the purpose of art is not to exist for its own sake (the late *Adrastea* and *Kalligone* are the most ferocious attacks on this doctrine, which he suspected both Kant and Goethe of advancing) or to be utilitarian, or propagandist or "social realist"; still less, of course, should it embellish life or invent forms of pleasure or produce artefacts for the market. The artist is a sacred vessel through which blows the spirit of his

[73] VIII, 33.
[74] II, 61.
[75] VIII, 252.
[76] It is odd that one of Hamann's most fruitful observations—that the poetry of Livonian peasants in the country round Riga and Mitau, which he knew well, was connected with the rhythms of their daily work—evidently made no impression on his disciple. Herder is fascinated by the intimate relation of action and speech—e.g., in his theory of why it is that (as he supposed) verbs precede nouns in primitive speech—but ignores the influence of work. This was made good much later under Saint-Simonian and Marxist influence.

time and place and society; he is the man who conveys, as far as possible, a total human experience, a world. This is the doctrine that, under the impulsion of German romanticism and French socialism, profoundly affected the conception of the artist and his relation to society, that animated Russian critics and writers from the late eighteen-thirties until, at any rate, *Doctor Zhivago*. The theory of art as total expression and of the artist as a man who testifies to the truth—as opposed to the concept of him as a purveyor, however gifted and dedicated—or as a priest of an esoteric cult, entered the practice of the great Russian novelists of the nineteenth century, even of such "pure" writers as Turgenev and Chekhov, very deeply. Through their works it has had a great, indeed a decisive influence, not only on the literature and criticism but on the moral and political ideas and behavior of the West, and indeed of the entire world. Consequently, Herder was perhaps not altogether mistaken when he so confidently proclaimed the part to be played by the artist in the world to come. Whether as an aesthetic critic, or as a philosopher of history, or as a creator of the notion of the non-alienated man, or as the most vehement critic of the classifiers and dividers, Herder (with Hamann) emerges as the originator of the doctrine of the unity of art and life, theory and practice. He is the most eloquent of all the preachers of the restoration of the unbroken human being, by progress to civilization, to *Humanität*, whether by an act of water divining whereby the buried stream of the true humanist tradition may be found and continued, or, as Rousseau demanded, by some social transformation that will destroy the shackles that crib and confine men and allow them to enter or re-enter the Garden of Eden, which they lost when they yielded to the temptation to organize and dominate each other's personalities. Once the walls that separate men are knocked down—walls of state or class or race or religion—they will "return to themselves" and be men and creative once again. The influence of this part of his teaching on the ideas of others, who spoke more articulately and acted with greater political effect, has been very great. [77]

[77] Like other passionate propagandists, Herder pleaded for that which he himself conspicuously lacked. As sometimes happens, what the prophet saw before him was a great compensatory fantasy. The vision of the unity of the human personality and its integration into the society round it by "natural" means was the polar opposite of Herder's own character and conduct. He was, by all accounts, a deeply divided, touchy, resentful, bitter, unhappy man, in constant need of support and praise, neurotic, pedantic, difficult, suspicious, and often insupportable. When he speaks about the "wholly irreplaceable feeling of being alive" (XIII, 337) and compares it with the carefully tended, overarranged world of, say, the critic Sulzer, he is evidently speaking of a sentiment for which he longed but must often have lacked. It has frequently been remarked that it is tormented and unbalanced personalities—Rousseau,

VIII

Finally, I come to what is perhaps the most revolutionary of the implications of Herder's position. Men, according to Herder, truly flourish only in congenial circumstances, that is, where the group to which they belong has achieved a fruitful relationship with the environment by which it is shaped and which in turn it shapes. There the individual is happily integrated into the "natural community,"[78] which grows spontaneously, like a plant, and is not held together by artificial clamps, or soldered together by sheer force, or regulated by laws and regulations invented, whether benevolently or not, by the despot or his bureaucrats. Each of these natural societies contains within itself the "ideal of its own perfection, wholly independent of all comparison with those of others."[79] If this is so, how must we answer the question, put by men throughout recorded history and settled with such clarity and authority by the great *lumières* of the eighteenth century, namely: What is the best life for men? And, more particularly, What is the most perfect society? There is, after all, no dearth of solutions. Every age has provided its own formulas. Some have looked for the solution in sacred books or in revelation or in the words of inspired prophets or the tradition of organized priesthoods; others found it in the rational insight of the trained metaphysician, or in the combination of scientific observation and experiment, or in the "natural" good sense of men not "scribbled over" by philosophers or theologians or perverted by "interested error." Still others have found

---

Nietzsche, D. H. Lawrence—who celebrate with particular passion physical beauty, strength, generosity, spontaneity, above all unbroken unity, harmony and serenity, qualities for which they had an insatiable craving. No man felt less happy in the Prussia of Frederick the Great, or even in the enlightened Weimar of Goethe and Wieland and Schiller, than Herder. Wieland, the most amiable and tolerant of men, found him maddening. Goethe said that he had in him something compulsively vicious—like a vicious horse—a desire to bite and hurt. His ideals were at times a mirror image of his own frustrations.

[78] This is the real community which was later (even before Tönnies) contrasted with the artificial *Gesellschaft;* e.g., Fichte's *Totum* as contrasted with his *Compositum*. But in Herder there are still no explicitly metaphysical overtones: the *Kräfte* realized in communal life—the dynamic forces which he derives from Leibniz—are neither discovered nor act in any *a priori* or transcendent fashion: but neither are they described as being susceptible to scientific tests; their nature, a puzzle to his commentators, evidently did not seem problematic to Herder.

[79] This is, in effect, the central thesis of *Yet Another Philosophy of History*. Meinecke discusses this in *Die Entstehung des Historismus* (II, 438) and his conclusions are subjected to penetrating criticism by G. A. Wells in *The Journal of the History of Ideas* (XXI [Oct.–Dec., 1960], 535–36). Despite Mr. Wells's strictures, Meinecke's thesis—that the heart of Herder's doctrines is a systematic relativism—seems to me to be valid.

it only in the uncorrupted heart of the simple good man. Some thought that only trained experts could discover great and saving truths; others that on questions of value all sane men were qualified to judge. Some maintained that such truths could be discovered at any time, and that it was mere bad luck that it had taken so long to find some of them, or that they had been so easily forgotten. Others held that mankind was subject to the law of growth; and that the truth would not be seen in its fullness until mankind had reached maturity—the age of reason. Some doubted even this, and said men could never attain to such knowledge on earth; or if they did, were too weak to follow it in practice, since such perfection was attainable only by angels or in the life hereafter. But one assumption was common to all these views: that it was, at any rate in principle, possible to draw some outline of the perfect society or the perfect man, if only to define how far a given society or a given individual fell short of the ideal. This was necessary if one was to be able to measure degrees of imperfection. But this belief in the objective solution had not been absolutely universal. Relativists held that different circumstances and temperaments demanded different policies: but though the routes might differ, the goal—human happiness, the satisfaction of human wishes— was one and the same. Some skeptical thinkers in the ancient world— Carneades, for example—went further and uttered the disquieting thought that some ultimate values might be incompatible with one another, so that no solution could logically incorporate them all. There was something of this doubt about the logic of the concept of the perfect society not only among the Greeks, but in the Renaissance too, in Pontano, in Montaigne, in Machiavelli, and after them in Leibniz and Rousseau, who thought that no gain could be made without a corresponding loss.[80] It was present, too, in the works of the great dramatists, Sophocles, Euripides, Shakespeare. Nevertheless, the central stream of the Western tradition was little affected by this fundamental doubt. The central assumption was that problems of value were in principle soluble, and soluble with finality. Whether the solutions could be implemented by imperfect men was another question, a question which did not affect the rationality of the universe. This is the keystone of the classical arch which, after Herder, began to crumble.

If Herder's view of mankind was correct—if Germans in the eighteenth century cannot become Greeks or Romans or ancient Hebrews or simple shepherds, still less all of these together; and if each of the civilizations

---

[80] See footnote 88.

into which he infuses so much life by his sympathetic *Einfühlen* are widely different, and indeed uncombinable—then how could there exist, even in principle, one universal ideal, valid for all men, at all times, everywhere? The "physiognomies" of cultures are unique: each presents a wonderful exfoliation of human potentialities in its own time and place and environment. We are forbidden to make judgments of comparative value, for that is measuring the incommensurable. And even though Herder himself may not be at all consistent in this respect, since he condemns and praises entire civilizations, his doctrine, at least in his most original works, does not permit this. Nor can it be doubted that he himself made valiant efforts to live up to his earlier principles: for all his dislike of the rigidly centralized Egyptian establishment, or Roman imperialism, or the brutal chivalry of the Middle Ages, or the dogmatism and intolerance of the Catholic Church, he sought to be not merely fair to these civilizations, but to represent them as each realizing an ideal of indefeasible validity which as an expression of a particular manifestation of the human spirit was valuable in itself, and not as a step to some higher order. It is this rejection of a central category of the Enlightenment which saw each civilization either as a steppingstone to a higher one, or as a sad relapse to an earlier and lower one, that gives force, sense of reality, and persuasive power to his vast panoramic survey. It is true that in the *Ideen* he enunciates the general ideal of *Humanität* toward which man is slowly climbing, and some of Herder's interpreters have faithfully attempted to represent his earlier relativism as a phase of his thought which he "outgrew," or else to reconcile it with his hazy notion of a single progressive movement toward *Humanität*. Thus, Professor Max Rouché thinks that Herder conceives of history as a drama, each act, perhaps each scene, of which can and should be understood and evaluated independently; which does not prevent us from perceiving that, taken together, these episodes constitute a single progressive ascent.[81] Perhaps Herder did come to believe this, or to believe that he believed it. But it remains a vague conception; his skill and imagination, even in the *Ideen*, goes into the evocation of the individual cultures and not of the alleged links between them. The whole thrust of the argument both in such early works as the *Aelteste Urkunde des Menschengeschlechtes, Von deutscher Art und Kunst, Vom Geist der Ebräischen Poesie*, the *Kritische Waelder*, and in the late and mildly worded *Briefe zu Befoerderung der Humanität*, and the *Ideen* itself, not to speak of his classical statement of historical relativism in *Auch Eine Philosophie der Geschichte*,

[81] *Op. cit.*, Introduction.

is to show and celebrate the uniqueness, the individuality, and, above all, the incommensurability with one another of each of the civilizations which he so lovingly describes and defends. But if all these forms of life are intelligible and valuable—each in its own terms—"organic" wholes, patterns of ends and means which cannot be resurrected, still less amalgamated, they can scarcely be graded as so many links in some impersonal, rigorously determined progress, some stages of which are rendered automatically more valuable than others by their relationship—say, proximity to, or mirroring of—the final goal toward which humanity, however uncertainly, is marching. This places Herder's *Weltanschauung*, so far as it is consistent at all, despite all the insights that it shares with them, outside the "perfectibilian" philosophies of modern times, as remote from the divine tactic of Bossuet (or even Burke) as from the doctrine of progress determined by the growth of reason preached by Voltaire or Lessing or Condorcet, or from the ideal of self-understanding and self-emancipation, spiritual or social, Hegelian or Marxist.

If Herder's notion of the equal validity of incommensurable cultures is accepted, the concepts of an ideal state or of an ideal man become incoherent. This is a far more radical denial of the foundations of traditional Western morality than any that Hume ever uttered. Herder's relativism is a doctrine different from that of the Greek sophists or Montesquieu or Hume. These thinkers were agreed, by and large, that what men sought was happiness; they merely pointed out that differences of circumstance and the interplay of environment—"climate"—with men's nature, conceived as fairly uniform, created different characters and outlooks and, above all, different needs which called for dissimilar institutional means of satisfying them. But they recognized a broad identity or similarity of purpose in all known forms of human activity, universal and timeless goals of men as such, which bound them in a single human species or Great Society. This would, at least in theory, enable a socially imaginative and well-informed universal despot, provided he was enlightened enough, to govern each society with a due regard to its individual needs; and to advance them all toward universal harmony, each marching along its own path toward the self-same purpose—happiness and the rule of reason, virtue, justice. This is precisely Lessing's conception, which he expresses by the famous parable of the three rings in *Nathan the Wise*.[82]

Herder had deep affinities with the *Aufklärung*, and he did write with optimism and eloquence about man's ascent to ideal *Humanität* and uttered

[82] It has found an unexpected reincarnation not long ago in Mao Tse-tung's celebrated image of the many flowers.

sentiments to which Lessing could have subscribed no less than Goethe; yet, despite the authority of some excellent scholars,[83] I do not believe that anyone who reads Herder's works with the *Einfühlung* for which he asks, and which he so well describes, will sustain the impression that it is this—the ideal of enlightened Weimar—that fills his mind. He is a rich, suggestive, prolix, marvellously imaginative writer, but seldom clear or rigorous or conclusive. His ideas are often confused, sometimes inconsistent, never wholly specific or precise, as, indeed, Kant pointedly complained. As a result, many interpretations can be (and have been) put upon his works. But what lies at the heart of the whole of his thought— what influenced later thinkers, particularly the German Romantics and, through them, the entire history of populism, nationalism, and individualism—is the theme to which he constantly returns; that one must not judge one culture by the criteria of another; that differing civilizations are different growths, pursue different goals, embody different ways of living, are dominated by different attitudes to life; so that to understand them one must perform an imaginative act of "empathy" into their essence, understand them "from within" as far as possible, and see the world through their eyes—be a "shepherd among shepherds" with the ancient Hebrews, or "sail the Northern seas in a tempest" and read the Eddas again in "the dark, dangerous, grimly disciplined atmosphere of "a ship struggling through the Skagerrak." These widely differing societies and their ideals are not commensurable. Such questions as which of them is the best, or even which one would prefer, which one would judge to be nearer to the universal human ideal, *Humanität*, even subjectively conceived—the pattern most likely to produce man as he should be or one thinks he should be—are, therefore, for a thinker of this type, meaningless. "Not a man, not a country, not a people, not a natural history, not a state, are like one another. Hence the True, the Good, the Beautiful in them are not similar either."[84] Herder wrote this in his Journal in 1769. The cloven hoof of relativism, or rather pluralism, shows itself even in his most orthodox discussions of universal ideals; for he thinks each image of *Humanität* to be unique and *sui generis*.[85] It is this, and not the commonplace universalism that he shares with his age, that struck, and perhaps shocked, the *Aufklärer*, the Kantians, the progressive thinkers of his time.

[83] E.g., Rudolf Stadelmann, *Der Historische Sinn bei Herder* (Halle, 1928); R. A. Fritzsche, *Herder und die Humanität, Der Morgen*, Bk. III (Halle, 1928); H. Vesterling, *Herder's Humanitätsprinzip* (Halle, 1890).
[84] IV, 472.
[85] XIV, 210, 217, 230.

For this goes directly against the notion of steady progress on the part of mankind as a whole, which, despite difficulties and relapses, must, or at least can, go on; a proposition to which the German no less than the French or Italian Enlightenment was fully committed.[86]

Herder is not a subjectivist. He believes in objective standards of judgment that are derived from understanding the life and purposes of individual societies and are themselves objective historical structures, and require, on the part of the student, wide and scrupulous scholarship as well as sympathetic imagination. What he rejects is the single overarching standard of values, in terms of which all cultures, characters, and acts can be evaluated. Each phenomenon to be investigated presents its own measuring rod, its own internal constellation of values in the light of which alone "the facts" can be truly understood. This is much more thoroughgoing than the realization that man is incapable of complete perfection, as, for instance, Winckelmann allowed,[87] Rousseau lamented, and Kant accepted; or the doctrine that all gains entail some loss.[88] For what is here entailed is that the highest ends for which men have rightly striven and sometimes died are strictly incompatible with one another. Even if it were possible to revive the glories of the past as those pre-historicist thinkers (Machiavelli or Mably, for instance) thought, who called for a return to the heroic virtues of Greece or Rome, we could not revive and unite them all. If we choose to emulate the Greeks, we cannot also emulate the Hebrews; if we model ourselves on the Chinese, whether as they are in reality, or in Voltaire's *opéra bouffe* version, we cannot also be the Florentines of the Renaissance, or the innocent, serene, hospitable savages of eighteenth-century imagination. Even if, *per impossibile*, we could choose among these ideals, which should we select? Since there is no common standard in terms of which to grade them, there can be no final solution to the problem of what men as such should aim at. The proposition that this question must be capable, at least in principle, of one

---

[86] Among modern thinkers, Herder's relativism most resembles Wyndham Lewis's protest against what he called "the demon of progress in the arts." In the tract which bears this title that acute, if perverse, writer denounced, with characteristically vehement and biting eloquence, the notion that valid universal criteria exist in terms of which it is possible to assert or deny that (I cannot recollect his specific examples) Phidias is superior or inferior to Michelangelo or Maillol, or that Goethe or Tolstoy represent an improvement on, or decline from, Homer or Aeschylus or Dante or the Book of Job.

[87] E.g., in his *Die Geschichte der Kunst des Alterhums*, ed. J. Lessing (Berlin, 1869–70).

[88] Leibniz (ed. Gerhart), II, 589; Boulainvilliers, *Histoire de l'ancien gouvernement de la France* (1727), I, 322; Rousseau in the letter to Mirabeau of July 26, 1767; Wegelin in his *Philosophy of Hispasstory* (1770) im.

correct answer, which few had doubted since Plato had taken it for granted, is undermined. Herder, of course, condemns the very wish to resurrect ancient ideals: ideals belong to the form of life which generates them, and are mere historical memories without them: values—ends— live and die with the social wholes of which they form an intrinsic part. Each "collective individuality" is unique, and has its own aims and standards, which will themselves inevitably be superseded by other goals and values—ethical, social, and aesthetic. Each of these systems is objectively valid in its own day, in the course of "Nature's long year" which brings all things to pass. All cultures are equal in the sight of God, each in its time and place. Ranke said precisely this: his theology is a complacent version of Herder's theses, not of those of Hegel or Montesquieu. But if this is so, then the notion of the perfect civilization in which the ideal human being realizes his full potentialities is patently absurd: not merely difficult to formulate, or impossible to realize in practice, but incoherent and meaningless. This is perhaps the sharpest blow ever delivered against the classical philosophy of the West, to which the notion of perfection—the logical possibility of universal, timeless solutions of problems of value—is essential.

The consequences of Herder's doctrines did not make themselves felt immediately. He was thought to be a bold and original thinker, but not a subverter of common moral assumptions. Nor, of course, did he think so himself. The full effect was felt only when the Romantic Movement, at its most violent, attempted to overthrow the authority both of reason and of dogma on which the old order rested. The extent of its explosive potentialities was not fully realized until the rise of modern anti-rationalist movements—nationalism, fascism, existentialism, emotivism, and the wars and revolutions made in the name of two among them; that is to say, not until our own time, and perhaps not altogether even today.

IX

Herder's works, as might be expected, bristle with contradictions: on the one hand, "The power which thinks and works in me, is in its nature as eternal as that which holds together the sun and the stars; wherever and whoever I shall be, I shall be what I am now, a force in a system of forces, in the immeasurable harmony of God's world."[89] Whatever can be, will be. All potentialities will be realized. Herder believes in plenitude, in the great chain of being, in a nature with no barriers. Influenced by

[89] XIII, 16.

the naturalists, by Ritter, by von Haller, he sees man as an animal among animals: man is what he is because of slowly working natural causes, because he walks upright, or because of a cavity in his skull. Yet he also believes, with Aristotle and the Bible, in natural kinds, and in the special act of creation. Again, he believes in a general human essence, a central human character: it is, as Leibniz taught in the *Nouveaux essais*, like a vein in marble, to be brought out by reason and imagination. Men are the Benjamins, the "darlings of Nature's old age," the peak of the creative process. Yet, of course, he also believes that this human essence takes conflicting forms; types differ and the differences are unbridgeable. There is a curious effort to bring together the monistic notion of the logically rigorous interconnection of all real entities in Spinoza's world (although in Herder's case it takes the form of something more flexible and empirical) with the dynamic, self-developing individuated entities of Leibniz. [90] There is a tension between Herder's naturalism and his teleology, his Christianity and his enthusiastic acceptance of the findings of the natural sciences; between respect for some, at any rate, of the achievements of the French Encyclopedists, who believed in quantitative methods, precision and a unified schema of knowledge, and the qualitative approach of Goethe and Schelling and their vitalistic followers. Again, there is a contradiction between his naturalistic determinism, which at times is very strong, and the notion that one can and should resist natural impulses and natural forces; [91] for people who do not resist are overwhelmed. The Jews were crushed by the Romans; their disastrous destiny was avoidable; yet it is ascribed to natural factors; the Romans too are held to have succumbed to vices which they could have resisted successfully. Herder was not sensitive to the problem of free will as, say, Kant was; there are too many conflicting strains in him. He may have believed, like most self-determinists, that men were free when they did what they chose, while it was, in some sense, idle to ask whether men were free to choose, since they obviously were not; but his writings give evidence that he sought escape in this time-honored, but hardly satisfactory, "solution." [92] Again, there are the separate strands of *Humanität* as a general human ideal (to be realized fully, perhaps, only in the world to come) and the *Gang Gottes über die Natur*—a phrase and a concept which Hegel later

[90] This is developed at length in *God: Some Conversations*, in which he defends Spinoza against Jacobi's charges of atheism and pantheism.

[91] See the magnificent paean to human freedom and man's powers of resistance to nature, XII, 142–50.

[92] Wells, *Herder and After*, argues strongly for this interpretation.

appropriated—and, on the other side, his more frequent and characteristic pluralism and relativism. There is noticeable tension between his passion for his German kinsmen, real and imaginary, for the ancient German tribal life which seemed to him spontaneous, creative, free, and his reluctant admiration for Rome, and even more for the Church, with their universalism and order and power of rational organization. More far-reaching still is the contrast between, on the one hand, the notion of the continuity of overflowing nature, the *Natura naturans*, the energy that is one in magnetism and electricity, in plants and animals and men, in language and in art—a universal, continuous life force of which everything is a manifestation, of which laws can be discovered in the form both of the physical sciences of his time, and of biology, psychology, and the particular brand of historical geography and anthropology that he favored; and on the other hand, the crucial role attributed to the unaccountable leaps of genius, miraculous events, sheer chance, the unanalyzable process of true creation—as opposed to the impossibility of achieving anything great or lasting solely by the application of techniques; or, what goes with this, the incommunicability of the central core of what individuates men or cultures and gives them all the color and force and value they possess, something that is open only to the eye of imaginative intuition, incapable of being reduced to communicable, teachable scientific method. Finally, there is the ban on moralizing, but also the impassioned apostrophes to the great moments of human existence, the curses heaped on the enemies of human unity and creativity—the bloodstained conquerors, the ruthless centralizers, the shriveling of the spirit by narrow and superficial systematizers—and at the head of them all, the odious Voltaire, with his devitalizing ironies and pettiness and lack of insight into what men truly are. All the confusions of his time seem richly reflected in his shapeless, sprawling, but continuously suggestive works.

X

Herder is in some sense a premonitory symptom, the albatross before the coming storm. The French Revolution was founded on the notion of timeless truths given to the faculty of reason with which all men are endowed. It was dedicated to the creation or restoration of a static and harmonious society, founded on unaltering principles, a dream of classical perfection, or at least to the closest approximation of it feasible on earth. It preached a peaceful universalism and a rational humanitarianism. But its consequences threw into relief the precariousness of human institutions; the disturbing phenomenon of change; the clash of irreconcilable values and ideas; the insufficiency of simple formulas; the complexity of men and societies; the poetry of action, destruction, heroism, war; the effectiveness of mobs and of great men; the power of chance; the feebleness of reason and the power over it of fanatically believed doctrines; the unpredictability of events; the part played in history by unintended consequences and the ignorance of the workings of the sunken two-thirds of the great human iceberg, of which only the visible portion had been studied by scientists and taken into account by the ideologists of the great Revolution. This, too, could be said of the Russian Revolution. Its ideals are too familiar to rehearse; and its results, too, threw doubts, whether justified or not, on the effectiveness of the kind of democracy for which liberals and radicals in the nineteenth century had pleaded; on the ability of rational men to allow for and control the forces of unreason; on revolution as an instrument for the promotion of freedom, a wider culture and social justice. It awakened men forcibly to the effectiveness of resolute conspiracies by disciplined parties; the irrationality of the masses; the weakness of liberal and democratic institutions in the West; the force of nationalist passions. As Durkheim, Pareto, and Freud stand to the Russian Revolution, to the ideas of democracy and liberty, and to the forces of social cohesion and disintegration that are discussed today, so Herder stands to the events of 1789. The craving for fraternity, for self-expression, disbelief in the capacity of reason to determine values dominated the nineteenth century—tendencies that have reached their climax in our own time. Herder lived until 1803. He did not attempt to draw the moral of his own doctrines in relation to the fate of Germany or Europe, as Saint-Simon and Hegel and de Maistre, in their very different fashions, had attempted to do. Perhaps he died too early in the century. Nevertheless, he, more than any of his contemporaries, had a sense of the insecurity of the foundations of enlightened beliefs in his own time, even while he half accepted them. In this sense, those who thought of him as endowed with special powers—we are told that he was sometimes called a magician and was a model for Goethe's Faust[93]—did him no injustice.

---

[93] E.g., by Günter Jacobi in *Herder als Faust* (Leipzig, 1911). Goethe himself detested such identifications (for a discussion of this, see Robert T. Clark, Jr., *Herder: His Life and Thought* [Berkeley and Los Angeles, 1955], pp. 127f.).

The Term and Concept of

"Classicism" in Literary History

BY RENÉ WELLEK

◄◄◄◄◄◄◄◄◄◄◄◄◄ ☼ ►►►►►►►►►►►►►

Today it seems impossible to write about English eighteenth-century literature without using the term "classicism" or, possibly even more frequently, "neoclassicism." There are books such as *The Course of English Classicism*, articles called "The Tendency toward Platonism in Neo-Classical Esthetics," or " 'Distrust' of Imagination in English Neoclassicism," and chapters in literary histories on the "Rise of Classicism," "The Disintegration of Classicism," etc.[1] But what seems to us a matter of course was not so even sixty years ago, and a hundred years ago the term was not used or hardly used at all. The English classicists or neoclassicists did not, of course, call themselves by that name; they spoke, at most, of the imitation of the ancients, of the observance of the rules, or similarly. When early in the nineteenth century their reputation declined and they were looked upon as belonging to a bygone age, the age was called The Augustan Age, The Age of Pope, The Age of Queen Anne, but not the Age of Classicism. Macaulay, in 1828, spoke of "The Critical School of Poetry"; some enemies referred to it as "The French School."[2] The issue

---

[1] I allude to Sherard Vines (London, 1930); L. I. Bredvold's "Tendency . . . ," *ELH*, I (1934), 91–119; D. F. Bond's, "Distrust . . . ," in *Philological Quarterly*, XIV (1935), 54–69, and to the chapters by George Sherburn in Albert C. Baugh (ed.), *A Literary History of England* (New York, 1948), pp. 699ff., 967ff.

[2] In "John Dryden" (1828), reprinted in *Miscellaneous Works* (New York, 1880), I, 145. "French School," e.g., in *Edinburgh Review*, CCVII (July, 1858), 1—a review of Bell's edition of Dryden and of Scott's edition of Dryden, referring to the term as customary.

whether Pope was a poet or not or whether he was a poet of the highest rank, first raised in Joseph Warton's *Essay on Pope* (1756), was debated in terms of a contrast between natural and artificial poetry or of a distinction between high imaginative, pure poetry and didactic or ethical poetry, but not in terms of a contrast between classicism and romanticism.

It took a long time before the term "classicism" was applied to the style of Dryden and Pope. Why was this so? Can we account for it? Is there any significance to the lack of the term? If we believe with Croce that an idea is not there until it is expressed we must ascribe great importance to the question of terminology. Such terms, I would agree, as Renaissance, romanticism, baroque, and realism crystallize ideas, formulate the problem of periodization and pervasive style, however uncertain and disputable may be the extension, valuation, and precise content of each term. They have become indispensable tools of historiography, and their absence shows a lack of interest in abstraction, in the whole problem of period style, and the characterization and generalizations implied in these terms. The England of the nineteenth century is a case in point.

It seems significant that during the nineteenth century a whole set of alternative terms to "classicism" was used sporadically: the need for a term was felt, and different words were tried and dropped. "Classicalism" is now completely out of use, but it occurs, e.g., in a letter by Elizabeth Barrett in 1839. She praises Landor as "the most classical, because the freest from mere classicalism." [3] Ruskin in the first volume of *Modern Painters* (1846) refers to "the hybrid classicalism" of the landscape painter Richard Wilson; [4] Arnold in his preface to *Merope* (1857) complains that people have been "taught to consider classicalism as inseparable from coldness." [5] Leslie Stephen, in his *History of English Thought in the Eighteenth Century* (1876), calls the "classicalism of the time . . . midway between the taste of the Renaissance and that of modern times." [6] W. J. Courthope, in his *Life of Alexander Pope* (1889), speaks of the "classicalism which reached its height in the 'Botanical Garden' of Erasmus Darwin." [7] There was the alternative term "classicality," which Ruskin used when he contemptuously referred to the "vile classicality of Canova." [8] Slowly, in the anti-eighteenth-century atmosphere of Victorian literary studies, the terms "pseudo-classical," "pseudo-classicism," and "pseudo-classicalism"

---

[3] Quoted in John Foster, *W. S. Landor* (London, 1869), II, 298.
[4] *Modern Painters*, I, *Works*, ed. Cook-Wedderburn (London, 1902–12), III, 230.
[5] In *On the Classical Tradition*, ed. R. H. Super (Ann Arbor, Mich., 1960), p. 38.
[6] (London, 1876), II, 355.
[7] (London, 1889), p. 374. Used also on p. 61.
[8] *Modern Painters*, I, *Works*, ed. Cook-Wedderburn, III, 230.

emerge. Ruskin referred to Claude Lorrain as "pseudo-classical" in 1856,[9] and James Russell Lowell, in his essay on Pope (1871), speaks of a "pseudo-classicism, the classicism of red heels and periwigs."[10] In 1885 the word appears for the first time on the title page of an English, or rather American, book. Thomas Sergeant Perry, an early friend of Henry James, wrote *From Opitz to Lessing: A Study of Pseudo-Classicism in Literature*.[11] But Leslie Stephen, in 1876, used the new term "pseudo-classicalism" to refer to poetry after Pope.[12]

The more neutral term "neoclassical" appeared somewhat earlier. William Rushton, of whom I know nothing, gave a lecture, "The Classical and Romantic Schools of English Literature" (1863), which shows that he was aware of making an innovation. "When we speak of the classical school in English Literature," he says, "we refer to those writers who have formed their style upon the ancient models, and, for the sake of distinction, we might call them the Revived Classical or the Neo-Classical school." Later he refers again to "the development of the neo-classical school" in the works of Dryden and Pope.[13] But as far as I know the term is exceedingly rare in the following decades. Saintsbury in his *History of Criticism* (1902) has a chapter "The Neo-classic Creed," but the word becomes common only in the nineteen-twenties.[14]

The term "classicism" was victorious after all. At first it was definitely an import from the Continent and referred to events on the Continent. Carlyle, in the essay on Schiller (1831), seems to have used the word for the first time in English, complacently and prematurely reflecting that "we are troubled with no controversies on Romanticism and Classicism."[15] Facetiously, in *The French Revolution* (1837), Carlyle enumerates "Catholicism, Classicism, Sentimentalism, Cannibalism; all isms that make up Man in France."[16] Carlyle's hostility to those abstractions seems somewhat odd, since he wrote his *History of the French Revolution* very much in such terms, personifying Constitutional Patriotism, Sansculottism, and Monarchism on almost every page. But as late as 1837 John Stuart Mill had to explain patiently that "this insurrection against the old traditions

---

[9] *Modern Painters*, III, *Works*, ed. Cook-Wedderburn, V, 244.
[10] *Literary Essays* (Boston, 1891), IV, 8.
[11] Boston, 1885.
[12] *History of English Thought in the Eighteenth Century* (London, 1876), II, 357.
[13] "The Classical and Romantic Schools of English Literature," *The Afternoon Lectures on English Literature* (London, 1863), pp. 44, 63, 72.
[14] "The Crystallising of the Neo-Classic Creed," *A History of Criticism* (Edinburgh, 1902), II, 240ff.
[15] *Critical and Miscellaneous Essays* (Centenary ed.; London, 1899), II, 172.
[16] *French Revolution* (Centenary ed.; London, 1899), III, 205.

of classicism was called romanticism" in France.[17] I cannot find the term in English for many years to come and certainly the standard discussions of Pope and Dryden get along without it. It occurs in Arnold's essay on Heine (1863) when he speaks of his "utter rejection of stock classicism and stock romanticism."[18] Walter Pater, in his essay on "Romanticism" (1876), which was later reprinted as the Postscript to *Appreciations* (1889), quotes Stendhal on classicism and romanticism,[19] but otherwise does not use the term even when he discusses Winckelmann and Goethe. Edward Dowden, in 1878, speaking of Landor, is satisfied that "the attempts made . . . to bend our literature to classicism were not of native origin" and thus could not succeed for any length of time.[20] Even Edmund Gosse, in his *Modern English Literature* (1898), knows only a "classical" poetry during the lifetime of Pope and puts the term "classical" in quotation marks.[21] In Oliver Elton's *Augustan Ages* (1899), the terms "French Classicism" and the English "representatives of classicism" are used,[22] and Herbert Grierson in a later volume of the same series, *The First Half of the Seventeenth Century* (1906), says casually that "in our period the classicism of the Augustan ages is taking shape."[23] I could not prove it with statistical accuracy, but I believe that only Emile Legouis' and Louis Cazamian's *Histoire de la littérature anglaise* (1925), which calls a whole section "Classicism (1702–1740)," established the academic usage, particularly in the United States, as Legouis-Cazamian was the standard history of English literature when I was a student in the twenties.

Some of the evidence here presented is undoubtedly far from complete. Some of the dates for first occurrences of the terms, though they antedate the examples given in the *NED*, could probably be pushed back further. But in its general outlines the sketch must be correct: the late acceptance of the term "classicism" for English literature of the late seventeenth and early eighteenth centuries shows that English literary thinking for a long time shied away from the abstraction and the shorthand implicit in the use of the term. It shows also that attention was turned elsewhere. When we read what nineteenth-century authors have to say about Pope, Dryden, Swift, and Addison, we get almost exclusively discussions of their lives, personalities, and ethics, and possibly of their religious and

[17] "Armand Carrel," *Dissertations and Discussions* (2nd ed.; London, 1867), I, 233.
[18] *Lectures and Essays in Criticism*, ed. R. H. Super (Ann Arbor, Mich., 1962), p. 122.
[19] *Appreciations* (London, 1924), p. 245.
[20] "W. S. Landor," *Studies in Literature 1785–1877* (London, 1878), p. 182.
[21] (London, 1898), pp. 214, 215.
[22] (Edinburgh, 1899), pp. 265–66.
[23] (Edinburgh, 1906), pp. 376–77.

political views. If we get criticism, it is usually content with anthologizing or some general reflections still very much in the tradition of the eighteenth-century debates: Was Pope a poet? Were Pope and Dryden classics of our prose? The idea of a period as a unit of style is late and was later in England than on the Continent. But it would be a mistake to ignore the fact that the older terms, The Augustan Age, The Age of Queen Anne, The Age of Pope, etc., did imply some awareness of a definite period in English literature which, during the early nineteenth century, became a target of attack or a banner of defiance against the new taste. In my earlier paper on "The Concept of Romanticism" (1949), I argued that even without the term many English writers "had a clear consciousness that there was a movement which rejected the critical concepts and poetic practice of the 18th century."[24] Jeffrey, who wrote in 1811 that "Pope was much the best of the classical Continental school,"[25] sums up what most of us would think today.

Jeffrey's word "Continental" raises the crucial problem. English classicism was assumed to be an importation from France: the direct result of the Restoration of 1660, when the Stuarts returned from exile. Pope stated this in well-known lines:

We conquer'd France, but felt our captive's charms:
Her Arts victorious triumph'd o'er our Arms.[26]

De Quincey, in 1851, saw the difficulty of this chronological sequence and perversely interpreted the English conquest of France as referring to the battle of Agincourt in 1415 instead of the victories of Marlborough over the armies of Louis XIV, which Pope must have had in mind. De Quincey, in his contempt for the French, goes so far as to deny that "either Dryden or Pope was even slightly influenced by French literature" and to assert that "the thing they did they would have done though France had been at the back of China."[27] A little later, Hippolyte Taine, in his *Histoire de la littérature anglaise* (1864), devoted some eloquent pages to contrasting the gentle, wise, and polite Molière with the brutal, gross and vulgar Wycherley, and the refined and elegant Racine with the bombastic and obscene Otway. The characters of English Restoration

---

[24] Reprinted in *Concepts of Criticism* (New Haven, 1963), p. 152.
[25] "The Dramatic Works of John Ford" (1811), *Contributions to the Edinburgh Review* (London, 1844), II, 292.
[26] "The First Epistle of the Second Book of Horace," ll. 263–64, in *Imitations of Horace*, ed. J. Butt, (London, 1939), p. 217.
[27] *Collected Writings*, ed. D. Masson (London, 1896), XI, 61.

tragedies, Taine concluded, are as much like Racine's as "the cook of Madame de Sévigné is like Madame de Sévigné."[28] Katherine E. Wheatley, in a recent book, *Racine and English Classicism* (1956), displayed, with some pedantic glee, all the misinterpretations and mistranslations of English translators and adapters of Racine. She argues that there was a deep gulf between the two literatures and suggests that the English lacked a psychological tradition comparable to the French *moralistes* and the Racinian analysis of passion.[29] Henri Peyre, in his *Qu'est-ce que le classicisme?* (1935), emphasized the distinctness and uniqueness of French classicism and argued that "the relations between French literature of the 17th century and that of antiquity" were much looser than it is usually assumed.[30] As to English literature, P. S. Wood had pointed to "Native Elements in English Neo-Classicism" (1926),[31] and since then many scholars have demonstrated the continuity between the Elizabethan Age and the Restoration. As early as 1898 Felix Schelling proclaimed Ben Jonson the father of the English "Classical School."[32]

Surely, in an international history of criticism these arguments for the divorce between French and English literature of that time are not convincing. They merely push the matter back into the past, to the common sources of the neoclassical, i.e., Aristotelian and Horatian theory, which was formulated first in Italy early in the sixteenth century and a little later by Scaliger, an Italian active in France, and then again by Dutch scholars such as Vossius and Heinsius. Ben Jonson, it has been shown long ago, paraphrased and translated these writers,[33] and the French seventeenth-century critics were clearly influenced by them at least in dramatic theory.[34] English classicism is, in critical theory, part and parcel of the huge Western European neoclassical tradition. It was in direct contact with France, particularly with Boileau,[35] but drew also on the sources of French classical theory in Antiquity and in Italian and Dutch

---

[28] (2nd ed.; Paris, 1866), III, 216: "la cuisinière de Mme de Sévigné à Mme de Sévigné."

[29] Austin, Texas, 1956.

[30] Quoted from expanded edition, *Le Classicisme français* (New York, 1942), p. 32: "Combien lâches sonts les rapports entre la littérature française de XVII*e* siècle et celle de l'antiquité."

[31] In *Modern Philology*, XXIV (1926), 201–8.

[32] "Ben Jonson and the Classical School," *PMLA*, XIII (1898), 221–49; reprinted in *Shakespeare and "Demi-Science"* (Philadelphia, 1927).

[33] See J. E. Spingarn, "The Sources of Jonson's *Discoveries*," *Modern Philology*, II (1905), 451–60, and the edition of *Timber, or Discoveries* by M. Castelain (Paris, 1906).

[34] See Edith G. Kern, *The Influence of Heinsius and Vossius upon French Dramatic Theory* (Baltimore, 1949).

[35] Cf. A. F. Clark, *Boileau and the French Classical Critics in England* (Paris, 1925).

humanism. English classicism is rightly named so. My little history must have shown that it was named on the analogy of French classicism.

But how did the French come to speak of classicism? It will be necessary to go farther into the history of the term. Every dictionary tells us that the word *classicus* occurs first in Aulus Gellius, a Roman author of the second century after Christ, who in his miscellany *Noctes Atticae* refers to "classicus scriptor, non proletarius," transferring a term of the Roman taxation classes to the ranking of writers.[36] *Classicus* thus meant originally "first class," "excellent," "superior." The term seems not to have been used in the Middle Ages at all, but reappears in the Renaissance in Latin and soon in the vernaculars. The first recorded occurrence in French, in Sébillet's *L'Art poétique* (1548), refers, surprisingly, to "les bons et classiques poètes françois comme sont entre les vieux Alain Chartier et Jean de Meun."[37] The names of two medieval poets show that the word had no association with classical antiquity and simply meant "standard," "superior," "excellent." I am not aware of any study that traces the process by which the term became identified with the ancients as in the term "classical antiquity," though the reason for the shift is obvious enough. "Classical" came to mean Roman and Greek, and it still implied superiority, authority, and even perfection. Nor am I aware of any study that shows how "classical" came to be associated with the classroom, with the texts taught in schools, though again the reason for the shift in meaning is obvious enough: the ancient classics were the only secular authors studied, and they were studied as models of style and sources of ideas. Ernst Robert Curtius, in *Europäische Literatur and lateinisches Mittelalter* (1948), has raised the question of the formation of a canon of ancient authors and of the great writers in the modern literatures. It would be worthwhile to trace the process in detail for every literature. Pope, in 1737, said that "who lasts a century can have no flaw: I hold that Wit a Classic, good in law,"[38] and George Sewell, in his introduction to Shakespeare's *Poems* (a part of Pope's *Shakespeare*, 1725), had asked for careful editions of English authors, which "we in justice owe to our own great writers, both in Prose, and Poetry. They are in some degree our Classics: on their Foundation we must build, as the Formers

---

[36] *Noctes*, 19, 8, 15: "Vel oratorum aliquis vel poetarum, id est classicus assiduusque aliquis, scriptor, non proletarius."

[37] Quoted from Edmond Huguet, *Dictionnaire de la langue française du seizième siècle*, II, 308, or Sébillet, *Art poétique* (Paris, 1910), Ch. III, p. 26.

[38] As in note 26 above. Pope paraphrases Horace's: "Est vetus atque probus, centum qui perficit annos" (ll. 55–56, p. 199).

and Refiners of our Language."[39] Sewell thinks of Shakespeare as deserving and getting such treatment. We are back at the meaning of "classic" that Sébillet assumed. Shakespeare is a standard author.

The same meaning of the term is recorded also in France, though surprisingly somewhat later than in England. Pierre-Joseph Thoulier D'Olivet, in his *Histoire de l'Académie* (1729), complains that "Italy had classical authors and we as yet have none."[40] In a letter to the same Abbé D'Olivet, Voltaire in 1761 proposed to edit the "classical authors" of the French, reserving Corneille for himself as a special favorite.[41] Certainly Voltaire's own *Siècle de Louis XIV* (1751) puts the age and its writers next to other golden ages: that of Leo X, of Augustus and Alexander. Characteristically, the age of Pericles is still missing from the list.[42] In all these discussions the implication of "classicity" as model and standard is dominant. The remoter model behind the great modern writer in antiquity is assumed as a matter of course, but not more so than when Dante is considered a "classic" in Italy or when Spaniards speak of their Golden Age. The matter of style did not enter.

The decisive event for the development of the concept of "classicism" was, after all, the great romantic-classical debate begun in Germany by the brothers Schlegel. I have discussed these questions at length in several of my writings, largely with emphasis on the romantic side, and I do not wish to repeat myself.[43] For my immediate purpose the transformation of the meaning of the word "classical" from a term of valuation to a term for a stylistic trend, type, or period, in which differences of quality are allowed to exist, is the crucial turning point. The historistic revolution brought about the awareness of the existence, side by side, of at least two literary traditions. The Schlegelian dichotomy was first expounded in France by Madame de Staël in *De l'Allemagne* (1814), but a few months before the delayed publication of the book August Wilhelm Schlegel's *Vorlesungen über dramatische Kunst und Literatur* appeared in a

---

[39] Quoted by J. C. Maxwell in *Notes and Queries*, X, No. 6 (June, 1963), 220. From the preface to Pope's *Shakespeare*, VII, vii.

[40] Ed. Livet (Paris, 1858), II, 47. "L'Italie avait des auteurs classiques, et nous n'en avons point encore de tels."

[41] Voltaire, *Correspondence*, ed. T. Bestermann (Geneva, 1959), XL, 275. See also a letter to C. P. Duclos, p. 274. Both letters were written on April 10, 1761.

[42] Ch. XXXII, ed. René Groos (Paris, 1947), II, 129. "Le siècle de Louis XIV a donc en tout la destinée des siècles de Léon X, d'Auguste, d'Alexandre."

[43] "The Concept of Romanticism," *Concepts of Criticism* (New Haven, 1963), and *A History of Modern Criticism* (New Haven, 1955), Vol. 2.

translation by her cousin, Madame Necker de Saussure. [44] In her preface (1813) the translator commented perceptively: "In Mr. Schlegel's work, the epithet 'classical' is a simple designation of a genre, independent of the degree of perfection with which the genre is treated." [45] We all know the violent polemics which Madame de Staël's book stirred up. But if we examine the texts of the classical-romantic debate we do not find the term "classicisme." It is not in Eggli-Martino's very full collection, *Le Débat romantique 1813–1816*, though the word "romantisme" occurs twice in 1816. [46]

We must go to Italy to find the first occurrence of "classicismo." A very complete collection by Egidio Bellorini, *Discussioni e polemiche sul romanticismo*, would seem to furnish a check on the emergence of the term. In September, 1818, Giovanni Berchet speaks, in a note, quite casually of "la pedantesca servilità del classicismo," [47] and Ermes Visconti in November and December of the same year uses the term frequently and freely in "Idee elementari sulla poesia romantica." He distinguishes, for example, between the "admirable classicism of the ancients" and the "scholastic classicism of the moderns." [48] It is difficult to believe that the term could have emerged so casually and be used as a matter of course. I suspect that it must have existed before in the discussions about the revival of Antiquity in the fine arts initiated by Winckelmann and David. But I have failed to find the word in all the obvious texts: Milizia, Cicognara, Ennio Quirino Visconti, or in the many writings about Canova.

What matters for my purposes here in that Stendhal picked up the term in Milan—he read and paraphrased Visconti, whom he also knew personally—and then gave, in his *Racine et Shakespeare* (1823), the famous facetious definitions of classicism and romanticism. "Romanticism is the art of presenting to different peoples those literary works which, in

[44] Madame de Staël's *De l'Allemagne* was printed in 1810 but suppressed by Napoleon. It appeared in French in London, October, 1813, and was reprinted in Paris in May, 1814. Schlegel's *Cours* appeared in December, 1813, in Paris, in French translation.

[45] "Dans l'ouvrage de M. Schlegel, l'épithète de classique est une simple désignation de genre, indépendante du degré de perfection avec laquelle le genre est traité."

[46] *Le Débat romantique en France 1813–1830*, eds. Edmond Eggli and Pierre Martino (Paris, 1933). "Romantisme" on pp. 445, 472–73.

[47] "Del Criterio ne' discorsi," in Giovanni Berchet, *Opere* (Bari, 1912), II, 65n. Not in Bellorini.

[48] *Discussioni e polemiche sul romanticismo*, ed. Egidio Bellorini (Bari, 1943), I, 436: "il classicismo degli antichi, originale e ammirabile, il classicismo dei moderni . . . scolastico."

the existing state of their habits and beliefs, are capable of giving them the greatest possible pleasure. Classicism, on the contrary, presents to them that literature which gave the greatest possible pleasure to their great-grandfathers."[49] But it would be an error to think that classicism became an established term in France soon after Stendhal's use. It occurs only infrequently in the great debate of the next years, which led to the preface to *Cromwell* (1827). In a careful monograph devoted to the debate of the year 1826 I found it only twice in a pamphlet by Cyprien Desmarais, *Le Temps présent*.[50] No doubt the old word "classique" sufficed for most purposes and "classicisme" was felt to be an ugly neologism. It is called a neologism as late as 1863 in Littré's *Dictionary*, and it has never gained admittance into the Dictionary of the French Academy. Champfleury, the champion of the new term "realism," perceptively remarked, in *Le Réalisme* (1857), that "the power of the word 'classique' prevented in spite of the efforts of some people (Stendhal among others) the adoption of the designation 'classicisme.' "[51] In Italy, Niccolò Tommaseo, the great lexicographer, apparently felt the same. In his *Dictionary of the Italian Language* (1858ff.), "classicismo" is defined as "the party of those who say they honor the classics by imitating their forms and using them as a whip against their enemies," and he adds with heavy irony: "Parola elegante come la cosa."[52] Other nations apparently did not so strongly feel the aesthetic objections to the word: Goethe uses the term reporting on "Klassiker und Romantiker in Italien" (1820),[53] and Pushkin in 1830 praises a poet, F. N. Glinka, for "not professing either ancient or French classicism and not following either Gothic or modern Romanticism."[54]

---

[49] *Racine et Shakespeare* (Paris, 1905), pp. 32–33: "Le *romanticisme* est l'art de présenter aux peuples les oeuvres littéraires qui, dans l'état actuel de leurs habitudes et de leurs croyances, sont susceptibles de leur donner le plus de plaisir possible. Le *classicisme*, au contraire, leur présente la littérature qui donnait le plus grand plaisir possible à leurs arrière-grands-pères."

[50] Christian A. E. Jensen, *L'Evolution du romantisme. L'Année 1826* (Geneva, 1959), pp. 50, 120.

[51] Champfleury, *Le Réalisme* (Paris, 1857), Preface. "Ce qui fait la force du mot classique c'est que malgré les efforts de quelques-uns (Stendhal entre autres), la désignation de classicisme n'a pu être adopté."

[52] *Dizionario della lingua italiana* (New ed.; Torino, 1915), II, 1465: "Partito di coloro che dicono d'onorare i Classici imitandone le forme, e servendosi di quelli come de scudiscio contro i loro avversarii."

[53] *Sämtliche Werke*, Jubiläumsausgabe, XXXVII, 118. Note that the text (uncorrected in the critical edition) speaks of "Romantizismus und Kritizismus" as "zwei unversöhnliche Sekten."

[54] Review of *Kareliya*, in *Pushkin o literature*, ed. N. V. Bogoslovsky (Moscow, 1934:) "On ne ispoveduet ni drevnego, ni frantsuzkogo klassitsizma, on ne sleduet ni goticheskomu, ni noveishemu romantizmu."

At the end of Chapter VII of *Evgeny Onegin* (1828), Pushkin paid ironic "homage to classicism" by addressing belatedly the Epic Muse and announcing his theme: "I sing of a young friend."[55] In Spain the word seems to occur quite late: the date 1884 is given in Corominas' *Diccinario.*[56]

In France an important development took place, whatever term was used: the exaltation of the French seventeenth century as the classical age in sharp contrast to the eighteenth century, which to us may seem stylistically and in critical theory a direct continuation of the seventeenth. But in the early nineteenth century the two periods were contrasted for reasons which are easy to understand: the seventeenth century appealed to the conservative, political, and religious reaction, while the eighteenth century bore the onus of preparing and even causing the French Revolution. The men who were responsible for the definition of this ideology do not, I think, use the term "classicism" or use it very rarely. Désiré Nisard's *Histoire de la littérature française* (4 vols., 1844–61) is dominated by a conception of the French spirit which reaches its perfection in the seventeenth century, while everything since appears as decadence. Nisard had actually been the first who accused the Romantics of decadence. His *Etudes des moeurs et de critique sur les poètes latins de la décadence* (2 vols., 1834) was a harshly critical discussion of the writers of Silver Latinity that led up to an explicit indictment of the French literature of Nisard's own age. Modern French poetry, he argues, shows all the symptoms of the decadence of late Antiquity, while the age of Louis XIV parallels that of the great Augustus. With the triumphs of Rachel on the stage in the seventeenth-century tragedies, the dismal failure of Hugo's *Les Burgraves,* and the great success of Ponsard's "classical" tragedy *Lucrèce* in 1843, something like a comeback of classicism seemed to be accomplished. Ponsard rather coyly pretended hardly to remember that one used to distinguish between "classics and romantics, or people who were called something like that."[57] Ponsard later (1847) asserted that "innovation or reaction, romanticism or classicism are only words which fit formulas" and concluded that "in art there is nothing but good or bad,"[58] a sentiment which would have found the approval of Croce.

[55] *Onegin,* VII, stanza 55, l. 13: "Ja klassitsizmu otdal chest."
[56] *Diccionario crítico etimológico de la lengua castellana* (Madrid, 1954), I, 817.
[57] *Revue de Vienne,* III (1840), 490. Quoted in Camille Latreille, *La Fin du théâtre romantique et François Ponsard* (Paris, 1899), p. 302n: "Des classiques et des romantiques, ou des gens qu'on appelait à peu près ainsi."
[58] "A propos d'Agnès de Méranie," *Oeuvres complètes* (Paris, 1876), p. 356: "L'innovation ou la réaction, le romanticisme ou le classicisme, sont des mots qui s'appliquent à des formules. L'art ne connaît que le bon et le mauvais."

But nothing came of the new "classical" revival: the new enthusiasts for classical antiquity spoke rather of the "pagan school" or called their style "néo-grecque." It was definitely a new Hellenism which saw itself as very different from the tradition of French classicism. Sainte-Beuve's famous essay "Qu'est-ce qu'un classique?" (1850) must be seen in this context. While insisting on the Greco-Latin tradition, Sainte-Beuve aims at enlarging the concept. He recognizes the existence of something transcending the tradition: Homer, Dante, and Shakespeare are classics, though they do not conform to the demands of what we would call French classicism. This kind of classicism, with its rules, he knows, is definitely a thing of the past. Still, he pleads, we must preserve the notion and the cult of the classics and at the same time widen it and make it more generous.[59]

Sainte-Beuve and Taine do not use the word "classicism." Sainte-Beuve, however, restated the sense of the classical tradition, while Taine dealt it a severe blow when, in *Origines de la France contemporaine* (1874), he associated the abstract utopianism of the Jacobins with the rationalism of the Cartesian tradition and made the Revolution appear to be the logical outcome of the classical spirit.[60] Later in the century, the new champion of French classicism, Ferdinand Brunetière, hardly ever used the term. Only in a review of a book by Emile Deschanel, *Le Romantisme des classiques* (1882), does Brunetière use the term several times, infected as he is by Deschanel's frequent use;[61] while Jules Lemaître, reviewing the same book, got along without it.[62] I cannot, of course, exclude the possibility that the term might be found elsewhere, but I have the impression that it became fully established only about 1890. In 1889 Georges Pellisier's *Le Mouvement littéraire aux XIXᵉ siècle* contains an introductory chapter entitled "Le Classicisme," Eugène François Lintilhac published an important article in 1890, "J. D. Scaliger, fondateur du classicisme,"[63] and in 1897 Louis Bertrand put the term on the title page of his book *La Fin du classicisme et le retour à l'antique*, a careful study of the late eighteenth-century classical revival. But Gustave Lanson, in his standard *Histoire de la littérature française* (1894), still avoids the term in the text,

---

[59] *Causeries du Lundi* (Paris, 1945), III, 38–55.

[60] Ch. II of Livre troisième, in Vol. I: *Ancien régime* (Paris, 1947), pp. 288ff.

[61] "Classiques et romantiques," *Etudes critiques sur l'histoire de la littérature française* (2nd ed.; Paris, 1890), III, 293, 299, 315, 319, 320, 321, 325.

[62] "Le Romantisme des classiques," *Les Contemporains* (8ème série, Paris, 1918), pp. 159–75.

[63] In *La Nouvelle revue*, LXIV (1890), 333–46, 528–47.

though the title of a chapter calls Guez de Balzac, Chapelain, and Descartes "Trois ouvriers du classicisme," and a caption speaks of "a union of Cartesianism and art in classicism."[64]

Louis Bertrand later belonged to a group of conservatives who, after the turn of the century, launched the anti-romantic campaign which accused romanticism, contrary to Taine, of all the evils of the French Revolution and the anarchy of our own time. Charles Maurras, the founder of the *Action française*, Pierre Lasserre, who praised Maurras in a pamphlet *Charles Maurras et la Renaissance classique* (1902) and then wrote the spirited *Le Romantisme français* (1907), and the Baron Ernest Seillière, who wrote a good dozen books on the romantic disease, made "classicism" a new slogan which was also a political and philosophical war cry. The implication in the Dreyfus affair and in the anti-German campaign before 1914 is obvious: Germans and Nordics in general were equated with romanticism, classicism with Latinity and France. The fierce and exclusive nationalism of this interpretation of the classical spirit would, one might have thought, limited its appeal to France. Still, Irving Babbitt's *Rousseau and Romanticism* (1919) draws its basic ideas and attitudes from this French group, even though Babbitt, as a good American and republican, finally shrank from its political consequences.[65] But T. S. Eliot, during his stay in Paris (1910–11), absorbed these ideas and recognized even later that Maurras' *L'Avenir de l'intelligence* (1905) had exerted a great influence on his intellectual development.[66] In England, T. E. Hulme drew heavily on these new French classicists. "Romanticism and Classicism" (published in 1924, but written in 1913) provided the most quoted statement of the new classicism. I cannot help thinking that this is unfortunate: Hulme's essay is confused and contradictory and makes classicism amount to a belief in original sin, in the stability of human nature, the impossibility of progress, and the possibility of a new dry, visual verse.[67] French seventeenth-century classicism was universal in its appeal, at least in ambition. The new classicism is an arid creed and has, with Maurras, Hulme, and Ezra Pound, definite fascist overtones. It is no wonder that it has not caught on in spite of T. S.

[64] (Paris, 1894), 1912 edition quoted, p. 391: "union du cartésianisme et de l'art dans le classicisme."

[65] Cf. "Racine and the Anti-Romantics" (originally in *The Nation*, November 18, 1909), reprinted in *The Spanish Character and Other Essays* (Boston, 1940), p. 90, and Marcus Selden Goldman, in F. Manchester and O. Shepard (eds.), *Irving Babbitt: Man and Teacher* (New York, 1941), p. 235, reporting on Babbitt's views in 1923.

[66] See *Nouvelle revue française*, IX (November, 1923), 619–25.

[67] In *Speculations*, ed. Herbert Read (London, 1924), pp. 113–40.

Eliot's defense of a much more generous and inclusive tradition. His *What Is a Classic?* (1944) restates even in detail, Sainte-Beuve's conception, though Eliot assures us that he had not read Sainte-Beuve's essay for some thirty-odd years. "The blood-stream of European literature," Eliot formulates, "is Latin and Greek—not as two systems of circulation, but one, for it is through Rome that our parentage to Greece must be traced."[68]

A rejection of this view is precisely the distinguishing feature of German classicism, or rather what Germans call their "Klassik." "Klassik" is the pervasive term in German books on literature. Nobody seems to be aware of the fact that it is a new term, and nobody has traced its history. In such a solid scholarly enterprise as *Grundriss der germanischen Philologie*, in the volume *Deutsche Wortgeschichte* (1942), we are given the false information that "Romantik" is a parallel and analogous formation to the word "Klassik."[69] Actually "Romantik" was used by Novalis in 1800, But I cannot find "Klassik" before the year 1887. There is, however, one quite isolated instance. Friedrich Schlegel, in notes published only in 1963, but dated 1797, jotted down these somewhat mystifying statements: "Absolute Classik also annihilirt sich selbst"; and "Alle Bildung ist Classik, Abstraction."[70] This is at least the provisional result of my search. Otto Harnack uses it in his *Goethe in der Epoche seiner Vollendung* (1887), first in quotation marks and then in the phrase about Euphorion as "der geniale Spross der vermählten Klassik und Romantik."[71] Harnack seems to have felt that the word is an innovation, as in a later book, *Der deutsche Klassizismus im Zeitalter Goethes* (1906), he explains in his preface: "I could not this time avoid the unpleasant expressions 'classicism' and 'classicist,' for which I usually substitute 'Klassik' and 'klassisch,' because usage has given the word 'klassisch' a special narrow meaning in relation to German poetry."[72] Harnack draws a distinction between "Klassizismus," the imitation of antiquity, and "Klassik," a term designating the works of the great German classics, Goethe and Schiller.

---

[68] (London, 1945), pp. 8, 31.

[69] Friedrich Kainz, "Klassik und Romantik," in F. Maurer and F. Stroh, *Deutsche Wortgeschichte* (2nd ed.; Berlin, 1959), II, 322.

[70] *Philosophische Lehrjahre*, Vol. 1, ed. Ernst Behler (Munich, 1963) [Vol. 18 of *Sämtliche Werke*], p. 23.

[71] (Leipzig, 1887), pp. 133, 152.

[72] (Berlin, 1906), Introduction: "Die unschönen Ausdrücke 'Klassizismus' und 'klassizistisch', für die ich sonst 'Klassik' und 'klassisch' zu setzen pflege, habe ich diesmal nicht vermeiden können, weil der Sprachgebrauch dem Worte "klassisch" in Bezug auf die deutsche Poesie eine besonders enge Bedeutung gegeben hat."

The term "Klassik" caught on, at first, only slowly. Eugen Wolff and Heinrich Hart use it in manifestoes of naturalism, or what they call "Die Moderne," in 1888 and 1890.[73] Carl Weitbrecht, in his book *Diesseits von Weimar. Auch ein Buch über Goethe* (1895), recommends that "klassisch" and "klassizistisch" should be sharply distinguished, as he argues that "Klassizismus" "derailed" Goethe's genius from its proper path.[74] Otto Harnack used the new term in the title of his *Deutsches Kunstleben im Zeitalter der Klassik* (Weimar, 1896). So Teutonizing a literary historian as Adolf Bartels adopted it in 1906 for a chapter of his *Handbuch zur Geschichte der deutschen Literatur.*[75] Also at the other end of the German cultural spectrum, with Friedrich Gundolf, the disciple of Stefan George, the new term replaces the older "classicism." In *Shakespeare und der deutsche Geist* (1911), the final chapter is called "Klassik und Romantik."[76] In his *Goethe* (1916), we are given a definition of the difference. "Klassizismus ist bewusste und gewollte, nicht naive Klassik";[77] and in 1922, Fritz Strich put the term on the title page of his *Deutsche Klassik und Romantik: oder Vollendung und Unendlichkeit* (Munich, 1922), the most influential German typology, which applies Wölfflin's principles of art history to literature. Since then the term is ubiquitous. There is a thesis by Alexander Heussler, a pupil of Fritz Strich, *Klassik und Klassizismus in der deutschen Literatur* (1952),[78] which elaborates the distinction between the two terms without any awareness of its novelty. "Classicism" for Heussler is Gottsched and Johann Elias Schlegel, while "Klassik" is Goethe and Schiller. The triumph of the new term was, however, not general at first. Oskar Walzel, in 1922, consistently speaks of "Klassizismus" when referring to Goethe.[79] Paul Merker, in a report on literary scholarship in the same year, does not know the new term,[80] and Franz Schultz, in a paper dating from 1928, expressly disavows the use of the neologism. "Recently," he says, "one has got accustomed to separating—

[73] Eugen Wolff, "Die jüngste Litteraturströmung und das Prinzip der Moderne," *Literarische Volkshefte* (1888), p. 44, reprinted in Erich Ruprecht (ed.), *Literarische Manifeste des Naturalismus* (Stuttgart, 1962), p. 138.—Heinrich Hart, "Der Kampf um die Form in der zeitgenössischen Dichtung," *Kritisches Jahrbuch*, I (1890), 76; reprinted in Ruprecht, *Literarische Manifeste*, p. 191.

[74] (Stuttgart, 1895), p. 35: "Aus dem Geleise gebracht." Cf. pp. 33–34.

[75] Leipzig, 1906. He uses also "Nachklassik".

[76] (Berlin, 1911), pp. 310, 321.

[77] (Berlin, 1916), p. 428.

[78] Bern, 1952.

[79] "Zwei Möglichkeiten deutscher Form," *Vom Geistesleben alter und neuer Zeit* (1922). Cf. pp. 117, 119, 122–23, 130, 141.

[80] *Neuere deutsche Literaturgeschichte* (Stuttgart, 1922), pp. 74ff.

apparently under the influence of Fritz Strich— 'Klassizismus' and 'Klassik.' 'Klassizismus' is seen as the older strivings for an imitation of antiquity, 'Klassik' as the opposite of 'Romantik' at the turn of the 18th and 19th centuries, i.e., the thought, theory and poetical practice of Goethe and Schiller. I should like to keep to the older concept and call 'Klassizismus' the movement" which began with Winckelmann and ended with Hegel.[81] But Schultz himself succumbed to the new fashion: he later wrote two volumes entitled *Klassik und Romantik der Deutschen* (1935, 1940).[82]

We can account for the success of the new term. "Classicism," in a sense resembling that of French classicism or the classicism in the plastic arts at the end of the eighteenth century, is not a very appropriate term for most of the writings of Goethe and Schiller if one excepts the stages in their careers when they consciously aimed at the imitation of the ancients, i.e., when Schiller wrote "Die Götter Griechenlands" (1788) and speculated on "Classizität" in a letter to Koerner about a planned epic on Frederick the Great,[83] and when Goethe wrote *Iphigenie auf Tauris*, went to Italy, and then produced *Römische Elegien*, the fragment *Achilleis*, the idyll, *Hermann und Dorothea*, and in the plastic arts advocated a rigid classicism of themes and forms. But classicism is clearly a term which does not fit *Goetz von Berlichingen* and *Werther*, or *West-östlicher Divan* and *Faust* and even less *Die Räuber*, *Wallensteins Lager* and *Die Jungfrau von Orleans*, subtitled by Schiller himself "eine romantische Tragödie." The term "Klassik" resumes the old meaning of standard or model, while the stylistic association with the ancients almost ceases to be felt. It has become a term such as "Goethezeit" or "deutsche Bewegung,"[84] which pries the German classics loose from international classi-

---

[81] "Der Mythus des deutschen Klassizismus," *Zeitschrift für deutsche Bildung*, IV (1928), 3: "Man hat sich neuerdings daran gewöhnt—wohl unter dem Einfluss von Fritz Strich—Klassizismus und Klassik zu sondern, unter Klassizismus die älteren Bestrebungen zur Nachahmung der Alten und unter 'Klassik' das Gegenstück zur 'Romantik' um die Wende des 18. und 19. Jahrhunderts zu erblicken, d.h. die Gedankenwelt, Kunstanschauung und Kunstübung der beiden Weimaraner Goethe und Schiller und ihre Nachwirkungen. Ich möchte bei der älteren Begriffsbildung bleiben und unter dem deutschen Klassizismus jene Bewegung verstehen, die von Winckelmann . . . bis Hegel führte."

[82] Stuttgart, 1935, 1940.

[83] Letter to Koerner, March 10, 1789, in *Briefe*, ed. F. Jonas (Stuttgart, 1893), II, 252. Cf. an earlier letter using "Classizität," to Friedrich Schröder, December 18, 1786, *ibid.*, I, 320.

[84] H. Korff's *Geist der Goethezeit*. "Deutsche Bewegung" is a term invented by Herman Nohl.

cism and yet resists the Western tendency to call Goethe and Schiller romantics.

In German literature we have, as in French literature, a little-explored process: the establishment of the great eighteenth-century writers as "Klassiker" and the Weimar period as the "classical" age. Germans still recognize six "Klassiker": Klopstock, Lessing, Wieland, Herder, Goethe, and Schiller,[85] an extremely heterogeneous group of which Klopstock today would appear to belong to what might be called preromanticism or sentimentalism; Lessing, in spite of his polemics against the doctrines of French tragedy, would appear as a rationalistic classicist who worshipped Aristotle; Wieland would appear as a man of the Enlightenment whose art strikes us often as rococo; Herder would seem an irrationalistic preromantic. How can a writer be called "klassisch" who, as Herder did in 1767, exclaimed "O the cursed word 'Classisch!'"[86] and who attacked Goethe's and Schiller's turn toward classicism as a betrayal of his teachings?

But Goethe and Schiller did not call themselves "Klassiker" and had an ambiguous and complex attitude toward the whole enterprise of establishing a classical literature. Goethe, in 1795, in a remarkable article, "Literarischer Sansculottismus," argues that no German author considers himself "klassisch" and that he would not desire "the revolutions which could prepare classical works in Germany."[87] The paper was written when the French Revolution had not yet run its course: Goethe feared the dangers of centralization and the abolition of the little German states, with one of which he was so closely identified, since "classical" meant to him writing which would express the unity of a nation. Only after the Schlegels had excited the great debate did Goethe use the term more freely, either denying the distinction and clinging to the older meaning of excellence or taking sides against the Romantics. A letter in 1804 reports that Goethe rejected the difference between the romantic and the classic because "everything excellent is *eo ipso* classic."[88] But

---

[85] See, e.g., Wilhelm Münch, "Über den Begriff des Klassikers," *Zum deutschen Kultur- und Bildungsleben* (Berlin, 1912), p. 248.

[86] *Sämtliche Werke.* ed. B. Suphan (Berlin, 1877ff.), I, 412: "O, das verwünschte Wort, Classisch!"

[87] *Sämtliche Werke*, Jubiläumsausgabe, XXXVI, 139–44; p. 141: "Wir wollen die Umwälzungen nicht wünschen, die in Deutschland klassische Werke vorbereiten könnten."

[88] A letter by Heinrich Voss, Jr., to L. R. Abeken, January 26, 1804, reporting Goethe as saying, "Alles was vortrefflich sei, sei *eo ipso* klassisch." In *Goethes Gespräche. Auswahl*, ed. F. von Biedermann (Wiesbaden, 1949), p. 163.

later in 1829 Goethe made his famous pronouncement: "I call the Classic the healthy, the Romantic the sickly."[89] One should, however, remember the historical context: Goethe was disturbed by the excesses of such German writers as Zacharias Werner and E. T. A. Hoffmann, and he disliked the new French *roman frénétique*. Later he called Hugo's *Notre Dame de Paris* the "most disgusting book ever written."[90] He had lost sight of the original, much wider meaning of the contrast, though in a conversation with Eckermann in 1830 Goethe claimed wrongly that the Schlegels merely renamed Schiller's distinction between the naive and the sentimental.[91] Goethe himself always professed to stand above the battle: in *Helena* and specifically in the figure of Euphorion Goethe aimed at a "reconciliation of the two poetic forms."[92]

While Goethe viewed the debate rather detachedly, he was, during his lifetime, fast becoming the German "Klassiker" or at least one of the two great "Klassiker." It is still not common knowledge that Goethe, after the international success of *Werther*, fell into comparative oblivion and that only the success of *Hermann und Dorothea* (1797) and the effect of the *Xenien*, written in collaboration with Schiller, gave him a commanding position in German literature. But even in the late eighteenth century, Goethe had many enemies: orthodox Christians who suspected him of atheism and paganism, utilitarian enthusiasts for the Enlightenment who thought him too aesthetic, and radical irrationalists who thought him too cold, commonsensical, and classicistic.[93] Goethe's towering reputation was secured first by the Schlegels, who played him up against Schiller yet did not consider either Schiller or Goethe classics. Friedrich Schlegel hoped as early as 1800 that Goethe would accomplish the task of "harmonizing the classical and romantic."[94] In August Wilhelm Schlegel's *Dramatic Lectures* (1809–11) Goethe is discussed along with the romantic drama written in the wake of Shakespeare.

We know only in very general terms how Goethe and Schiller became the German "Klassiker." Certainly claims for Goethe's transcendent

[89] To Eckermann, April 2, 1829: "Das Classische nenne ich das Gesunde, und das Romantische das Kranke," J. P. Eckermann, *Gespräche mit Goethe*, ed. Houben (Leipzig, 1948), pp. 263–64.

[90] *Ibid.*, p. 604, June 27, 1831: "Das abscheulichste Buch das je geschrieben worden." Cf. letter to Zelter, June 28, 1831.

[91] *Ibid.*, March 21, 1830, pp. 322–23.

[92] *Ibid.*, December 16, 1829, p. 299: "wo beide Dichtungsformen, . . . eine Art von Ausgleichung finden."

[93] Cf. Albert Bettex, *Der Kampf um das klassische Weimar 1788–98* (Zurich, 1935).

[94] "Gespräch über die Poesie" (1800), in *Kritische Schriften*, ed. Wolfdietrich Rasch (Munich, 1956), p. 334: "Die Harmonie des Klassischen und Romantischen."

greatness were made very early: e.g., Friedrich Schlegel, in 1798,[95] called Goethe, Dante, and Shakespeare "the great trichord" of modern poetry and classed *Wilhelm Meister* with Fichte's philosophy and the French Revolution as the great epoch-making events of the age,[96] and in Ludwig Tieck's *Zerbino* (1799), Goethe, Shakespeare, Cervantes, and Dante appear as "the sacred four" in the Garden of Poetry.[97] In a book by K. A. Schaller, in 1812, I found Goethe called "admittedly the first poet of Germany and at this time certainly without any serious rival among the other nations of Europe."[98] We all know Byron's dedication of *Sardana-palus* as that of a "literary vassal to his liege-Lord," though Byron—who knew no German—could hardly have had an adequate conception of Goethe's eminence,[99] and we know of the constant stream of admiring visitors in Goethe's later years. They did not come only from Germany, but included Madame de Staël, Benjamin Constant, Jean-Jacques Ampère, Thackeray, Mickiewicz, Oehlenschläger, Kollár, and many others.[100]

Goethe seems to have penetrated very early into German schools.[101] But adoption as reading in schools is only a symptom of the success with the wider public, with audiences in the theater and, most decisively, with the authorities who guided the educational systems of Prussia and the other German states. The role of Wilhelm von Humboldt and the other founders of the German *Gymnasium* must have been most important precisely because of the alliance between the ideal of Greek culture, *paideia*, and Goethe's and Schiller's pedagogical or pedagogically exploited classicism. The twentieth-century tendency to divorce Goethe and Schiller from classicism is a symptom of the decay of the classical *Gymnasium* and the whole ideal of liberal culture as it was, partly with Goethe in mind, formulated also in England by Matthew Arnold. I can only allude to the role of Bettina von Arnim's *Goethes Briefwechsel mit einem Kinde* (1835) and Eckermann's *Gespräche mit Goethe* (1835) in shaping

---

[95] Athenäums-fragment No. 247, in *Kritische Schriften*, p. 52: "der grosse Dreiklang der modernen Poesie."

[96] Athenäums-fragment No. 216, in *Kritische Schriften*, p. 46.

[97] In *Romantische Dichtungen* (Jena, 1799): "die heilige Vier."

[98] *Handbuch der klassischen Literatur der Deutschen* (Halle, 1812), p. 21: "Anerkannt der erste Dichter Deutschlands und gewiss gegenwärtig auch ohne gültigen Mitbewerber unter den übrigen europäischen Nationen."

[99] Quoted in Fritz Strich, *Goethe und die Weltliteratur* (Bern, 1946), p. 301.

[100] See *ibid.*, Eckermann, etc.

[101] A chapter, "Goethe im Deutschunterricht," in Wolfgang Leppmann, *Goethe und die Deutschen* (Stuttgart, 1962). This chapter is an addition of the German version of Leppmann's *The German Image of Goethe* (Oxford, 1961).

Goethe's image as an Olympian in spite of the political and liberal attacks of the Young Germans or Heine's attempt to relegate Goethe to a past "Kunstperiode." Soon after Goethe's death his position as the German *Klassiker* was secure, though apparently in the forties and fifties there was a temporary decline of his position, at least in relation to Schiller.

Still, in literary histories Goethe and Schiller were not considered "Klassiker" or as representing "classicism" for a long time. For example, in Franz Horn's *Geschichte und Kritik der deutschen Poesie und Beredsamkeit* (1805), the handbook used by Carlyle, we hear only of a "Klopstock-Lessing-Goethe period."[102] The whole early nineteenth-century in Germany, dominated as it was by romantic theory and taste, would not have considered the term "classicism" as flattering. Friedrich Schlegel, in 1800, pronounced most contemptuously on "the so-called classical poets of the English: Pope, Dryden and whoever else."[103] August Wilhelm Schlegel's Berlin and Vienna lecture courses treated all forms of classicism, French, English and German, with polemical harshness. The most influential literary histories avoided the terms "classicism" and "classical." Thus Gervinus, in his *Geschichte der poetischen Nationalliteratur der Deutschen* (5 vols., 1835–42), never, I think, refers to Goethe and Schiller as "klassisch" or "Klassiker," though once he describes Schiller's review, *Die Horen*, as having stabilized style and taste so that the "classical period" of the language could begin. But Gervinus also freely refers to the new edition of *Faust* (1808) as putting Goethe "in the vanguard of romantic trends."[104] A. F. C. Vilmar, who wrote an extremely popular *Geschichte der deutschen Nationalliteratur* (1857), calls Goethe the "greatest genius of our modern times" and refers to his period as the "second period of the flowering of German literature,"[105] but never uses the word "classical" or "classicism." In a now forgotten valuable book which is expressly concerned with the classical tradition, Carl Leo Cholevius' *Geschichte der deutschen Poesie nach antiken Elementen* (2 vols., 1856), Goethe and Schiller are described as "accomplishing a unification of the Romantic and the Antique," though Cholevius speaks also of the *Roman Elegies* as having

[102] (Berlin, 1805), p. 190.

[103] "Gespräch über die Poesie" (1800), in *Kritische Schriften*, p. 288: "die sogenannten klassischen Dichter der Engländer . . . den Pope, den Dryden oder wer sonst noch Klassiker sei."

[104] *Geschichte der deutschen Dichtung* (5th ed.; Leipzig, 1871–74), V, 492: "ihre klassische Periode." P. 789: "auf die Spitze der romantischen Richtungen."

[105] (Marburg, 1857), II, 168: "dieser grösste Genius unserer Neuzeit." P. 226: "Unsere zweite Blüteperiode."

been written during Goethe's "classical period."[106] As far as I could ascertain, the term "Klassizismus" first becomes common in Hermann Hettner's *Literaturgeschichte des achtzehnten Jahrhunderts* (6 vols., 1856–70). Hettner, however, reserves "Klassizismus" for the French, who were supposedly "overthrown" by Goethe and Schiller. In the last volumes of his great history, Hettner refers to the "classical age of German literature"—but that was in 1870.[107] Before that Rudolf von Gottschall's popular *Die deutsche Nationalliteratur des 19. Jahrhunderts* (1854) had referred to Goethe and Schiller consistently as "die Klassiker,"[108] and no doubt this had become the accepted convention, which was immensely strengthened when, in 1867, the privileges protecting the reprinting of the works of Goethe and Schiller were abolished and "Klassikerausgaben" began to proliferate.[109] The German middle classes acquired sets of the great and not so great writers, and with the founding of the Empire the works of Goethe and Schiller more and more assumed the role of a national palladium: a cultural heritage surrounded by almost superstitious awe. The founding of the *Goethe-Gesellschaft* (1885),[110] the long-drawn-out publication of the Weimar edition of Goethe's complete works, and the simultaneous emergence of a whole new profession, *Goethe-Philologie*, are symptoms of this victory. But as to terminology we still observe the same vacillations as in France and England. A. Kuhn, in *Schillers Geistesgang* (1863), speaks, e.g., of "the time of 'Classizität' in our literature,"[111] a term preferred also by the Danish critic Georg Brandes in his *Hauptströmungen der Literatur des neunzehnten Jahrhunderts*.[112] Others stuck to "classicism": e.g., Julian Schmidt speaks of the break of the Schlegels with "Classizismus,"[113] but in Wilhelm Scherer's standard *Geschichte der deutschen Literatur* (1883), the term "classicism" occurs only in the Table of Contents, while the text speaks of "classische Mode." Only once, I

[106] Leipzig, 1856: "Schiller und Goethe vollenden die Ineinsbildung des Romantischen und des Antiken" (Inhaltsangabe to p. 118). "Classische Periode" (p. 297).

[107] *Literaturgeschichte des achtzehnten Jahrhunderts* (6 vols.; Braunschweig, 1856–70). E.g., Vol. II (1859), "Lessing, Goethe und Schiller haben den französischen Klassizismus gestürzt." V (1870), 25: "Das klassische Zeitalter der deutschen Literatur."

[108] Sixth ed., Breslau, 1891, reprints "Vorrede" to 1st ed., 1854, p. viii.

[109] See Peter Frank, "Chancen und Gefahren von Klassikerausgaben," *Merkur*, XVII (1963), 1201.

[110] A detailed sociological and statistical study in Leppmann, *Goethe und die Deutschen.*

[111] (Berlin, 1863), p. 354: "In der Zeit der Classizität unserer Literatur."

[112] See G. Brandes, *Die Emigrantenliteratur* (Berlin, 1914), p. 223, or *Die Reaktion in Frankreich* (Charlottenburg, 1900), p. 248. These lectures appeared in 1872 and 1874.

[113] *Geschichte der deutschen Literatur* (Berlin, 1890), Vol. IV: "Der Bruch der Schlegel mit dem Classizismus, 1797."

think, does Scherer refer to "our modern classical period."[114] One can see how the dissatisfaction with the term "classicism" came about and why the new term "Klassik" replaced it. In the atmosphere of the last eighty years, the German "Klassiker" were more and more Teutonized and romanticized as national assets, while the term "classics" clung to them in an almost Pickwickian sense.

In retrospect, it is obvious that the term "classicism" belongs to the nineteenth-century. It occurs first in Italy in 1818, in Germany in 1820, in France in 1822, in Russia in 1830, and in England in 1831. In Germany about 1887 the term "Klassik," invented by Friedrich Schlegel in 1797, displaced "Klassizismus." Clearly the terms have something in common: the implied reference to excellence, to authority, and to the relation to Antiquity. But obviously in the three countries discussed "classicism" refers to three distinct bodies of literature:—the French seventeenth-century, the English late seventeenth and early eighteenth-centuries, and the German very late eighteenth-century—which differ widely in substance and form, claim to authority and greatness, and even in their relation to Antiquity. To characterize these differences would mean writing the literary history of three countries in two centuries. I remark only briefly that French and German classicism have preserved an authority which is absent from English classicism in spite of the attempts to reinstate it in its position and the increased and, I believe, deserved scholarly interest in the great writers of the period: Pope and Swift in particular. T. S. Eliot seems right in saying that "we have no classic age, and no classic poet, in English," though he reminds us that "unless we are able to enjoy the work of Pope, we cannot arrive at a full understanding of English poetry."[115] I can only hint that French and English classicism are far more Latin than German classicism, which is more definitely and self-consciously Greek. In a history of European styles of literature based on an analogy with art history, French seventeenth-century classicism will appear as clearly baroque; a muted, subdued baroque as Leo Spitzer has shown in a fine essay;[116] while English classicism seems most enlightened, commonsensical, even realistic, though on occasion it has affinities with what could be called rococo. This seems at least true of Pope's *Rape of the Lock.*[117] German classicism, even in its

[114] (Berlin, 1883), p. 615; p. 576: "Der Geist unserer modernen classischen Litteraturperiode."

[115] T. S. Eliot, *What Is a Classic?* (London, 1945), p. 17.

[116] "Die klassische Dämpfung in Racines Stil," *Romanische Stil- und Literaturstudien* (Marburg, 1931), Vol. 1, pp. 135–268.

[117] Cf. Friedrich Brie, *Englische Rokoko-epik* (Munich, 1927).

most self-consciously neoclassical stage, will appear to us as romantic or possibly nostalgic and utopian, as was also the contemporary classicism elsewhere. The elegiac note is prominent in Chénier and the painters and sculptors of the return to antiquity, David, Canova, and Thorvaldsen, who have a sentimental streak. The dream of the golden age is never far away.[118] The Empire style of Napoleon is classicistic; but Napoleon carried *Werther* and Ossian about with him.

The ramifications of my subject are endless. I have barely touched the surface, and, I am sure, can be corrected on dates and details. But I am not thinking of my topic as only a contribution to lexicography or the history of terminology. I have the model of the late Leo Spitzer in mind. Spitzer is probably best remembered as a student of stylistics and etymology, but he was also a master of what he called "historical semantics." His papers on *Classical and Christian Ideas of World Harmony* and on *"Milieu and Ambiance"*[119] show how he could focus on the learned keywords of our civilization and write word history within a general history of thought, that is, combine lexicography with the history of ideas. This is also the ambition of this sketch, which I should like to see as paralleling and suplementing my older papers on the concepts of baroque, romanticism, and realism.[120] I am ultimately working toward a history of literary periodization, a key concept of my old project: a history of literary history and literary scholarship within a history of modern criticism.

Bibliographical Note

The history of the term "classicism" has hardly been investigated. Some remarks are to be found in Pierre Moreau, *Le Classicisme des romantiques* (Paris, 1932); Henri Peyre, *Le Classicisme français* (New York, 1942), Ch. II, "Le Mot Classicisme," deals with "classique" and has nothing to say about "classicisme" as a word; Ernst Robert Curtius, *Europäische Literatur und lateinisches Mittelalter* (Bern, 1948), esp. pp. 251ff.; Harry Levin, "Contexts of the Classical," in his *Contexts of Criticism* (Cambridge, Mass., 1957), pp. 38–54; George Luck, "Scriptor Classicus," in *Comparative Literature*, X (1958), 150–58.

[118] Cf. Rudolf Zeitler, *Klassizismus und Utopia* (Uppsala, 1954).

[119] *Classical and Christian Ideas of World Harmony*, ed. Anna G. Hatcher. Foreword by René Wellek (Baltimore, 1963). *"Milieu and Ambiance," Essays in Historical Semantics* (New York, 1948), pp. 179–316.

[120] Now collected in my *Concepts of Criticism* (New Haven, 1963).

Most other discussions of classicism are analytical, ideological, or historical. Here is a small selection: P. Van Tieghem, "Classique," in *Revue de synthèse historique* XLI (1931), 238–41, purely analytical; Gerhart Rosenwaldt, "Zur Bedeutung des Klassischen in der bildenden Kunst," in *Zeitschrift für Aesthetik*, XI (1916), 125, contains a striking definition: "Klassisch ist ein Kunstwerk das vollkommen stilisiert ist, ohne von der Natur abzuweichen, so dass dem Bedürfniss nach Stilisierung und Nachahmung in gleicher Weise Genüge getan ist." Helmut Kuhn, " 'Klassisch' als historischer Begriff," in Werner Jaeger (ed.), *Das Problem des Klassischen und die Antike* (Stuttgart, 1933, reprinted 1961), pp. 109–28; *Concinnitas: Beiträge zum Problem des Klassischen. Heinrich Wölfflin zum achtzigsten Geburtstag . . . zugeeignet* (Basel, 1944); Kurt Herbert Halbach, "Zum Begriff und Wesen der Klassik," in *Festschrift Paul Kluckhohn und Hermann Schneider gewidmet . . .* (Tübingen, 1948), pp. 166–94.

Fritz Ernst, *Der Klassizismus in Italien, Frankreich und Deutschland* (Zürich, 1924) is a thin sketch. Sherard Vines, *The Course of English Classicism from the Tudor to the Victorian Age* (London, 1930) is lively but confused. Two books on Goethe's fame are relevant: Reinhard Buchwald, *Goethezeit und Gegenwart* (Stuttgart, 1949) and Wolfgang Leppmann, *The German Image of Goethe* (Oxford, 1961), the German version of which is *Goethe und die Deutschen* (Stuttgart, 1962).

Two encyclopedia articles merit attention: Antonio Viscardi, "Classicismo," in *Dizionario letterario Bompiani delle opere . . .* (Milan, 1947), I, 22–43, and Henri Peyre, "Le Classicisme," in *Encyclopédie de la Pléiade. Histoire des littératures* (Paris, 1956), II, 110–39.

Diderot and Historical Painting

BY JEAN SEZNEC

◀◀◀◀◀◀◀◀◀◀◀◀◀ ☼ ▶▶▶▶▶▶▶▶▶▶▶▶▶

In 1767 Diderot had been a professional art critic for eight years for the *Correspondance littéraire* of his friend Grimm, an association that was to continue for another fourteen years. It was in this capacity that he reviewed the exhibition of painting and sculpture in the Salon of 1767, which was one in a series of biennial exhibitions held at the Louvre since the seventeenth century.

Fig. 1 gives a general view of the Salon of 1767. To hang and to present such a number of exhibits was no mean task. The man in charge of these arrangements was called *le tapissier*. For most of the exhibitions attended by Diderot, the *tapissier* was Chardin.

The catalogue, or *livret*, which was sold at the door to the visitors, makes it clear that the Salon was a very official affair. Only the fellows of the Academy were allowed to exhibit; and the whole show was placed under the high supervision of a Minister, the Director General of Fine Arts— namely, during those years, Marigny, the brother of Madame de Pompadour. It is also to be noticed that the artists in the catalogue are not listed in alphabetical order but in order of dignity, according to their titles and offices. First came the *Premier peintre du Roi*, then the *Rector*, then the *Assistant Rector*; after them came the *Professors*, the *Academicians*, and the *Agréés*. In his reviews of the Salons Diderot follows that order; but he does not accept the hierarchy; far from it: he is apt to upbraid a *Rector*, or a *Premier peintre*, as fiercely as a mere *Agréé*.

Please note in Fig. 1 how the paintings are arranged along the walls. On the very top are the great canvases depicting historical subjects. They have been placed up there because, being huge, they can be seen from a distance; however, they are not on top in the physical, literal sense only. Their towering position is symbolic: they dominate all the other types of painting—portraits, landscapes, still lifes, etc.—because they are held to be the first in importance. According to the academic doctrine, there is a hierarchy among works of art: the supreme rank belongs to historical painting; everything else is considered more or less inferior. The doctrine had been formulated in the seventeenth century by Félibien in a lecture delivered in 1667 to the Academy itself. Félibien reminds his listeners that painting is an intellectual pursuit. To draw lines and mix colors does not qualify one as an artist, but as a simple craftsman; it is a purely mechanical activity—whereas painting concerns the mind. Félibien goes on to unfold the consequences of this principle. Inasmuch, he says, as artists concern themselves with more difficult and more noble objects, they emerge from the lower regions of their art and rise to a more dignified status. For instance, a painter who deals with landscapes is above another who paints only fruits, flowers, or shells; again, a painter who represents living animals deserves more esteem than the one who represents only lifeless things; and since the human figure is God's most perfect work on earth, the painter who imitates God by depicting human figures is far superior to anyone else.

Now, just as there is a hierarchy of subjects based on their nature, there is another hierarchy based on the importance of the scene represented when it includes human figures. A portrait painter, for instance, although he does represent the human figure, has not yet reached the summit of painting; nor can he claim the honor due only to the most excellent. The most excellent are the artists who know how to represent a group of figures borrowed either from history or from mythology. To be truly superior, one must depict either great actions, like the historians, or pleasing scenes, like the poets. Such is the doctrine; and such are the ascending steps of painting.

Diderot, who does not accept the official hierarchy of ranks among the artists, does accept the hierarchy of the categories of paintings—which means, in fact, the hierarchy of subjects. He has the highest regard for historical paintings, for what he calls "les grandes machines" and what his friend Galiani called "le macchine da stupire." For him they are *the* important part of an exhibition—so much so that he rates the quality and the interest of a Salon according to the number of historical paintings. For example, he starts the review of the Salon of 1769 with the following complaint: "What a poor Salon we had this year! Almost no historical painting—no great composition at all."

This attitude may come as a surprise to us, but this is simply because our perspective and our values are different. When we think of eighteenth-century French painting today, the pictures which are likely to come first to our mind are images such as Fragonard's *L'Escarpolette* ("The Swing"): to us it looks like an epitome not only of Fragonard's spirit but of the mood of a frivolous age. Let us realize, however, that for Diderot *L'Escarpolette* was a very minor production indeed: his praise and admiration went to a different Fragonard, the serious, tragic, melodramatic one, the Fragonard who painted *The Great Priest Corésus Sacrificing Himself In Order To Save Callirhoé*. Correspondingly, in the eyes of their contemporaries the great eighteenth-century painters were not, or at least were not always, the ones whom we consider great: they were Pierre, Vien, Lagrenée, Taraval, Doyen, Hallé, and Durameau. Most of them are forgotten today; but let us remember that in their own day they were big men.

Historical painting derives its subjects from three main sources: Scripture and the lives of Saints, ancient history, and pagan mythology. Painters drew alternately from these sources, a practice, as Diderot observes, which produces some awkward results; for while they shift constantly from the Bible to the Fable, and vice versa, painters end up in representing Ulysses as a St. Joseph, the child Jesus as a Cupid, or in placing an apostle's head on the shoulders of a Roman senator.

Fig. 2 is *St. Denis Preaching the Christian Faith in Gaul* by Vien. The picture was painted for St. Roch, and it is still there today, facing another picture exhibited at the same Salon of 1767, *The Miracle of the Plague-Stricken* by Doyen (Fig. 3). The public, according to Diderot, was divided between these two canvases, and certainly, he says, they are both great compositions: "ce sont deux grandes machines." Their merits, however, are very different. The *St. Denis* is widely painted in a free, broad style; the figures are correctly drawn; the drapery is nobly arranged; the expressions are simple and natural; there is no agitation, and everything is beautifully peaceful.

The contrast of Doyen's picture with Vien's is striking. Vien was quiet, effortless, harmonious. He reminded one of Le Sueur, while Doyen reminds one of Rubens. As you turn to Doyen, says Diderot, everything becomes vigorous and fiery, and Vien appears lifeless and cold by comparison. There is however a particular element which attracts Diderot, besides the verve—namely horror. The picture is full of gruesome details—corpses, dying people, sick people covered with sores; there are even two feet sticking out from a sewer. Now, Diderot feasts his eyes on all these details.

These two big naked feet are a wonderful invention; so is this frantic man rushing out of the hospital, and this other moribund man who scratches and lacerates his own flesh; and again this dead man whose naked arms and hair are hanging from the terrace.

I know that some pusillanimous visitors have recoiled from this canvas, and refused to look at it; but what do I care? I am not pusillanimous; I am not one of those fainthearted people, who have a timid, overrefined taste. Furthermore, where should I expect to find horrible scenes, terrifying sights, if I don't find them in a plague, a famine, an epidemic?

In fact, this kind of sight can be found somewhere else, namely, in the annals of the Christian religion. Christianity, being a creed of fanatics, is rich in episodes of terror and cruelty; from this point of view, it is far superior to paganism, because (as Diderot explains) it is far more favorable to the fine arts.

Those who think otherwise have no idea of the proud attitude of Christians facing the praetorian tribunal; they are unaware of the cold ferocity of the priests; they have not seen those men, possessed with the demon of fanaticism, interrupting a sacrifice, overthrowing an altar, tearing down the idol of a pagan god, insulting a pontiff, defying a magistrate, and undergoing martyrdom.

Here lies a mine of great tragedies and of frightening pictures. Such as *St. Andrew Refusing to Sacrifice to the Gods* by Deshays; or *St. Cyr and Ste Julitte Delivered unto the Hands of the Executioners* by Durameau (Fig. 4).

Diderot incidentally does not distinguish between the victims and the torturers. The important thing is that there should be bloodshed. Christians cause blood to be shed. Therefore, Christianity is a storehouse of ghastly subjects for historical painters. This is Diderot's version of *Le Génie du Christianisme*.

Let us now turn to ancient history. At the Salon of 1765, a big canvas by Carle Van Loo was exhibited; it represented *Augustus Ordering the Doors of the Temple of Janus To Be Closed*, which means proclaiming the return of peace. This painting and two others had been commissioned for the king; the choice of the subjects was inspired by political circumstances and philosophical intentions. Peace had just been signed in 1763, after the Seven Years' War—and not a victorious peace. Cochin, secretary to the Academy, had been invited by Marigny to submit a program of decoration for Choisy, one of the royal residences. This is what he suggested:

For too long have painters celebrated warlike deeds, which result only in the destruction of mankind; would it not be sensible, for once, to illustrate some of those generous, beneficent acts through which good monarchs of the past have achieved the happiness of their peoples? I therefore beg to submit to you some of the deeds performed by the Emperors Augustus, Trajan, and Marcus Aurelius.

Nothing, for instance, could be more in keeping with the peace-loving disposition of our own monarch than a picture of *Augustus Closing the Doors of the Temple of War.* Another episode, quite worthy of the king's kindness, would be *Trajan, on His Way to a Military Expedition, Stops and Dismounts from His Horse In Order To Grant Justice to a Poor Woman.* A third episode would be: *Marcus Aurelius Relieving the Sufferings of His People at a Time of Famine and Pestilence.*

Cochin, a friend of the *philosophes*, was very pleased with this humanitarian program celebrating enlightened despots, the ultimate purpose of which was to flatter the king; but the king was neither pleased nor flattered. Louis XV did not care for serious, moralizing pictures; he preferred nymphs. He had the paintings removed from Choisy.

They were not lost forever, though. Two of them, *Marcus Aurelius* and *Augustus*, are in the Museum of Amiens today. A peace between England and France was signed at Amiens in 1802; and since Bonaparte wanted appropriate pictures to decorate the room where the treaty was to be signed, he was glad to use those which had been rejected by Louis XV.

Diderot of course approved of the program and the subjects; but he was far from satisfied with the way they had been dealt with.

M. Van Loo, your Augustus is miserable. Haven't you in your studio a pupil who had the courage to tell you that he is stiff, short, ignoble? Do you call *that* an Emperor? With this long palm leaf which is stuck against his shoulder, he looks like a member of the brotherhood of Jerusalem—coming back from the procession.

And that priest, behind him, what does he mean with his casket and his awkward gesture? and that senator, all hampered and entangled by his cloak and his paper? And what is the meaning of the whole, anyway? Where is the interest of the scene? Where is the subject? To close the doors of the Temple of Janus means announcing peace throughout the Empire; it is a public rejoicing: it is a festival. I look in vain in the canvas for the slightest trace of joy. Everything is cold, insipid, silent, mournful: it is the funeral of a vestal.

So much for Van Loo. Now for Hallé.

> M. Hallé, your Trajan is flat; he lacks nobility, expression, character. He seems to be saying to this woman: My good woman, you do look tired; I would gladly lend you my horse — unfortunately, it is as skittish as the devil.
> The officers in the Emperor's escort are just as ignoble as himself.

Vien does not fare any better.

> The face of your Marcus Aurelius is without expression—and indeed expression is absent from all the characters in your picture.
> This long, lean, thin young man resembles the child Jesus preaching in the Temple; and why did you make these senators look like apostles?
> This expiring young girl is cold; what shall I say of this colossal woman, spread all over the steps of the terrace? Is she asleep? Is she dead? I don't know. And that baby? Is this the way a baby should behave over the corpse of his mother? I am looking for some trace of famine and pestilence, for some of the horrible incidents which characterize such calamities. I am looking in vain. There are none. Everything is stiff, dry and cold. What a picture for a sensitive man!

Diderot, then, is severe upon all three pictures, and essentially for the same reasons. What he blames in each case is the *conception* of the subject. In each case the artist had a great subject, but to begin with he failed to realize its dramatic or pathetic possibilities. Also, none of the three artists has been able to rise to the dignity of Roman history; none of them has been able to *imagine* an emperor. Do you call *those* emperors? he exclaims again. They are puny, stingy, wretched little fellows, incapable of anything great. A poor, flat imagination which can conceive only insipid physiognomies and mean, petty personalities—this to Diderot is the curse of historical painters.

From this point of view, those who deal with mythological subjects are just as bad as those who deal with ancient history. Take La Grenée, for instance; his *Ceres and Triptolemus* or his *Bacchus and Ariadne*. Again, the great sin of the painter is the lack of style.

> What shocks me in this kind of subject is the childish type of the figures. I would rather have peasants with all their rusticity than

this bastard race that does not belong to any condition, any time, or any country.

This goddess, for instance, instead of showing me that inexpressible quality of greatness, of vigor, that denotes the divine, is just a suburban wet nurse with a lot of fine linen and no bust. This half-god, who should look passionate, noble and proud is nothing but an effeminate boy of eighteen.

As for the Bacchus, he looked like a vapid St. John.

Diderot feels that historical painting, like tragedy and epic, calls for "a great module" and large-scale characters; saints, emperors, and gods require superhuman proportions. These are petty and diminutive. Worse still, they are cold.

Now Boucher certainly lacked majesty. His goddesses and his nymphs looked like so many young ladies of easy virtue; at best, they looked like some marquise *en déshabillé;* but Boucher, at least, had a compensating grace: his nudes were voluptuous. La Grenée is pale, dull, and anemic by comparison. True, but Boucher is at the very end of his career. Voluptuousness is no longer the fashion. The eighteenth century, alas, is becoming virtuous.

As early as 1750, Rousseau, in his famous *Discours*, declaimed against sensuous pictures.

Our gardens, he wrote, are full of statues; our galleries are full of paintings. What do you suppose these paintings, these statues represent? You might think that these masterpieces, exhibited in public places, celebrate the defenders of the fatherland, or perhaps, those even greater men whose virtues added to the glory of the nation. Not at all. What you see are pictures of every perverted passion, carefully borrowed from ancient mythology; these are the scenes that are offered to the curiosity of our children, so that they have under their eyes, even before they can read, examples of vicious actions!

Amorous mythology was going out of fashion. "Avoid nudities; exhibit decent pictures"; such is now the official motto. On the eve of the opening of the Salon of 1775, Marigny's successor as Superintendent of the Arts, d'Angiviller, wrote to the committee in charge of the selection of pictures that they must banish from the Slaon any lascivious subject; no picture should be admitted to the Exhibition which could imperil morality. D'Angiviller added that such was the wish of the King himself, and the

King is no longer Louis XV, but the dull, honest Louis XVI. Anyway, the change in taste was the general tendency of the century. Following the lead of Jean-Jacques, *philosophes*, critics, men of letters were clamoring for moral subjects: they firmly believed that from now on historical painting should be a school for virtue.

Let us now consider *La Vertueuse Athénienne* by Vien. Ever since 1763 Diderot had been writing ecstatically about these Greek girls offering sacrifices on tripods borrowed from Herculaneum; he had praised their artlessness and their innocence. Ten years later, in 1773, to decorate her pavilion at Louveciennes, Madame du Barry herself preferred Vien's anemic virgins to those delightful figures by Fragonard which are today one of the glories of the Frick Gallery. In her eyes, Fragonard panels were old-fashioned, first, because they were not *à la grecque*, but also because they illustrated the progress of love with too much liveliness.

The Piety of Fabius Dorso (Fig. 5) by Lépicié, exhibited at the Salon of 1781, is even more edifying. The subject is explained in the catalogue. During the siege of the Capitol by the Gauls, Fabius Dorso, in order to perform a sacrifice instituted by his family, came out of that fortress, taking with him all the paraphernalia needed for the ceremony. He walked through the enemy camp, went up the Quirinal Hill, there performed the sacrifice, and then returned to the Capitol, having inspired respect and admiration from both the Romans and the Gauls. The picture shows him returning to the Capitol. Here is Diderot's comment:

> They say that the main figure is well put together; that its clothing is well draped; that the head is handsome and noble. As for myself I don't even know whether it is a man or a woman; it is a broomstick, a beanpole. There is nothing to characterize the action: Fabius carries his gods as if he were taking them from one apartment to another. No shadow of expression appears on any of the other faces; the soldiers see Fabius get out, and go back, as if this was of no concern to them.

Once more Diderot is blaming not the subject but the deficiency of the artist, who has neither the sense of the sacred nor the gift of dramatic imagination.

Now this kind of subject was not exceptional. In 1777 d'Angiviller had selected the following scenes for a set of Gobelins tapestries:

1. An example of religious piety among the Greeks: Cleobis and Biton, sons of a priestess, being afraid that their mother would be

late for a sacrifice because the oxen which were to drive her chariot to the temple had been delayed, decide to place themselves under the yoke and to drag the chariot.

2. An example of religious piety among the Romans: Lucius Albinus, having met Vestals who were on foot while carrying the sacred vases, orders his own wife and children to get off his carriage, and invites the Vestals to get aboard in their place.

In his Salon of 1767, Diderot tells us, not without a certain pride, that painters sometimes come to him to ask for a subject. This he is only too pleased to give; he likes to think of himself as a provider of subjects for the artists. For instance, he says an artist comes and asks me: "Give me a historical subject"; and I answer: "You should paint the *Death of Turenne*." This answer is surprising at first. How is it that Diderot, fond as he is of Antiquity, now recommends a modern subject taken from national history? National history, in fact, is in the process of invading painting, just as it is invading literature (remember Voltaire's tragedies).

At the same Salon of 1767, Cochin exhibited some drawings destined for the illustration of President Hénault's *Abrégé chronologique de l'histoire de France*. There was, among them, *King Louis VII Leaving for the Crusade* (Fig. 6).

> The fiery Saint Bernard is dragging his monarch to the Crusade, in spite of the wise Suger. The king has drawn his sword; Bernard seizes him by that hand which holds the sword. Suger seizes the other hand: he speaks, he argues, he prays, he urges earnestly — all in vain. The monk is very imperious; the Abbé, very sad.

Diderot however does not approve of the allegorical trappings of the picture; this mixing of real characters with imaginary beings, this *galimatias* as he calls it, is both confusing and shocking. Apart from this defect, he is pleased with Cochin's undertaking; he acclaims this illustration of scenes from our history. This new source will provide painters with an inspiration just as fruitful as that of ancient history.

Take for instance *William the Conqueror Landing in England* by Lépicié. "What a wonderful subject for a painter!" Diderot exclaims, provided of course the painter is not Lépicié; for alas, Lépicié depicting William the Conqueror shows no more intelligence, no more genius than his colleagues when they try to represent Augustus or Caesar.

> One sees in this picture a few idle, dumb, motionless soldiers; then all by himself a big short man, his arms extended, screaming.

(I asked him a hundred times what was the matter with him—but I still don't know.) Then comes William, in the center, on horseback, the man and the horse equally monstrous. The whole army is on the march in the background. No noise, no tumult, no military enthusiasm. It is a thousand times duller than the march of a regiment passing along the walls of a provincial town, on the way to its garrison.

Such is Diderot's indignation at seeing the subject wasted, that he recomposes the whole picture, according to his own conception.

Rousseau deplored the fact that painting did not represent "the defenders of the fatherland, nor those even greater men whose virtues added to the glory of the nation." This is precisely what painters are now set to do: they celebrate, more and more often, the great men of France. First the good kings, of course, beginning with Henri IV, the king of toleration and of chicken in every pot, already celebrated in epic verse and on the stage, but also virtuous heroes, magnanimous and humane soldiers. Diderot suggested Turenne; Duguesclin and Bayard are now among the pet subjects of historical painters. A good example of this type of painting is *Bayard, Having Made a Girl Prisoner, Returns Her to Her Mother, and Provides Money for Her Dowry* (Fig. 7), which is an episode that is treated several times. A similar story is told about Scipio; and indeed *La Continence de Scipion* is also represented toward the end of the century (by Vien, for instance, in 1779), but chastity for chastity, Bayard's continency now has the preference. If the function of historical painting is truly to transmit to posterity great examples of honor and morality, some of these examples at least are being provided by France.

Yet, Antiquity remains the main repertory of subjects; but it is an increasingly graver, more grandiose Antiquity, and also a more and more rigid one, stiffened as it is by the influence of British painters such as Benjamin West and Gavin Hamilton. To begin with, the frivolous is now decidedly superseded by the grand, and the erotic by the epic. Ovid has been unthroned by Homer, and for good. Scenes borrowed from the *Iliad* become more and more numerous; this is just what Diderot wants, for the triumph of Homer over Ovid means the triumph of *le grand goût* over *le petit goût*. The trouble is that, once more, artists are not up to their subjects, incapable as they are to conceive Homeric majesty and poetic terror.

For instance, *Juno and Vulcan Coming to the Rescue of Achilles* by Deshays are again mean, puny figures. "Vulcan looks like a young boy. Where is

FIG. 1.—G. de Saint Aubin, *The Salon of 1767*. Private Collection. (Photo by Bulloz.)

FIG. 2.—Vien, *St. Denis Preaching the Christian Faith in Gaul*. St. Roch, Paris. (Photo by Archives Photographiques.)

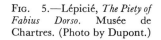
Fig. 5.—Lépicié, *The Piety of Fabius Dorso*. Musée de Chartres. (Photo by Dupont.)

Fig. 6.—Cochin, *King Louis VII Leaving for the Crusade*. Bibliothèque Nationale, Paris. (Photo by B. N.)

FIG. 7.—Brenet. *Bayard, Having Made a Girl Prisoner, Returns Her to Her Mother, and Provides Money for Her Dowry*. Musée de Grenoble. (Photo by Piccardy.)

FIG. 8.—David, *Belisarius*. Musée de Lille. (Photo by Bulloz.)

the vigorous, the formidable god of the foundries, of the blazing caverns? This is not the way the old poet pictures him." There lies, of course, the root of the misunderstanding. Diderot's mind, the mind of a humanist, is filled with imposing images: the poor painter, sometimes illiterate, cannot see through the eyes of Homer. In the same way, *The Battle between the Greeks and the Trojans around Patroclus's Body* by Brenet (1781) fails to convey the Homeric grandeur: it is too mannered, too affected. Achilles, who comes to the rescue on tiptoes like a dancer, is ridiculous.

If we now turn to Roman history, we shall find a stiff, severe Antiquity, the paragon of civic virtues. At the Salon of 1771 Beaufort exhibited *Brutus and Collatinus Swearing To Avenge Lucretia's Death, and To Expel the Tarquins from Rome*. Another great and proud subject, says Diderot; but

> the painter should have transported his imagination at Collatie; he should have visualized the stabbed Lucretia—and from that moment he should have become a Roman himself, burning with rage against the Tarquins. Instead, what do I see in Beaufort's picture? The forced and stilted figures of a painter who strives vainly to whip himself into a frenzy. As for Lucretia, O the ugly girl—much better to kill than to rape, if you ask me.

Yet with all its shortcomings this canvas is of great interest, for it points out the way to David (who indeed painted the same subject); and David is the very type of painter whom Diderot has in mind, the type of painter he is forever calling out for. Another composition points the same way: *The Fight between the Romans and the Sabines Interrupted by the Sabine Women* by Vincent. It prefigures the famous picture by David of the same subject.

But at the Salon of 1781, where this canvas was exhibited, David himself appeared for the first time. Diderot, who reviews the Salon for the last time, experiences at last the joy of finding a historical painter who fulfills his dearest wishes. Let us realize, however, that this advent, this arrival of David on the scene is also a resurrection: the resurrection of Poussin.

For Diderot, the absolute masterpiece of historical painting was *The Will of Eudamidas*. Eudamidas, a citizen of Corinth, was very poor, but he had two rich friends. When he died, he dictated his will: of one of his friends, he requested that he maintain his wife; of the other, he asked that he provide a dowry and a husband to his daughter. In Diderot's eyes, this is the supreme achievement of historical painting, because it combines a morally sublime subject with a sober, austere, style—the style of a bas-relief. Poussin is the master par excellence to whom French painters should return. Incidentally, Diderot here agrees with Napoleon. During his campaign in Egypt, Bonaparte had taken with him an engraving of that very same painting, and he once said to Denon: "After one has seen this austere composition, one cannot forget it; Denon, our school of painting has grown stale; we must bring it back into the ways of Poussin."

This will be David's task; and he had already started. At the Salon of 1781, Diderot stops in front of David's *Belisarius* (Fig. 8), in which Justinian's old general, now blind and destitute and reduced to begging his bread, is recognized by one of his old soldiers. At last, there is a young painter with a sense of nobility and restraint and a gift for the grand manner. *Il a de l'âme;* David feels the greatness, the gravity of his subject, and he knows how to express it, for he knows how to pose an attitude and arrange a piece of clothing in a way which is both natural and dignified. He has recaptured the moral austerity of the seventeenth century; at the same time, he has replaced the cheap or ridiculous travesties of his predecessors with a sculptural style which restores the heroes of Greece and Rome to their majestic stature. One should paint as they spoke in Sparta (*Peindre comme on parlait à Sparte*); this was Diderot's wish, and David carried it out.

Are we, then, going to make Diderot a champion of neoclassical painting? This would be to oversimplify his role and to restrict his taste. Let us remember that the same Diderot takes delight in violent and tumultuous scenes, in the horrors of plague and torture. This is the sign of another demand, of another tendency. Remember Doyen's canvas at St. Roch. Its gruesome, passionate features no longer forecast David; rather they forecast Gros, Géricault, and Delacroix. One can already discern the scattered elements of those great romantic melodramas, the *Massacre at Chios*, the *Plague-Stricken of Jaffa*, and *The Raft of the Medusa*.

Diderot's attitude in front of the historical pictures of his day is significant in other respects. Until his very last Salon, he seems to retain his admiration for that type of painting and his belief in its supremacy. When discussing pictures of another kind, a landscape, a domestic scene, or even a portrait, he is apt to deplore the absence of the dramatic element; he feels, for instance, that Loutherbourg's shepherds and animals, that Lépicié's family groups, or even Hubert Robert's ruins fail to interest the spectator because the artist has not been able to devise an anecdote, a story which would have animated the scene; and in each case Diderot remarks that only historical painters know how to invent such incidents.

But what about Greuze? He certainly knows how to tell a story; you can make a drama, or even a novel, out of his pictures; and indeed

Diderot seems almost ready to confer upon Greuze, in spite of his rustic or bourgeois subjects, the supreme title of *peintre d'histoire*. I protest, he says, that to me the *Ungrateful Son* or the *Village Bride* are truly historical paintings because they offer me all sorts of dramatic incidents. Greuze in fact thought that he could easily raise himself to the highest rank simply by selecting, for once, an antique subject where all his dramatic qualities would be displayed to the full. He decided to represent *Septimius Severus Reproaching His Son Caracalla for Having Tried to Assassinate Him;* and he submitted that picture to the Academy in 1769, precisely to support his application for the official title of *peintre d'histoire*. Alas, Greuze brought upon himself, on that occasion, the worst humiliation of his career. He was granted only the inferior rank of *peintre de genre:* the Academy decided that his picture was too mediocre to qualify him as historical painter.

The verdict of the Academy may seem unduly severe. After all, Greuze's *Septimius Severus* is no worse than Vien's *Marcus Aurelius* or Hallé's *Trajan*. Yet Diderot in this case agrees with the Academy. Greuze, he says, has proved himself unable to rise to that kind of exaggeration which is required by historical painting. His Septimius is ignoble; Caracalla is ignobler still. He would do very well in a rustic or domestic scene; for instance, he would make a *Bad Brother*, or an *Ungrateful Son*. In a word, Greuze has remained incurably, inevitably bourgeois. This would suggest that Diderot accepts the aristocratic character of historical painting. It is an exclusive club; any painter of common, ordinary scenes who tries to force the entrance to the club does so at his own risk.

Yet Diderot's faith in the dogma of academic hierarchy is not unshaken. One artist did oblige him to reconsider that dogma and to wonder about the whole question of subject in painting. There is obviously no story, no heroic episode, no dramatic interest in some pieces of crockery, two biscuits, a jar full of olives, two glasses of wine; and yet Diderot stops in front of such a still life and exclaims: "There is a painter for you! Chardin is not a historical painter, *but* he is a great man." Chardin indeed upsets the whole system of academic values and starts Diderot thinking. Historical painters, he says, look down on these humble artists and their humble subjects. They consider them as narrow minds devoid of lofty ideas and poetic genius, crawling miserably on the ground, never daring to lose sight of nature. To the historical painter such people are just copyists—at best, craftsmen, and nothing else. But for his part, the man who represents nature scrupulously sees historical painting as a fictitious and extravagant performance; he finds no truth in it, nor even any semblance of truth: everything is arbitrary, inflated, and hollow.

In short, it is the quarrel between prose and poetry. Diderot perceives the merits of prose, its integrity, its honest beauty, just as he perceives the weaknesses and the perils of poetry; and he realizes the flimsy character of historical painting. The fault of course rests first with the artists, but the genre itself carries with it the danger of unreality. How could one give back some substance to those vast compositions? Perhaps by injecting into them a dose of *vérité commune*. Ah, says Diderot, "if only a sacrifice, a battle, a triumph, a public scene could be rendered with the same truth in all its details as a domestic scene by Greuze or Chardin!" And Diderot dreams of the ways of bringing some prosaic solidity into poetic artifice. This is of course what he himself has been trying to achieve with his *drame bourgeois:* to stuff the empty nobility of classical tragedy with the substantial simplicity of everyday life. There we detect one of the many links which connect his art criticism with his attempts at renovating literary forms.

I feel that the problem of Diderot and historical painting, limited as it may appear, is, therefore, a central one: its aesthetic implications extend beyond the history of taste, and even beyond the field of fine arts. But I also feel that in this case one has to begin at the beginning: no generalization can be valid until one has *seen* the actual pictures which first provoked Diderot's reactions, and stimulated his thought.

Imitation, Eclecticism, and Genius

BY R. WITTKOWER

The theory of imitation is the main theme of my paper.[1] This theory had an enormous power of survival, not only—I suggest—because it was sanctioned by Antiquity, but also because *mimesis*, as Aristotle tells us in his *Poetics*, is instinctive in man from his infancy. Man is the most imitative of all animals and all men obviously receive pleasure from imitation. So far so good. But then Aristotle applies this empirical insight into the nature of man to the works of imitative art: the more exact the imitation, the greater the pleasure they evoke.[2]

For Aristotle this conclusion only appears as a first step in his analysis of the arts, yet imitation remained the center of his argument and countless generations followed him. In modern aesthetics, however, it is taken for granted that art has nothing to do with imitation. For a modern point of view, two of the three terms in the title of my paper, namely "imitation" and "eclecticism," belong together, and there is probably general agreement that eclecticism results from imitation. By contrast the third term, "genius," conjures up a spiritual, intellectual and creative frame of mind at the farthest remove from both imitation and eclecticism.

Our own reaction to these terms derives from deep changes of outlook and interpretation that came about toward the end of the eighteenth century. The link between imitation and eclecticism resulted, of course,

[1] In preparing this paper the following works were particularly helpful to me: J. E. Spingarn, *A History of Literary Criticism in the Renaissance* (New York, 1899 [2nd ed., 1924]); Irving Babbit, *The New Laocoon* (Boston & New York, 1910); Julius von Schlosser, *Die Kunstliteratur* (Vienna, 1924); Erwin Panofsky, *Idea* (2nd ed.; Berlin, 1960 [1st ed., 1924]).

[2] *Poetics*, 1448b.

from a new—and let me say at once—irrational conception of originality and genius.

These changes, long in preparation, have been studied by literary historians and historians of ideas perhaps more fully than by art historians. This is not surprising, for the development of modern art theory from its very beginning—i.e., from Alberti's *On Painting* (1435)—depended on ancient literary theories to which writers on art remained tied for no less than 350 years. I need hardly point out that art theorists took their cue from Horace's *Ut pictura poesis*[3] and could and did claim that literary and art theory had the same parentage. Thus we find a painter like Reynolds referring in his *Discourses* to Plato, Aristotle, Cicero, Horace, Quintilian, Valerius Maximus, Pliny and, among modern authors, to Boileau, Corneille, Pope, Dryden, and Burke.[4] I have to be more modest than Reynolds (since I have been asked to deliver one "Discourse" and not fifteen) and cannot go into the literary theory as much as my subject would demand.

To be sure, *mimesis* is the essence not only of literary and art theory but also of artistic practice, and this is true for most of the eighteenth century and even for the nineteenth. But the nature of *mimesis* is no less evasive than a chameleon's color. The ancients spilled a great deal of ink over the clarification of this problem, and as an introduction to the eighteenth century it may be helpful to start with the result of their discussions in tabulated form.

The first case, which has already been mentioned—the closer the imitation the more perfect the work of art—implies that art can never surpass nature.

Secondly, contrary to the first case, nature is regarded as accidental and imperfect, and for this reason the artist has to choose the most perfect parts from nature and to combine them in his work. Thus the work of art surpasses nature.

Thirdly, some ancient writers went a step further and postulated that the work of selection had been done, once and for all, by the great poets and artists of Antiquity, and, therefore, by turning to them and imitating them, one implicitly imitates what is most perfect in nature. This approach implies that the gifted imitator may combine the virtues of his models and create works of even higher quality. In other words, the elimination

---

[3] Rensselaer W. Lee, "*Ut Pictura Poesis:* The Humanistic Theory of Painting," *The Art Bulletin*, XXII (1940), 197ff. I owe a great debt to this fundamental study.

[4] Sir Joshua Reynolds, *Discourses on Art*, ed. Robert R. Wark (Huntington Library, San Marino, 1959), see Index.

of accidentals in nature or the idealization of nature can be advanced further and further if artists always stand on the shoulders of their great precursors. In this context the question was discussed whether it was preferable to select only one model for imitation or to choose the best from several models.

Fourthly, the artist can also render concepts of his imagination. Such concepts are formed by images stored up in his mind. This theory should not be confused with that of the Platonic ideas which are independent of sensory experience.

I said that all these aspects of the theory of imitation were elaborated in Antiquity and in reference to poetry rather than to the visual arts. Writers, theorists and artists of the Renaissance and post-Renaissance periods had this miscellaneous tradition constantly at hand in the works of Plato and Aristole, Cicero, Horace, Pliny, Quintilian, and Macrobius, [5] to which must be added Longinus' *On the Sublime*, effective after Boileau's French version of it. [6]

It is a memorable fact that few art critics had a philosophical mind. Not rarely do we find different and even mutually exclusive interpretations of *mimesis* side by side in the work of one and the same author. [7] Almost anything was possible at any time so far as the theory of imitation was concerned. In trying to distill from these treatises conservative or progressive trends we force the vagaries of history into half-true schemata. The glorious inconsistencies in Diderot's writings appear paradoxical only if one attempts to dissect his personality by separating his retardative from his advanced views. When Winckelmann propounded the axiom: "The only way for us to become great, nay if it were possible inimitable, is the imitation of the Ancients" [8]—who in 1755 could say whether this was the voice of a reactionary or a prophet and who can say it now? Nevertheless, at certain periods there was a consensus to value one aspect of

---

[5] The *mimesis* theories of antiquity were usually not correctly interpreted in the period under review. Above all, we now know that for Aristotle *mimesis* meant much more than pure imitation. For the Greek point of view, cf. Richard McKeon, "Literary Criticicm and the Concept of Imitation in Antiquity," *Modern Philology*, XXXIV (1936), 1ff., and H. Koller, *Die Mimesis in der Antike* (Bern, 1954). For the Roman point of view, see Arno Reiff, *Interpretatio, Imitatio, Aemulatio. Begriff und Vorstellung literarischer Abhängigkeit bei den Römern* (Cologne, 1959). Cf. also Harold Ogden White, *Plagiarism and Imitation during the English Renaissance* (Cambridge, Mass., 1935), pp. 3–19.

[6] Samuel H. Monk, *The Sublime. A Study of Critical Theories in XVIII-Century England* (Ann Arbor Paperback, 1960), pp. 10ff.

[7] Lee, "Ut Pictura Poesis," p. 203 and *passim*.

[8] *Gedanken über die Nachahmung der griechischen Werke in der Malerei und Bildhauerkunst* (1755).

mimesis higher than another, although there were always dissenters. After this caveat I will now proceed to comment on the various aspects of *mimesis* mentioned before.

The naïve realism adduced by Aristotle as one of the causes for the birth of poetry is reflected in the innumerable anecdotes told by Pliny and others regarding works so faithful to nature that they deceived the beholder.[9] *Ars simia naturae*[10] ("Art the ape of Nature"), reputedly an ancient phrase, became a title of honor for the procedure of artists from the fourteenth century onward. In the late sixteenth century the meaning of the metaphor changed. A differentiation became common between *imitatio sapiens* and *imitatio insipiens*. The ape now symbolized the foolish, faithful imitation of nature that was also condemned by most theorists of the seventeenth and eighteenth centuries. Nonetheless, the simian, slavish imitation of nature remained a valid measuring rod.

Let me quote the case of Giorgione. Everybody from the earliest critics on agreed that the revolutionary softness of his colorism opened up a new dimension in the history of painting. Surprisingly, Vasari (writing in 1550) explained that Giorgione wanted with his innovation to advance the rendering of living and natural objects and to portray them as best he could in color[11]—*ars simia naturae*. Following Vasari, seventeenth- and eighteenth-century writers regarded Giorgione's chromatic triumphs as a means by which to achieve verisimilitude in painting. I think it was the Venetian Anton Maria Zanetti[12] who as late as 1771 introduced new criteria by saying that Giorgione "added to solid cognition the free play of fantasy and imagination." The autonomy of the imagination was a late eighteenth-century concept. By projecting this notion into Giorgione's work, one was able to see him with pre-Romantic eyes. Whatever merits this critical breakthrough had, it is evident that the "naïve realism" approach did not do justice to Giorgione. But there were always writers, even during the eighteenth century, who regarded naïve realism as a satisfactory critical position. I shall only mention Dézallier D'Argenville, in whose popular work on famous painters the perfect imitation of nature remained the guiding principle.[13]

[9] Cf. Panofsky, *Idea*, p. 7; Ernst Kris and Otto Kurz, *Die Legende vom Künstler* (Vienna, 1934), pp. 69ff.

[10] For the following, Panofsky, *Idea*, p. 89f.; H. W. Janson, *Apes and Ape Lore in the Middle Ages and the Renaissance* (London, 1952), Ch. X, pp. 287ff.; Ernst Robert Curtius, *Europäische Literatur und Lateinisches Mittelalter* (Bern, 1954), p. 522f.

[11] Vasari, *Vite*, ed. G. Milanesi, IV, 91ff.

[12] *Della pittura veneziana e delle opere pubbliche de' Veneziani Maestri* (Venice, 1771).

[13] Ant. Jos. Dézallier D'Argenville, *Abrégé de la vie des plus fameux peintres* (3 vols.; Paris, 1745–52 [4 vols.; 2nd ed.; Paris, 1762]). Cf. also André Fontaine, *Les Doctrines d'art en France de Poussin à Diderot* (Paris, 1909), p. 194.

The basic problem of the naïve realistic approach is an epistemological one: the pre-condition for requesting a perfect imitation of nature as the ultimate goal of art would have to be an agreement on what nature is. Is it the nature represented by Giotto, whose works, according to Boccaccio, were taken for real life; is it the harmoniously ordered universe of Leonardo, who demanded mimetic faithfulness from the artist; is it Giorgione's poetical vision of nature; or is it contained in Vernet's theatrical land- and seascapes, which for Diderot were the supreme renderings of natural scenery?[14]

The second approach, the choice and combination of the most perfect parts in nature, was more sophisticated, not only because it implied an intelligible principle of order but also because one could, by a man-made set of rules, rationally determine wherein the perfection of nature consisted. Thus a binding contract united all those who were prepared to play the game. The shibboleth of ideal imitation remained valid for countless generations of artists and critics. Its first important statement takes us back to Xenophon's *Memorabilia* (III, 10, 1–6), where Socrates explains that since it is difficult to find a perfect body in nature, the artist has to select the most beautiful parts from many bodies. The story told of the fifth-century painter Zeuxis, who, when painting Helena chose five Croton girls as models and combined their most beautiful features in his picture, was transmitted to posterity through Pliny[15] and Cicero[16] and was endlessly repeated from Alberti to the close of the eighteenth century.

Writers on art of the eighteenth century were obsessed by this traditional concept and often lifted from Aristotle's dictum that artists imitate natural things "either as they were or are or as they are said or thought to be or to have been" only the last clause: "or as they ought to be."[17] Thus Richardson said in his *Essay on the Theory of Painting* (1715):[18] "No man sees what things are, that knows not what they ought to be." In 1760 Daniel Webb, in his *Inquiry into the Beauties of Painting*, explained that the Greek artists knew how to combine the scattered beauties in nature and therefore rose "from an imperfect imitative, to a perfect

[14] Arthur A. Lovejoy, "Nature as Aesthetic Norm," *Modern Language Notes* (1927), republished in *Essays in the History of Ideas* (New York, 1955), pp. 69ff., gives an enumeration of the aesthetic uses of the term mainly in the seventeenth and eighteenth centuries showing the innumerable meanings connoted with nature.

[15] *Hist. nat.*, XXXV, 64.

[16] *De invent.*, II, 1, i. Cf. also Denis Mahon, *Studies in Seicento Art and Theory* (London, 1947), p. 133f.

[17] *Poetics*, 1460b.

[18] P. 137.

ideal beauty."[19] The trouble with Raphael was that he did not sufficiently heed the lesson to be learned from the ancients and for this reason never ascended to their perfect idealization of nature.[20] As late as 1771 the Abbé Laugier propounded that the choice of the beautiful parts in nature is one of the great privileges of the painter.[21]

But the *locus classicus* for this concept is surely Batteux's *Les Beaux-Arts reduits à un même principe*, published in 1747.[22] He reasserts the principle that the choice of the best parts in nature creates a whole that is more perfect than nature. The rest is a long-winded exegesis of this principle. *Goût* (taste)—i.e., an inborn feeling rather than the scientific exploration of the Renaissance—is now made judge of the choice. The essence of art is not the *vrai*, but the *vraisemblable*. In other words, wise imitation "sees nature not as she is, but as she ought to be": we are back to Aristotle. Batteux calls improved nature *la belle nature*, which was, of course, a stock phrase of eighteenth-century criticism.

The selection theory rarely appears separate from the third and fourth aspects of my tabulation. It was a short step to approach *la belle nature* through the idea of it formed in the artist's mind as well as through the clearinghouse of ancient art. The one position may be called pseudo-Platonic, the other pseudo-Aristotelian: pseudo-Platonic because the imitation does not concern the idea existing *a priori* in the artist's mind; it is the idea resulting from the empirical study of nature. As Bellori expressed it in 1664 in his famous statement before the Roman Accademia di San Luca: "The Idea, originated in nature, supersedes its origin and becomes the origin of art"[23]—a programmatic formulation still valid through most of the eighteenth century. It was valid from Richardson's "a painter must raise his ideas beyond what he sees"[24] to Webb's images formed by a combination of studies from nature with the ideal or inventive part of art[25] and to Reynolds' dictum that the painter forms an ab-

[19] Quoted from the second edition, 1777, p. 40.

[20] *Ibid.*, pp. 59ff.

[21] Abbé Laugier, *Manière de bien juger des ouvrages de peinture* (Paris, 1771), p. 59.

[22] For the following, pp. 13, 14, 24f., 39, 58f.

[23] Gio. Pietro Bellori, "L'idea del pittore, dello scultore e dell' architetto, scelta delle bellezze naturali superiore alla natura," *Le vite de' pittori, scultori et architetti* (Rome, 1672), p. 3ff. Reprinted in Panofsky, *Idea*, pp. 130ff. The Italian text of the passage quoted above runs: "Questa Idea . . . originata dalla natura supera l'origine e fassi originale dell' arte."

[24] *Essay*, p. 162. The passage quoted in the text runs on: "and form a model of Perfection in his Own Mind which is not to be found in Reality . . ."

[25] *Inquiry* (4th ed., 1777), p. 4f. Webb differentiates between exact imitation of nature, which he calls "the mechanick or executive part of the art" (such "servile copiers of the works of nature" were the Dutch painters) and "the ideal or inventive" part. "Perfection of the art consists in an union of these two parts. Of all the moderns, Raphael seems to have come the nearest to this point."

stract idea of natural forms "more perfect than any original."[26] I shall
have occasion to point out that a proper Platonic or neo-Platonic position
as professed by late sixteenth-century Mannerist artists was not fully
embraced again until the discovery of original genius toward the end of
the eighteenth century.

Finally, I turn to the most common position, which I have just called
pseudo-Aristotelian. I have called it pseudo-Aristotelian because select
models—epitomes of ideal nature—rather than select nature were recom-
mended for imitation. This method had been suggested by ancient writers,
by Cicero, Horace, Quintilian, Macrobius, and others,[27] and the lesson
they taught was first taken up in the literary criticism of the Renaissance;
in Vida's *De arte poetica* (1527), in Daniello's *La poetica* (1536), in Scaliger's
Poetices (1561)—to mention only three of scores of treatises.[28] The discussion had been opened by an exchange of views in 1512 between
Pietro Bembo and Gianfrancesco Pico. Pico advocated the imitation and
reinterpretation of many ancient writers, while Bembo insisted on the
imitation of single models: Cicero for prose and Virgil for verse.[29]

From here stems ultimately a controversy which we still find carried
on through the eighteenth century. English neo-Palladianism of the first
half of the century was based on the imitation of one model, Palladio,
who was regarded as the most accomplished interpreter of the ideal
beauty in ancient architecture. English neoclassicism of the second half
of the century switched to a reinterpretation of many models chosen
from Antiquity.

Needless to say, it was Boileau who gave the theory its final *raison
d'être* by founding the "rules and literary practice of classical literature
on reason and nature." In the words of Spingarn: "For Vida, nature is
to be followed on the authority of the classics; for Boileau, the classics
are to be followed on the authority of nature and reason."[30] And so
Boileau remained the voice of the eighteenth century.

The effect on art theory of the new departure in literary theory is first
to be found in Paolo Pini's *Dialogo di pittura* (1548). He suggests that if
the talents of Titian and Michelangelo would have appeared in one

---

[26] *Discourses*, p. 44.
[27] Cf. above note 5, particularly the book by A. Reiff, who shows convincingly that
aemulatio rather than *imitatio* (i.e., faithful copying) was regarded as "good" literary
method in Rome.
[28] Cf. Spingarn, *A History*, particularly Ch. V.
[29] For this controversy, cf. Eugenio Battisti, "Il concetto d'imitazione nel Cinque-
cento italiano," *Rinascimento e Barocco* (Einaudi, 1960), pp. 176ff., with further literature.
[30] Spingarn, *A History*, p. 135.

person he would have been *lo dio della pittura* ("the god of painting)."[31] Vasari, in his Life of Raphael, first applied this concept historically. Raphael, he maintained, took the best from ancient and modern masters and by combining their different manners in a style of his own superseded them all.[32] The old issue of selective imitation of nature had shifted to the question of style, and who could doubt that the superstyle was the product of the best styles so far produced?

From the end of the sixteenth century onward the theoretical literature abounds with the request for imitation from many masters.[33] Later, by a strange freak of history, which Mr. Mahon has disentangled in his *Studies in Seicento Art and Theory*, the Carracci were incorrectly regarded as the originators of this concept. The legend was mainly disseminated through Malvasia's *Lives*, published in 1678.[34] But ten years earlier Charles Alphonse Du Fresnoy had written in his Latin poem *De arte graphica* that Annibale Carracci had taken from the great painters of the past all the excellence he found in them and had combined them in his work.[35] In the notes which Du Fresnoy's friend Roger de Piles appended to the second edition, Annibale is called wonderfully accomplished and of an universal genius.[36] Now Du Fresnoy's work had an enormous success not only in France but also in England. It was translated and published by Dryden with a long introduction of his own in 1695, and three new editions followed in the eighteenth century.[37] The third edition

[31] Modern art historians maintain that this remark adumbrates an eclectic program; cf. Schlosser, *Die Kunstliteratur*, p. 210f., Anthony Blunt, *Artistic Theory in Italy 1450–1600* (Oxford, 1940), p. 85.

[32] Further comments to Vasari's analysis in R. Wittkower, "The Young Raphael," *Allen Memorial Art Museum Bulletin* (Oberlin College), Vol. XX, No. 3, p. 166f.

[33] Mahon, *Studies*, pp. 120, 137.

[34] A spurious poem about Niccolò dell'Abate published by Malvasia in 1678 and attributed to Agostino Carracci praises Niccolò dell'Abate for having combined the manners of Michelangelo, Titian, Raphael, Tibaldi, Primaticcio, and Parmigianino; cf. Mahon, *ibid.*, p. 208.

[35] In the English edition of 1750 (*The Art of Painting*) which I am using, p. 76f. Cf. also Mahon, in *The Art Bulletin*, XXXIV (1952), p. 230.

[36] The second edition with a French translation and de Piles' notes appeared like the first in 1668. In his assessment of Annibale, de Piles has some interesting reservations. The whole passage in the English translation of 1750, p. 233, runs as follows: "He (Annibale) Imitated Correggio, Titian, and Raphael, in their different Manners as he pleas'd; excepting only, that you see not in his Pictures, the Nobleness, the Grace, and the Charms of Raphael: and his Out-lines are neither so pure, nor so elegant as his. In all other things, he is wonderfully accomplish'd, and of an Universal Genius."

[37] In 1716, 1750, and 1769. There were, moreover, translations into English by Wright (1728), Wills (1754), and Churchey (1789); the most important, however, was that by William Mason, because of Reynolds' annotations (Dublin, 1783). Some of these editions escaped the attention of W. Folkierski in his interesting paper "Ut Pictura Poesis ou l'étrange fortune du *De arte graphica* de Du Fresnoy en Angleterre," *Revue de littérature comparée*, XXVII (1953), 385ff.

of 1750 is particularly remarkable because it was dedicated to Richard, third Earl of Burlington, the man who had such an extraordinary influence on the formation of English taste in the first half of the eighteenth century. Roger de Piles, too, in his important *Abrégé de la vie des peintres*, assures us that no painter had been more universal than Annibale Carracci.[38] And even as late as 1771 the Abbé Laugier, in his posthumously published *Manière de bien juger des ouvrages de peinture*—a work that leaned heavily on Roger de Piles—continued this tradition.[39] Other artists were, of course, also judged by the same criteria.[40] In the same year, J. F. M. Michel,[41] in his biography of Rubens, argued that Rubens was the greatest painter because he had united Titian's color, Correggio's light, Raphael's nobility, Veronese's richness, and Annibale Carracci's grandeur. The principle had been clearly restated by the Abbé Du Bos. He wrote, nowadays (i.e. 1719) painters have more help from art than Raphael had. If Raphael could come back to this world, he would be even better than he was when he lived.[42]

But meanwhile the decisive term had been coined. In 1763 Johann Winckelmann, the father of classical archaeology, wrote that the Carracci were "Eclectici" who united the purity of the ancients and of Raphael with the knowledge of Michelangelo, the richness of the Venetians and

[38] First published in 1699. Second edition, 1715, p. 305: "Cependent nous ne voyons point de Peintre qui ait été plus universel, plus facile, ni plus assuré dans tout ce qu'il faisoit, ni qui ait eu une approbation plus général qu'Annibal." The entire passage starting on p. 303 contains a very fine and knowledgeable analysis of Annibale's art and development, far removed from any clichés.

[39] The passage is interesting enough to be quoted literally: "Les Carraches vous appliqueront, & vous intéresseront d'une maniere nouvelle, & sur-tout Annibal, le meilleur & le plus sublime des trois. C'est encore ici un auteur original, qui, profitant des découvertes faites par ceux qui l'avoient devancé dans la carriere, a pourtant trouvé le secret de traiter ses sujects d'une maniere qui n'est ni triviale, ni empruntée. Plus fier que Raphael, moins sauvage que Michel-Ange, il a dessiné savamment & de grand goût, prononçant les choses avec force et sans dureté. Il a su caractériser ses objets avec une justesse infinie; il a mis beaucoup d'esprit & de vivacité dans ses expressions ... C'est un artiste qui a trouvé le champ de la peinture tout défriché, & dont le travail a produit des fruits, non d'un caractere nouveau et inconnu, mais d'une qualité exquise" (p. 183f.). These remarks by the famed author of the *Essai sur l'architecture* (Paris, 1753) who had written simplicity and nature on his flag reveal how tenaciously established values were adhered to even among "progressive" critics.

[40] In a talk before the Académie Royale in Paris in 1664 Lebrun maintained that Poussin had united the good qualities of Raphael, Titian and Veronese. Cf. Mahon, *Studies*, p. 206.

[41] *Histoire de la vie de P. P. Rubens* (Brussels, 1771), p. 345, quoted by Mahon, *Studies*, p. 206.

[42] Abbé Du Bois, *Reflexions critiques sur la poésie et sur la peinture* (4th ed.; Paris, 1746), I, 380f.

the gaiety of the Lombard school.[43] Winckelmann adopted the term originally used to designate those late antique philosophers who—to paraphrase his own words[44]—tried to combine the ideas of previous schools, owing to their lack of vitality. But Winckelmann, the classicist, was far from condemning the method altogether.[45] In contrast to his predecessors, who regarded the selection of the best from many masters as a style-forming principle, he interpreted the method as pertaining to a certain stage in human history: just as the eclectic philosophers had summarized the systems of their great forerunners, so the eclectic painters (i.e., the Carracci and their school) summarized the manners of their great classical and Renaissance peers.

In his assessment of the Carracci, Winckelmann may have been influenced[46] by his friend Anton Raphael Mengs, who as a painter expressed most fully Winckelmann's neoclassical ideology and as a theorist firmly upheld the classical doctrine. According to Mengs, artists before Raphael sought only the pure imitation of nature with chaotic results. Raphael, Correggio, and Titian knew what to choose, but Raphael was undoubtedly the greatest. All later artists were inferior to these great masters.[47] Despite this theory of cultural despair, the Carracci come in for high praise, for after a period of decadence—so Mengs informs us— it was they who formed a new school "and became the first and most happy among the Imitators."[48]

Now Mengs is careful to differentiate between copying and imitating. The copyist proceeds without real understanding: "But he who effectively studies and observes the productions of great men with the true desire to imitate them, makes himself capable of producing works which resem-

---

[43] *Abhandlung von der Fähigkeit der Empfindung des Schönen in der Kunst*, quoted by Mahon, *Studies*, p. 213.

[44] In the *Geschichte der Kunst des Alterthums* (Dresden, 1764). Cf. Mahon, *Studies*, p. 206.

[45] Cf. Lee, in *The Art Bulletin*, XXXIII (1951), 209f.

[46] Carl Justi, *Winckelmann und seine Zeitgenossen* (Leipzig, 1898), II, p. 28.

[47] In *Gedanken über die Schönheit und den Geschmack in der Mahlerey*, first published in Zurich, 1762. I am using the English edition, *The Works of Anthony Raphael Mengs*, published by Joseph Nicholas D'Azara (London, 1796), I, 36ff.

[48] The passage, in Mengs's Letter to Don Antonio Pontz (*The Works*, II, 78), continues: "Hannibal was the most correct imitator, and reunited the style of the ancient statues with the grandeur of Lewis (i.e., Lodovico Carracci) but he despised the subtilty of the art, and philosophical reflections. From these Carracci's was formed a school of many able men. . . ."

Cf. also Mengs's "Letter to a Friend upon the Rise, Progress, and Decay, of the Art of Designing" (*The Works*, II, 140f.). From a long passage on the Carracci, I quote: "By good fortune, were born at Bologna, some great geniuses, which were the Carraccis. . . . To these Carraccis we owe the restoration of painting. . . ."

ble them, because he considers the reasons with which they are done . . . and thus it makes him an imitator without being a plagiarist." [49]

Mengs himself claimed to be an imitator in this sense, as he stated in a remarkable passage in his letter addressed to Falconet: "I have proposed to myself to imitate the most eminent parts which I have discovered in others, contenting myself to be the last of those who seek the good road. . . . " With no sign of false modesty he regarded his approach to imitation as the cause of his international success, for nations which understand art—this is his implied argument—compare the works of living artists with the best of the deceased masters and do not fail to perceive his (Mengs's) sound principles of imitation. [50]

At the same moment Reynolds made similar observations. Reynolds and Mengs had met in Rome, [51] but do not seem to have appreciated each other's company. Reynolds' first eight Discourses had appeared in print between 1769 and 1778, and in 1778 they were published in an Italian edition [52] which Mengs, then court painter in Madrid, castigated as dangerous for young artists because of Reynolds' "superficial principles." [53] Nonetheless, both artists' theoretical positions are very similar, although this would be hard to believe if one knew only their works.

Where Mengs differentiates between copying and imitating, Reynolds distinguishes between copying and borrowing. He regards mere copying as absurd. [54] But the sagacious imitator penetrates into the principles on which the work of his choice is wrought. "What is learned in this manner from the works of others," he maintains, "becomes really our own, sinks deep, and is never forgotten." [55] And he concludes, precisely as Vasari had two hundred years before in his discussion of Raphael, that the painter who brings together in one piece "those beauties which are dispersed among a great variety of individuals, produces a figure more beautiful than can be found in nature, so that the artist who can unite in himself the excellencies of the various great painters, will approach nearer to perfection than any one of his masters." [56] This method of incorporation, adaptation and digestion Reynolds calls "borrowing": "Such imitation is so far from having any thing in it of the servility of

[49] In the Letter to Pontz (*The Works*, II, 106).
[50] *The Works*, II, 25.
[51] F. W. Hilles, *The Literary Career of Sir Joshua Reynolds* (Cambridge, 1936), p. 61.
[52] *Ibid.*, pp. 279–87.
[53] *Ibid.*, p. 61f.
[54] *Discourses*, p. 29 (Disc. II).
[55] *Ibid.*, p. 101f. (Disc. VI).
[56] *Ibid.*, p. 103, also p. 106 (Disc. VI).

plagiarism, that it is a perpetual exercise of the mind, a continual invention."[57] In fact, this kind of borrowing appeared to him "the true and only method by which an artist makes himself master of his profession."[58]

These were ideas very close to Reynolds' heart. He often came back to them,[59] above all in the 12th Discourse of 1784, where he adduced the great Raphael as crown witness of judicious borrowing. He demonstrated that Raphael had incorporated figures from Masaccio's Brancacci Chapel into his tapestry cartoons[60] and that for the sacrificial ceremony of the Sacrifice at Lystra he had relied on an ancient relief,[61] then in the Medici collection and now in the Uffizi. Reynolds shrewdly remarked that everyone knew the Brancacci Chapel and that Raphael therefore could not have considered his borrowing as plagiarism. He draws a clear line between those who steal from "mere poverty" and the others who, like Raphael, "enrich the general store with materials of equal or of greater value than what they have taken; such men surely need not be ashamed of the friendly intercourse which ought to exist among Artists, of receiving from the dead and giving to the living. . . . "[62]

Mengs and Reynolds advocated and defended a theory of imitation which, as we have seen, had been in vogue for no less than two hundred years. In fact, the theory of selective borrowing from great masters and antiquity was central to artistic creativity from the Renaissance onward. It was consciously and unconsciously accepted by the vast majority of artists, from Raphael to Rubens and Poussin and on to Tiepolo and Reynolds.

In keeping with this undeniable fact, the most common empirical procedure of art historians is concerned with the tracing of influences and borrowings, and to that extent the method of selective borrowing is silently acknowledged as perfectly respectable. But when confronted with this very issue as an explicit theory, the same art historians paradoxically retract and stigmatize it as eclectic.

[57] *Ibid.*, p. 107.

[58] *Ibid.*, p. 110. The passage continues: "which I hold ought to be one continued course of imitation that is not to cease but with his life."

[59] Cf., e.g., his notes to William Mason's translation of Du Fresnoy's *The Art of Painting* (Dublin, 1783), p. 69, note iv: "the artist may avail himself of the united powers of all his predecessors. He sets out with an ample inheritance, and avails himself of the selection of ages."

[60] *Discourses*, pp. 216, 219 (Disc. XII) and plates iv and v. Cf. also *Discourses*, ed. Roger Fry (London, 1905), Fig. xxviii. One of the "Masaccio" figures Reynolds was alluding to was the St. Paul in the fresco of *St. Paul Visiting St. Peter in Prison*, actually painted by Filippino Lippi.

[61] *Ibid.*, p. 216.

[62] *Ibid.*, p. 217.

We found the term first creeping in with Winckelmann, but not until the romantic era did it assume purely negative connotations.[63] Basically, the term "eclecticism" is a deprecatory label for the theory and practice of selective borrowing. Before saying more about this *volte-face*, which uprooted the foundations of the classical ideology, some further observations seem to be in place.

The essential tenets of the Italian Renaissance conquered the whole of Europe and in a broad but direct sense remained valid for more than 350 years. The longer a homogeneous artistic culture lasts the larger, of course, is its serviceable repertory.[64] Almost all the artists of this long period looked back to antiquity as a shining beacon. But while Brunelleschi, the father of Renaissance architecture, had to create a new language from miscellaneous traditions, Palladio—150 years later—could operate with ideas and motifs worked out by such forerunners as Alberti, Bramante, Giulio Romano, Michelangelo, and Sanmicheli. Again 150 years later, Juvarra, one of the towering eighteenth-century architects, looked back on an infinitely richer architectural panorama: he ranged over the whole field of ancient and Italian architecture; he mastered the entire repertory from Brunelleschi to Bramante, Antonio da Sangallo, Sanmicheli, Palladio, and on to Bernini and Borromini. Yet he also fulfilled supremely the request made by the propagators of selective borrowing to mould all this material in a new, exciting, and personal way.

The case of Tiepolo is not different: Veronese and Rembrandt, Raphael, Giovan Benedetto Castiglione, Luca Giordano, and many others formed his style. Selective borrowing and transformation was the method. Tiepolo died in 1770. The immense vitality and ease of performance of this most fertile genius among the eighteenth-century painters depended on his unconditional absorption of the classical ideology. Precisely because of his alleged eclecticism modern art historians, men who deserve being listened to,[65] have played him down. But even though, in retrospect, a Chardin may convey a more significant message—a message, moreover, to which many of us may respond more readily—it remains a fact that from an eighteenth-century viewpoint, Tiepolo was infinitely more representative. And so was Sir Joshua Reynolds, the unchallenged leader of British art, who firmly upheld his classical convictions till his death in 1792.

[63] Cf. Rensselaer W. Lee, in *The Art Bulletin*, XXXIII (1951), 208ff., and Denis Mahon, *ibid.*, XXXV (1953), 228.
[64] R. Wittkower, *Art and Architecture in Italy 1600–1750* (Baltimore, 1958), p. 240.
[65] Roberto Longhi, *Viatico per cinque secoli di pittura veneziana* (Florence, 1946).

Sir Joshua's method of borrowing was, as a rule, more direct than that of his great Italian counterpart. Like Raphael in the cases I mentioned, Sir Joshua did not shrink from more or less literal quotations, but requested their adaptation to the specific task in hand. Thus, for his portrait of Caroline, Duchess of Marlborough, and her daughter,[66] he used one of Michelangelo's lunettes in the Sistine Chapel, but translated the brooding and sublime quality of the original into a playful and rather insipid mode. Or he used the pose and proportions of the Belvedere Apollo to give the portrait of Admiral Keppel[67] an aura of youthful sprightliness appropriate to the shipwrecked but undaunted commodore.[68]

A careful reading of Reynolds' remarks on borrowing seems to reveal a defensive note. He knew there were apostates who did not cherish his concept of selective borrowing. No less a man than Horace Walpole felt he had to rise in his defense.

Sir J. Reynolds has been accused of plagiarism for having borrowed attitudes from ancient masters. Not only candour but criticism must deny the *force* of the charge. When a single posture is imitated from an historical picture and applied to a portrait in a different dress and with new attributes, this is not plagiarism, but quotation: and a quotation from a great author, with a novel application of the sense, has always been allowed to be an instance of parts and taste; and may have more merit than the original.[69]

The advocates of imitation were faced with a growing number of artists in revolt. Their criticism is epitomized in Chardin's *Singe peintre* (Louvre) copying an antique statue which on his canvas turns into an ape.[70] Hogarth, in the tailpiece of the Spring Gardens Catalogue of 1761 used the same simian formula to ridicule the antiquarian adulation of masters of past ages.

[66] 1764–65, Blenheim Castle.

[67] 1753.

[68] Further on the problem of borrowing in Reynolds' theory and practice, see Edgar Wind, "Humänitatsidee und heroisiertes Porträt in der englischen Kultur des 18. Jahrhunderts," *Vorträge der Bibliothek Warburg* (1930–31), pp. 156ff., and "Borrowed Attitudes in Reynolds and Hogarth," *Journal of the Warburg Institute*, II (1938–39), 182ff.; Charles Mitchell, "Three Phases of Reynolds's Method," *Burlington Magazine*, LXXX (1942), 35ff.; E. H. Gombrich, "Reynolds's Theory and Practice of Imitation," *ibid.*, pp. 40ff.

[69] Horace Walpole, *Anecdotes of Painting in England*, ed. R. N. Wornum (London, 1876), I, xvii.

[70] Janson, *Apes*, pp. 311f., 324. Cf. also R. Wittkower, in *Journal of the Warburg Institute*, II (1938–39), 82.

We witness a new approach to the whole province of art, an approach that eventually destroyed the belief in the value and virtue of imitation. The toiling scholar-artist was replaced by the genius who invents—to quote Addison—"by the mere strength of natural parts and without any assistance of art and learning." His work was regarded as the gift of a unique mind sovereignly dictating his own laws, and from this point of view any form of imitation appeared to be plagiarism. His source of inspiration was no longer "nature methodized" (to use Pope's phrase), but the vast, wonderful and infinitely varied realm of God's creation. And the critic, no longer a studious judge of the rules of art, gave free play to his emotive reactions before the work of art.

But none of the new ideas arose like a phoenix from the ashes. The concept of genius had its origin in Plato's theory of the *furores* as well as in Aristotle's doctrine of the Saturnine temperament, the birthright of "all extraordinary men distinguished in philosophy, politics, poetry and the arts."[71] The Renaissance reconciled Aristotle's and Plato's views and accepted Ficino's conclusion that only the Saturnine temperament was capable of Plato's creative enthusiasm. Hence the Renaissance view of the *divino artista*, the divine artist who cannot be measured by ordinary standards; hence also the conviction that artists are born and not made, expressed by scores of Renaissance writers. Paradoxically, this conviction was never abandoned, not even by the most avid propagators of imitation and rule.

The philosophy of accommodation which required the taming and control of natural talent by reason and rule had innumerable facets during the eighteenth century. Shaftesbury, for instance, in his careful exposition of the Platonic concept of divine enthusiasm felt it must be "of Reason and sound Sense" to avoid being turned into fanaticism.[72] Nor does William Duff, the author of *An Essay on Original Genius* (1767),[73] despite his adulation of originality and exorcism of imitation, allow the free rein of an exuberant imagination. It must be restrained by a proportionable share of reason and judgment. At the same time, however, Edward Young, in *Conjectures on Original Composition* (1759),[74] had gone a step further by claiming that "An Original may be said to be of a vegetable nature, it rises spontaneously, from the vital root of Genius;

---

[71] For this and the following R. and M. Wittkower, *Born under Saturn* (New York, 1963), pp. 98ff.
[72] "A Letter concerning Enthusiasm," *Characteristicks* (ed. of 1732), I, 53f.
[73] Pp. 8, 19, 256 and *passim*.
[74] P. 12.

it grows, it is not made." Similarly, Diderot, following Young, acknowledged the spontaneity and autonomy of genius.[75] These ideas prepared for the romantic conception of genius. At the end of the century Schiller coined the well-known phrase "A true genius must be naïve or it is none."[76]

As I have indicated, the work produced by genius defies rational analysis. This concept, too, has its history. Ancient writers—Cicero, Quintilian, Pliny—made allowance for the irrational elements in works of art and called it *venustas* ("grace").[77] The classical ideology from the sixteenth century onward was permeated with this concept: "grace" for the Italians from Baldassare Castiglione to Vasari and beyond was *un non so che*, which in the French theory of the seventeenth century became the *je ne sais quoi* and in England, in Pope's immortal phrase, "A Grace beyond the Reach of Art." Professor Monk has pointed out that in the eighteenth century the old antithesis beauty (the definable element dependent on rules) and grace was supplanted by the antithesis beauty and sublimity. This is certainly correct so long as some tenets of the classical ideology had currency. But the romantic conception of genius resolved the old antithesis, and this is where I find the decisive break with the past.

While it may be true that at the end of the eighteenth century the artistic genius—in Herbert Dickmann's phrase[78]—"comes to be thought of as the highest human type," it is usually forgotten that the connotations of genius with the extraordinary, strange, extravagant, and even mentally unbalanced belong to the very late period. Throughout most of the eighteenth century, on the contrary, exalted, lofty, and harmonious qualities were associated with true genius. This was also the image James Northcote left of his master Reynolds: "He had none of those eccentric bursts of action, those fiery impetuosities which are supposed by the vulgar to characterize genius, and which frequently are found to accompany a secondary rank of talent, but are never conjoined with the first. . . ."[79] And so the eighteenth-century ideal of reasonableness was made the touchstone of true genius even at this late date.

[75] Cf. Herbert Dickmann, "Diderot's Conception of Genius," *Journal of the History of Ideas*, II (1941), 151–82.

[76] *Über naive und sentimentalische Dichtung* (1795–96).

[77] Samuel Holt Monk, "A Grace beyond the Reach of Art," *Journal of the History of Ideas* V (1944), 131ff., gives ample documentary material from antiquity to the eighteenth century.

[78] "Diderot's Conception of Genius," p. 151.

[79] James Northcote, *The Life of Sir Joshua Reynolds* (2nd ed.; London, 1818), II, 321.

Nevertheless, Sir Joshua did not remain unmoved by the new ideas which I have briefly sketched. He opposed the notion that "rules are the fetters of genius. They are fetters only to men of no genius."[80] He went so far as to suggest that the well-trained mind may indulge "in the warmest enthusiasm, and venture to play on the borders of the wildest extravagance."[81] He agreed that art is addressed to imagination and sensibility[82] and that the painter like the poet satisfies a love of novelty, variety, and contrast, and, with reference to Longinus, he refers to Michelangelo's "most poetical and sublime imagination."[83]

To be sure, such notions were concessions to the new climate of opinion. But they were marginal within Reynolds' classic-idealistic approach to art. The real breakdown of this tradition came in the next generation. I have only to recall the name of William Blake, the first forty-three years of whose life belonged to the eighteenth century. Blake's violent reaction to Reynolds' *Discourses* is well known, but I feel I should quote some of his annotations written when he was about fifty years old.

"Enthusiasm is the All in All" is Blake's answer to Reynolds' "mere enthusiasm will carry you but a little way." Reynolds' "solidity and truth of principle" based on reason, provokes the exclamation "What has Reasoning to do with the Art of Painting?"; and in another place: "Artists who are above a plain Understanding are Mock'd and Destroy'd by the President of Fools." Against Reynolds' dictum that man *learns* all that he knows, Blake argues: "I say on the Contrary that Man Brings All that he has or can have Into the World with him," and so it follows that "Taste & Genius are Not Teachable or Acquirable, but are born with us." "The Man who says that the Genius is not Born, but Taught— is a Knave." Against Reynolds' exaltation of the general idea, Blake's sarcastic: "To Generalize is to be an Idiot. To Particularize is the Alone Distinction of Merit. General Knowledge are those Knowledges that Idiots possess."[84]

It was germane to Blake's concept of great art—and implicitly of genius—that he returned to an unqualified Platonism. "One power alone makes a poet: Imagination, the Divine Vision," he exclaimed.[85]

---

[80] *Discourses*, p. 17 (Disc. I).

[81] *Ibid.*, p. 27 (Disc. II).

[82] *Ibid.*, p. 59 (Disc. IV) and p. 241 (Disc. XIII).

[83] *Ibid.*, p. 84 and *passim* (Disc. V). Cf. also R. R. Wark's Introduction to the Discourses.

[84] William Blake, *Poetry and Prose*, ed. Geoffrey Keynes (London, 1941), pp. 770ff.

[85] For this and the following, cf. Anthony Blunt, *The Art of William Blake* (New York, 1959), Ch. 3, pp. 22ff.

He quite logically maintained that "All Forms are Perfect in the Poet's Mind, but these are not Abstracted nor compounded from Nature, but are from Imagination." Visionary images are immensely precise; "they are minutely articulated beyond all that the mortal and perishing nature can produce." They are "infinitely more perfect and more minutely organized than anything seen by the painter's mortal eye." Hence the vigor of Blake's attack against Reynolds' principle of the universal and general, a principle deeply rooted in the classical doctrine. Reynolds shared the view held by many since the sixteenth century that the painter must rise above the accidental and the transient: he "must get above all singular forms, local customs, particularities, and details of every kind," and the passkey to his goal, is of course, selective borrowing.

In the same vein as Blake, Goya, the greatest genius of Blake's generation, commended his etched series of the *Caprichos* with these words: "The artist begs the public to be indulgent with him because he has neither imitated other works nor even used studies from nature. But an artist may also, surely, remove himself entirely from nature and depict forms and movements which to this day have only existed in his imagination."[86]

I cannot discuss the question of to what extent Goya, Blake, and other contemporaries[87] who expressed similar ideas deluded themselves. Obviously, no mind is a clean slate. Needless to say, these artists too worked with an imagery both inherited and observed. But it was the new attitude toward original creation that dethroned selective borrowing. Only now, therefore, did Winckelmann's term "eclecticism" assume a ring of utter contempt.[88] Since the term had made its entry into art-historical writing in connection with the Carracci and their school, the negative label "eclectics" remained attached to them right to our own days.[89] Mr. Mahon, who has dealt comprehensively with the seman-

---

[86] But it must be pointed out that the title page originally intended for the whole series, which shows the painter asleep and dreaming, bears the inscription: "The sleep of reason produces monsters." In his comment to this plate Goya added: "Imagination deserted by reason produces impossible monsters. United with reason, imagination is the mother of the arts and the source of their wonders."

[87] E.g., the Germans Carstens and Schick; cf. Bernhard Knauss, *Das Künstlerideal des Klassizismus und der Romantik* (Reutlingen, 1925), pp. 74ff.

[88] It may be true that Henry Fuseli in his *Lectures on Painting* of 1801 (the whole passage quoted in D. Mahon, *Studies*, p. 216f.) was the first to stigmatize eclecticism as despicable. But, paradoxically, he sided on the whole with Reynolds' theoretical views on art; cf. Eudo C. Mason, *The Mind of Henry Fuseli* (London, 1951), p. 38 and *passim*.

[89] Cf., e.g., Ellis K. Waterhouse, *Baroque Painting in Rome* (London, 1937), p. 6f.; R. W. Lee, in *The Art Bulletin*, XXXIII (1951), 211f.; Lionello Venturi, in *Commentari*, I (1950), p. 169.

tic confusion to which the term lends itself, suggested to give it a well-earned rest, and I cannot but support his plea.

At about the middle of the eighteenth century the term "plagiarism" made an ominous appearance, but only when the advocates of originality decried the entire method of borrowing as eclectic and unworthy was the individual act of borrowing also stigmatized as plagiarism. Nonetheless, the theory of imitation and particularly of judicious borrowing was hard to kill. The artist abided by it much longer than one might have expected, and even when they seemed to abandon it, it slipped in by the back door.

Let me conclude with the voices of Robert Adam and Piranesi. Robert Adam, who almost monopolized important architectural commissions in England between 1760 and 1790, held that the freedom permissible to genius gave him liberty "to transform the beautiful spirit of antiquity with novelty and variety." But at the same time he maintained that architecture needed "to be informed and improved by correct taste," and the models of correct taste were the works of the ancients. In his *Parere su l'architettura* (1765), Piranesi ridiculed simplicity, reason and rule and advocated imaginative instead of imitative art. In spite of this stress put on originality, he admonished his readers: "Let us borrow from their stock" (i.e., of the ancients), and at the end of his life he went to Paestum and left us a legacy of wonderful engravings of the Greek temples on Italian soil.

It would seem that the theory of imitation with its focus on reason, uniformity, and universality accorded with vital issues of the Age of Enlightenment, and this may account for its tenacious survival. But this is a question I would like to ask rather than to answer.

Taste, Style, and Ideology

in Eighteenth-Century Music

BY EDWARD E. LOWINSKY

◄◄◄◄◄◄◄◄◄◄◄◄◄ ✳ ►►►►►►►►►►►►►

One of the most curious episodes in the history of eighteenth-century music relates to the election of Johann Sebastian Bach to the cantorship of the St. Thomas Church in the city of Leipzig in 1723, following the death of Johannes Kuhnau. The city fathers, disappointed in their hope to lure Telemann from Hamburg, had next voted for Christoph Graupner, Kapellmeister in Darmstadt. Since the Landgrave of Hesse-Darmstadt was unwilling to dismiss Graupner, the council, according to the official minutes, decided that "since the best man could not be obtained, mediocre ones would have to be accepted." [1] And this is how Bach obtained his position in Leipzig in 1723 after he had composed such works as the six Brandenburg Concertos and the *Well-Tempered Clavier*, works as immortal on the stage of music as those of his rivals were transient. How is an event like this to be explained? Is it simply a matter of ignorance on the part of the city council? Is it a matter of taste? Is it an event peculiar to eighteenth-century Germany or did similar things happen elsewhere?

In 1728, in the city of London, where Handel charmed English ears with the melodies of his Italian operas, John Gay's and Pepusch's *Beggar's Opera* [2] ended with one blow the monopoly of Italian opera. Handel's

[1] Hans T. David and Arthur Mendel, *The Bach Reader* (New York, 1945), p. 88. For a full account of the proceedings see C. Sanford Terry, *Bach, A Biography* (2nd ed.; London, 1950), pp. 141–50.

[2] Facsimile edition, with commentaries by Louis Kronenberger and Max Goberman (Larchmont, 1961).

Herculean efforts to stave off defeat were of no avail; his musical genius was helpless in stemming the tide of the popular ballad opera.

What had Gay and Pepusch to offer that Handel's operas lacked? For one thing, they had an English instead of an Italian libretto; for another, scenes from London's underworld in unvarnished colors with characters irresistible in their lifelike realism instead of intricate plots from ancient history or mythology with artificial characters walking on stilts; and finally, popular hit tunes instead of the da-capo aria with its display of virtuoso coloraturas. Obviously, it was not a matter of Handel's art against that of Pepusch, who, in this case, did no more than select and arrange the tunes.[3] It was a contest between pretense on a high level of artistry and truth on the level of popular simplicity, between an art twice removed from reality—in tongue and in time—and a native art holding up a mirror to present-day times, characters, and mores; it was a contest between solemnity and irony, indeed, impudence. And impudence won because it had truth, native tongue, and laughter on its side. And laughter, frowned upon by kings, was enjoyed as the spice of life by the middle class. Of course, the *Beggar's Opera* also had social implications and political overtones that delighted its contemporary audience. No one living in the London of 1728 could have missed the vast political satire directed against the Prime Minister, Sir Robert Walpole, his wife, and his mistress.[4]

Again, was this event peculiar to England? Would it ever have come to pass if there had not been that fateful split between an English audience and an opera sung in Italian?

No such split occurred in eighteenth-century France. Yet, nearly twenty-five years later, an explosion no less powerful and unexpected than the one in London occurred on the operatic stage of Paris. And since the French are an argumentative breed they made a lot of noise about it, echoes of which reverberate in the innumerable pamphlets produced during that affair.

On the first of August, 1752, an Italian troupe made its debut on the stage of the Académie royale de musique in Paris, presenting Pergolesi's *La Serva padrona*,[5] the musical comedy of a young genius of twenty-three. Pergolesi had died in 1736 at the age of twenty-six. *La Serva padrona* was first performed in Naples in 1733 as intermezzo between the acts of an Italian opera. In Paris it was performed between the acts of an opera by Lully, who, though dead for sixty-five years, was still very much alive as

---

[3] See Max Goberman, "The Music of *The Beggar's Opera*," in *ibid.*, pp. xiv–xviii, xvi.
[4] See Louis Kronenberger's comments, *ibid.*, pp. vii–xiii, viii.
[5] *Opera omnia di Giovanni Battista Pergolesi*, ed. F. Caffarelli, Vol. 11a (Rome, n.d.).

an artistic force and exercised an astonishing influence on French opera and French taste.

The performance of this small work had unforeseen consequences. I shall set them forth in the words of a contemporary observer who, at the same time, was deeply involved in them. Jean-Jacques Rousseau, in his *Confessions*,[6] describes the events as follows:

> Paris was divided into two parties, more violently opposed than if it had been a matter of religion or of an affair of State. One, the more numerous and influential, composed of the great, the wealthy, and the ladies, supported the French music; the other, more lively, more proud, and more enthusiastic, was composed of real connoisseurs, persons of talent, and men of genius. This little group assembled at the Opera, under the Queen's box. The other party filled the rest of the pit and house; but its chief meeting-place was under the King's box. This was the origin of these celebrated party names, "King's corner" and "Queen's corner." The dispute, as it became more animated, gave rise to several brochures. If the "King's corner" attempted to be witty, it was ridiculed by the "Petit Prophète"; if it attempted to argue, it was crushed by the "Lettre sur la musique Française." These two little pamphlets, by Grimm and myself respectively, are all that have survived the quarrel; all the rest are already forgotten.
>
> But the "Petit Prophète" . . . was taken as a joke, and did not bring the least annoyance upon its author, whereas the "Lettre sur la musique" was taken seriously and aroused against me the whole nation, which considered itself insulted in its music.

In his pamphlet[7] published in 1753 Rousseau had declared that each national music draws its character from the native language and its prosody.[8] The French language with its poor prosody, lacking clarity of definition in the proportion of long and short syllables,[9] is incapable of producing either good rhythm or good melody, good airs or good recita-

---

[6] English translation in the Modern Library edition (New York, n.d.), pp. 396ff.

[7] *Lettre sur la musique françoise*, in Vol. XV in *Oeuvres complètes de J.-J. Rousseau*, (Paris, 1827), pp. 161–232.

[8] "J'ai dit que toute musique nationale tire son principal caractère de la langue qui lui est propre, et je dois ajouter que c'est principalement la prosodie de la langue qui constitue ce caractère" (*ibid.*, p. 172).

[9] "[J]e suppose que la même langue dont je viens de parler eût une mauvaise prosodie, peu marquée, sans exactitude et sans précision; que les longues et les brèves n'eussent pas entre elles, en durées et en nombres, des rapports simples et propres à rendre le rhythme agréable, exact, régulier" (*ibid.*, p. 173).

tives.[10] French composers, therefore, find themselves constrained to compensate for the lack of melody by inventing an infinite number of burdensome ornaments, by multiplying the harmony and the accompaniments, and by piling one voice upon another.[11] Add to this the use, or rather abuse, of fugues, imitations, double counterpoints, and other beauties of purely arbitrary convention which have no merit excepting that of being difficult to master, and all of this leads to nothing but noise equally unworthy of occupying the pen of a man of genius or the attention of a man of taste.[12] Counterfugues, double fugues, inverted fugues, ostinato basses, and other laborious nonsense that the ear can't stand nor reason justify, are remains of barbarism and poor taste comparable to the portals of our Gothic cathedrals existing only to the shame of those who had the patience to fashion them.[13]

[10] "Il est clair que la musique nationale, étant contrainte de recevoir dans sa mesure les irrégularités de la prosodie, n'en auroit qu'une fort vague, inégale et très peu sensible; que le récitatif se sentiroit sur-tout de cette irrégularité, qu'on ne sauroit presque comment y faire accorder les valeurs des notes et celles des syllabes; qu'on seroit contraint d'y changer de mesure à tout moment, et qu'on ne pourroit jamais y rendre les vers dans un rhythme exact et cadencé; que, même dans les airs mesurés, tous les mouvements seroient peu naturels et sans précision" (*ibid.*, pp. 173–74).

[11] Among the many passages in which Rousseau criticizes the style and technique of French music in its attempt to cover up for its poverty of expression and the true effects of music, I choose the following: "Comment le musicien vient-il à bout de produire ces grands effets? Est-ce à force de contraster les mouvements, de multiplier les accords, les notes, les parties? est-ce à force d'entasser dessins sur dessins, instruments sur instruments? Tout ce fatras, qui n'est qu'un mauvais supplément où le génie manque, étoufferoit le chant loin de l'animer, et détruiroit l'intérêt en partageant l'attention. Quelque harmonie que puissent faire ensemble plusieurs parties toutes bien chantantes, l'effet de ces beaux chants s'évanouit aussitôt qu'ils se font entendre à-la-fois, et il ne reste que celui d'une suite d'accords, qui, quoi qu'on puisse dire, est toujours froide quand la mélodie ne l'anime pas: de sorte que plus on entasse des chants mal-à-propos, et moins la musique est agréable et chantante, parcequ'il est impossible à l'oreille de se prêter au même instant à plusieurs mélodies, et que, l'une effaçant l'impression de l'autre, il ne résulte du tout que de la confusion et du bruit" (*ibid.*, p. 191).

[12] "Une autre chose qui n'est pas moins contraire que la multiplication des parties à la règle que je viens d'établir, c'est l'abus ou plutôt l'usage des fugues, imitations, doubles dessins, et autres beautés arbitraires et de pure convention, qui n'ont presque de mérite que la difficulté vaincue, et qui toutes ont été inventées dans la naissance de l'art pour faire briller le savoir, en attendant qu'il fût question du génie" (*ibid.*, pp. 196–97). And after, "Tout cela, n'aboutissant qu'à faire du bruit, ainsi que la plupart de nos choeurs si admirés, est également indigne d'occuper la plume d'un homme de génie et l'attention d'un homme de goût" (*ibid.*, p. 197).

[13] "A l'égard des contrefugues, doubles fugues, fugues renversées, basses contraintes, et autres sottises difficiles que l'oreille ne peut souffrir et que la raison ne peut justifier, ce sont évidemment des restes de barbarie et de mauvais goût, qui ne subsistent, comme les portails de nos églises gothiques, que pour la honte de ceux qui ont eu la patience de les faire" (*ibid.*, pp. 197–98).

Finally, in his peroration, which reads rather like the summary of the prosecution, Rousseau lets go with this double-barrelled blast:

I have shown, I believe, that French music has neither measure nor melody, the language being capable of neither; that French singing is but a continuous barking, insufferable to an unprejudiced ear; its harmony is crude, void of expression, except only in a tyro-like padding, French airs are no airs, French recitatives are no recitatives, whence I conclude that the French have no music nor can they have any, or that, should they ever have one, it will be so much the worse for them.[14]

To add injury to insult Rousseau, in the same essay, extols the virtues of Italian music born of the most musical language in Europe.[15] Italian music has a simple and pure harmony,[16] lively and brilliant accompaniments, a well-defined measure and rhythm, imaginative and moving modulations, and a highly varied and expressive melody.[17] Its appeal is universal.

Here, in Rousseau's own words, is an account of what happened upon the publication of sentiments so well conceived to hurt the national pride of France:

It was the time of the great quarrel between Parliament and clergy. The Parliament had just been banished; the ferment was at its height; everything pointed to an approaching outburst. From the moment the brochure appeared, all other quarrels were at once forgotten; nothing was thought of, except the perilous condition of French music, and the only outburst was against myself. It was such

---

[14] "Je crois avoir fait voir qu'il n'y a ni mesure ni mélodie dans la musique françoise, parceque la langue n'en est pas susceptible; que le chant françois n'est qu'un aboiement continuel, insupportable à toute oreille non prévenue; que l'harmonie en est brute, sans expression, et sentant uniquement son remplissage d'écolier; que les airs françois ne sont point des airs; que le récitatif françois n'est point du récitatif. D'où je conclus que les François n'ont point de musique et n'en peuvent avoir, ou que, si jamais ils en ont une, ce sera tant pis pour eux" (*ibid.*, p. 231).

[15] "Or, s'il y a en Europe une langue propre à la musique, c'est certainement l'italienne; car cette langue est douce, sonore, harmonieuse, et accentuée plus qu'aucune autre, et ces quatre qualités sont précisément les plus convenables au chant" (*ibid.*, p. 178).

[16] "[L]es Italiens ont rendu l'harmonie plus pure, plus simple, et donné tous leurs soins à la perfection de la mélodie . . . " (*ibid.*, p. 199).

[17] "C'est à l'aide de ces modulations savantes, de cette harmonie simple et pure, de ces accompagnements vifs et brillants, que ces chants divins déchirent ou ravissent l'ame, mettent le spectateur hors de lui-même, et lui arrachent, dans ses transports, des cris dont jamais nos tranquilles opéra ne furent honorés" (*ibid.*, pp. 190–91).

that the nation has never quite recovered from it. At Court, the
only doubt was whether the Bastille or exile should be the punishment; and the Royal warrant of arrest would have been drawn up,
had not M. de Voyer shown the ridiculous aspect of the affair.
Anyone who sees it stated that this brochure possibly prevented a
revolution in the State will believe that he is dreaming. It is, however, an actual truth, which all Paris can still attest, since it is at the
present day no more than fifteen years since this singular incident
took place.

Although my liberty was not attacked, I was unsparingly in-
sulted, and even my life was in danger. The Opera orchestra
entered into an honourable conspiracy to assassinate me when
I left the theatre.[18] . . . I learned that M. Ancelet, an officer in
the Musketeers . . . had prevented the plot from being carried out,
by causing me to be protected, unknown to myself, when I left
the theatre.[19]

Curiously enough, the man whom History regards as the inspirator of
the French Revolution sees himself here cast in the role of the man who
prevented a revolution. At any rate, the Paris performance of *La Serva
padrona* in 1752 was the beginning of the notorious war of the buffoons, the

[18] This is perhaps not so strange as it seems if one reads some of the remarks in
which Rousseau either attacks the orchestra musicians of the Opera or, worse yet,
damns them with faint praise. A sample of the latter is the following: "As one has
assured me that there are among the orchestra musicians of the Opera not only very
good string players, which, I confess, almost all of them are, taken individually, but
truly honorable men who do not lend themselves to the intrigues of their colleagues
to the disservice of the public, I hasten to add this distinction so as to make amends,
as much as is in my power, for the possible wrong toward those for whom this is true."
("Comme on m'a assuré qu'il y avoit parmi les symphonistes de l'Opéra non seulement de très bons violons, ce que je confesse qu'ils sont presque tous, pris séparément,
mais de véritablement honnêtes gens, qui ne se prêtent point aux cabales de leurs
confrères pour mal servir le public, je me hâte d'ajouter ici cette distinction, pour
réparer, autant qu'il est en moi, le tort que je puis avoir vis-à-vis de ceux qui la méri-
tent") [*ibid.*, p. 177n].
    At another point Rousseau asks why it is that French musicians perform Italian
music tolerably well, but Italian musicians are incapable of making any sense out of
French music. The reason, he notes, lies not, as our musicians in their accustomed
haughtiness argue, in the superiority of French musicianship, but in the pre-eminence
of Italian music, which unlike French music, has melody and therefore can be readily
understood by musicians everywhere (*ibid.*, pp. 185–86n). But certainly he reached
the height of insult when he favorably compared the keyboard accompaniment of a
mere ten-year-old Italian boy with that of Sieur Noblet of the Opera, although he
"did not doubt that he, Noblet, was a good harmonist and accompanied very exactly" (*ibid.*, p. 203).
    For the combination of disarming candor and the most innocent-faced malice,
Rousseau has no equal.
[19] *Confessions*, pp. 396–97.

querelle des bouffons. It came at a time when the controversy on the merits of French and Italian music was at its height. Whereas in London the success of the *Beggar's Opera* was caused in part by its being written in the native tongue, the revolution of French opera style was brought about by a work presented in Italian and contending with one written in French.

Pergolesi's opera was performed as an intermezzo between the acts of Lully's *Acis et Galathée*, called "Pastorale Héroique." Old and new styles could hardly have been presented in more perfect examples. Lully's opera was peopled by pagan deities and a whole array of mythological, allegorical, and pastoral characters. Pergolesi's intermezzo, on the other hand, portrayed in deft strokes and realistic colors the characters and scenes of a bourgeois home: a wealthy but stingy old bachelor who has foresworn marriage, and a winsome young witch of a servant girl who tricks her rich master into marrying her. Between these two stands the comic figure of a male servant buffeted around by the two contending parties without ever opening his mouth.

In Lully's *Acis et Galathée* we find the whole apparatus of baroque opera: the ballets, the choruses, the orchestra that accompanies not only the airs but also the recitatives and which performs instrumental numbers such as symphonies, preludes, marches, etc. Lully's style is solemn, as behooves the court composer of Louis XIV, while his technique is contrapuntal. Compared with this, Pergolesi used an unpretentious score of a string quartet with harpsichord; since, however, the viola usually plays in octaves with the cello, we have here actually nothing but a string trio with harpsichord accompaniment. There are no ballets, no choruses, Lully's heavy-footed recitatives accompanied by orchestra are replaced by the so-called "recitativo secco," a lively, truly speechlike recitative merely punctuated by sparingly used harmonies of the harpsichord and rendered expressive by effective modulations. All solemnity is gone; the prevailing note is wit and irony, lightness and grace. The heavy garment of the many-voiced counterpoint is exchanged for the airy and transparent dress of homophony. Lully called his operas *tragédies en musique*. A historian of opera has characterized them in the following manner:

> The action, unrolling with majestic indifference to realism, presented a series of personages discoursing lengthily on *l'amour* or *la gloire* in the intervals of all kinds of improbable adventures. There were no comic figures, except in *Cadmus* and *Alceste;* everything was stately, formal, and detached from ordinary life. [20]

[20] Donald Jay Grout, *A Short History of Opera* (2 vols.; New York, 1947), I, 119.

The contrast created by Pergolesi's *opera buffa* could hardly have been more outspoken. That this was also a contrast of a social character, or royal versus middle-class entertainment, and that overtones of a class struggle were heard during the long and bitter quarrel over Italian versus French opera may be deduced from Rousseau's statement, quoted before, when he described the two parties as follows: "One, the more numerous and influential, composed of the great, the wealthy, and the ladies, supported the French music; the other, more lively, more proud, and more enthusiastic, was composed of real connoisseurs, persons of talent, and men of genius." Needless to say, this was a highly partisan view. It suffices to point out that Rameau, the greatest living composer in France at that time, was on the French side of the controversy.[21] But Rousseau saw correctly that the great quarrel that divided Paris was not only a matter of taste and style but involved questions of social ideology as well.

The stylistic concepts underlying the two operatic styles are of course those of baroque and rococo. A characteristic expression of the French baroque was the so-called "French overture," featuring a majestic slow opening with an array of dotted rhythms, a moderately animated fugue, and a return to the ceremonial beginning. Louis XIV, for whose pleasure Lully wrote his operas, frowned upon lively melodies.[22] The Italian rococo, on the contrary, loved the fast tempos—no tempo designation is used as frequently as *allegro*. *La Serva padrona* has no more than one slow aria, a *larghetto*, and this one is a pseudo-*larghetto* at best in which Serpina woos her recalcitrant master in the affected tones of simulated love. Everything else moves at a brisk pace within a narrow scale from *allegretto* to *allegro spiritoso*. Royal entertainment demands ceremony and dignity; middle-class entertainment echoes the brisk pace of everyday life.

[21] Rameau, however, is said to have confided to a friend: "If I was thirty years younger, I would go to Italy; Pergolese would be my model. . . . But at over sixty one realizes that one must stay where one is" (C. Girdlestone, *Jean-Philippe Rameau* [London, 1957], p. 492).

[22] In criticizing the famous monologues of the French opera Rousseau complains about their uniformly slow tempos. "Nothing is so dragging, so sluggish, so dull as these beautiful monologues which all the world admires while yawning. They pretend to be sad, but are only boring, to touch the heart, but afflict only the ear." ("Rien n'est si traînant, si lâche, si languissant, que ces beaux monologues que tout le monde admire en bâillant: ils voudroient être tristes, et ne sont qu'ennuyeux; ils voudroient toucher le coeur, et ne font qu'affliger les oreilles" [*Lettre*, p. 213].)
Rousseau praises the Italians for the manner in which their lively accompaniments with subdivisions of notes render their *adagio* more agreeable and more energetic while also keeping time. It would seem that he speaks here of Alberti basses, which we shall treat presently.

An essential aspect of the change in the style of music from baroque to rococo lies in the transition from polyphony to homophony. In both cases several voices are employed. In polyphony each voice has a melodic line of its own; in homophony the highest voice carries the melody, the other voices accompany. The fugue is a symbol of the baroque, the "classical" sonata of the emerging rococo. But the baroque, too, had a homophonic style. Failure to differentiate between baroque and rococo homophony is the reason why there is still confusion about a proper delineation of the two styles in music. Two examples will illustrate the difference:

Handel, Sarabande from Suite in D minor

Pergolesi, Sonata in B♭ major

In Handel's Sarabande the melody is in the highest voice just as in Pergolesi. But there is a world of difference between these two homophonic styles. Handel's texture is heavy and saturated, Pergolesi's is light and airy; Handel has a preference for a strong and low bass, Pergolesi favors the middle and high registers. More fundamental, however, are these differences:

1. Handel's bass is actually a melodic line; Pergolesi's is mere accompaniment;

2. Handel almost always gives the full harmony, and the bass has preferably the root of the harmony—these are the reasons for the heaviness of his texture. Pergolesi shies away from full harmony—so much so that for most of the time he employs no more than two voices—and he abandons the one-sided preference for the root in the bass. These are the reasons for the lightness of his texture. As a substitute for the full harmony of the baroque, Pergolesi uses the broken triadic movement said to have been invented by a Venetian dilettante, Domenico Alberti (1710–40), and therefore called "Alberti" basses. These broken triadic figures dissolve the heaviness of harmony and enliven the pace of the music.[23] They replace, as it were, the weightiness of dialogue between bass and

[23] It is astonishing with what clarity of perception Rousseau recognizes these elements of stylistic change. The accompaniment, he says, rather than constituting a real melodic line, should be a light murmur comparable to the sound of a brook or the twittering of the birds ("un accompagnement contraint et continu, qui fît plutôt un léger murmure qu'un véritable chant, comme seroit le bruit d'une rivière ou le gazouillement des oiseaux" [ibid., pp. 195–96]). Again, Rousseau seems to describe the effect of the Italian Alberti basses.

Mozart, Sonata in C major, K. 545*

*From Nathan Broder's edition of *Mozart Sonatas and Fantasies for the Piano*. Used here with kind permission of Theodore Presser Company, Bryn Mawr, Pa.

melody in the baroque with the graceful and lively conversation of the rococo, a conversation which loses in depth what it gains in animation.

3. Finally, Handel tries to give to each tone of the melody its own harmony: harmonic change equals—and at times surpasses—melody in importance. Indeed, it is a question whether melody here is not really an exponent of harmony rather than harmony being an accompaniment of melody. At any rate, if one plays the Sarabande melody without its harmonic base, little remains. Harmony is too powerful an element in baroque music to be left out without irreparable loss. Pergolesi, on the other hand, restricts change of harmony to a bare minimum. Melody emerges as the leading element of his musical conception. If one plays his sonata without accompaniment, it is incomplete, to be sure, but its essence emerges intact.

Mozart's indebtedness to the world of Italian rococo is evident in his characteristic Sonata in C major (K. 545), where there is greater thematic coherence, longer breath, stronger continuity; yet the basis of his style already exists in Pergolesi, who died twenty years before Mozart was born. What then distinguishes a baroque from a rococo melody? For one thing, the rhythm. In Mozart's melody the long notes fall naturally on the strong beat. The rhythmic pattern is utterly simple; it nevertheless dominates the whole melody without receiving either supplement or contradiction from the rhythm of other voices, notably the bass.[23a]

[23a] Simplicity, regularity, symmetry are the basis of rococo rhythm and meter. But to these Mozart adds, particularly in his later years, the elements of variety and surprise and the principle of increased rhythmic motion, a rhythmic discovery peculiarly his own (see Edward E. Lowinsky, "On Mozart's Rhythm," *The Musical Quarterly*, XLII [April, 1956], 162–86).

Bach, Italian Concerto, 2nd movement

Handel's Sarabande seems at first no less simple than Mozart's *Allegro*. But there are essential differences: the long notes go against the beat, producing an interesting conflict between rhythm and meter. (The rhythmic pattern is characteristic of the Sarabande in general, certainly; but then the Sarabande is characteristic of the baroque; the rococo and the classicism following in its wake discontinue the Sarabande.[24]) Moreover, Handel's bass not only has an independent melodic line, but it also complements rhythmically the motion of the melody. This demonstrates the baroque desire for rhythmic continuity as against the striving of the rococo for neat, small, symmetrical forms.

To penetrate more deeply into the nature of baroque versus rococo style we shall choose examples of the highest art in both styles. We begin with the *Andante* from Bach's Italian Concerto.

The slow movement of Bach's Italian Concerto operates, as it were, on three levels: the accompaniment is formed by an independent melody with its own logic and continuity; this accompanying melody is interrupted, or rather articulated, by the rhythmic motif of a repeated bass tone, a bell motif, likewise consistent and continuous. Over these is spanned a melody that surges on and on in a free, irregular, complex rhythm constantly going against the natural beat marked by the accompaniment and eschewing easy divisions into clear phrases.

The surging melody conceals the motivic form of the substructure. This motivic form is one of the essential aspects of Bach's musical organism. The prototype of Bach's music, the fugue, reveals the relationship between the part and the whole, the fugal subject and the fugal form. This relationship also governs his preludes, his suites, his concertos, each time in a different form: it is fundamental to Bach's thought. The B-flat minor prelude from the *Well-Tempered Clavier* (Pt. I) illustrates how, even in the free form of the prelude, the closest relationship exists between the smallest part and the whole.

[24] The one Sarabande to be found in the keyboard Suite in E major by Pergolesi is a most interesting example of stylistic change: it begins in the characteristically heavy Sarabande rhythm: ♩ ♩ ♪ ♩ | ♩ ♩ ♪ , but immediately goes on to dissolve the ancient pattern into livelier rhythms: ♩ |♫ ♫ ♫ ♫ ♫ ♫ ♩♫|♩ ♪♩ ♪ ♩ | ♫ ♫ ♫ ♫ ♫ ♫|♫ ⁓

Bach, B♭ minor Prelude from *Well-Tempered Clavier* (I)

The relationship between the germinating motif ♫♫ ♪ and the prelude as a whole is not sufficiently understood in its complexity if one says "the whole grows out of this motivic germ." While this is true on one level, it is false on another. Obviously, an entirely different form, indeed, a work of art of a decidedly inferior character, could grow out of the same motif, a form lacking the power, the great line, the expressive individuality of Bach's prelude. To do justice to Bach's work we must acknowledge the existence in the composer's mind of a vision of the whole which is not conditioned by the germinating motif. It might be closer to the truth to say that the germinating motif is conditioned by the vision of the whole. But we might be closest to the truth if we say that the whole and the parts, including the smallest elements, the motives, are inseparable and are in constant mutual influence upon each other.

Bach's music may be viewed as a perfect symbol of the universe as seen by Gottfried Wilhelm Leibniz (1646–1716), a universe formed by Monads,[25] which are defined as simple,[26] individuated,[27] energetic substances in a constant flux of activity and change,[28] related to other Monads through a pre-established harmony.[29] In this picture of the universe the Monad stands for the motif, the pre-established harmony for the vision of the whole. A Bach motif can indeed be defined in terms of a Leibniz Monad, whose main attribute is force and energy; it is con-

[25] Leibniz wrote the *Monadology* in 1714. It is interesting to note that there is an interval of only eight years between this philosophical work and Bach's *Well-Tempered Clavier* (Pt. I), which was written in 1722. I use the following edition: Leibniz, *The Monadology*, trans. with introduction and notes by Robert Latta (Oxford, 1898 [second impression 1925]). The *Monadology* is arranged in ninety paragraphs. The following quotations refer to paragraphs.

[26] "The Monad . . . is nothing but a *simple* substance . . ." (§ 1).

[27] "[E]ach Monad must be different from every other" (§ 9).

[28] "[E]very . . . Monad is subject to change . . . this change is continuous in each" (§ 10) and "the natural changes of the Monads come from an *internal principle*" (§ 11).

[29] Leibniz' famous dictum that "Monads have no windows" (§ 7) means that each Monad follows in its continuous activity only its own individual principle. The fact that the infinite numbers of Monads nevertheless act in accord with each other is due to the pre-established harmony in which God created them: "the influence of one Monad upon another is only ideal, and it can have its effect only through the mediation of God, in so far as in the ideas of God any Monad rightly claims that God, in regulating the others from the beginning of things, should have regard to it" (§ 51). In like manner Leibniz explains "the union or rather the mutual agreement of the soul and the organic body. The soul follows its own laws, and the body likewise follows its own laws; and they agree with each other in virtue of the pre-established harmony between all substances, since they are all representations of one and the same universe" (§ 78).

stantly active and variable, but in the nature of its action and change it follows its own inner principle; the Monad is a mirror of the whole,[30] even as the whole consists of the Monads. Yet, each Monad mirrors the whole, the universe, in its own individual fashion,[31] so that the immense order and harmony of the universe is accompanied by infinite variety.[32]

In a Bach fugue we find the most perfect order together with the greatest possible variety. The fugal subject is at once identical throughout and variable throughout. It appears in constantly varying pitches, keys, shapes, time forms, and directions. Yet, it never loses its identity.

So far we have dealt with order and variety in temporal succession. There exists also an order of the simultaneous: "In my philosophy continuity governs in the order of temporal succession; it governs likewise in the order of the simultaneous. Owing to this principle [of continuity] the universe is completely filled,[33] and empty spaces are to be relegated to the realm of imagination."[34]

Bach's polyphony corresponds to Leibniz' simultaneousness or *plenum;* as the multiplicity of Monads is regulated by a pre-established harmony so is the multiplicity of Bach's temporal and polyphonic figurations governed by the pre-existent laws of counterpoint and harmony.

[30] "Now this connexion or adaptation of all created things to each and of each to all, means that each simple substance has relations which express all the others, and, consequently, that it is a perpetual living mirror of the universe" (§ 56).

[31] "And as the same town, looked at from various sides, appears quite different and becomes as it were numerous in aspects; even so, as a result of the infinite number of simple substances, it is as if there were so many different universes, which, nevertheless are nothing but aspects of a single universe, according to the special point of view of each Monad" (§ 57).

[32] "And by this means there is obtained as great variety as possible, along with the greatest possible order; that is to say, it is the way to get as much perfection as possible" (§ 58).

[33] Leibniz ordinarily uses the term *plenum* to express at once his idea of a universe filled with Monads and his opposition to the notion of the vacuum held by the atomists (see *Monadology*, p. 72n). In his *Principles of Nature and Grace*, written at the same time as, and as a prelude to, the *Monadology*, Leibniz puts it this way: "All nature is a *plenum*. There are simple substances everywhere, which are actually separated from one another by activities of their own, and which continually change their relations. . . . Since the world is a *plenum* all things are connected together and each body acts upon every other. . . . Hence it follows that each Monad is a living mirror, or a mirror endowed with inner activity, representative of the universe, according to its point of view, and as subject to rule as is the universe itself" (*Monadology*, pp. 408–9).

[34] Letter to Varignon in G. W. Leibniz, *Philosophische Werke*, ed. Ernst Cassirer (5 vols.; 3rd ed.; Leipzig, 1915), II, 556–59; translated in *ibid.*, pp. 75–78; discussed in H. J. Kanitz, *Das Übergegensätzliche gezeigt am Kontinuitätsprinzip bei Leibniz* (Hamburg, 1951), p. 53.

The Law of Continuity[35] formulated by Leibniz in 1687 as originating in the infinite and producing a world in which everything is connected with everything else, and the principle of the preservation of energy[36] stated one year earlier, find an artistic symbol of extraordinary force in Bach's music with its surging dynamics and its unbroken line of continuity. The logic of Bach's continuity can be defined in the same terms in which Leibniz defines the Monad: "every present state of a simple substance [Monad] is naturally a consequence of its preceding state, in such a way that its present is big with its future."[37]

An analogy such as the one between Bach's music and Leibniz' philosophy is not so much a fantasy of a modern interpreter of baroque music as it is an idea thoroughly at home in baroque thought itself. It is perhaps sufficient to point to Johannes Kepler, who published his *Harmonices mundi* in 1619, presenting in it his vision of the mathematical beauty of the world, conceivable in numbers mathematically, in tones musically. Indeed, he did not refrain from presenting the motions of the planets in musical notation to indicate their harmonious relationship. This concept, rooted in Pythagoreanism and in Platonic thought, was taken up in Renaissance philosophy by Nicholas of Cusa; it was indeed the *spiritus rector* of Copernicus' new astronomy. Kepler, as a youth, had drunk deeply from Copernicus' cup; he felt its intoxicating power till the end of his life. Leibniz was thoroughly at home in the Pythagorean tradition[38] and in its more modern presentations through Nicholas of Cusa, Copernicus, and Kepler. "Music," he wrote in the famous passage of a

[35] Latta defines Leibniz' Law of Continuity in this manner: "Everything is continually changing, and in every part of this change there is both a permanent and a varying element. That is to say, at any moment everything both 'is' and 'is not,' everything is becoming something else—something which is, nevertheless, not entirely 'other' " (*Monadology*, p. 223n). Is there a better way to describe the unity of constancy and change, permanence and flux in a Bach fugue?

[36] Leibniz holds that nature always preserves the same quantity of force (see *Monadology*, pp. 90–91). Kuno Fischer, *Gottfried Wilhelm Leibniz* (Heidelberg, 1902), pp. 394–99, discusses the principle of "Die Erhaltung der Kraft" and some of the ideas on rest and motion following from this principle in the following manner; I translate (p. 398): "All bodies are in constant motion, even in the state of rest; the moving force is always alive, even in the state of inertia: therefore, rest and motion are not opposites, but gradual differences. Were they opposites, no transition from one to the other could take place, or that transition would have to be made by a leap, which is contrary to nature's principle. Rest, therefore, must be considered as an infinitely small motion, inertia as infinitely small activity, dead force as the beginning of the element of the living force (*vis elementaris*)."

[37] *Monadology*, § 22.

[38] In a recent article in *Musik in Geschichte und Gegenwart*, Vol. VIII (1960), cols. 498–503, Rudolf Haase speaks of his philosophy as a "secularized Pythagoreanism."

letter of April 17, 1712, "is unconscious mathematics."[39] To put it differently: music is a sounding symbol of the cosmic harmony based on mathematical laws. In the preface to the *Théodicée* of 1710, the only work published in his lifetime, he says:

> God is the ocean, of which we have received but a few drops; in *us* resides some power, some knowledge, some kindness, but in God they exist in all their plenitude. Order, symmetry, harmony delight us; painting and music are sparks of it. But God is all order, He always observes the right proportions, and He is the architect of the universal harmony.[40]

No wonder, then, that Leibniz, in his attempt to clarify the marvelous concord of body and soul, chooses (aside from the well-known simile of the two clocks) the following musical metaphor:

> this concomitance, which I maintain, is comparable to several different bands of musicians or choirs, playing their parts separately, and so placed that they do not see or even hear one another, which can nevertheless keep perfectly together by each following their own notes, in such a way that he who hears them all finds in them a harmony that is wonderful and much more surprising than if there had been any connexion between them.[41]

[39] "Musica est exercitium arithmeticae occultum nescientis se numerare animi" (*Leibnitii epistolae ad diversos*, ed. Fr. Korthold [Leipzig, 1734–42], letter 154). In the *Principles of Nature and Grace* (*Monadology*, p. 422), he wrote: "Music charms us, although its beauty consists only in the harmonies of numbers and in the counting (of which we are unconscious but which nevertheless the soul does make) of the beats or vibrations of sounding bodies, which beats or vibrations come together at definite intervals." Kuno Fischer has made an attempt—unsuccessful, I believe—to deny the obvious meaning of this statement and to ascribe to Leibniz a genuine aesthetic judgment that would make him almost a predecessor of Kant's aesthetics (in *Gottfried Wilhelm Leibniz*, pp. 500–4).

[40] G. W. Leibniz, *Die philosophischen Schriften*, ed. C. I. Gerhardt (7 vols.; Berlin, 1875), Vol. VI: *Essais de théodicée sur la bonté de Dieu*, etc., p. 27.

[41] *Monadology*, p. 47; see also Kanitz, *Das Übergegensätzliche*, p. 143. It is perhaps not superfluous to add that the present writer is fully aware of the precariousness of analogies between an artistic form and a philosophical system. He has attempted to follow the standards set up by himself in another context:

"1) The phenomena that are examined in two or more fields must be studied exactly and independently of each other;

2) The chronological connection must be convincing;

3) The phenomena studied should not be of a peripheral but of a structural character;

4) The analogy should consist in basic concepts that underlie the structure of the different branches of expression in question;

5) Any evidence to the effect that the analogies correspond to the philosophy or vision of a particular time would be most welcome as irrefutable corroboration, but

Leibniz' ideas on music reverberated in the circle of Bach's friends and admirers, however partial the echo may have been.[42] It may suffice to refer to Lorenz Mizler (1711–78), who studied with Bach in Leipzig and was promoted to *magister* following his dissertation on the thesis that music is a part of philosophy.[43] Mizler was a follower of Christian Wolff (1679–1754), translator and systematizer of Leibniz' philosophy who attempted a conciliation between Leibniz, Descartes, and Spinoza. Mizler's conviction that "the same reason that governs the universe also governs music"[44] was in the best Leibniz tradition.

Mizler was founder and editor of the *Neu eröffnete musikalische Bibliothek* (1739–54),[45] organ of the Korrespondierende Sozietaet der musikalischen

---

it should not be judged indispensable—because basic concepts may work in the human mind both consciously and subconsciously" (Edward E. Lowinsky, "The Concept of Physical and Musical Space in the Renaissance," *Papers of the American Musicological Society for 1941* [1946], pp. 57–84, 64).

Analogies between Bach's music and Leibniz' philosophy have been attempted before. I refer merely to Hans H. Eggebrecht's "Bach und Leibniz," in *Berichte über die wissenschaftliche Bachtagung* (Leipzig, 1951), pp. 431–42, where the reader will also find mention of previous literature on the question. The present attempt was worked out independently.

[42] It is not without interest that the old and venerable medieval division of music into *musica mundana, humana*, and *instrumentalis* can still be found in the work of the great Bach apostle Johann Philipp Kirnberger, *Die Kunst des reinen Satzes in der Musik, Zweyter Theil, Dritte Abtheilung* (Berlin, 1779). On pp. 176–77 Kirnberger writes on "Eintheilung der Musik" and mentions "die Musik der *Welt*, die *menschliche* und die *harmonische*, oder die, so durch Werkzeuge hervorgebracht wird." He defines the "music of the world" as consisting "in a proportionate order of the colors, the elements, and the natural bodies which are all harmonically ordered"; the "human music" as consisting "in a harmonious relation between soul and body singly as well as united"; the "harmonic music" as formed by "natural sounds apt to produce tunes and melodies."

In the preceding paragraph he quoted the "definition of music as given by Caesar Capranica in the year 1591 in Rome." Here music is said to "comprehend all science and even philosophy," and is held to occupy, according to Boethius, "the first place among the seven liberal arts"; "its order in number, weight, and measure is well proportioned."

[43] *Dissertatio, quod musica ars sit pars eruditionis philosophicae* (1734).

[44] "[D]ass die Vernunft, die über alles herrschet, auch in der Musik herrschen müsse" (H. G. Hoke, in *Musik in Geschichte und Gegenwart*, Vol. IX [1961], cols. 388–92).

[45] The most cursory examination of Mizler's *Musikalische Bibliothek* reveals its preoccupation with the mathematical foundation of music. The first volume of 1739 opens programmatically with "Meiboms Vorrede über die Scribenten von der alten Griechischen Musik" (that is, the preface of Marcus Meibom to his celebrated edition of ancient authors on music in Greek accompanied by translations in Latin [Amsterdam, 1652]). In the dedication to Queen Christina of Sweden, Meibom speaks of music as that discipline that, in ancient times, comprised every branch of learning and wisdom, and as the art tied to nature by eternal laws. He speaks of ancient musical thinkers and starts their line with Pythagoras and ends it with Boethius.

Wissenschaften,[46] likewise founded by him, which Bach joined in 1747, offering a triple canon for six parts and the canonic variations over *Vom Himmel hoch* as his contribution. It has been calculated that the triple canon for six parts can be resolved in 480 different ways,[47] and it is not

---

He insists that all Pythagoreans learned and performed music. And Pythagorean ideas are of course discussed time and again in the treatises by the seven ancient authors edited by him.

The volume continues with "Printzens Musikalische Kunst-Übungen," dealing with the doctrine of musical intervals (Dresden, 1689); it contains two writings by the great theoretician of musical temperament Andreas Werckmeister, a *Horologium Musicum* (!), David Kellner's *General-Bass*, and, amazingly enough, a translation of Henricus Cornelius Agrippa's chapter on music in his treatise *De incertitudine et vanitate scientiarum* (*ca.* 1544). This great skeptic, who delivers in his treatise a devastating critique of all sciences, also criticizes the music of his time for its frivolity and lasciviousness. At the same time he is a great admirer of the ancient philosophy of music and a fiery adherent of Pythagorean principles. Unquestionably, Mizler translated this chapter with the intention of commenting on his own time and his own ideas.

Of particular interest is the publication of Chapter XIII of Erhard Weigel's *Idea der ganzen Mathematik* (1669), which deals with music; for Weigel, famous professor of mathematics at the University of Jena, was the teacher of Leibniz.

It is well known that Mizler did all in his power to defend Bach against the attack of Scheibe. He published Magister Birnbaum's defense, as well as that of Christoph Gottlieb Schröter, and probably wrote some unsigned pieces himself (see David and Mendel, *The Bach Reader*, pp. 237–52, for the highlights of the controversy). It is significant that Bach's second defender, Christoph Gottlieb Schröter, appears in the *Musikalische Bibliothek* with an essay on "Die Notwendigkeit der Mathematik bey gründlicher Erlernung der musikalischen Composition" (Vol. II, No. 2, pp. 201–76 [1746]).

[46] Even in the founding and naming of this society Mizler seems to have followed Leibniz, who founded the "Sozietät der Wissenschaften."

[47] Friedrich Smend, *Johann Sebastian Bach bei seinem Namen gerufen* (Kassel, 1950), pp. 11–24; Smend goes on to show how by various applications of numerological procedures the names of Bach and Handel can be found in the notes of the canon. I take no stand here on the validity of either all musical resolutions or of the numerological procedures involved. I am indebted to my young colleague, composer John M. Perkins, for tackling the problem of canonic permutations posed by Bach's triple canon. His calculations, made independently, are more explicit than those of Smend and so useful that I shall quote them here in their entirety:

"The number of possible permutations of *n* different things is equal to *n*!. Thus, neglecting for the moment the musicality of the results, any 6-voice piece may be written out in $6! = 6 \times 5 \times 4 \times 3 \times 2 \times 1 = 720$ different "inversions," by octave transposition of the lines. If not only the original form but also the true (mirror) inversion, retrograde, and retrograde-inversion (page upside-down) forms are counted, there are $4 \times 720 = 2880$ potential solutions. In the case of the Bach canon, it may be felt that only one of the 6 lines in each form serves well as the bass (primarily because of the resolution of $^6_4$ chords). This eliminates 5/6 of the possibilities, leaving $2880/6 = 480$. (In other words, each of the four forms is counted as having $(6-1)! = 5! = 5 \times 4 \times 3 \times 2 \times 1 = 120$ solutions.) The musical quality of the inversion, retrograde, and retrograde-inversion forms is a separate question of course; and it seems likely that in a perpetual canon by inversion the inversion and retrograde-inversion forms will not differ very fundamentally from the original and retrograde

unlikely that Bach, well aware of the musico-mathematical philosophy of his friend, admirer, and former student, chose the canon with great deliberation.[48] The unsurpassed master of canon and fugue introduced himself to the new and exclusive society[49] by a recondite form which was the most intriguing symbol of universal harmony conceivable: it represented a sound image of the most perfect unity, multiplicity, and harmony. It also represented the religious symbol of the Trinity in the perfect union of its three diverse themes.

The canon had become a shibboleth in the struggle between old and new. In 1723 Mattheson gave over a hundred pages of his *Critica musica*[50] to a debate entitled "Anatomy of the Canon" between himself and Heinrich Bokemeyer, Cantor of Wolfenbüttel, on the merits of the canon. Bokemeyer saw in the canon the true guide to the pinnacle of art.[51] Mattheson demanded to know where the listener was whose heart was ever stirred by a canon.[52] "Truly," he exclaims, "it takes more *connoissances* to compose a single *monodiam* to stir the heart than to produce a thousand *canones*."[53] Bokemeyer concedes that canons, as syllogisms in logic, are being ridiculed nowadays; but he insists that the syllogism remains the only way to find truth as, in his time, the learned Leibniz, and, following him, Professor Wolff, have solidly proven; likewise, the canon remains the foundation of all art.[54] The connection between canonic art and Leibniz' logic is noteworthy, and so is the fact that Bokemeyer belonged to Mizler's Musical Society, where he was accepted

---

forms, respectively. But I think all 120 solutions of the original form are good (all tritones are satisfactory, etc.) although not really very different from one another."

[48] The canon appeared on the portrait (Haussmann, 1746) that Bach, as a new member of the society, had to contribute. But "it was also printed separately for distribution among the members" (see *The Bach Reader*, p. 177, where the canon is reproduced in the form in which Mizler printed it in Vol. IV, Pt. 1 of his *Musikalische Bibliothek*).

[49] Bach was the fourteenth member and the Society was limited by statute to twenty members—a number it failed to reach when Leopold Mozart declined its invitation. (The reason for this declination may be guessed from Leopold Mozart's remarks on Mizler's Society in his *Gründliche Violinschule* of 1756 [paragraph 6 of the first chapter of the Introduction], where, after a suitable compliment on the founding of the Society, he says that its learned members, in his opinion, would render a greater service to music by precise investigations of how to build better violins than by long-winded discourses on parallel fifths and octaves or whole series of measurements of "paper intervals.")

[50] Hamburg, 1722–25; facsimile ed. by Frits A. M. Knuf (Amsterdam, 1964), pp. 235–368: *Die Canonische Anatomie*.

[51] *Ibid.*, p. 240.

[52] *Ibid.*, p. 233.

[53] *Ibid.*, p. 262.

[54] *Ibid.*, p. 250.

as a member in the same year, 1739, as Stölzel and Telemann.[55] Finally, it should be recalled that Mizler, founder and president of the Musical Society, assumed the symbolic name Pythagoras, thereby confessing his musical creed in an unmistakable fashion.

If Bach's polyphony has its ideological background in Leibniz' philosophy, another world opens in the music of the young Mozart. We choose the *Andante* from the Sonata in D major K. 311, composed in 1778, as a suitable example for comparison.

Mozart, instead of operating on a multiplicity of levels, concentrates on one single melody, subordinating everything else thereto. This is the homophonic texture of the *style galant:* one melody and a light accompaniment that renounces any claims on independence, melodic or rhythmic. The rhythm is simple, the accents are regular, the phrases are clear-cut: the smallest unit consists of two measures, which it expands to four and eight measures. These eight-measure phrases are organized into question and answer, or—to use ordinary musical terminology—into antecedent and consequent. The consequent repeats the melody of the antecedent; only the ending differs: the antecedent remains open, the consequent concludes the phrase, or—again in musical terminology—the antecedent cadences in the dominant, the consequent in the tonic. Instead of one great line of melody, a number of shorter melodies follow each other; more precisely, the first alternates with a second melody and then returns, giving the listener the pleasure of recognizing an already familiar tune. The movement is in rondo form and more alternations and returns follow.

The play between *forte* and *piano* in short intervals highlights the sectional structure as well as the conversational character of this music. Whereas Bach's music sounds, in Goethe's words, "as if the eternal harmony conversed with itself," Mozart's *Andante* reflects something of the dialogue character of the new style. Instead of mirroring the universe, this new style addresses itself to the listener. Mozart's movement presents an art of easy orientation. Its clear order, its constant references and

---

[55] Mattheson prints the answers of Heinichen and Telemann to a questionnaire on the use and significance of the canon at the end of his "dialogue" with Bokemeyer. Heinichen rejects the canon completely; Telemann, interestingly enough, takes a careful position in the middle, admitting the use of the canon in the composition of church music and in the teaching of composition but denying that it is the foundation of music; rather, the canon is like one of many rooms in the great palace of the musical art (*ibid.*, pp. 358–60). As a final triumph, however, Mattheson publishes a letter from Bokemeyer announcing his abject surrender: "I have now the unexpected good fortune to be guided by Your Excellency to melody, and thus, as it were, *a peripheria ad centrum,* as the only real fountain of the true art of music."

Mozart, Sonata in D major, K. 311, 2nd movement

Andante con espressione

repetitions, its symmetry, its concentration on one main musical event, the melody, render it rational and comprehensible to all. Indeed, its ingratiating quality and natural simplicity rest on its basis in folk song. We need only to strip the melody of a few ornamental notes to reduce it to a form that reveals its folk song-like character:

The simplicity of rococo melody in general contrasts with the excess of ornamentation which characterizes baroque melody.[56] Rococo ornamentation never obscures the melody, it merely graces it. Baroque ornamentation covers the melody with a growth so luxuriant as to change the lightest song into a more or less ponderous affair. This is well illustrated in one of Couperin's most charming melodies, *La Pastorelle*, from the *premier ordre* of the first book of *Pièces de clavecin* of 1713 (see page 189).

The mere title with the added indication *naïvement* is evidence that Couperin intended to create a small, unpretentious form of a pastoral and folklike character. And if the ornamentations were left out he would have succeeded fairly well. The form is simple. Aside from its various repetitions, it can be schematically expressed in this manner: A B A'. The melody is constructed in two- and four-measure phrases; the rhythm and melody have undeniable charm and grace, which are the reasons why Couperin is so often characterized as a rococo composer. Yet, the basis of Couperin's art remains baroque in character, essentially for two reasons:

1. The interminable ornamentations prevent his melodies from achieving the typical fast rococo gait; they obstruct the intended lightness of character.

[56] If baroque melody appears simple in its notation, as for example in a Corelli sonata for violin and figured bass, it is because the performer was expected to improvise virtuoso ornamentations. Corelli himself executed his sonatas in this manner. We are fortunate to have an edition of his sonatas, published in Amsterdam (1715), where the ornamentations (*agréments*) of his Adagio movements were printed "comme il les joue." (Hans-Peter Schmitz, *Die Kunst der Verzierung im 18. Jahrhundert* [Kassel, 1955], pp. 55–61, prints three slow movements in their original, simple notation and with Corelli's ornamentations; Ernst T. Ferand, *Die Improvisation, Das Musikwerk* [Cologne, 1956], No. 27, pp. 112–13, publishes a fourth Adagio in the same manner.)

Couperin, *La Pastorelle*

2. Couperin's bass never abandons its fundamental baroque character: it is always motivic, always independent and melodic. In the most homophonic of his pieces there are always two lines. But "singleness of melody" is an inalienable property of the rococo style in music. And this was well understood by the protagonists of the new style, the greatest, most articulate, and most passionate of whom was Jean-Jacques Rousseau. [57]

Rousseau laid down most of his ideas on music in his *Dictionnaire de musique*, the result of sixteen years of labor, originating in the articles on music he had written for the great *Encyclopédie*. [58] To be sure, this is the most personal dictionary on music ever written; it is also the most delightful and readable one. If it is often not objective, for that very reason it is a vitally important document of the musical creed of the time. If Rousseau had been asked which of the articles in his *Dictionnaire de musique* he considered the most important, he would undoubtedly have replied, the article on *unité de mélodie* (which must be translated not with "unity," but with "singleness of melody"). It is this article to which, time and again, he refers the reader; it expresses his musical philosophy in a nutshell, and it is a superb summary of the new aesthetics.

I shall translate some of the most striking passages from Rousseau's article "Unité de mélodie": [59]

All fine arts have some unity of subject matter, the source of the pleasure which they afford the spirit. For a divided attention cannot come to rest, and when our attention is occupied by two subjects, that is proof that neither of them satisfies us. There exists in music a successive unity with regard to the subject, by which all voices well linked together form a single whole, which can be grasped in its ensemble and in all its relations.

Evidently, Rousseau refers here to the successive unity of a fugue held together by the use of one single subject. "But," he continues,

---

[57] It may seem that Johannes Mattheson (1681–1764) deserves credit, and priority, for this role. In the endless stream of his writings he stresses time and again the leading role of melody. But for Mattheson, Scheibe, and their partisans, melody was only the *principal* voice; the bass never lost its double function as the foundation of harmony and independent, continuous line (neither in their writings nor in their compositions). Mattheson, who after all wrote a *Generalbass Schule*, is the representative of stylistic transition, Rousseau the spokesman of the stylistic revolution achieved.

[58] Rousseau complains in the "Préface" that he was given no more than three months for that task: "true to my word, at the expense of my reputation, I worked hastily and poorly." To compensate for this he undertook the writing of the *Dictionnaire*.

[59] *Dictionnaire de musique* (Paris, 1768), pp. 536–39.

there exists another unity of subject, finer, more simultaneous, from which springs without one's realizing it the energy of music and the force of its expressions.

When I hear our psalms sung in four parts

—and here Rousseau, the native Calvinist from Geneva, speaks of the Huguenot psalter for four voices by Claude Goudimel—

I am always ravished in the beginning by that full and strong harmony; and the first chords, when they are intoned properly, move me to the point of trembling. But as soon as I have heard the continuation for some minutes my attention slackens, the loud sound gradually dulls my senses, soon it fatigues me — and I end up by feeling bored because I hear nothing but chords. This never happens to me when I hear modern music though its harmony be less vigorous. And I recall that at the Opera in Venice a beautiful aria well performed, far from ever boring me, however long it may have been, aroused an always fresh attention and I heard it with more interest at the end than at the beginning.

This difference stems from that of the character of the two musical styles, one of which is nothing but a sequence of harmonies, whereas the other is a sequence of song. Now the pleasure in harmony is a pleasure of the senses pure and simple, and the pleasure of the senses is always brief; saturation and boredom follow it quickly. But the pleasure in melody and song is a pleasure of interest and feeling which speaks to the heart and which the artist can always sustain and renew through the force of genius.

Music, therefore, must necessarily sing in order to move, to please, to sustain interest and attention. But

—and this is a stab against Rameau and his *Traité de l'harmonie*[60]—

how in our systems of chords and of harmony should music begin to sing? When each part has its own melody, all the parts heard together destroy each other mutually and there will be no melody at all anymore; when all parts sing the same melody, one will have no harmony and the concert will be reduced to a unison.

The manner in which a musical instinct, a certain secret feeling of genius, has resolved this difficulty without seeing it, and has even drawn advantage from it, is very remarkable. Harmony, instead of choking melody, animates, reinforces it, determines it; the diverse parts collaborate without confusion toward the same effect. And

[60] Rameau is indeed named and criticized in Rousseau's article.

although each of them would seem to have its own melody, in all of these united parts one hears only one and the same song emerge. That is what I call singleness of melody. . . . I conclude by declaring that from the principles here established it follows firstly that any music that does not sing is boring, whatever its harmony; secondly that any music in which one distinguishes several simultaneous melodies is bad, and that it results in the same effect as two or more orations pronounced simultaneously in the same tone. [61]

No longer is polyphony a metaphysical cypher; it is merely an art appealing to the senses. In Rousseau's view of music all echoes of a harmony of the universe are dead. Only the listener is alive, and the listener ought to receive music not merely with his senses, but he ought to seek instead "a pleasure of interest and feeling which speaks to the heart. . . . Music, therefore, must necessarily sing in order to move. . . ." The turn from the contemplation of celestial harmony and mathematical order to the heart of man, the feeling, suffering, rejoicing, sympathetic heart of the individual, could not have been stated more emphatically. Man had always been Rousseau's prime concern. The outstanding

[61] Rousseau had already pronounced his theory on *unité de mélodie* in his letter on French music in 1753. He writes there: "To render music interesting, to have it bring to the soul the feelings one wishes to arouse, it is necessary that all parts concur in strengthening the expression of the subject matter, that harmony serve only to render it more energetic, that the accompaniment embellish it without covering it up or disfiguring it, that the bass, in a uniform and simple gait, guide in some fashion singer as well as listener without either of them becoming aware of it. In one word, the whole ensemble must present only one single melody to the ear and one single idea to the mind. This singleness of melody appears to me an indispensable rule no less important than the unity of action in the tragedy; for it is based on the same principle and directed toward the same goal." ("Pour qu'une musique devienne intéressante, pour qu'elle porte à l'âme les sentiments qu'on y veut exciter, il faut que toutes les parties concourent à fortifier l'expression du sujet; que l'harmonie ne serve qu'à le rendre plus énergique; que l'accompagnement l'embellisse sans le couvrir ni le dé-figurer; que la basse, par une marche uniforme et simple, guide en quelque sorte celui qui chante et celui qui écoute, sans que ni l'un ni l'autre s'en aperçoive: il faut, en un mot, que le tout ensemble ne porte à-la-fois qu'une mélodie à l'oreille et qu'une idée à l'esprit" [*op. cit.*, pp. 191–92].)

That Rousseau felt that he had discovered this principle appears in a passage later on where he says that this is a "rule of which no theorist whom I know has talked to this day, which Italian composers alone have felt and practiced, perhaps without ever questioning its existence, and on which depends all sweetness of song, the force of expression, and almost all charm of good music."—("règle dont aucun théoricien, que je sache, n'a parlé jusqu'à ce jour, que les compositeurs italiens ont seuls sentie et pratiquée, sans se douter peut-être de son existence, et de laquelle dépendent la douceur du chant, la force de l'expression, et presque tout le charme de la bonne musique" [*ibid.*, p. 202].)

sciences to him were those concerned with man: psychology, philosophy, aesthetics, ethics, social sciences, education. A man's workshop is society; his laboratory is the self. Rousseau's autobiography, therefore, was much more than a literary exercise in self-revelation; it was for him what anatomy is to a physician. He himself declares his intent in writing the *Confessions* in these words: "I was determined to make it a work unique of its kind, by an unexampled veracity, which, for once at least, would enable the outside world to behold a man as he really was in his inmost self." [62]

It cannot be surprising that to such a man music's chief task would be the portrayal of human emotions. He gives no less than six pages of his *Dictionnaire de musique* to the article on "Expression," which he defines as that "quality through which the musician feels vividly and renders with energy all the ideas that he must render, and all the feelings that he must express." [63] The instructions that Rousseau gives the composer to this end are astonishing in their acuteness, richness, sensitivity, and musicality. They reflect his own musicianship. For he was a singer, [64] he played the *clavecin*, [65] he was capable of performing moderately well on violoncello, zither, and flute, he copied music and for years made a living at it, and, of course, he composed. But when we compare Rousseau, the composer, with Rousseau the aesthetician, we make a strange discovery: as a writer, in his article on expression, but also in those on imitation, harmony, and melody, he made an important contribution to the aesthetic philosophy of the *Sturm und Drang;* as a composer, he was careful not to step beyond the boundaries of the prevailing rococo style. The man who, in his literary work, subordinated everything to veracity, as a composer subordinated veracity to pleasantness. True, in discussing the aesthetics of the imitation of passions, he had already issued this warning:

> Above all, it is well to remember that music's charm lies not only in the imitation, but in an agreeable imitation; and that even declamation, to make a great effect, must be subordinated to the melody in such a manner that one cannot paint the sentiment

---

[62] *Confessions*, p. 534.

[63] "Qualité par laquelle le Musicien sent vivement & rend avec énergie toutes les idées qu'il doit rendre, & tous les sentimens qu'il doit exprimer" (*Dictionnaire*, p. 210).

[64] "He had a voice of ravishing sweetness and his singing was full of expression," said a contemporary (Mercier, *De J.-J. Rousseau*, in the appendix to the *Confessions* of Petitain, quoted by Julien Tiersot in his *Jean-Jacques Rousseau* [2nd ed.; Paris, 1920], pp. 174–75).

[65] "Le clavecin fut pour lui un ami de toute la vie" (*ibid.*).

without giving it that secret charm which is inseparable from it, nor touch the heart without pleasing the ear.[66]

And he continues:

Do not mistake the baroque for the expressive, nor harshness for energy, nor give a shocking presentation of the passions you wish to render, nor do, in a word, as one does at the French opera, where the passionate tone resembles the cries of colic rather than the transports of love.[67]

Rousseau's idea of expressive truth is modified by the Italian concept regarding appeal to the ear. But to get to the core of his musical philosophy, we must now test his ideas by his own compositions, of which none is more famous and historically more important than *Le Devin du village*, "The Village Soothsayer."

We recall that the successful performance in Paris of Pergolesi's *La Serva padrona* took place in August, 1752. In his enthusiasm, Rousseau, at his own expense, had Pergolesi's score engraved and published that same year. But more than that: a few weeks after the run of Pergolesi's intermezzo had started, Rousseau retired to the country to execute his own plans for an intermezzo in the French language modeled along the lines of Pergolesi's work.

With what incredible speed Rousseau wrote libretto and music may be seen from the title page of his score, which, in translation, reads as follows: "The Village Soothsayer, Intermezzo presented at Fontainebleau before their Majesties on the 18th and 24th of October 1752 and in Paris

[66] "Surtout il faut bien observer que le charme de la Musique ne consiste pas seulement dans l'imitation, mais dans une imitation agréable; & que la déclamation même, pour faire un grand effet, doit être subordonnée à la Mélodie: de sorte qu'on ne peut peindre le sentiment sans lui donner ce charme secret qui en est inséparable, ni toucher le coeur si l'on ne plaît à l'oreille" (*Dictionnaire*, p. 211). In reading these words—"nor touch the heart without pleasing the ear"—we feel reminded of that famous passage in Mozart's letter of September 26, 1781, to his father in which, writing about operatic expression, he says: "But passions, violent or not, must never be expressed to the point of tedium, and music, even in the most horrible situation, must never offend the ear but please it even then, hence it must always remain music . . . (*Mozart, Briefe und Aufzeichnungen*, ed. W. A. Bauer and O. E. Deutsch [4 vols.; Kassel, 1963], III, 162).

[67] "N'allez donc pas prendre le baroque pour l'expressif, ni la dureté pour de l'énergie; ni donner un tableau hideux des passions que vous voulez rendre, ni faire en un mot comme à l'Opéra François, où le ton passionné ressemble aux cris de la colique, bien plus qu'aux transports de l'amour" (*Dictionnaire*, pp. 211–12).

at the Royal Academy of Music on the first of March 1753 by J.-J. Rousseau."[68]

If Pergolesi had two actors, excluding the mute servant, Rousseau has three: the shepherd, Colin, the shepherdess, Colette, and the village soothsayer. The plot is of the slightest. Colette has lost Colin's love; in her despair she asks for the assistance of the village soothsayer, who spreads a charm for Colin and advises Colette to be a bit more coy. Colin returns, Colette pretends coldness, and after a bit of a lovers' quarrel in which he threatens to harm himself, Colin is readmitted to Colette's good graces. The village soothsayer unites them in marriage. The rest—and it is the longer part, which shows the weakness of Rousseau as a dramatist—is given to celebrations of various sorts. Rousseau's score is more ambitious than Pergolesi's. He adds choruses, dances, pantomimes, instrumental preludes, and the like.

Rousseau's musical taste is accurately reflected in Colette's airs from the first act, "J'ai perdu tout mon bonheur," and "Si des Galans de la Ville." I quote the initial measures of both airs.

If we compare the text with the music, if we weigh the words "J'ai perdu tout mon bonheur, j'ai perdu mon serviteur" with the easy-going melody in F major, we must admit that the same melody might be sung to the words "J'ai trouvé tout mon bonheur." But there is no denying Rousseau's gift for felicitous melody, astonishing in one who was, after all, a musical dilettante and entirely self-taught as a composer.

While, superficially seen, *Le Devin du village* is nothing but an innocent pastoral play, closer examination reveals a number of social overtones and innuendoes that form a strange, muted counterpoint, a sort of shadow play, accompanying the main play. Though confined to hints, pantomimes, and stage directions, its presence makes itself seen and felt. When Colin throws himself at Colette's feet to ask her forgiveness, she points to a luxurious ribbon that he had received from the lady, "un Ruban fort riche qu'il a reçu de la Dame," the implication is unmistakable; it was a lady of rank who had stolen Colin's affections. To this Colette responds in her second air when she sings that she, too, might have formed tender ties with "les Galans de la Ville," if she had wanted to. The stage directions continue: "Colin throws the ribbon away with disdain. Colette gives him a simpler one, with which she had been adorned, and he receives it with delight."

More explicit is the "Pantomime" which forms a part of the village

[68] *Le Devin du village* (Paris, n.d.).

Rousseau, *Le Devin du village*

Rousseau, *Le Devin du village*

celebration. Not a word is said, but the action, accompanied by instrumental music, evolves in the following manner:

1. entry of the village girl
2. entry of the courtier
3. the courtier catches sight of the village girl; she dances while he observes her
4. he offers her money
5. she refuses it contemptuously
6. he gives her a necklace
7. she tries it on, gazing with delight at her image in the fountain
8. enters the villager
9. noticing the villager's distress, the girl returns the necklace
10. the courtier sees him; he threatens him
11. the girl tries to appease him and makes a sign to the villager to leave; he refuses and the courtier threatens to kill him
12. they both throw themselves at the feet of the courtier, who is moved and unites them
13. all three rejoice—the villagers in their union, the courtier in his good deed.

In this seemingly naïve little pantomime, whose topic goes back to the medieval *pastourelle* and ultimately to ancient bucolic poetry, Rousseau manages to condense his social philosophy. Only two years earlier he had published his first *Discours*, in which he blamed the advance of civilization for the decline of human morals and happiness. Whereas in the traditional *pastourelle* the knight woos the shepherdess, the pantomime portrays the aristocrat as willing to corrupt the country girl: he tries to buy her favors. He is also shown ready to kill her lover. The simple people from the country, on the other hand, are good. The girl rejects the money, but her feminine vanity is tempted by the necklace. The villager is brave; he refuses to leave his sweetheart to the amorous attentions of the courtier. In the play itself, the village soothsayer is content to accept as payment the happiness of the young couple.

Obviously, the pantomime is not the place for a tragedy. Rousseau could not permit it to come to a showdown between the courtier and the villager. Thus the courtier allows himself to be deflected from his purpose and, to the satisfaction of all concerned, including of course the public, he unites the lovers—a happy, if somewhat incongruous, ending. But the attentive spectator must have noticed the ominous implications—the pantomime was the summer lightning, the thunder was yet decades off. Rousseau's intentions were made clear in the music accompanying the two protagonists: the courtier appears to sounds which are characteristic of the feudal pastime *par excellence*, the hunt: fast tempo, 6/8 time, major key, and triadic figures;[69] the villager enters to the sounds of a veritable revolutionary march: major key, a dignified tempo, dotted rhythms of a martial character, and a melodic line irresistibly going forward and underlining the air of determination by a climactic unison of all instruments.

In 1752 Rousseau wrote the prototype of revolutionary music which compares astonishingly well with the revolutionary hymn of a much greater musician, the so-called "seconde Marseillaise" of Etienne Nicolas Méhul,[70] written in 1794.

Le Devin du village makes it easier to understand Rousseau's ideas on music and the style of his own compositions. The musical expression of his operetta is suitable for the simple and unspoiled people of the countryside. An excess of individuality, an exaggeration of feeling, would be out of place. As folk song expresses the joys and sorrows of the people in a simple, unexaggerated, but nevertheless touching manner, so Rousseau wanted to create melodies at once simple and moving. And he succeeded so well that his operetta remained on the stage, with interruptions, till 1828 and became the subject of numerous imitations and parodies. The success of Rousseau's operetta was astonishing, even at court, where the King was

---

[69] See Alexander L. Ringer, "The *Chasse* as a Musical Topic of the 18th Century," *Journal of the American Musicological Society*, VI (1953), 148–59.

[70] See the score in A. Lavignac, *Encyclopédie de la musique, Premier partie, Histoire de la musique, France* (Paris, 1914), pp. 1587–90.

Rousseau, *Le Devin du village*

said to have gone around singing Colette's opening air "with the most execrable voice in the Kingdom and utterly out of tune. . . . " Indeed, the King was ready to grant Rousseau a pension, but Rousseau declined to be presented to him.[71]

Obviously, this success did not rest on Rousseau's musical superiority over Lully, let alone Rameau. On the other hand, I do not share the

[71] See Rousseau's own account in his *Confessions*, pp. 389–92.

opinion that Rousseau's music had nothing to do with his success;[72] notwithstanding its dilettante character, it is both ingratiating and melodious. Notwithstanding its dilettante character? Or, perhaps, because of it? Rather than giving too dogmatic an answer, let us hint at this paradoxical truth: there are changes of style in which a dilettante has the advantage over the professional precisely because he is not burdened by training, tradition, or genius—three forces that were in the way of Rameau, and even more so of Bach, with regard to a rapprochement to the new style. The absence of all three elements in Rousseau's musicianship was a help rather than a hindrance in his struggle for a new French opera style. The dilettante made the breakthrough, the professionals followed. And no one realized more clearly the dilettante character of the whole undertaking, no one understood its necessity better, than Rousseau himself:

> Nothing in my operetta goes beyond the elementary rules of composition with regard to learning and technique: a student of three months could write the "Devin," whereas a learned composer would find it hard to embark upon a course of such decided simplicity.[73]

In no other work of the eighteenth century have taste, style, and ideology met in such felicitous fusion. Of no other work can it be said that its creator was not only the author of libretto and music but also the foremost social ideologist of the century.[74]

The musical characteristics of rococo style, all present in Rousseau's score, are simplicity, pleasantness, melodiousness, homophony, symmetry, regularity in phrase structure and in rhythm and accent. Repelled by the artificiality of courtly taste and style, the creator of the new ideology extolls the virtues of the simple people. Pastoral life, which had been before a mere disguise for the playful characters of noble society, becomes an ideal in and for itself. This new ideology is characterized by a profound faith in the original goodness of man and a complementary belief in the

---

[72] Rousseau himself reports about the première at court: "The piece was very badly acted, but the singing was good, and the music well executed . . . I heard around me women, who seemed to me as beautiful as angels, whispering and saying to each other in a low tone, 'Charming! delightful! every note speaks to the heart!' " (*ibid.*, p. 390).

[73] See Albert Jansen, *Jean-Jacques Rousseau als Musiker* (Berlin, 1884), p. 176.

[74] On Rousseau's ideological position in eighteenth-century thought, see Ernst Cassirer, *The Question of Jean-Jacques Rousseau*, trans. and ed. by Peter Gay (Bloomington, 1963).

corrupting influence of riches, power, and the institutions designed to maintain them. But any faith based on such simple notions of good and bad must needs ignore the ambivalent character of man himself, no matter what the institutions under which he lives. The undeniable shallowness present in much of the art and music of the rococo has its roots in the oversimplification of the views on man and life in the governing philosophy of the era.

Yet such shallowness is often inseparable from a break with tradition. It takes a new simplicity, and even simpleness, to arrive at a new profundity.[75] The new profundity came in the reform operas of Gluck, in the music of the mature Haydn, the late Mozart, and Beethoven. It may seem paradoxical that the deeper exploration of man's emotional life in the works of these composers had an intimate connection with Rousseau's philosophical, literary, and musical writings,[76] whereas Rousseau's own music remained aloof from the emancipation of emotion that he helped initiate. It may seem no less paradoxical that the deepening of Haydn's and Mozart's music was inseparably tied to their discovery of the music of Bach, who had been rejected by the "progressives" of his own generation. In 1781, the year of Haydn's new thematically conceived quartets (op. 33), and the year in which Mozart heard Bach's music for the first time in the house of the Viennese patron of music, Baron van Swieten, the stylistic revolution had come full cycle. The new style was well established. And great musicians such as Haydn and Mozart, and later Beethoven, were now able to appreciate—across the boundaries of styles—the immense musicality of Bach's genius. From that year on, one may say, Bach has never ceased to play a role in the musical life of the world: classics, romantics, moderns have admired him; he had something to say to each of them; he has instructed all of them.

[75] That the ideologists of the new style were keenly aware of this dilemma may be deduced from parts of Grimm's satire on French opera written in the wake of the performances of Pergolesi's intermezzo and Rousseau's operetta and published in Paris in 1753. Here he says: "And I shall teach them to be simple without being flat . . . and I shall teach them to write music which will have character and exact and distinct movement, and which will not be void of expression" (see Oliver Strunk, *Source Readings in Music History* [New York, 1950], p. 632). Two paragraphs later Grimm praises Rousseau's *Devin du village* as a model of the new music.

[76] The connection between the new language of passion in the works of Gluck, Haydn, Mozart, Beethoven, and Rousseau's writings would be a subject worthy of investigation. Gluck and Rousseau met personally, at the composer's insistence, in Paris in 1774. Gluck was deeply imbued with Rousseau's ideas on opera. Rousseau, in his *Observations sur l'Alceste, de Gluck* (*Oeuvres*, pp. 295–322) wrote a magnificent critique of the dramatic weaknesses in Gluck's *Alceste*, but furnished there and elsewhere (*Extrait ... sur un morceau de l'Orphée de M. le Chevalier Gluck*, in *ibid.*, pp. 323–30)

evidence of his great admiration for the German composer. Haydn's change of style from the *galant* to that of *Sturm und Drang* has been connected with the immense liberating force of Rousseau's ideas (Karl Geiringer, *Haydn* [2nd ed.; New York, 1963], pp. 272, 278). During his two visits to Paris (1763–64 and 1778) Mozart must have heard time and again of Rousseau, whose libretto of *Le Devin du village* he set to music in a German adaptation (*Bastien und Bastienne*). Mozart's musico-dramatic rendering of the relationship between the Count and Susanna in *Le Nozze di Figaro* and between Don Giovanni and Zerlina finds its first adumbration in the pantomime of Rousseau's intermezzo. Mozart's librettist da Ponte was so inflamed by Rousseau's first *discours* that he created a scandal by using its topic in the examinations of the seminary in Treviso and found himself summarily dismissed (see *Memoirs of Lorenzo da Ponte*, trans. E. Abbott [2nd ed.; New York, 1959], pp. 27ff.). Many of the ideals that Mozart espoused as a Freemason—he joined a Viennese lodge in 1784—accorded with those of Rousseau's, and there is much similarity in the tender, childlike, sensitive, open-minded, frank characters of both men. A posthumously published cantata, *Die ihr des unermesslichen Weltalls Schöpfer ehrt* (K. 619), had as author of its text a German Rousseau enthusiast (see G. de Saint-Foix, *W.-A. Mozart* [5 vols.; Paris, 1936–46], V, 214–16).

Beethoven, more radically than Haydn and Mozart, had caught fire with Rousseau's social ideas (one has only to ponder the libretto he chose for his only opera, *Fidelio*) and his love of nature. Indeed, he had already been compared by his contemporaries with Rousseau (see Edouard Herriot's account of Baron de Trémont's visit to Beethoven in 1809, and the Baron's comparison of Beethoven with Rousseau in his book *The Life and Times of Beethoven* [New York, 1935], pp. 240–42). As his Conversation Books prove (January, 1820, Blatt 61a; *Ludwig van Beethovens Konversationshefte*, ed. G. Schünemann [Berlin, 1941], I, 207), Beethoven had read the *Contrat social*, which opens with these words: "Man is born free, yet goes everywhere in chains." Recently, the thesis was put forward that Beethoven's *Sonate pathétique* was named after Rousseau's article "Pathétique" in the *Dictionnaire de musique* (pp. 372–73) in which we read at the end: "The true *pathétique* lies in the impassioned accent which is not determined by rules, but which the genius finds and the heart feels without art's being able to formulate its laws in any manner whatsoever" (see Edward E. Lowinsky, "Musical Genius—Evolution and Origins of a Concept," *Musical Quarterly*, L[1964], 328). It would be hard to find a sentiment better suited to express the young Beethoven's frame of mind or to characterize the explosive strength and novelty of the *Sonate pathétique*. But there is more to this thesis: in his *Observations sur l'Alceste* (*Oeuvres*, pp. 300–1) Rousseau distinguishes between three kinds of harmony: diatonic, chromatic, and *pathétique*. Diatonic harmony is the simplest of the three and perhaps the most natural. Chromatic harmony consists in constant changes of key through bass progressions by fifths, "and finally, the harmony that I call *pathétique* consists in combinations of augmented and diminished chords in favor of which one wanders through keys far removed from each other: one strikes the ear with rending intervals and the soul with rapid and fiery ideas designed to disturb and to agitate." Rousseau's concept of *harmonie pathétique* fits the style of the opening movement of Beethoven's *Sonate pathétique* with its minor key, its array of diminished seventh chords and dissonances, its far-flung modulations, its contrasting themes and the rapidity of their change with such perfection that one may indeed regard his sonata as an homage to Rousseau; and this the more so if one considers the second movement, which offers a beautiful example of *unité de mélodie* and a music touching the heart. Rousseau's *Observations*, although left by him in a fragmentary form, were published posthumously in 1781 and made a deep impression on the public interested in music. It is very likely that Beethoven, who admired both Rousseau and Gluck, was acquainted with the *Observations*. That Romain Rolland's (*Beethovens Meisterjahre* [Leipzig, 1930], p. 108) sharp ear detected a close relationship between

If we now, in conclusion, return to the episode in Bach's life that was the point of departure for our investigation, we are compelled to conclude that, whatever their individual competence as musical arbiters, the judgment of the city fathers of Leipzig was in precise accord with the "progressive" taste in London and in Paris. Moreover, it reflected a large current of contemporaneous German opinion; indeed, in terms of chronology, it was considerably ahead of it. The famous critique of Johann Adolph Scheibe on Bach's music, published in 1737, contains a sentence critical of Bach's style that might have been lifted out of Rousseau's *Dictionnaire*, except that it appeared thirty-one years earlier: "All the voices must work with each other and be of equal difficulty, and none of them can be recognized as the principal voice."[77] Here we have a clear anticipation of Rousseau's rejection of counterpoint and polyphony, although, as previously mentioned, the demand for clear audibility of the principal voice is not yet Rousseau's demand for *unité de mélodie*. It is, however, its harbinger.

George Philipp Telemann was the first choice of the council at Leipzig and, indeed, Telemann's music was the ideal fulfillment of the wishes of Mattheson, Scheibe, and their followers. While still rooted in the style of baroque counterpoint, Telemann was the chief pioneer of the "progressive" group that strove for melodiousness, homophony, and simplicity.

---

the impetuous first theme of the first *Allegro* and the aria and duet of the second act of Gluck's *Orfeo* adds further interest. (Rolland must have meant the aria and duet of the third act, *Fortune ennemie*, *Allegro*, in C minor, which, aside from its agitated character, shows a thematic similarity in measures 10–13 of the introduction, and also later in the aria, to Beethoven's first Allegro theme.)

Concerning Gluck's admiration for Rousseau, see his letter to the editor of the *Mercure de France* of février, 1773, pp. 182–84, translated by Oliver Strunk in *Source Readings in Music History*, pp. 681–83. Here Gluck writes: "I admit that I should have produced it [*Iphigénie*] in Paris with pleasure, since by its effect and with the aid of the famous M. Rousseau of Geneva, whom I was planning to consult, we might perhaps together have been able, by searching for a melody noble, affecting, and natural, with an exact declamation according to the prosody of each language and the character of each people, to determine the means which I have in view of producing a music suitable for all the nations and of causing the ridiculous distinctions of national music to disappear. The study which I have made of the works on music of that great man, among others the letter in which he analyzes the monologue in Lully's *Armide*, proves the sublimity of his attainments and the sureness of his taste, and has filled me with admiration. From it I have retained the profound conviction that if he had chosen to apply himself to the practice of that art, he would have been able to accomplish in reality the marvelous effects which antiquity attributed to music. I am charmed to find here the opportunity of rendering to him publicly the tribute of praise which I believe him to merit." Surely, a more enthusiastic testimony for Rousseau's vision in matters musical, and from a more competent source, could hardly be imagined.

[77] *The Bach Reader*, p. 238.

In a song anthology of 1741 Telemann confesses his defect in not having fully realized his ideal, "die Kunst niedrig zu schreiben" ("the art to write in a lowly style"), or, to put it better, the art of simplicity.[78] Telemann eagerly studied the Italian and French music of his time; he absorbed the Polish-Czechoslovakian folk music that he heard when his court temporarily transferred close to the Polish border and later to Cracow. He imitated and used all these styles, and his connections with the new taste in Italy and France were manifold. A few years before Pergolesi he set to music the libretto *Pimpinona*, or "The Uneven Marriage," which anticipates the plot of *La Serva padrona*. When Pergolesi's intermezzo was performed in Paris in 1752 between the acts of a Lully opera, an overture by Telemann preceded the performance. Telemann visited Paris in 1737, supervising the performance of a motet for chorus, soli, and orchestra on Psalm 71, which was executed at the *Concert spirituel*. He wrote a great number of instrumental and vocal works specifically for the Parisians. At the same time he had close ties with Handel in London and with Bach in Leipzig.

It does appear in retrospect that events that took place in musical centers as diverse as Leipzig, London, and Paris were, after all, not unconnected with each other. The revolutions in taste, style, and ideology in Italy, France, Germany, England were different, yet similar: they were different in form, similar in substance. The international aspirations of the eighteenth century appear perhaps as clearly in no other art as in music. The style born out of the travail and struggle of change, the style of the Viennese classics, has become the most international style of music; it has conquered audiences the world over. Lully, in his operas, addressed the French court; Bach, in his church music, the German Protestants. But Haydn, in the instrumental music of his later years, Mozart, in his operas, Beethoven, in his symphonies, address mankind. And mankind has listened to them with a fervor and a devotion that have no parallel in the realm of the arts.

Postcript: There is justifiable doubt about the authenticity of Pergolesi's sonata in B-flat major (pp. 172–73). The only point that really matters in our context is the stylistic contrast between baroque and rococo. Any one of a score of other sonatas would have served the purpose as well.

[78] See Erich Valentin, *Telemann in seiner Zeit* (Hamburg, 1959), p. 35.

Secretum Iter:
Some Uses of Retirement Literature in the Poetry of Pope

BY MAYNARD MACK

I

Among the opposites that Pope liked to think were (or might be) reconciled in a well-regulated temperament and world—drought and rain, wild heath and fruitful field, gravity and gaiety, carelessness and care, "Carthusian fasts" and "fulsome Bacchanals," "mad Good-nature" and "mean Self-love," Montaigne's *aperçus* and Lockes' generalized principles, St. Paul and Aristippus, and dozens more—no polarity is more important for him than that between the life of action and the life of retreat. In his first published letter, printed in the *Spectator* of June 16, 1712, he is already engaged by this question, arguing that neither extreme is tenable—

> in the former Men generally grow useless by too much Rest, and in the latter are destroyed by too much Precipitation—

yet conceding at the end that there is "a sort of People who seem designed for Solitude," and aligning himself with them:

> As for my Part, I am one of those of whom *Seneca* says, *Tam umbratiles sunt, ut putent in turbido esse quicquid in luce est.* Some Men, like Pictures, are fitter for a Corner than a full Light; and I believe

such as have a natural Bent to Solitude, are like Waters which may
be forced into Fountains, and exalted to a great Height, may
make a much nobler Figure, and a much louder Noise, but after
all run more smoothly, equally and plentifully, in their own
natural Course upon the Ground.[1] The Consideration of this
would make me very well contented with the Possession only of
that Quiet which Cowley[2] calls the Companion of Obscurity.

We know of course that this was not consistently Pope's view. He was
to show himself in due course a busy manager of fame and fortune, as
artful in manipulating his auctorial world of booksellers and printers
as Walpole in Parliament; also an eminent amateur landscape architect;
an opener of doors and promoter of benefactions; a political rallying
point; a gregarious acquaintance and tireless friend. Yet the notion that
he belongs to those "designed for Solitude" never dims in him. In part
it motivates his retirement at Twickenham. It starts up on page after
page of his correspondence, often cheek by jowl with the acknowledgment
(not always distinguishable from a boast) that he is harassed by more

---

[1] This interesting contrast derived from the various possible applications of water in
landscape-gardening was to reappear two decades later in Pope's characterization
of the Man of Ross, whose inner nature finds expression in his characteristic use of
outward nature:

> Who hung with woods yon mountain's sultry brow?
> From the dry rock who bade the waters flow?
> Not to the skies in useless columns tost,
> Or in proud falls magnificently lost,
> But clear and artless, pouring through the plain
> Health to the sick, and solace to the swain.

> (*Epistle to Bathurst*, 253–58)

[2] The influence of Cowley's "Several Discourses By Way of Essays, in Verse and
Prose," published posthumously in the *Works* (1668), on the dissemination of retire-
ment attitudes generally and on Pope particularly, is very considerable. Its eleven
informal essays, whose collective import may be gathered from their titles ("Of
Liberty," "Of Solitude," "Of Obscurity," "Of Agriculture," "The Garden," "Of
Greatness," "Of Avarice," "The Dangers of an Honest Man in Much Company,"
"The Shortness of Life and Uncertainty of Riches," "The Danger of Procrastination,"
"Of Myself"), together with the poems and translations accompanying them, give
graceful and sometimes powerful expression to that whole body of convictions, *exempla*,
and images about the priority of ethical and aesthetic self-cultivation—far from the
madding crowd of courts and cities—which the seventeenth and eighteenth centuries
in England inherited from the Roman poets. The reader of these essays and poems
will be struck by the frequency with which some part of them seems to have lingered
in Pope's mind.

The phrase Pope quotes in the *Spectator* letter is from Cowley's translation of the
second chorus of Seneca's *Thyestes* (appended to his essay "Of Obscurity"). See below,
pp. 232–33.

"business" than any mortal should allow himself to be. And it plays, I believe, rather a larger role than has been appreciated in the complex of attitudes, reminiscences, assumptions, and value symbols (everything that constitutes a sensibility and habit of mind) on which his poems draw from first to last. The voice that twentieth-century criticism of Pope has listened to with most discernment is the voice of the man whose restless appetite for "some new thing" is recorded in the proper names we annotate and who tells us, in the characteristic epic-like tones of the *vita activa*,

> Yes, I am proud; I must be proud to see
> Men not afraid of God, afraid of me.

> (*Epilogue to the Satires: Dialogue* ii, 208–9)

We have listened less attentively to another voice that speaks from this tame poetic personality and calls on a tradition and vocabulary of retirement literature which was as "available" to his contemporaries, and as fully charged with imaginative meanings, as the traditions of satire or epic. Elsewhere I intend to discuss this aspect of Pope's life and work in some detail. Here I wish simply to point out that it is a pervasive element in his work, appearing in a variety of unexpected places and forms.

II

I begin with some passages whose connection with the literature of retirement has not been noticed, or at least not stressed. They serve to indicate the extent to which the vocabulary of this tradition was present to the poet's mind and should therefore be present to ours, though the specific source of the vocabulary, in any given instance, may escape us. The following lines from the imitation of Donne's second satire, for instance, make their point adequately if we observe that they discriminate hospitality, in the Tudor sense of manorial and parochial responsibility, as an act whose basis is religious and whose continuance is inseparable from the well-being of the nation, like the maintenance of the Vestal fire at Rome.

> We see no new-built Palaces aspire,
> No Kitchens emulate the Vestal Fire.   (111–12)

It is not imperative, in other words, that we see behind the Vestal allusion, which is Pope's addition to his original, a reminiscence of Cowley's paraphrase of Martial[3] on the happy retired life:

> Let constant Fires the Winters fury tame;
> And let thy Kitchens be a Vestal flame.[4]

Yet once we recognize it, this echo of one of the great set pieces of Roman retirement literature, coming through Cowley, himself an influential spokesman of *beatus ille* sentiment, adds a certain weight to Pope's expressed concern in the poem for the right use of wealth, and associates it, as in so many of his other poems, to a particular way of life.

Something similar may be said of these lines in the *Epistle to Cobham:*

> Court-virtues bear, like Gems, the highest rate,
> Born where Heav'n's influence scarce can penetrate:
> In life's low vale, the soil the virtues like,
> They please as Beauties, here as Wonders strike.   (93–96)

Here it is enough to catch the general reference to retired innocence, and to mark the characteristic gulf that poetry in this vein always places between court or city and "the soil the virtues like." Yet in any account of the genesis of the passage, we should have to note that Pope apparently remembers in its third verse an image from Cowley's paraphrase of Virgil's *O fortunatos nimium:* "In Life's cool vale let my low Scene be laid."[5] The Virgilian passage masses behind Pope's contrast of court and country the most authoritative of all literary precedents:

> si non ingentem foribus domus alta superbis
> mane salutantum totis vomit aedibus undam,
> nec varios inhiant pulchra testudine postis
> inlusasque auro vestis Ephyreiaque aera,
> alba neque Assyrio fucatur lana veneno,
> nec casia liquidi corrumpitur usu olivi:
> at secura quies et nescia fallere vita,
> divus opum variarum, at latis otia fundis.

---

[3] X, xlvii.

[4] *Cowley's Essays*, eds. J. R. Lumby and Arthur Tilley (Cambridge, 1923), p. 113. Hereafter referred to as *Essays*.

[5] *Ibid.*, p. 47.

(speluncae vivique lacus et frigida Tempe
mugitus boum mollesque sub arbore somni)
non absunt; illic saltus ac lustra ferarum,
et patiens operum exiguoque adsueta iuventus,
sacra deum sanctique patres: extrema per illos
Iustitia excedens terris vestigia fecit.[6]

("What though no stately mansion with proud portals disgorges
at dawn from all its halls a tide of visitors, though they never
gaze at doors inlaid with lovely tortoise-shell or at raiment
tricked with gold or at bronzes of Ephyra, though their white wool
be not stained with Assyrian dye, or their clear oil's service spoiled
by cassia? Yet theirs is repose without care, and a life that knows
no fraud, but is rich in treasures manifold. Yea, the ease of broad
domains, caverns, and living lakes, and cool vales, the lowing of
the kine, and soft slumbers beneath the trees — all are theirs.
They have woodland glades and the haunts of game; a youth
hardened to toil and inured to scanty fare; worship of gods and
reverence for age; among them, as she quitted the earth, Justice
planted her latest steps.")

Likewise, Cowley's essay "Of Agriculture," to which this paraphrase of
Virgil is one of his several verse appendices, may easily lurk somewhere
in the genetic background of Pope's lines, its theme being precisely the
superiority of country to court or city as a nourisher of virtues. "We walk
here," Cowley writes (contrasting dark and light in a way that may have
helped father Pope's contrast of mine and garden), "in the light and open
wayes of the Divine Bounty; we grope there in the dark and confused
Labyrinths of Human Malice";[7] and a little later, referring to the poets'
traditional fondness for retreat, he lapses into verses that perhaps also
lingered in Pope's mind, though the horticultural image is of course a
commonplace:

As well might Corn as Verse in Cities grow;
In vain the thankless Glebe we Plow and Sow,
Against th' unnatural Soil in vain we strive;
'Tis not a Ground in which these Plants will thrive.[8]

[6] *Georgics*, II, 461–74. Translations of Latin authors, unless otherwise noted, are
those of the Loeb editions.
[7] *Essays*, p. 37.
[8] *Ibid.*, p. 41.

Such passages, one supposes, show at most reminiscence, not allusion. We move somewhat closer to the latter (though without quite reaching it) in the couplet that begins Pope's description of a visit to Timon's villa in the *Epistle to Burlington:*

> At Timon's Villa let us pass a day,
> Where all cry out, "What sums are thrown away!"
>
> (99–100)

Should we happen to turn from this to William Temple's essay on "The Gardens of Epicurus," we find the following:

> The perfectest figure of a garden I ever saw . . . was that of Moor Park in Hertfordshire, when I knew it about thirty years ago. It was made by the Countess of Bedford, esteemed among the great wits of her time, and celebrated by Dr. Donne; and with very great care, excellent contrivance, and much cost; but *greater sums may be thrown away without effect or honour if there want sense in proportion to money*, or *if nature be not followed; which I take to be the great rule in this, and perhaps in everything else . . . And whether the greatest of mortal men shall attempt the forcing of Nature*, may but be judged, by observing how seldom God Almighty does it himself, by so few, true, and undisputed miracles . . . For my own part *I know not three wiser precepts for the conduct either of princes or private men, than* —
>
> *servare modum, finemque tueri, naturamque sequi.*[9]

It would be rash to claim that Pope's account of Timon's villa insists on our remembering Temple's paragraph. We are given sufficient indication without it that the poet speaks in the guise of the Twickenham garden-philosopher who understands and respects nature, and who therefore knows that the criterion of true possession is not ownership but enjoyment. Yet quite evidently we have in the paragraph an important instance of the body of opinion with which the speaker of the poem allies himself and even possibly the germ of his references to "sums . . . thrown away," the priority of "Sense" over "Expence," and the error of forcing rather than following nature. Moreover, the picture of the foolish Timon's villa stands out with added clarity if we allow ourselves to glimpse beyond it the "perfectest figure of a garden I ever saw"—made by one who was among "the greatest wits" of her time, who esteemed poetry and

---

[9] *The Gardens of Epicurus*, ed. A. F. Sieveking (London, 1908), p. 50. Italics mine.

poets, and knew how to treat them (as Timon does not), and who, though building with much cost, did not throw her "sums" away.

III

A more complicated instance, involving allusion unmistakably, occurs in the *Epistle to Bathurst*. Here, at several points, Pope's commentary on the corrupting power of gold echoes with recollections of one of the primary classical texts in praise of rural innocence and simplicity— Horace's sixteenth ode of the third book:

> aurum per medios ire satellites
> et perrumpere amat saxa, potentius
> ictu fulmineo: concidit auguris
>   Argivi domus, ob lucrum
>
> demersa exitio; diffidit urbium
> portas vir Macedo et subruit aemulos
> reges muneribus; munera navium
>   saevos inlaqueant duces.
>
> crescentem sequitur cura pecuniam
> maiorumque fames. . . .
>
> contemptae dominus splendidior rei,
> quam si, quidquid arat impiger Apulus
> occultare meis dicerer horreis,
>   magnas inter opes inops.
>
> purae rivus aquae silvaque iugerum
> paucorum et segetis certa fides meae
> fulgentem imperio fertilis Africae
>   fallit sorte beatior.
>
>   . . . multa petentibus
> desunt multa; bene est, cui deus obtulit
>   parca quod satis est manu.   (9–18, 25–32, 42–44)

("Gold loves to make its way through the midst of sentinels and to break through rocks, for 'tis mightier than the thunderbolt. 'Twas for the sake of gain that the house of the Argive prophet plunged to destruction and fell in ruins. 'Twas by gifts of gold that the Macedonian burst open gates of cities and overthrew rival kings; gifts ensnare bluff admirals too. Yet as money grows, care and greed for greater riches follow after . . . [I am] a more glorious master of the wealth I spurn than were I said to hide within my barns the produce of all the acres that the sturdy Apulian ploughs, a beggar in the midst of mighty wealth. My stream of pure water, my woodland of few acres, and sure trust in my crop of corn bring me more blessing than the lot of the dazzling lord of fertile Africa, though he know it not. . . . To those who seek for much, much is ever lacking; blest is he to whom the god with chary hand has given just enough.")

   Much of what Pope has to say about the wrong and right use of riches in the *Epistle to Bathurst* could be regarded as (in a general way) inspired application of these attitudes and of the rhetoric of paradox in which they are expressed: "magnas inter opes inops" ("a beggar in the midst of mighty wealth"), "multa petentibus desunt multa" (To those who seek for much, much is ever lacking"), "contemptae dominus splendidior rei" ("a more glorious master of the wealth I spurn"), etc. The Horatian phrases point precisely to the two worlds of Pope's epistle: that which contains Bathurst, Oxford, and the Man of Ross, on the one hand, and that which contains Cotta, Villiers, Hopkins, Cutler, and all the rest who manifest "Want with a full . . . purse," on the other. Possibly there are also links of a more explicit sort between what Horace says about the power of gold to pierce all barriers and Pope's apostrophe to "Blest paper-credit," which corrupts closer home than Horace's Argos and Asia:

.   .   .   .

> Gold imp'd by thee, can compass hardest things,
> Can pocket States, can fetch or carry Kings;
> A single leaf shall waft an Army o'er,
> Or ship off Senates to some distant Shore.

.   .   .   .

> Pregnant with thousands flits the Scrap unseen,
> And silent sells a King, or buys a Queen.   (71–74, 77–78)

Again, however, the analogies may belong as much to prehistory and composition as to meaning, until we come to the story of Balaam. Here Pope's "Tempter," who failed with Job, and therefore nowadays "tempts by making rich, not making poor," pours wealth on his victim:

> Till all the Daemon makes his full descent,
> In one abundant show'r of Cent. per Cent.,
> Sinks deep within him, and possesses whole . . . . (371–73)

The allusion to Zeus's possession of Danaë is clear enough without Horace, but the application of this ancient story to the seductions of money directs our attention squarely to the ode we have been discussing, where, in two stanzas I have so far left unquoted, Horace makes this application his introduction to praise of the retired life:

> Inclusam Danaën turris aënea
> robustaeque fores et vigilum canum
> tristes excubiae munierant satis
>   nocturnis ab adulteris,
>
> si non Acrisium virginis abditae
> custodem pavidum Iuppiter et Venus
> risissent: fore enim tutum iter et patens
>   converso in pretium deo.   (1–8)

("Towers of bronze, doors of oak, and the strict guard of watch-dogs had quite protected imprisoned Danaë from nocturnal lovers, had not Jupiter and Venus laughed at Acrisius, anxious keeper of the hidden maiden. For they knew that the way would be safe and open, when the god had turned to gold.")

Horace's "converso in pretium deo" ("when the god had turned to gold") obviously anticipates the metamorphosis of Satan in Pope's poem. It also anticipates the materialism of Balaam's worship. Beginning by "solemnizing" the Lord's Day with "an added pudding," then salving his conscience for theft by going to church twice on Sunday, he is presently vouchsafed the "full descent" of the Satanic Comforter, whereupon he arrogates the role of Providence to himself:

> What late he call'd a Blessing, now was Wit,
> And God's good Providence, a lucky Hit—   (377–78)

translates the observances of worship to his counting-house;

> Things change their titles, as our manners turn:
> His Compting-house employ'd the Sunday morn—
>
> (379–80)

and by a predictable progression eventually curses God and dies. Through the Danaë analogue, Pope makes a comment in sexual terms on the perversion implicit in Balaam's possession not by a God but by his own wealth. By deliberately vulgarizing the greatest spiritual drama of the Old Testament into a mercantile success story, he makes a comment on perversions of a deeper and more inclusive kind. To these he adds through Horace the constructive perspectives of the literature of retirement, as earlier in the poem he had set beside his gallery of wealth-abusers the figure of the Man of Ross. In the context of the Roman allusion, we are invited to hear not simply the voice of Horace but the authority implicit in a long tradition of philosophical self-cultivation, telling us there are less costly ways than Balaam's to the discovery that

> multa petentibus
> desunt multa; bene est, cui deus obtulit
> parca quod satis est manu.

I suppose the most insistent of Pope's overt allusions to the idiom of retirement literature in these poems of the thirties occurs in his imitation of the fourth satire of Donne. Pope's poem, like Donne's, comes to a point about midway, when the speaker's narrative of his visit to court is punctuated by his longed-for escape from an impertinent courtier and his return home. There—in a "trance," as Donne has it; Pope's word is "vision"—he relives his visit as if it were a glimpse of hell, experiencing yet stronger repugnance at what he sees.

In Donne, the flight from court is simply a flight to the poet's house, accomplished to the accompaniment of mock pity:

> At home in wholesome solitariness
> My piteous soul began the wretchednesse
> Of suiters at court to mourn, and a Trance
> Like his, who dream't he saw hell, did advance
> It self o're me: Such men as he saw there
> I saw at Court, and worse, and more . . . .   (155–60)

In Pope the escape from court to solitude is marked more sharply. It is signaled by a break from narrative to imprecation, and it brings into play a *mise-en-scène* wholly characteristic of retirement literature, inhabited by characteristic figures:

> Bear me, some God! oh quickly bear me hence
> To wholesome Solitude, the Nurse of Sense:
> Where Contemplation prunes her ruffled Wings,
> And the free Soul looks down to pity Kings.
> There sober Thought pursu'd th' amusing theme
> Till Fancy colour'd it, and form'd a Dream.
> A *Vision* Hermits can to Hell transport,
> And force ev'n me to see the Damn'd at Court.
> Not *Dante* dreaming all th' Infernal State,
> Beheld such Scenes of *Envy*, *Sin*, and *Hate*.   (184–93)

Pope's alteration of Donne's "at home" to a special habitat of retirement virtues is interesting, partly because, like all his other changes, it sharpens the attack on court life, but chiefly because of its ancestry. The place where Contemplation prunes ruffled wings and the free Soul looks down has probably its antecedent in those medieval gardens where the souls of the just are represented by birds, though it is by no means clear that Pope knew this. What he surely did know is that this garden situation is the normal habitat of that bird-of-the soul which materializes so often in seventeenth-century poetry, most familiarly in Marvell's "The Garden":

> There like a Bird it sits and sings,
> Then whets, and combs its silver Wings,
> And, till prepar'd for longer flight,
> Waves in its Plumes the various Light—   (53–56)

and which has reappeared in our time in versions (and gardens) as different as those of Burnt Norton and the palace of the emperor of Byzantium.

Pope's personified "Solitude," "Sense," and "Contemplation" pruning ruffled wings also have a history, as his editors point out. They look directly back to the speech of the elder brother in *Comus* on the integrity and security of virtue even when most exposed:

> Virtue could see to do what virtue would
> By her own radiant light, though Sun and Moon
> Were in the flat Sea sunk. And Wisdom's self
> Oft seeks to sweet retired Solitude,
> Where with her best nurse Contemplation
> She plumes her feathers, and lets grow her wings
> That in the various bussle of resort
> Were all to-ruffl'd, and sometimes impair'd.
> He that has light within his own claer brest
> May sit i'th centre, and enjoy bright day.   (373–82)

The allusion to *Comus*, clearly one we are not meant to overlook, marshals beside the figure of Pope's garden-sage, whose free soul is proof against the corruption of courts, the particular image of Milton's virtuous Lady, who as easily resists Comus' seduction and for the same reason: "Thou canst not touch the freedom of my mind" (662). The inclination of Pope's "Soul" to look down and pity "Kings" (specifically) no doubt owes more to the teachings of Platonized stoicism he had rendered recently in the *Essay on Man* (and perhaps to his view of the House of Brunswick)—

> Awake, my St. John! leave all meaner things
> To low ambition and the pride of Kings—   (I, 1–2)

than to Milton or seventeenth-century garden mysticism. But Solitude, Contemplation, and the bird-of-the soul are another matter.[10] These make a background for the ensuing vision of the court as hell that could hardly be improved on, and remind us how profoundly Pope's mind is penetrated by the conceptions of the century into which he was born.

---

[10] Pope's "free Soul" and the general character of his apostrophe to "some God" suggest that, whether or not he is remembering Marvell, he is remembering Dryden's:

> my free Soul, aspiring to the Height
> Of Nature, and unclouded Fields of Light;

and also his

> Some God conduct me to the sacred Shades
> .   .   .   .
> Or lead me to some solitary Place
> And cover my Retreat from Human Race—

from the translation of Virgil's *O fortunatos nimium* (*Georgics*, II, 686, 692, 696–97). If so, the passage has a further link with retirement literature.

The comparison between the "free Soul" and the Lady tempted by Comus *may* imply an analogy between the seductions of Comus and those of the Court. This analogy seems to reappear overtly in the "Wizard old" (Sir Robert Walpole) with his corrupting "cup" at the close of the *Dunciad*, IV, 517ff.

IV

I come next to what is rather a network of values and assumptions in Pope's poetry of the thirties than a series of explicit allusions. That they are inherited assumptions does not make them less deeply felt—quite the contrary: Pope's most powerful vein is often elegiac. Their genealogy can be traced in the work of Jacobean and Stuart poets, particularly those who wrote celebrating English country-houses and the landscape and way of life of which such houses were at their best a center. Mr. G. R. Hibbard has written eloquently on this subject, locating in certain poems of Jonson's, Carew's, and Herrick's, and in parts of Marvell's *Upon Appleton House,* a body of poetry "truly Augustan in the sense that it voices and defines the values of a society conscious of its own achievement of a civilized way of living, and conscious also of the forces that threatened to undermine and overthrow that achievement."[11] He concedes that the period in which such poetry could be written was brief, terminated by changes in domestic architecture and social organization each of which mutually hastened the other; but argues that the poetry remained influential because of its high quality, and that the attitudes it inculcated survived into the next century, remarkably, and to some extent, uniquely, in Pope. "Pope's conception of what the great house should be," he concludes, referring to the *Epistle to Burlington:*

> was, of course, different from that of Ben Jonson and his successors, in the purely architectural sense. Where they set up the traditional Elizabethan house in opposition to the baroque, Pope set up the classical designs of Palladio. But underneath the surface difference he is wholly in agreement with them that the right and proper end of building is use, not show; and that the proper aim of the individual should be the subordination of himself to the service of the community, not exploitation of the community for his own personal ends.[12]

Mr. Hibbard is surely right in associating Pope to this tradition. If not strictly in the main current of seventeenth-century retirement literature, it incorporates nevertheless its values and derives from the same classical texts; and Pope draws from it, I think, many of the predis-

[11] "The Country House Poem of the Seventeenth Century," *Journal of the Warburg and Courtauld Institutes,* XIX (1956), 159.
[12] *Ibid.,* p. 174.

positions that gleam unstated behind his criticism of such phenomena as Timon's villa. The absurd Brobdingnagian grandeur of that place—

> To compass this his building is a Town,
> His Pond an Ocean, his parterre a Down—   (105–6)

recalls not only the conspicuous consumption of certain contemporary Whig magnates, but equally the stress laid by Jonson, Carew, Herrick, and Marvell on dwellings built for use not show, each one "arisen, as it were, out of the earth it stands on"[13] to be a true home to its "lord":

> Now, Penshurst, they that will proportion thee
> With other edifices, when they see
> Those proud ambitious heaps, and nothing else,
> May say their lords have built, but thy lord dwells.[14]
>   (99–102)

Marvell, too, proposes in his opening lines on Appleton House an antitype—an anti-dwelling, so to speak—which incorporates some of the eccentricities of Timon's villa, as well as other follies recorded in the *Epistle to Burlington*. Marvell's "Architect"—who would so exhaust quarries as to reduce them to caves:

> Within this sober Frame expect
> Work of no Forrain *Architect;*
> That unto Caves the Quarries drew,
> And Forrests did to Parterres hew—   (1–4)

clearly belongs in the ancestry of Timon, who has made his house "a labour'd Quarry above ground"; just as the man who "Forrests did to Parterres hew" has a family likeness to Sabinus' son, who cut away all the trees in which Sabinus had taken joy:

> His Son's fine Taste an op'ner Vista loves,
> Foe to the Dryads of his Father's groves,
> One boundless Green, or flourish'd Carpet views,
> With all the mournful family of Yews;
> The thriving plants ignoble broomsticks made,
> Now sweep those Alleys they were born to shade.   (93–98)

---

[13] *Ibid.*, p. 164.
[14] See the close of "Upon the Duke of Marlborough's House at Woodstock," variously attributed to Swift, Pope, Abel Evans, and William King.
> I find, by all you have been telling,
> That 'tis a house, but not a dwelling.

Marvell's query about the proportionableness of his anti-dwelling to its owner—

> What need of all this Marble Crust
> T 'impark the wanton Mote of Dust?— (21–22)

exhibits the same concern that Pope feels for right relations between house and man—

> Who but must laugh, the Master when he sees,
> A puny insect, shiv'ring at a breeze! (107–8)

Marvell's comic vision of the house as a palace filled, like Aeolus's, with draughts—

> But He, superfluously spread,
> Demands more room alive than dead.
> And in his hollow Palace goes
> Where Winds as he themselves may lose— (17–20)

if it has not inspired, at any rate looks forward to Pope's emphasis on impractical grandeur:

> Greatness, with Timon, dwells in such a draught
> As brings all Brobdignag before your thought— (103–4)

and on the general propensity of such grandeur to favor appearance against comfort, calling even

> the Winds thro' long Arcades to roar,
> Proud to catch cold at a Venetian door. (35–36)

Altogether, the contrast that Marvell establishes between his hypothetical grandee, dwarfed by his showy house, and Fairfax, whose unpretentious dwelling barely contains his greatness—

> Height with a certain Grace does bend,
> But low Things clownishly ascend— (59–60)

has the same ethical base as that which Sidney had established with respect to Kalander's house—

> The house it selfe was built of faire and strong stone, not affecting so much any extraordinarie kinde of finenes, as an honorable representing of a firme statelines. The lightes, doores and staires, rather directed to the use of the guest, then to the eyes of the Artificer—[15]

and that which Pope makes the ground of his distinction between the architecture of "Imitating Fools" and the architecture of Burlington, who shows us

Rome was glorious, not profuse.   (23)

Pope's criticism of contemporary ostentation speaks here from a long and (in the best sense) "classical" tradition.

V

Much else in Pope gains in clarity if we see it in the light of seventeenth-century conventions and conceptions, to which he is one of the latest heirs. Digressing for a moment to his earlier work, we are helped to understand the lines in *Windsor Forest* which have been so often absurdly misread[16] if we call to mind their Elizabethan, Jacobean, and Stuart antecedents:

> Not proud *Olympus* yields a nobler Sight,
> Tho' Gods assembled grace his tow'ring Height,
> Than what more humble Mountains offer here,
> Where, in their Blessings, all those Gods appear.
> See Pan with Flocks, with Fruits *Pomona* crown'd,
> Here blushing *Flora* paints th' enamel'd Ground,
> Here *Ceres'* Gifts in waving Prospect stand,
> And nodding tempt the joyful Reaper's Hand,
> Rich Industry sits smiling on the Plains,
> And Peace and Plenty tell, a Stuart reigns.   (33–42)

[15] *The Countess of Pembroke's Arcadia*, Bk. I: *Works*, ed. A. Feuillerat (Cambridge, 1939), I, 15.

[16] E.g., in Bernard Groom's "Some Kinds of Poetic Diction," *Essays and Studies by Members of the English Association*, Vol. XV (1929).

Pope's description follows the convention of Tudor and Stuart allegorical painting, where monarchs regularly lead and control figures of "Peace and Plenty," together with more orthodox members of the classical Pantheon. Behind his tableau lies also, we may guess, the tradition of emblematic pageants (this is a Windsor landscape after all, and the monarch is its climax) such as were acted at court and put on for royal progresses in the reigns of Elizabeth and James. In addition, "To Penshurst" and other poems like it have contributed to these lines their vision of an English countryside so profoundly oriented toward man that its fruits and living creatures are emulous to feed him,[17] as the grain in Pope's lines seems consciously to "tempt" the reaper's hand. Especially to be noticed is the characteristically Renaissance way of understanding the presence of pagan gods in a modern setting. It is seen by Pope as a relation between the gifts of those gods and their "apparition" or theophany: "Where, in their Blessings, all those Gods appear." Carew, Pope's anticipator and perhaps model in this, makes it a contrast of the god's gifts and their icons:

> Amalthea's horn
> Of plenty is not in effigy worn
> Without the gate, but she, within the door,
> Empties her free and unexhausted store;
> Nor, crown'd with wheat in wreaths, doth Ceres stand
> In stone, with a crooked sickle in her hand;
> Nor on a marble tun, his face besmear'd
> With grapes, is curl'd unscissor'd Bacchus rear'd:
> We offer not an emblem to the eyes
> But to the taste, those useful deities.
>
> (*To My Friend G. N., from Wrest*, 59–66)

What is true of *Windsor Forest* remains true, *mutatis mutandis*, in the satires of the thirties. They are unmistakably Augustan, yet the pressure of the preceding age often swells visibly beneath the contemporary surface. The expression of responsibilities and pieties remains patriarchal in its feeling for the relation between master and dependents:

> Where are those Troops of poor, that throng'd of yore
> The good old Landlord's hospitable door?
>
> (*The Second Satire of Dr. John Donne*, 113–14)

[17] Cf. "To Penshurst," 29–38, and Carew's "To Saxham," 19–30.

The land continues to be seen as a locus of invisible presences:

> The woods recede around the naked seat,
> The Sylvans groan. . . .
>
> (*Epistle to Bathurst*, 209–10)

The objects of satire have an Elizabethan and Jacobean substance for all their contemporary dress: they are to a large extent, as in the preceding century, lawyers, embezzlers, extortionists, courtiers, affected females, royal favorites, Italianate returned travelers—and what is equally significant in this connection is that Pope chose to paraphrase two satires by Donne and contemplated paraphrasing one of Hall's.

One's attention is especially struck in these poems by the old-fashioned notions of what constitutes national and individual virtue, and the emotions which reverberate in the verse whenever such virtue is mentioned. These attitudes have long roots, often reaching as far back as Rome, but all seem to be nourished and extended in Pope's case by his wide reading in the seventeenth-century poets. Essentially, it is *their* vision of his country that he makes his own—the new Eden, the new Jerusalem, the new Rome. It is their feeling for the life of considerate use that pulses behind much of his social criticism, though the immediate vehicle be Horace. Their picture of the country gentleman living on his estate and so far as possible by it, seeking no city gain or court preferment, radiating through the land practices of provident abundance, occupying a great house "rear'd with no man's ruin, no man's groan," caring for his tenants and so loved by them that:

> all come in, the farmer, and the clowne:
> And no one empty-handed, to salute
> [The] lord and lady, though they have no sute—
>
> ("To Penshurst," 48–50)

this is Pope's picture, too, whenever in the satires he allows the positive ideals underlying his criticism to emerge:

> His Father's Acres who enjoys in Peace,
> Or makes his Neighbours glad, if he encrease;
> Whose chearful Tenants bless their yearly toil,
> Yet to their Lord owe more than to the soil;

> Whose ample Lawns are not asham'd to feed
> The milky heifer and deserving steed;
> Whose rising Forests, not for pride or show,
> But future Buildings, future Navies grow:
> Let his Plantations stretch from down to down,
> First shade a Country, and then raise a Town.

(Epistle to Burlington, 81–90)

This passage is highly characteristic of Pope. Yet its deep sense of reciprocities between man and man and man and nature, eventuating in a whole whose every part is responsive to every other (where tenants "bless," soil can be "owed" a debt, lawns are "not asham'd," forests rise but not for "pride," etc.), is a sense rare among eighteenth-century poets. It belongs in outlook, though not in phrasing, to the Renaissance.

When Pope thinks of hospitality, it is invariably again a Tudor-Stuart picture that comes to his mind. With Jonson and his successors he sees a gate which turns no one away, homebred fare, a host who gives himself along with the meal. In his imitation of Horace's second satire of the second book, Horace's own passing references to the hospitality of Ofellus are intensified by Pope, first, with an allusion to a well-known turbot in Juvenal,[18] and then with a proud specificity as to the homebred character of the meal he offers, the pride belonging as fully to seventeenth-century English housekeeping attitudes as to Horatian Rome.

> Tis true, no Turbots dignify my boards,
> But gudgeons, flounders, what my Thames affords.
> To Hounslow-heath I point and Bansted-down,
> Thence comes your mutton, and these chicks my own:
> From yon old Wallnut-tree a show'r shall fall;
> And grapes, long-lingring on my only wall,
> And figs, from standard and Espalier join:
> The dev'l is in you if you cannot dine.   (141–48)

The stress in Pope's original is on the sufficient though simple character of the meal, which did not require "fish sent from town." Pope incorporates within this a notably seventeenth-century English sense of proprietorship and place.[19]

---

[18] *Satire IV*, pp. 37ff.

[19] One may also notice Dryden's "homebred plenty," in *Georgics*, II, 657, his own insertion.

Or if it is manorial hospitality which comes to Pope's mind, he thinks of the great halls celebrated by an earlier age, where lord, tenants, neighbors, guests, travelers, and poor were alike welcome and shared alike from a bounteous table. His portrait of Cotta in the *Epistle to Bathurst* consists precisely in inverting this:

> Old Cotta sham'd his fortune and his birth,
> Yet was not Cotta void of wit or worth:
> What tho' (the use of barb'rous spits forgot)
> His kitchen vy'd in coolness with his grot?
> His court with nettles, moats with cresses stor'd,
> With soups unbought and sallads blest his board.
> If Cotta liv'd on pulse, it was no more
> Than Bramins, Saints, and Sages did before;
> To cram the Rich was prodigal expence,
> And who would take the Poor from Providence:
> Like some lone Chartreux stands the good old Hall,
> Silence without, and Fasts within the wall;
> No rafter'd roofs with dance and tabor sound,
> No noon-tide bell invites the country round;
> Tenants with sighs the smoakless tow'rs survey,
> And turn th' unwilling steeds another way:
> Benighted wanderers, the forest o'er,
> Curse the sav'd candle, and unop'ning door;
> While the gaunt mastiff growling at the gate,
> Affrights the beggar whom he longs to eat.   (179–98)

We do less than justice to such lines if we do not imagine, crowding in behind them, like the disapproving ghosts who haunt the tent of Shakespeare's Richard III the night before Boswell Field, the Sidneys of Penshurst, the Wroths of Loughton House and Durrants, The Crofts of Saxham, the Greys of Wrest, the Pembertons of Rushden, the Fairfaxes of Nunappleton, and all those others who took seriously in their time the responsibilities of rank and wealth. Old Cotta's cold kitchen and miser's view of "barb'rous spits" are to be seen against the "liberall board" of Penshurst, flowing "With all that hospitalitie doth know" (60), or the great hall of Wrest:

> Where, at large tables fill'd with wholesome meats,
> The servant, tenant, and kind neighbour eats,

> (Carew, *To My Friend G. N., from Wrest*, 35–36)

or, especially, the mighty kitchen at Rushden:

> The fat-fed smoking Temple, which in
> The wholesome savour of thy mighty chines
> Invites to supper him who dines,
> Where laden spits, warp't with large Ribbs of Beefe,
> Not represent, but give reliefe
> To the lanke Stranger and the sowre Swain;
> Where both may feed, and come againe. . . .
>
> (Herrick, *A Panegyrick to Sir Lewis Pemberton*, 6–12)

Cotta's "soups unbought and sallads," as has often been pointed out, cross his image ironically with that of the old Corycian in Virgil's fourth Georgic, the type figure of contentment on little ("regum aequabat opes animis" ["he matched in contentment the wealth of kings"], says Virgil); but they further cross it with the seventeenth-century English countryman's pride in self-sufficiency, expressed in Carew's praise of Wrest, where grow
> Such native aromatics as we use:
> No foreign gums, nor essence fetch'd from far—   (14–15)

and Jonson's of Robert Wroth:

> [Thou] canst at home in thy securer rest
> Live with unbought provision blest.
>
> (*To Sir Robert Wroth*, 13–14)

When Cotta leaves the poor to "Providence," we are to recall those who acted by another code—for instance, the Greys of Wrest, who did not fill their dining room with "statues" but with "living men" (33–34), and the Fairfaxes, whose "open Door" was adorned with "a stately Frontispiece of Poor" (65–67); and we are also to recall their successors in Pope's own day, the Oxfords, Bathursts, Burlingtons, all who carry on the tradition of wealth applied to social ends, among whom "English Bounty," like *Iustitia* among the *O fortunatos nimium* of the second Georgic,

> yet a-while may stand,
> And Honour linger ere it leaves the land.
>
> (*Epistle to Bathurst*, 247–48)

Even Cotta's gaunt mastiff, who gives solid expression to the philosophy of "sav'd candle" and "unop'ning door," has possibly among his literary ancestors a figure whose absence is dwelt on in seventeenth-century descriptions of country houses properly run. In Jonson, it is the officious waiter, who is not to be found at Penshurst:

> Here no man tells my cups, nor, standing by,
> A waiter doth my gluttony envy:
> But gives me what I call, and lets me eate.   (67–69)

In Carew, it is the surly porter who does not guard the gate at Saxham:

> Thou hast no porter at thy door
> T' examine or keep back the poor;
> Nor locks nor bolts: thy gates have bin
> Made only to let strangers in,
> Untaught to shut, they do not fear
> To stand wide open all the year.
>
> ("To Saxham," 49–54)

In Herrick, it is both porter and waiter, neither of whom is employed at Rushden:

> For no black-bearded *Vigil* from thy doore
> Beats with a button'd-staffe the poor:
>
> .   .   .   .
>
> Thus like a *Roman Tribute*, thou thy gate
> Early setts ope to feast, and late;
> Keeping no *currish Waiter* to affright
> With blasting Eye, the appetite.
>
> (*A Panegyrick to Sir Lewis Pemberton*, 13–14, 45–48)

VI

The end product of the influence of retirement literature on Pope's poems of the thirties is the ingratiating semirural figure whose value-system colors them all, and whose personality and vocabulary are impressed at some point on most. Essentially, this is the figure of the *beatus vir* of literary tradition, a composite of Roman outlines shaped to English seventeenth-century and Augustan circumstances, or, to restate the matter in rhetorical terms, a collecting of traditional *topoi* into something like an identifiable physical presence by the voice of a speaker who is at once Pope of Twickenham and a universal type.

In the tradition on which Pope draws, this figure normally speaks from a small homestead of inherited land—his *rura paterna,* as Horace has it in the second Epode (1.3)—about which he has feelings of the kind expressed by the elder shepherd in Shakespeare's *Winter's Tale:*

> To die upon the bed my father died,
> To lie close by his honest bones. (IV, iv, 467–68)

Here the happy man was born, and here he stays. For in the words of Claudian's *De sene Veronensi,* one of the main Latin sources of the figure:

> Felix, qui propriis aevum transegit in arvis,
> ipsa domus puerum quem videt, ipsa senem. (1–2)

("Happy he who has passed his whole life mid his own fields, he of whose birth and old age the same house is witness.")

Partly he is bound to his birthplace by natural pieties of the sort Vaughan praises in his man of "constancy" (in his translation of Casimir Sarbiewski), who can contentedly

> *dine* and *sup*
> Where his *old parents* bred him up.
>
> (*Lib. 4. Ode 15,* 29–30)

Partly he is bound by the conviction that "Fair quiet" and Innocence her "Sister dear" are best sought after elsewhere than "In busie Companies of Men."[20] Jonson had stated the point memorably in his verses to Lady Aubigny, subsequently recalled by Gray:

> In single paths, dangers with ease are watch'd.
> Contagion in the prease is soonest catch'd.
> This makes, that wisely you decline your life,
> Farre from the maze of custome, error, strife,
> And keepe an even, and unalter'd gaite . . .
>
> (*To Katherine, Lady Aubigny,* 57–61)

[20] Marvell, "The Garden," 10–12.

The *beatus vir* therefore shuns "the Forum's madness,"[21] never on any account goes to law,[22] cherishes independence like all who, having learned "the Great Art of cheerful Poverty,"[23] "can endure to stoop"[24] as they enter their humble doorways, and hugs himself that he has got free of the world and its ways:

> Let others trust the Seas, dare death and hell,
> Search either Inde, vaunt of their scarres and wounds;
> Let others their deare breath (nay silence) sell
> To fools, and (swolne, not rich) stretch out their bounds
> By spoiling those that live, and wronging dead;
> That they may drink in pearl, and couch their head
> In soft, but sleepless down; in rich but restless bed.[25]

His conscience is quiet. His sleep at night is unbroken by fears or cares.[26] His health is sound because his diet is spare and got by labor or hunting:

> . . . all the Rivers, and the Forests nigh,
> Both Food and Game, and Exercise supply.[27]

He keeps a warm ever-blazing hearth,[28] values his friends, has a wife (if he has a wife at all) who is a paragon of chastity,[29] reverences his ancestors,

[21] *Georgics*, II, 502: "insanumque forum"; cf. also Cowley's "The Wrangling Barr" in "Of Myself" (*Essays*, p. 112). This is the *beatus vir*'s usual view of law courts, and may account for Pope's rendering Donne's "the termes of law" as "the bawling Bar" (*Imit. Donne*, IV, 55).

[22] Martial, II, xc, 10: "sit nox cum somno, sit sine lite dies" ("Let me have night with sleep, have day without a lawsuit").

[23] Cowley's translation of "patiens operum exiguosque adsueta" (*Georgics*, II, 472), in his rendering of *O fortunatos nimium* at the close of his essay "Of Agriculture" (*Essays*, p. 46).

[24] Martial, II, liii, 8: "si tua non rectus tecta subire potes" ("if you can endure to stoop as you enter your dwelling"). This gesture became a standard emblem in retirement literature, probably owing in part to the great stress laid on it in Virgil's episode of Evander's house (*Aeneid*, VIII, 362ff.); Shakespeare puts a version of it into the mouth of Belarius in *Cymbeline*, III, iii, 1ff.

[25] Phineaus Fletcher's adaptation of *O fortunatos nimium* (II, 503–6) in the *Purple Island*, st. xxvi.

[26] Cf. for example Horace, *Epistles*, I, x, 18: "est ubi divellat somnos minus invida Cura?" ("Is there any [place] where envious Care less distracts our slumber?")

[27] Cowley's rendering of "illic saltus ac lustra ferarum" (*Georgics*, II, 471) in his version of *O fortunatos nimium* in "Of Agriculture" (*Essays*, p. 46).

[28] Martial, X, xlvii, 4: "focus perennis."

[29] *Ibid.*, p. 10: "non tristis torus et tamen pudicus" ("a wife not prudish and yet pure"); *Georgics*, II, 524: "casta pudicitiam servat domus" ("his unstained home guards its purity").

worships his God, and bridles his will. He neither fears the approach
of death nor longs for it,[30] but when it comes, "Serenely as he liv'd,
resigns his breath."[31]

The essential features of this portrait remained recognizable for
nearly two millenia. This we may see by placing the following versions of
it side by side. First, the Virgilian version, in which preference oscillates
between the life of the happy farmer and that of the retired poet-sage:

> O happy, if he knew his happy State!
> The Swain, who, free from Business and Debate,
> Receives his easy Food from Nature's Hand.
>
> .   .   .   .
>
> Give me the Ways of wandring Stars to know;
> The Depths of Heav'n above, and Earth below.
> Teach me the various Labours of the Moon,
> And whence proceed th' Eclipses of the Sun.
> Why flowing Tides prevail upon the Main,
> And in what dark Recess they shrink again.
>
> .   .   .   .
>
> But, if my heavy Blood restrain the Flight
> Of my free Soul, aspiring to the Height
> Of Nature, and unclouded Fields of Light:
> My next Desire is, void of Care and Strife,
> To lead a soft, secure, inglorious Life.
> A Country Cottage, near a Crystal Flood,
> A winding Vally, and a lofty Wood.
>
> .   .   .   .
>
> Happy the Man, who, studying Nature's Laws
> Thro' known Effects can trace the secret Cause.
> And happy too is he, who decks the Bow'rs
> Of Sylvans, and adores the Rural Pow'rs:
> Whose Mind, unmov'd, the Bribes of Courts can see.[32]

---

[30] Martial, X, xlvii, 13: "summum nec metuas diem nec optes."

[31] George Granville, "An Imitation *of the second* Chorus *in the second* Act *of* Seneca's
Thyestes," 29.

[32] Dryden's translation: *Georgics*, II, 639–41, 677–82, 685–91, 698–99, 702–4.

Next, Martial's epigram *Ad Seipsum* (X, xlvii), as Englished by Ben Jonson:

> The Things that make the happier life, are these,
> Most pleasant Martiall; Substance got with ease,
> Not Labour'd for, but left thee by thy Sire;
> A Soyle, not barren; a continewall fire;
> Never at Law; seldome in office gown'd;
> A quiet mind; free powers; a body sound;
> A wise simplicity; friends alike-stated;
> Thy table without art, and easy-rated:
> Thy night not drunken, but from cares layd wast;
> No sowre, or sullen bed-mate, yet a Chast;
> Sleep, that will make the darkest houres swift-pac't;
> Will to bee, what thou art; and nothing more:
> Nor feare thy latest day, nor wish therfore.

Third, part of Seneca's second chorus in *Thyestes* in Cowley's rendering at the close of his essay "Of Obscurity":

> Upon the slippery tops of humane State,
> > The guilded Pinnacles of Fate,
> Let others proudly stand, and for a while
> > The giddy danger to beguile,
> With Joy, and with disdain look down on all,
> > Till their Heads turn, and down they fall.
> Me, O ye Gods, on Earth, or else so near
> > That I no Fall to Earth may fear,
> And, O ye gods, at a good distance seat
> > From the long Ruines of the Great.
> Here wrapt in th' Arms of Quiet let me ly;
> Quiet, Companion of Obscurity.
> Here let my Life, with as much silence slide,
> > As Time that measures it does glide.
> Nor let the Breath of Infamy or Fame,
> From town to town Eccho about my Name.
> Nor let my homely Death embroidered be
> > With Scutcheon or with Elegie.
> > An old *Plebean* let me Dy,
> Alas, all then are such as well as I.
> > To him, alas, to him, I fear,

The face of Death will terrible appear:
Who in his life flattering his senceless pride
By being known to all the world beside,
Does not himself, when he is Dying know
Nor what he is, nor Whither hee's to go.

Fourth, Pope's ode *On Solitude*, probably his first poem, an Augustan landmark in this tradition:

Happy the man, whose wish and care
A few paternal acres bound,
Content to breathe his native air,
       In his own ground.

Whose herds with milk, whose fields with bread,
Whose flocks supply him with attire,
Whose trees in summer yield him shade,
       In winter fire.

Blest! who can unconcern'dly find
Hours, days, and years slide soft away,
In health of body, peace of mind,
       Quiet by day,

Sound sleep by night; study and ease
Together mix'd; sweet recreation,
And innocence, which most dost please,
       With meditation.

Thus let me live, unseen, unknown,
Thus unlamented let me dye,
Steal from the world, and not a stone
       Tell where I lye.

Fifth, the version of the type-figure which Pope adopts for *Windsor Forest*, compressing in one Virgil's alternatives of happy rural innocent and retired philosopher, but with a heavy bias toward the latter:

Happy . . . who to these Shades retires,
Whom Nature charms, and whom the Muse inspires,
Whom humbler Joys of home-felt Quiet please,
Successive Study, Exercise and Ease.

He gathers Health from Herbs the Forest yields,
And of their fragrant Physick spoils the Fields:
With Chymick Art exalts the Min'ral Pow'rs,
And draws the Aromatick Souls of Flow'rs.
Now marks the Course of rolling Orbs on high;
O'er figur'd Worlds now travels with his Eye.
Of ancient Writ unlocks the learned Store,
Consults the Dead, and lives past Ages o'er.
Or wandring thoughtful in the silent Wood
Attends the Duties of the Wise and Good,
T' observe a Mean, be to himself a Friend,
To follow Nature, and regard his End.
Or looks on Heav'n with more than mortal Eyes,
Bids his free Soul expatiate in the Skies,
Amid her Kindred Stars familiar roam,
Survey the Region, and confess her Home!   (237–56)

Finally, a passage by Pope not usually associated with the tradition, though obviously dependent on it:

Born to no Pride, inheriting no Strife,
Nor marrying Discord in a Noble Wife,
Stranger to civil and Religious Rage,
The good Man walk'd innoxious thro' his Age.
No Courts he saw, no Suits would ever try,
Nor dar'd an Oath, nor hazarded a Lye:
Un-learn'd he knew no Schoolman's subtle Art,
No Language, but the Language of the Heart.
By Nature honest, by Experience wise,
Healthy by Temp'rance and by Exercise:
His Life, tho' long, to sickness past unknown,
His Death was instant, and without a groan.
Oh grant me thus to live, and thus to die!
Who sprung from Kings shall know less joy than I.

The last passage is, of course, Pope's portrait of his father in the *Epistle to Dr. Arbuthnot* (392–405). What is especially interesting about it is the fusion of reality with something else, as we are now in a position to see. The lines give us a true character of Pope's father, so far as we can judge from the evidence we have; this is certainly how Pope felt about his father, as letters to Caryll show: "I have lost one whom I am even more obliged to as a friend, than as a father"; "I heartily beg of God to give me just such a death, on condition he will in his mercy allow me just such a life."[33] Yet the portrait which the poet actually creates follows in every essential detail the type-figure of the happy man and rounds it off with a well-placed echo of Virgil's praise of the old Corycian: "he matched in contentment the wealth of kings."[34]

Painters, it has been pointed out, are as often prone to see what they know how to draw as to draw what they see.[35] Something of the sort is also true of poets: Pope sees his father, in poetry, through the lens of a traditional image, very much as Shakespeare sees his kings in poetry through another traditional image, that of the sleepless head which wears a crown.

VII

When Pope looks at himself through the lens of this genial image, the portrait that confronts him does not correspond at every point with the one we have just examined, for the poet is a man of affairs and fame, as his father was not; nor are the traditional features of the *beatus vir* represented equally in every poem. Yet there is an identifiable poet-speaker in all the poems of the thirties who incorporates a large number of the *topoi* with which we have here been concerned.

Beneficiary of a true old-fashioned education, this figure has been "bred up at home" and taught "to know the good from bad" by a father who can bear injustice without repining or wavering from principle:

> For Right Hereditary tax'd and fin'd,
> He stuck to Poverty with Peace of Mind;
> And me, the Muses help'd to undergo it;
> Convict a Papist He, and I a Poet.
>
>   *(Imit. Hor., Ep.* II, ii, 64–67)

[33] [October 28, 1717?], November 6, 1717: *Correspondence*, ed. George Sherburn (Oxford, 1956), I 448, 449.

[34] *Georgics,* IV, 132: "*regum aequabat opes animis,*" For a much more detailed account of the attributes of the type-figure than I have had occasion to give here, see Maren-Sofie Rostvig's *The Happy Man* (2 vols.; Oslo, 1954, 1958), to which I am in debt.

[35] See especially on this theme E. H. Gombrich, *Art and Illusion* (London, 1960), p. 86, and the whole chapter.

Son and father, subscribing to a faith that costs something—in the son's case, poetry as well as popery—have stood necessarily withdrawn in a world to which the Old Religion is as alien as old-fashioned costumes or scruples, [36] and in which lust of gain drives peeress and butler to the same gaming table. [37] In the son's case, a competence of means has been reached, "thanks to Homer," [38] which enables him to "piddle" along happily on "Broccoli and mutton," entertaining his "ancient friends," [39] now ceremonially with "Feast" and "Bowl," [40] now simply, like a good bourgeois, with "Beans and Bacon":

> My Friends above, my Folks below,
> Chatting and laughing all-a-row,
> The Beans and Bacon set before 'em,
> The Grace-cup serv'd with all decorum.
>
> (*Imit. Hor., Sat.* II, vi, 35–38)

In either case the diet is staunchly homebred like himself and serves as index and metaphor of a way of life where duties to neighbors, friends, parents, and one's Creator are cheerfully carried out: "And what's more rare, a Poet shall say Grace." [41] True, he knows the tug of nostalgia for a time when there was no double taxing of Roman Catholics, when no "Laws, by Suff'rers thought unjust" [42] were on the statute books: "My lands are sold, my Father's house is gone"; [43] but the proper response to this—"I'll hire another's, is not that my own?" [44]—cannot be long in occurring to a mind schooled to the central principle of the retirement creed: "Fix'd to no spot is Happiness sincere." [45] Though he had formerly somewhat more of this world's goods, he was then no better off:

> In *South-sea* days not happier, when surmis'd
> The Lord of Thousands, than if now *Excis'd;*
> In Forest planted by a Father's hand
> Then in five acres now of rented land.
>
> (*Imit. Hor., Sat.* II, ii, 133–36)

---

[36] *Imit. Donne,* II, 121–24; *Imit. Hor., Ep.* II, ii, 116–26; *Epilogue to the Satires: Dial.* i, 39–40.

[37] *Epistle to Bathurst,* 137 ff.

[38] *Imit. Hor., Ep.* II, ii, 68.

[39] *Ibid., Sat.* II, ii, 137–39.

[40] *Ibid., Sat.* II, i, 127–28.

[41] *Ibid., Sat.* II, ii, 150. Cf. *Georgics,* II, 473: "sacra deum sanctique patres."

[42] *Ibid., Ep.* II, ii, 60.

[43] *Ibid., Sat.* II, ii, 155.

[44] *Ibid.,* 156.

[45] *Essay on Man,* IV, 15–16.

And though he should lose much of what he has, he would be no worse off: he could shrink back to his "Paternal Cell," following again his father's example.

> There dy'd my Father, no man's Debtor,
> And there I'll die, nor worse nor better.
>
> (*Ibid.*, *Ep.* I, vii, 79–80)

For the true test of ownership, at Twickenham as at Penshurst, Wrest, and Rushden, is use:

> Well if the Use be mine, can it concern one
> Whether the Name belong to Pope or Vernon?
>
> (*Ibid.*, *Sat.* II, ii, 165–66)

> Delightful Abscourt, if its Fields afford
> Their Fruits to you, confesses you its Lord;
>
> (*Ibid.*, *Ep.* II, ii, 232–33)

and the true use of what one owns is to keep one free. Free of the penalties exacted by the world of those who are at its mercy:

> South-sea Subscriptions take who please,
> Leave me but Liberty and Ease.
> 'Twas what I said to Craggs and Child,
> Who prais'd my Modesty and smil'd.
> Give me, I cry'd, (enough for me)
> My Bread, and Independency.
>
> (*Ibid.*, *Ep.* I, vii, 65–70)

And free of the worse penalties exacted by the inner world of desire, when not taught to remember that "Man? and *for ever?*" [46] have no connection in the natural scheme of things:

> Grac'd as thou art, with all the Pow'r of Words,
> So known, so honour'd at the House of Lords;
> Conspicuous Scene! another yet is nigh
> (More silent far) where Kings and Poets lye.
>
> (*Ibid.*, *Ep.* I, vi, 49–51)

[46] *Imit. Hor.*, *Ep.* II, ii, 252.

In this autobiographical figure of the thirties, a variety of strains merge. It is a Roman figure, derived from many works and authors, of whom Horace is only one. It is also a recognizable seventeenth-century figure, hero of a thousand poems in praise of virtuous retirement, sprung up in part from the dragon's teeth sown before and during the Civil Wars, and from the abyss sensed between one vision of England and another which was to be institutionalized after 1688. And it is very plainly a version of the historical Alexander Pope. Its effectiveness is precisely in its seamlessness, as we may see from two further expressions of it, one having to do with the poet's life, the other with his works.

Over the entrance to his grotto, Pope inscribed the words: *Secretum iter et fallentis semita vita* ("a secluded journey along the pathway of life unnoticed"). The inscription was obviously suitable to the place and, as eighteenth-century practitioners of retirement go, to the man who placed it there: it had a personal valency, as we have seen. This same sentiment, however, is Cowley's theme in his essay "Of Obscurity," and its flavor perfectly suits many a well-known poet and poem of that age. Thus it has an historical valency too, pointing to a long tradition of self-seclusions, some of them partly engendered by political exclusions, like Pope's own situation at Twickenham. Finally, the inscription is an Horatian tag, with a philosophical valency of sorts, bringing to the reader a context from Horace's eighteenth epistle of Book I that could serve as epigraph equally for the ethical teaching of his satires and epistles as a group or that of the *Essay on Man:*

> Inter cuncta leges et percontabere doctos,
> qua ratione queas traducere leniter aevum,
> num te semper inops agitet vexetque cupido,
> num pavor et rerum mediocriter utilium spes,
> virtutem doctrina paret Naturane donet,
> quid minuat curas, quid te tibi reddat amicum,
> quid pure tranquillet, honos an dulce lucellum,
> an secretum iter et fallentis semita vitae.   (96–103)

("Amid all this you must read and question the wise, how you may be able to pass your days in tranquillity. Is greed, ever penniless, to drive and harass you, or fears and hopes about things that profit little? Does wisdom beget virtue, or Nature bring her as a gift? What will lessen care? What will make you a friend to yourself? What gives you unruffled calm—honour, or the sweets of dear gain, or a secluded journey along the pathway of life unnoticed?")

Roman ethical culture, the tradition of withdrawal from political action
inspired by seventeenth-century British history, the personal tastes of
Pope of Twickenham on one side of his nature: all are joined together in
the consensus of a line from Horace.

Our other example comes from Pope's imitation of Horace's second
epistle of Book II:

> Well, on the whole, plain Prose must be my fate:
> Wisdom (curse on it!) will come soon or late.
> There is a time when Poets will grow dull:
> I'll e'en leave Verses to the boys at school.
> To rules of Poetry no more confin'd.
> I'll learn to smooth and harmonize my Mind,
> Teach ev'ry thought within its bounds to roll,
> And keep the equal Measure of the Soul.   (202–5)

This is pure Horace, one is obliged to confess, particularly the conception
of life as a poem to be "formed." But it is pure "Moral philosophy," too,
of a kind often enunciated in seventeenth-century *vade-mecums*. And it is
likewise pure Pope, sealed as his by the wry grimace, the easy diction,
the formidable rhythms, and the immediately ensuing lines which tie
Horace's undifferentiated speaker to a specifically realized Twickenham
setting:

> Soon as I enter at my Country door,
> My Mind resumes the thread it dropt before;
> Thoughts which at Hyde-Park-Corner I forgot,
> Meet and rejoin me, in the pensive Grott.
> There all alone, and Compliments apart,
> I ask these sober questions of my Heart. . . .   (206–11)

The lines are also sealed as Pope's by the personal concern which we
know from other sources invested this problem for him. He raises it in the
Epistle to Dr. Arbuthnot:

> Heav'ns! was I born for nothing but to write?
> Has life no joys for me? or (to be grave)
> Have I no friend to serve, no Soul to save?

In his letters it concerns him repeatedly. The young man's acknowledgment of the price of his art, stated in the early days as a discovery lately made—

> To follow Poetry as one ought, one must forget father and mother and cleave to it alone—[47]

deepens as time wears on into those "sober questions" about perfection of the life or of the work which, in our own day, Yeats has understood so well:

> To write well, lastingly well, Immortally well, must one not leave Father and Mother and cleave unto the Muse? Must one not be prepared to endure the reproaches of Men, want and much Fasting, nay Martyrdom in its Cause? Tis such a Task as scarce leaves a Man time to be a good Neighbour, an useful friend, nay to plant a Tree, much less to save his Soul.[48]

And in still another moving letter filled with harassments—the poet has been looking after repairs to Fortescue's house before rushing off to see Peterborough in his last illness—there comes a question at the close, in words belonging obviously to the retirement tradition yet having in them the home-felt pressure of the individual case:

> . . . When shall you & I sit by a Fireside, without a Brief or a Poem in our hands, & yet not idle, not thoughtless, but as Serious, and more so, than any Business ought to make us, except the great Business, that of enjoying a reasonable Being, & regarding its End. The sooner this is our case, the better: God deliver you from Law, me from Rhime![49]

Here too, Pope of Twickenham, seventeenth-century Christian humanism, and Roman and Horatian precedents speak with a single voice.

VIII

For a final instance of the way in which the retirement tradition moves always under the surface of Pope's consciousness and may at any time

[47] To Jervas, August 16, 1714: *Correspondence*, I, 243.
[48] To Bolingbroke, April 9, 1724: *Ibid.*, II, 227.
[49] To Fortescue, August 23, 1735: *Ibid.*, III, 486.

break out, we may look to the *Epistle to Dr. Arbuthnot.* The eloquent shape of this poem comes in large part from the poet's tying his "Bill of Complaint"[50] against others to a progressive enlargement of vision in himself.[51] This takes him from amused self-centered harassment at the opening to otherward-looking serenity at the close, and the proud commemorative portrait of his father, quoted above in the sequence of retirement figures marks the final stage in a process of sloughing off distraction and detraction and other vanities of worldly fame to reach a single-minded vision of true innocence. This way of life the poet then identifies with his own best longings— "O grant me thus to live, and thus to die!"—and, in the final prayerful lines for Arbuthnot and his mother, seems to make his own for time to come. To put the progress of the poem in another way, at its beginning the poet's known personal ill-health is seen in part as the "disease" of worldly success, a "Plague" no "*Drop* or *Nostrum*" can cure,[52] which makes its address to the physical Arbuthnot a stroke of imagination as well as friendship. At its end, now identified with a father whose life excluded all such "sickness," the speaker has in a sense changed places with the physician; he is possessed of "lenient Arts" of his own for smoothing the "Bed of Death" and for "extending" the breath of the living (earlier, line 27, it was Arbuthnot who "prolonged" life), and it is he who is given the final healing prayer for the physician's preservation and well-being, as well as his own.

To this extent, the poem's debt to retirement attitudes is obvious. There may, however, have been a more circumstantial debt. One of the many classic delineations of the *beatus vir* is found in the closing portion of the second chorus of Seneca's *Thyestes*, a favorite passage with Pope, often referred to in his correspondence;[53] and one of the most influential imitations of Seneca's lines is Cowley's rendering, already quoted. It may be that thinking about his father in connection with the tribute he wished to pay him in the epistle put Pope in mind of the Senecan passage, and that this reminded him of Cowley's essay "Of Obscurity," to which these

[50] Pope's phrase in the poem's *Advertisement.*

[51] This view is further argued in " 'The Shadowy Cave': Some Speculations on a Twickenham Grotto," *Restoration and Eighteenth-Century Literature: Essays in Honor of A. D. McKillop,* Chicago (1963), pp. 71–72.

[52] See E. F. Mengel, Jr., "Patterns of Imagery in Pope's *Arbuthnot,*" *PMLA,* Vol. LXIX (1954).

[53] To Atterbury, March 19, 1722 (in this instance, Pope quotes from Granville's version of the Senecan lines: see above, note 31); to Caryll, October 26 [1722]; to Broome, June 29 [1725]; *Correspondence,* II, 109, 140, 302.

lines formed the afterpiece.[54] It may be that Pope was put in mind of Cowley's essay by his own reference to it in his letter of 1712 to the *Spectator*, which he would perhaps have been going over at about the time he was composing the epistle, with an eye to the publication of his literary correspondence in 1735. It may be that occasionally Pope took down his copy of Cowley to reread, and had done so near the time of writing *Arbuthnot*. Or it may be that there is no connection whatever between the epistle and the passages I am about to quote, that the resemblances are coincidental.

What will be striking in any case, to a reader who has just come from a close perusal of the structure of the *Epistle to Dr. Arbuthnot*, is that Cowley's essay begins with an analysis of the Horatian line that Pope adopted for the archway of his Grotto: *Secretum iter et fallentis semita vita*—a line eminently calculated to remind Pope of his father and of his own (at times) desires for himself. The essay then proceeds rapidly to words of counsel that it is easy to suppose were tumbling in Pope's brain when he reached the important realization that his poem must begin from a position of invaded privacy.

If we engage into a large Acquaintance and various familiarities, we set open our gates to Invaders of most of our time: we expose our life to a *Quotidian Ague* of frigid impertinencies, which would make a wise man tremble to think of.

Even the disease image is here, crying out to be elaborated.

The sentence just quoted leads immediately to further counsel about staying out of the world's view

(I sought no homage from the Race that write;
I kept, like *Asian* Monarchs, from their sight. . . .)

and about avoiding all fame but that of virtue

---

[54] One detail in the portrait of his father ("Death . . . without a groan"), not to be found in Seneca's Latin except by inference, may possibly be a reminiscence of Marvell's version of this chorus (8–11):

Thus when without noise, unknown,
I have liv'd out all my span,
I shall dye, without a groan,
An old honest Country man.

But see below, p. 243, the passage from Cowley's "Of Obscurity," where this detail is also found.

(Curst be the Verse, how well soe'er it flow,
That tends to make one worthy Man my foe. . . .)

Then comes the most striking resemblance of all: Cowley's prose sketch
of the stock retirement figure, in which it would certainly have been hard
for Pope *not* to recognize his father, and again, one aspect of himself:

> Upon the whole matter, I account a person who has a moderate
> Minde and Fortune, and lives in the conversation of two or three
> agreeable friends, with little commerce in the world besides, who
> is esteemed well enough by his few neighbours that know him, and
> is truly irreproachable by any body, and so after a healthful quiet
> life, before the great inconveniences of old age, goes more silently
> out of it than he came in, (for I would not have him so much as
> Cry in the *Exit*). This Innocent Deceiver of the world, as *Horace*
> calls him, this *Muta persona*, I take to have been more happy in his
> Part, than the greatest Actors that fill the Stage with show and
> noise . . . .

There follows the chorus from *Thyestes*.

Perhaps a stricter relevance than we had thought lies behind the tribute
Pope paid, less than three years after the *Epistle to Dr. Arbuthnot*, in the
Epistle to Augustus (75–78):

> Who now reads Cowley? If he pleases yet,
> His moral pleases, not his pointed wit;
> Forgot his Epic, nay Pindaric Art,
> But still I love the language of his Heart.

The English Poet and

the Burden of the Past, 1660–1820

BY W. J. BATE

◄◄◄◄◄◄◄◄◄◄◄◄ ☼ ►►►►►►►►►►►►

I

The theme of this essay could be expressed by a remark Johnson quotes from Pliny in one of the *Ramblers* (No. 86): "The burthen of government is increased upon princes by the virtues of their immediate predecessors." And Johnson goes on to add: "He that succeeds a celebrated writer, has the same difficulties to encounter."

I have often wondered whether we could find any more comprehensive way of taking up the whole of English poetry from the middle seventeenth century down to the present—or for that matter the modern history of the arts as a whole—than by exploring the effects of this accumulating anxiety and the question it so directly presents to the poet or artist: What is there left to do? Yet this is not a subject we seem tempted to pursue. As critics or historians, we too often tend to focus on one of two things. We either concentrate on the writer's "subjects" (what he is obviously writing *about*, or what he says elsewhere is concerning him), or, if we prefer to be more indirect or subtle and try to look beneath the surface, we concentrate on what interests us and what we therefore feel should be interesting or motivating him, whether it be a "climate of ideas" or psychoanalytic preoccupations.

Unlike the poet, the critic or historian always has a subject matter—literature itself (or the other arts). And as for finding a new "idiom" in which to express himself, any difficulties in doing so are not only rudimentary in comparison but usually unnecessary. Relatively unbothered by any sharp personal experience of the same sort, we continue to remain oblivious because of the natural pride and embarrassed silence of the writer himself. The writer or artist may be self-revealing enough in other ways. But when his anxiety has to do with the all-important matter of his craft, and his achievement or impotence there, he naturally prefers to wrestle with it privately or to express it only indirectly. The subject, in other words, is not one for which we can compile a clean-cut reading list. We begin to sense its importance only when we look between the lines, or follow closely the life of writer after writer, or weigh the context of self-defensive manifestoes or fatalistic excuses in eras of militant transition in style, and, above all, when we note the nagging apprehension, from generation to generation, that the poet is somehow becoming increasingly powerless to attain (or is in some way being forbidden to try to attain) the scope and power of the earlier poetry that he so deeply admires.

We need, as historians, to keep in mind what it means to artists and writers to come immediately after a great creative era. We need to keep in mind the natural anxieties, the intimidations, the temptations to paralysis, their understandable desire to establish themselves, and the appeal of different procedures from those they have been accustomed to admire. The burden of the past upon the writers of eighteenth-century England is an immensely fruitful subject—fruitful for understanding the general situation, in some ways the nature of the achievement, not only of this period but also of the Romantics, the Victorians, and the twentieth century. We could, in fact, make a very good argument that this remorseless deepening of self-consciousness, before the rich and intimidating legacy of the past, becomes the greatest single problem that modern art (art, that is to say, since the close of the seventeenth century) has had to face, and that it will become so increasingly in the future.

In comparison, most of the "ideas" or preoccupations that we extract (as conflicts, goals, or anxieties) and then picture as so sharply pressing on the mind of the artist are often less directly urgent. We need, as Johnson often reminds us, to remember that the critic or historian of the arts as well as the artist himself have very different vocations, however much their interests overlap or intertwine. The critic or historian of the arts, as we have said, can always find a subject matter. He may have his own anxieties and uncertainties. But he is at least not in competition with Shakespeare or Milton, Dryden or Pope, Wordsworth or Keats. The poet, on the other hand, is unavoidably aware, in a very direct and concrete sense, of previous writers, and never so much as when he tries to establish

a difference; and he is keenly aware of them in a way that he is not (if he
is writing in the early eighteenth century) of Newton, Locke, or Shaftesbury. Newtonian philosophy, ideals of order and decorum, or Shaftes-
burian benevolence may all have concerned eighteenth-century poets.
It is taken for granted that they have an important place in our consideration of what the English poetry of the eighteenth century became. The
point is merely that these poets also had one very direct problem that was
at least as absorbing to them, and often far more so: the stark problem of
what and how to write.

So with the English Romantics. Keats, who certainly faced enough
personal difficulties, would become really despondent (except after his
fatal illness began) only when, as he told his friend Richard Woodhouse,
he felt that "there was nothing original to be written in poetry; that its
riches were already exhausted—and all its beauties forestalled." Goethe
rejoiced that he was not born an Englishman and did not have to com-
pete with the achievement of Shakespeare. The situation is the same when
we move on to the Victorians or to the first half of the twentieth century:
these writers, we say, were faced with a difficult situation, which we then
proceed briskly to document—the decline of faith, the lack of certainty in
moral as well as religious values. All this is true (and is true of certain
earlier eras). But the pessimism we explain with such a cumbersome
machinery of ideas has often an even sharper, more immediate spur—the
nagging questions: what is there left to write? and how, as craftsmen, do
we get not only new subjects but a new idiom? A great deal of modern
literature—and criticism—is haunted, as Spender says, by the thought of a
"Second Fall of Man," and almost everything has been blamed: the
Renaissance loss of the medieval unity of faith, Baconian science, British
empiricism, Rousseau, the French Revolution, industrialism, nineteenth-
century science, universities and academicism, the growing complexity of
ordinary life, the spread of mass media. But whatever else enters into the
situation, the principal explanation is the writer's loss of self-confidence as
he compares what he feels able to do with the rich heritage of past art and
literature. Scientists, we notice, are not affected with this despondency.
And we do not account for that interesting exception, or for any number
of other exceptions that enter into the picture, if we try to attribute it to
mere insensitivity.

II

If you took up English neoclassicism solely in the light of what we call
the "history of ideas," it could still remain one of the great unresolved

puzzles of literary history. No explanation for it—at least no explanation why it caught on so quickly and firmly after 1660—would satisfy anyone for very long except the person who provides it.

Let me hurry to say that I am not speaking of English neoclassic *theory*—that is of neoclassic critical writing. It is only too easy, if we confine ourselves to the history of critical theory, to trace an ancestral line through Sidney and Ben Jonson down to the Restoration (the history of critical theory is by definition a history of *ideas*). And if we want more help, we have merely to turn to the intellectual history of England during the sixteenth and seventeenth centuries and we can find any number of ideas, if not ancestral at least collateral, to enrich our genealogical chart. But once the glow of discovery has faded, the result is not really very persuasive except to the confirmed Hegelian, of which there are twentieth as well as nineteenth-century varieties. Our consciences begin to remind us that, as historians of ideas, we are naturally swayed by special interests. We have a vocational interest in presupposing that there is a relatively clean-cut influence of "ideas" on artists, meaning, by "ideas," concepts that we, as historians, have abstracted from a large, diverse period of human life, and which may very well have struck our attention only because they are so susceptible of genealogy. Of course we all say—and say it quite sincerely—that what we are really interested in is the *reciprocal* influence of ideas and art. But it is so difficult to put neatly the influence of art, in all its diversity, on the climate of ideas. To the orderly mind of the historian, this task is as elusive, or as unmanageably messy, as having to describe and categorize the influence of people on ideas. We find ourselves feeling that it is better to leave all that for some future, more leisurely consideration. Hence, in our actual practice if not in ultimate ideal, we lean radically toward the simplicities of thinking in terms of a one-way traffic.

A sense of all this begins to nag the conscience after we trace our genealogies of ideas in order to explain English neoclassicism: the rephrasing, by sixteenth- and seventeenth-century critics, of classical ideals; the premium on decorum, refinement, regularity, and the ways in which they are particularized; the confidence in method; the influence of mathematics. Are these ideas, these concepts and values, that we have abstracted, not progenitors after all of the actual neoclassic literature to come, but only midwives, escorts, even (to quote Eliot) "attendant persons"? Putting it another way: were these particular concepts and ideas such that they would have been left undeveloped, would have fallen on deaf ears, unless there had also been *other* considerations, equally or perhaps more important?

We know very well, for example, that English literature itself, from the time of Elizabeth down into the middle seventeenth century, showed a diversity that has been unrivaled since the most fertile days of Athens. We also know that it showed, at its best, a power or intensity in its diversity (in idiom, in metaphor, in cadence) that has haunted English literature ever since that time. And this literature was written at the same time as those more theoretical works to which we are looking for the ancestry of English neoclassicism. We know that the intensity and diversity of that literature (or, putting it more truthfully, an intensity both of, and within, diversity) far outweighs our thin sketch of theoretical or merely critical concepts through the Elizabethan and Jacobean eras. To put it bluntly: it is not at all from English life and English experience in its widest sense, from the time of Elizabeth through that of Cromwell, that a really developed neoclassicism came so suddenly. We know perfectly well that systematized and pervasive neoclassicism is very much a French product, and that it was in fact viewed as that (whether with respect, restiveness, or antagonism) by the English themselves, from Dryden, Rymer, and Temple down to Hazlitt and Francis Jeffrey, a century and a half later.

Then why did English neoclassicism occur? We are always being reminded that these values of the "New Classicism" of France never sat too easily on the English mind. Of course they did not. In fact, they were always being qualified by native English attitudes; and (though we have recently tended to exaggerate the amount) there was a good deal of open dissent. But this makes the matter all the more curious: Why should it have flourished so rapidly when there was this much tendency to dissent and qualify? There is, in fact, nothing else in the whole of the long literary history of England quite like this brisk transition. There is no other instance, after the invention of printing, where you find a settled group of literary premises and aims imported almost bodily, adopted with such dispatch, and then transformed into orthodoxy, or near-orthodoxy, for so long a time (a full seventy or eighty years), despite a large undercurrent that runs counter to it. Of the three really great transitions in English poetry since the Elizabethans and Jacobeans, this is the first. The second is found in the large shift that took place in the late eighteenth and early nineteenth centuries, and the third in the radical change of idiom and mode during the first half of the twentieth century. But the second of these transitions, to which we apply the loose word "romantic," was the reverse in almost every way from what we are considering now. To begin with, it was slower and longer prepared for in the actual writing (as distinct from critical theory) that preceded it. It emerged from within the neoclassic stronghold, opening the walls one by one. To a large extent it was demonstrably—even dramatically—a nationalistic movement in England (as it was in another, more pronounced way, in Germany). When we turn to our own era, we have to admit that the transition to the new poetic idiom of the early and middle twentieth century was rapid, and that it was analogous to the neoclassic transition in speed as well as in other ways. On the other hand, this radical modern change was less metaphysically rationalized; in some ways it was closer to its own imme- diate past (the English romantics) than Pope ever was to Shakespeare or Milton; nor was it—despite the influence of the French Symbolists and of others—a continental importation: too much else, by that time, was already going on within the English-speaking world generally.

III

To the England of the Restoration and the early eighteenth century, the mature and sophisticated neoclassicism of France had an irresistible appeal. It gave them a chance to be different from their own immediate English predecessors while at the same time, it offered a counterideal that was impressively—almost monolithically—systematized. French neo- classicism appeared to have answers ready for almost any kind of objection to it. And most of the answers had this further support: they inevitably referred—or pulled the conscience back—to the premises of "reason" and of ordered nature that the English themselves were already sharing, though not perhaps in the same spirit as the French. To dismiss an argu- ment that led directly back to "reason" was something they were not at all prepared to do. Even the more articulate writers still lacked the vocabu- lary to express any hesitations they might have felt. And in any case, had not their own English Newton already helped to disclose the universal architecture, and to an extent that no Frenchman had done?—Newton, as James Thomson later said, "whom God / To mortals lent to trace his boundless works."

But to the English—if not the French at this particular time—there was a built-in conflict in what this welcome new body of ideals carried. On the one hand, they found themselves embracing the classical ideal that really great art was *general;* and this, by definition, seemed to imply that great

art naturally concerns itself with the most widely applicable subjects and
in doing so reaches a wide audience. Yet at the same time this new classical art, this neoclassicism of France, openly cultivated what the English
eighteenth century (and, in a curious way, the English romantics) called
"refinement." The French could meet and absorb this challenge; the
English could not. "Refinement," in this new systematized model of how
to proceed, could be admitted as both new and desirable. But the ideal
of "generality" brought back to the English mind their own past creative
achievement—Shakespeare and Milton especially. Critics could tell them
that Waller and Denham had brought to English poets the new, cherished
values of "refinement"—cleanliness, smoothness, urbanity, and sophistication. But, after admitting this, where was the "generality" (generality in
the grander sense of the word—"the *grandeur* of generality," to use Johnson's phrase)? Dryden—however bland, self-controlled, self-confident,
and, in the best sense of the word, negligent—had himself slightly chafed
beneath this dichotomy. He swung back and forth. But always, in thinking
of the rich English past, he was aware of "the giants before the flood" (we
see this in the *Essay of Dramatic Poesy:* the dice there are secretly loaded on
the side of his great English progenitors), and, in speaking of Shakespeare,
he could say enviously that "All the images of nature were *still present* to
him." Pope also would speak differently at different times. But one thing
that remained with him was that early advice from William Walsh:
"Mr. Walsh . . . used to tell me that there was *one way left of excelling;* for
though we had several great poets, we never had any one great poet that
was correct; and he desired me to make that my study and aim." Pope
could say that "Nature and Homer were the same"; he could himself
translate Homer; and he could contemplate writing a blank-verse epic
on a legendary British hero. Nevertheless this gifted poet—certainly one
of the eight or ten greatest in the entire history of English letters—settled
in practice for the more specialized (and newer) quality of "refinement";
this at least, for the English poet, remained as "one way left of excelling."

   But whatever Pope's individual success (and that itself created a further
problem for still later poets) the classical ideal of generality, of scope in
subject and breadth of appeal, continued to bring back the question: what
has happened to the "greater genres," to epic and dramatic tragedy?
That question, and all it implies, was to haunt the English poet henceforth. Take just three instances, purposely selected because each writer is
so masculinely vigorous and independent. Johnson, loathing any cant
about "decline" or anything else that reflected on man's freedom—
Johnson who was "always angry," as he said, "whenever he heard earlier

periods extolled at the expense of the modern"—could still permit Imlac
to say that, whatever the nation and language and however different
the explanations offered, "it is commonly observed that the early writers
are in possession of nature, and their followers of art: that the first excel in
strength and invention, and the latter in elegance and refinement."
Keats could compare the ancients and the Elizabethans to "Emperors of
vast Provinces," while by contrast "each of the moderns like an Elector of
Hanover keeps his petty state." And, to glance ahead another hundred
years, there are those lines of Yeats:

> Shakespearean fish swam the sea, far away from land;
> Romantic fish swam in nets coming to the hand;
> What are all those fish that lie gasping on the strand?

IV

By the middle of the eighteenth century, after a hundred years of the
English neoclassic adventure in the arts, we find an almost universal
suspicion that something had somehow gone wrong. And nothing could be
historically more shortsighted and parochial than to associate that feeling,
as has so often been done, merely with a budding "romanticism" restive
against "neoclassic restriction." The uneasiness went far deeper and
afflicted those who sympathized with the stylistic mode, or modes, of
neoclassic poetry. This is especially true by the second half of the century.
Who are the conservatives who leap to mind? They are men like Burke,
who hungered for amplitude and the "sublime," or the classically minded
Reynolds, who found himself, as he grew older, thinking of Michelangelo
and longing for the scope and power associated with the lost "sublime."
As conservatives in poetry we think of Johnson and Goldsmith. Yet there
is that illuminating moment when Boswell tells Johnson of a dispute
between the Augustan-minded Goldsmith and Robert Dodsley the pub-
lisher. Goldsmith had maintained that there was no

> poetry produced in this age. Dodsley appealed to his own Collec-
> tion, and maintained, that though you could not find a palace like
> Dryden's "Ode on St. Cecilia's Day," you had villages composed
> of very pretty houses; and he mentioned particularly "The
> Spleen." JOHNSON. "I think Dodsley gave up the question.
> He and Goldsmith said the same thing; only he said it in a softer
> manner than Goldsmith did; for he acknowledged that there was
> no poetry, nothing that towered above the common mark."

These conservatives are simply thinking and reacting in the vein typified by Sir William Temple, two or three generations before: that of an intelligent and well-read Englishman who has been brought up on the classics, and who is looking for the exemplification of broad classical values in the literature of his own day. (To say this is not to deny that Temple also said some silly things. It is easy to pick holes in what he says about literature; but we, as historians, have the accumulated labors of two and a half centuries of criticism and scholarship to permit us our superiority.)

Whatever else can be said of the spate of critical writing that suddenly begins in the middle of the eighteenth century, we can describe it as an attempt (however confused) to reground the entire thinking about poetry in the light of one overwhelming fact: the obviously superior originality and at least an apparently greater immediacy and universality of subject and appeal in the poetry of earlier periods. The regrounding brought with it the fear—more openly expressed than ever before in history—that literature and the other arts as well were threatened with decline.[1] This was not at all the result of reading Vico (of whom few had heard) or of reading reflections by others who had read Vico. Nor is the matter disposed of by saying that "progress" is a "romantic" idea and that thoughts of the "Golden Age" or of historical cycles are natural to a neoclassical period. Least of all do we show much insight when we mutter that this apprehension is an old one and cite once again the sixteenth- and seventeenth-century writers who dwell on the "decay of nature." The sort of anxiety of which we are now speaking is very different from the idea of the "decay of nature." In fact, the people who felt it most strongly were those who believed most in progress in other ways—for whom the decline in the arts was the unfortunate by-product of the increase in knowledge, communication, taste, and general civilization. And in any case we should remember that the practicing writer is quite capable of falling into apprehensions without the aid of the philosopher—especially when the cards appear to be stacked against him. This has been possible for a very long time. I think of the poignant epigram left by an Egyptian writer of 2000 B.C. (Khakheperresenb): "Would I had phrases that are not known, utterances that are strange, in new language that hath not been used, free from repetition, not an utterance which hath grown stale, which men of old have spoken."

[1] See the article of John D. Scheffer, "The Idea of Decline in Literature and the Fine Arts in Eighteenth-Century England," *Modern Philology*, XXXIV (1936–37), 155–78.

Several diagnoses were advanced, many of them dovetailing with the discussion of other matters. There were the outright primitivists (so often discussed apart from this pressing, personal concern on the part of the writer). Earlier, more primitive folk, as Thomas Blackwell said in his *Enquiry into the Life and Writings of Homer* (1735), "lived naturally": their passions were simple, direct and intense; their conversation did not consist of "the Prattle, and little pretty Forms that enervate a polished Speech" in the later periods of a culture. This approach continues without interruption and with increasing sophistication until it culminates in Wordsworth's great preface to the *Lyrical Ballads* at the end of the century. It can be hopeful (as it is in Wordsworth)—assuming that we are free, if we want, to get back to the "essential passions." But more often it assumes that the door is closed. The best example I can think of is William Duff's *Essay of Original Genius* (1767), the concluding chapter of which bears the long title (here abbreviated): "That Original Poetic Genius Will in General Be Displayed in Its Ultimate Vigour in the Early . . . Periods of Society . . . and That It Will Seldom Appear in a Very Great Degree in Cultivated Life."

Other diagnoses, which included a fair admixture of the primitivistic spirit, focused on specific factors. An example is John Brown's *Dissertation on the Rise, Union, and Power, the Progressions, Separations, and Corruptions of Poetry and Music* (1763). The tendency of the arts to "divide" and specialize was also applied to language itself. Few of the rhetorics and general studies of language, during the later eighteenth century, failed to note that metaphor and with it poetic "suggestiveness" in general are gradually lost as a language becomes more exact and denotative through use and through the growth of a more analytic writing. Before long everyone was agreeing. Typically, when a small discussion group was founded in Manchester (The Literary and Philosophical Society of Manchester), one of the papers in their first volume (1781–83) could stress that a language was more poetic in its earlier stages; that poetic feeling later becomes "minced into finer portions," and that therefore a "strong poetic character may be expected to decline, as Taste improves."

Still others, in searching for an explanation, found it in the self-consciousness and timidity created by the growth of criticism—a growth considered inevitable as a culture grows older and a part of the price paid for the spread of literacy. Sir William Temple had implied as much. But it is now, in the mid-eighteenth century, that the thought is really grasped at, in the hope of finding some simple explanation. There is the well-known remark in Joseph Warton's *Essay on Pope* (1756)—well-known because even Johnson thought it one that "deserves great attention": "In no polished nation, after criticism has been much studied, and the rules of writing established, has any very extraordinary work ever appeared." This is a central point in Goldsmith's *Enquiry into the Present State of Polite Learning* (1759), and Goldsmith did much to popularize it. Yet the idea, however common, is never treated too seriously (partly, of course, because critics—who would naturally be the ones to pursue the idea—were not eager to argue against the basis of what they themselves spent their time pursuing).

The real interest of this attitude appears indirectly: that is, in its underlying sense of how much intimidation may have to do with the writer's fluency and what he tries to attain. And Edward Young, in the *Conjectures on Original Composition* (1759), faces the whole matter of intimidation directly, though he is thinking less about the effect of criticism than about the intimidating pressures, on the practicing writer, of great models of the past—those great models on whom the present writer has naturally been educated. Young's approach appears at first to be far more interesting and valuable. The disappointment comes in Young's rather easy conclusion of what the writer should do about it. In effect Young suggests that the writer pull himself up by his own bootstraps. Let us imitate the general spirit of the past writers we admire (their boldness, their openness, their range) but keep selecting our own means of working toward it: He that imitates the *Iliad* is not imitating Homer.

V

Meanwhile the essence of the problem was being put by David Hume, though relatively few people cared to dwell on it. In his essay "Of the Rise and Progress of the Arts and Sciences," he considers different facets of the subject and then advances his "fourth observation": "That when the arts and sciences come to perfection in any state, from that moment they naturally, or rather necessarily, decline, and seldom or never revive in that nation where they formerly flourished." The observation, he admits, is theoretically puzzling and seems to be "contrary to reason."

Is not the answer that "a noble emulation is the source of every excellence"? If, in a period just before us, an art seems to have attained a "perfection," this very achievement, pressing on the artist that follows, will "extinguish emulation, and sink the ardor of generous youth." Hume does not elaborate at the moment on what happens when emulation proves so difficult. But in his essay "Of Simplicity and Refinement" (where he states that "the excess of refinement is now more to be guarded against than ever") he goes a little further: after an art has reached a high level, "the endeavor to *please by novelty* leads men wide of simplicity and nature."

There are two points made by Hume, whose uncanny perceptions in so many other ways have continued to arouse or bedevil our thinking since his time. First, he implies that decline is inevitable (and not for any Spenglerian reason—Hume is no post-Hegelian believer in the determinism of the *Zeitgeist*—but rather for empirical reasons that have to do with the way that human nature insists on behaving). But we need not linger on this matter of inevitability: Hume was no dogmatist; he could quickly change his position when given additional facts to consider. The second point is the important one: that, because of the spirit of emulation—because of the need of the artist to feel that he has a chance before the accumulated "perfection of the past"—he is in danger either of giving up, or else of manicuring the past, or, finally, of searching, in compensation, for novelty for its own sake.

In bringing up this directly human problem of emulation, Hume resurrects some remarks by Velleius Paterculus, written about the year 30 A.D. (*Historiae Romanae*, I. xvii): when we feel ourselves unable to excel (or even to equal) the great predecessors immediately before us, hope and emulation languish; we gradually resign the pursuit in which they have excelled and try to seek out a new one. This is one of those instances when an idea or attitude, expressed by a long-forgotten writer, becomes alive once again and is repeated in a new context because it seems to make sense. Velleius touched home to very few people before Hume; but henceforth we find him briefly quoted or echoed by those who knew or had read Hume, such as Lord Kames or Archibald Alison. The speculations of men like Kames or Alison, however, are limited and indirect, revealing a general, unlocalized suspicion that they are unwilling to apply to literature in any detail. Kames, for example, in his *Sketches of the History of Man* (1774), cites the effect of Newton on mathematics in Great Britain since Newton's day—the whole study of it has since languished. Kames also speculates about the ultimate effect of the great painters of the Italian Renaissance, and compares Raphael, Michelangelo, and Titian to large oaks that intercept new plants from the "sunshine of emulation."

I suspect that one reason this large problem of the burden of the past and of its effect on emulation was not followed up, but rather bruited around as a premise, is because it was most clearly seen by men who were fundamentally conservative (in the broad sense of the word): by men who valued the gains in general insight (and, if you will, "progress" and "refinement") that had been won since the Middle Ages and the Renaissance. All of these men, however different in other ways, are the reverse of nostalgic primitivists—they include not only Johnson, Burke, and Goldsmith, but also such men as Hume and Voltaire. For Hume, however radical his ultimate effect as a philosopher, in most respects wanted to conserve what he conceived to be the gains of his age. So did Voltaire, in another way. Being independent and original people themselves, and at the same time hoping to conserve recently attained values, they especially felt the tensions, the contradictions, the embarrassments. It can be seriously argued that the most truly original ideas that have persisted from the eighteenth century (leaving aside Rousseau)—ideas that have since been developed or merely repeated—have come from men who, in general spirit, wished to conserve the gains of the time and its immediate past. Themselves so energetic, so appreciative of the appeal of novelty ("No man," said Johnson, "ever yet became great by imitation."), these men were especially clairvoyant in recognizing to what the pressure for novelty at all costs could eventually lead. So with Voltaire, whose essay on taste written for the *Encyclopédie* (1757) was soon translated and widely read in England. If a period of art immediately behind us has little to be said for it, the pressure to be different can be valuable. But if "artists through the apprehension of being regarded as mere imitators" feel it necessary to "strike out into new and uncommon paths" after a really great period of art, the direction is probably going to be downward. And Richard Hurd, in ending his long *Discourse on Poetical Imitation*, felt himself justified in one general conclusion that "they who have a comprehensive view of the history of letters, in their general periods, . . . will hardly dispute": that though many other causes may contribute to decline, "yet the *principal*, ever, is this *anxious dread of imitation* in polite and cultivated writers."

VI

Meanwhile, in its restive attempt to lift the burden of the past, or at least to shift it a little to one side, the English eighteenth century had struck back at its own most recent inheritance (neoclassicism) with two relatively new ideals (new at least for art) that were henceforth to haunt almost every English writer, and in time almost every Western European and American artist: the ideals of *originality* and *sincerity*.

Like most compensatory ideals that become rigid through anxiety, they only complicated the problem further (and, for that matter, also conflicted with each other). That is, they quickly became the sort of ideals that you can neither live with nor live without. You cannot openly deny them. You cannot afford to come out and say that you want to be "unoriginal" or "insincere." Yet if you are never to write a line unless you are convinced that you are totally "sincere," then when do you start? You can be sure that something is going to happen both to your fluency and your range. David Perkins, in his new book, *Wordsworth and the Poetry of Sincerity*, has brilliantly and sympathetically shown the dilemma that Wordsworth inherited and then—through his own individual success— powerfully deepened. Similarly, if you are exhorted to be "original" at all costs, then how do you take even the first step—especially if what you have been taught most to admire is represented by great predecessors from whom you must distinguish yourself, and, even worse, if your "original" departure from those admired models must spring from an "originality" that is itself "sincere"?

This was the fearful legacy of the great Romantics who come at the close of the eighteenth century—who in this, as in so many other ways, are so much the children of the eighteenth century: a legacy that consisted not of just one but a whole series of conflicting demands. To begin with, you were exhorted to be "original" at all costs, and yet reminded that you could not be "original" about the most important things. [2]

[2] Francis Jeffrey is characteristic—all the more so because (despite some of his remarks on Wordsworth) he was in general so warm a champion of the new effort in literature. Here is just one excerpt (from his review of Scott's *Lady of the Lake*): "As the elements of poetical emotion are necessarily limited, so it was natural for those who first sought to excite it, to avail themselves of those subjects, situations, and images, that were most obviously calculated to produce that effect . . . after-poets were in a very different situation. They could neither take the most general topics of interest, nor treat them with the [same] ease and difference . . . because this was precisely what had been done. . . . " Jeffrey then takes up the alternatives that appear to be shaping up: an increasing and more detailed realism in the study and presentation of character; a more careful (but more "limited") exploration of the emotional life; or, thirdly, a self-conscious "distortion" of object and idiom, either by "affectation" of an obvious sort or through "dissecting" a subject—or a "narrow corner" of it— "with such curious and microscopic accuracy" that its "original form" is "no longer discernible to the eyes of the uninstructed." Elsewhere Jeffrey speculates that the promising new genre of the novel will give us something of what we find in the great dramatic poetry of the Elizabethans and Jacobeans. We sometimes have the feeling, as we look through Jeffrey's reviews, that we are reading an earlier version of Edmund Wilson's essay, "Is Verse a Dying Technique?" And Keats himself, "cowering," as he said, "under the wings of great Poets," occasionally wonder whether epic poems (though he himself was about to begin one—*Hyperion*) were not "splendid impositions" on the modern world.

Twenty-five centuries of past poetry had virtually insured that. You were told that the "inner life" still remained to be explored, and yet the whole character of your education and idealism was dominated by the great past examples of objective art (above all, poetic drama); and the "inner life" seemed by contrast hopelessly specialized in appeal as well as fraught with all the dangers of self-absorption. At the same time, as the eighteenth century passed into the nineteenth, the critical intelligence of England and Scotland was turning, with more delicacy and more historical understanding than ever before, to the great works of the English Renaissance—the Elizabethans and Jacobeans. Hazlitt, with sharp impatience, weighed the modern movement against that rich past. The title of his little essay, "Why the Arts Are Not Progressive," suggests a a point of view that persists through almost every critical work he wrote, and which is all the more persuasive because of his robust liberalism: Where are the greater "genres"—the direct turning to "nature," with simplicity and confidence—that we find dawning so splendidly in Chaucer and then reaching a high norm from the time of Shakespeare to the middle seventeenth century? Coleridge, in his own way, was ending with an ideal of poetry by which, as he "freely" admitted, he was himself no poet—an ideal that looked back to the great poetic dramas of another era. The interesting thing, as we pass the year 1800, is that it is the major figures (or the near-major figures) who betray this anxiety. Among reviewers, it is the best of them, Francis Jeffrey, who especially looks for a poetry (or, if not a poetry, at least a prose fiction) that will give back to us a literature that will have something of the older range and strength of the epic and poetic drama. Thomas Love Peacock was not a major critic. But he was a realistic and shrewd man. His *Four Ages of Poetry* put, with distilled irony, the helplessness of his contemporaries if they really wanted to write poetry comparable to that of the envied past. After a primitive "iron" age comes the "golden" age (the great days of Greece, in the ancient world; or the era of Shakespeare in the English Renaissance). Then the Silver Age takes over—Rome, and Augustan England. And what is now about to appear is an Age of Brass.

VII

Was there no way of getting out of this self-created prison? For of course it *was* self-created. How the oriental artist, during all those centuries that he followed his craft, would have stared—or laughed—if told that these past artists by whom, and through whom, he had been taught should suddenly represent territory that was *verboten:* that he had studied them only in order to be different! Take any of the great past eras we say we admire: Would not the Greek artist, the Renaissance artist, be complimented if he was told he could be virtually mistaken for his greatest predecessors; and, if he was able to go still further than they, did he not assume that it would be through assimilating the virtues and techniques of his predecessors while perhaps capping them with just a little more? Was it not a sufficient triumph even to recapture a few of the virtues of our greatest predecessors, as Sir Joshua Reynolds said in his last discourse to the students at the Royal Academy?—that last discourse in which he disowned his earlier willingness to abide by "the taste of the times in which I live" and said that, "however unequal I feel myself to that attempt, were I now to begin the world again, I would tread in the steps of that great master [Michelangelo] . . . [since] to catch the slightest of his perfections would be glory and distinction enough." It requires no heroic effort to be different from the great.

Nature—life in all its diversity—is still constantly before us. Cannot we *force* ourselves to turn directly toward it? And some of the Romantics tried to do just that. I quote, because it is so short, a remark from a letter of the painter John Constable (October 31, 1820): "In the early ages of the fine arts, the productions were more affecting and sublime"; and why? Only because "the artists, being without human exemplars, *were forced to have recourse to nature.*" "Force yourselves to have that recourse" was, in effect, the advice of two of the greatest men of letters that the eighteenth century produced—Johnson and Goethe. Over and over again, though Johnson allowed Imlac in *Rasselas* to admit that "the first writers took possession of the most striking objects," he himself kept stressing that "there are qualities in . . . nature *yet* undiscovered, and combinations in the powers of art yet untried." Granted (in fact it is tautological) that over-all characteristics remain the same. But the poet can still observe the "alterations" that "time is always making in the modes of life." The complaint "that all topics are pre-occupied" is repeated only by the timid or by the militantly conservative, a complaint "by which some discourage others and some themselves." And Goethe could point out the mistake of the new "subjective" writer who concentrates solely on expressing his individual feelings in the frantic hope of being "original." He will have his reward. He has "soon talked out his little *internal* material, and is at last ruined by *mannerism,*" by mere repetition of what his small inner fountain provides, while the poet who turns directly to nature, to external reality, will tap a perennial fountain of subject matter and, in doing so, become "inexhaustible and forever new." To some extent, that salutary counsel was followed.[3] The Romantics opened up the subjective world; but they did so greatly, and with profound and wide appeal, because some of them could simultaneously cling to the other ideal.

But problems still remained—problems that sharply anticipate these that we now face a century later. Take just one. Assume that you can still pull yourself up by your bootstraps and can energetically and freshly begin, by some miracle, to write in the "larger *genres*" of poetry—the epic, poetic drama, or at least analogous equivalents. There is still the fact that your audiences, your readers, are different now from what they were in the past. At least they threaten to be so. Even if they, and the critics who assail you, could somehow put "originality" out of their minds (which they will not), and could be as open as they enthusiastically say that Shakespeare's audience was, is it not also a fact that this more literate modern audience, living in its more complex world, has been deriving its "imaginative exercise"—its *katharsis*, to use Aristotle's term—from literature itself, from the large accumulated heritage of imaginative literature? Hazlitt shrewdly raised that question. The Aristotelian *katharsis* that comes in seeing a great tragedy (with us it too often comes in merely *reading* great tragedies) "substitutes an *artificial and intellectual* interest for real passion." It does this automatically. But in that case could we not say that

> Tragedy, like Comedy, must therefore defeat itself; for its patterns must be drawn from the living models within the breast, from feeling or from observation; and the materials of Tragedy cannot be found among a people, who are the habitual spectators of Tragedy, whose interests and passions are not their own, but ideal, remote, sentimental, and abstracted. It is for this reason chiefly, we conceive, that the highest efforts of the Tragic Muse are in general the earliest; where the strong impulses of nature are not lost in the refinements and glosses of art.

And John Wilson could develop, from this premise, a question that would strike home to every poet of the time (and still more to every poet since). The human imagination, when both fed and challenged constantly by a

[3] The routine historian of criticism or historian of ideas shows only his own parochialism when he tries to "periodize" the great. Greatness, when it reaches a certain level, finds itself meeting the great of other eras in what Keats calls "an immortal freemasonry." Johnson has far more in common with the great English Romantics— with the greatest writers in the English language since the Romantics—than with the minor figures of his day. He also bears that same relation to the past (he is in some ways, as Whitehead says, "of the essence of the seventeenth century").

rich but unsystematized life, may move freely and instinctively into the "larger genres," in its hope to convey or understand its experience. But if the habitual, daily use of our imaginations (no longer submitting to *real* life and constantly dwelling in the mesh of it) turns largely for compensatory nourishment and exercise to past poetry, shall we not end with merely a lyric—or, if not a lyric, at least a shorter-breathed—poetry, a poetry produced largely from the soil of past poetry?

VIII

And yet, with all the strikes against them, the greater Romantics still succeeded (astonishingly so when we remember that, in England, we are dealing with only some twenty-five years, in a nation with about a twenty-fifth of the population of the English-speaking world now). To try even to touch on what each of them did would demand another essay— perhaps another ten essays. If we were forced to put it quickly and to overlook completely the step-by-step drama of each writer's life (and it is from this that we could learn what, in Johnson's phrase about biography, we could "put to use"), I suppose we could still draw a few morals. And whatever morals we draw, we come back to the heart of the eighteenth century. For in its rather traumatic reconsideration of what next to do (and this is the first of the periods that have followed the Renaissance— and thus the first to face the situation we ourselves face now), the eighteenth century was to some extent self-corrective. While it created further embarrassments for itself and for the century and a half that has followed, an important part of it never lost its hold upon essentials but rather came, after struggle and self-division, to a deeper appreciation of them. Perhaps the greatest lesson it learned from comparing its own experience with the larger past was the value of boldness; not the boldness of negativism, of grudgingly withholding one's assent, of talking out of the side of the mouth as we seek to establish our identities or reach into our pockets for our mite of "originality." None of us, as Goethe said, is really very "original" but gets most of what he attains in his short life from others. The boldness desired involves a direct facing up to what we admire, and then trying to be like it (the old Greek ideal of education, of *paideia*, of trying to be like the excellence, or *arêtê*, that we have come to admire— whatever our self-defensive protests). It is like that habit of Keats of beginning each large new effort by rereading *Lear* and of keeping always close at hand that engraving of Shakespeare which he found in the lodging house in the Isle of Wight when he went off to begin *Endymion;* in a sense, what this typifies was true of them all: true at least of the greatest artists (Wordsworth, looking constantly back as he did to Milton; Beethoven, who in his last days kept rereading the scores of Handel; Goethe, who constantly returned to the Greeks or to Shakespeare). In effect, they ended—at their best—in violating the taboo that they inherited and that so many of their contemporaries were strengthening.

IX

To reduce that taboo to size, to get ourselves out of this self-created prison, to heal or overcome this needless self-division, has been the greatest single problem for modern art. And in saying this, we are also speaking of something even larger—the freedom of man (that freedom so indispensable to achievement) to follow openly and directly what he most values: what he has been taught to value, what he secretly or openly wishes he had done or could do.

For the brute fact remains that in *no other* aspect of life (only in the arts during the last two centuries, and hardly ever in the arts before then) do you have a situation where the whole procedure of what to do with your life, your vocation, your craft—the whole process of learning and achievement—is crazily split down the middle by two opposing demands. On the one hand, we have the natural human response to great examples that, from childhood up, are viewed as prototypes (in statecraft, science, religion, or anything else—including even the hero worship and desire for emulation in gangsters). In no case do you have this natural response of the human heart and mind exercised through education, encouraged, and gradually absorbed into the conscience and bloodstream—and, at the same time have suddenly blocking it a *second* injunction: the injunction that you are forbidden to be very closely like these examples. In no other case are you simultaneously enjoined to admire and at the same time to try, at all costs, *not* to follow closely what you admire, not merely in any of the details but in over-all procedure, in general object, in any of the broader conventions of mode, vocabulary, or idiom. Yet here, in the arts this split is widening with every generation, and not only widening but dramatized, with a helpless and blind militancy on each side.

The essence of neurosis is conflict. It becomes especially so when you face obviously conflicting demands: when the pressures (or what we imagine the pressures to be) are ones that enjoin us to move in two different—in fact, two *opposing*—directions at once. And what do you do then? I think of the fable of the donkey that starved when he was confronted, on each side, with two equally distant bales of hay. The arts stutter, stagger, pull back into paralysis and indecision before such a conflict of demand. As such they mirror the greatest single cultural problem we face, assuming that we physically survive: that is how to use a heritage, when we know and admire so much about it, how to grow by means of it, how to acquire our "identities," how to be ourselves.

As we now try to reground our thinking, to discover what next to do, we have the salutary example of the greatest writers of that short period a century and a half ago that came at the close of the eighteenth century. Naturally any number of problems have increased, or been newly created, since their time. An example of the latter is the disastrous modern split between "popular" and "sophisticated" art that has become so great in the middle twentieth century—a split where each tries to be as unlike the other as possible. But in many ways we are better off.

X

As you can guess, I am chiefly interested in the nineteenth and above all the twentieth century aspect of this subject, and I know the modern situation has influenced my reflections about art. Nevertheless, my concern here is to illustrate the perennial relevance of the eighteenth century. This brilliant, and on the whole honest, era was the first of the modern periods to follow the Renaissance. It was the first in any number of respects to face dramatically what we ourselves face today.

The Influence of

English Fiction on the French

Mid-Eighteenth-Century Novel

BY GEORGES MAY

◄◄◄◄◄◄◄◄◄◄◄◄◄ ☼ ►►►►►►►►►►►►►

Not so long ago a certain brand of French academic criticism and literary historiography enjoyed indulging in comfortably chauvinistic simplifications such as the following: French literature can be distinguished in the seventeenth, eighteenth, and nineteenth centuries by its changing attitude toward foreign literatures. At one end, the seventeenth century marked the apex of the beneficial influence of the classical literatures of Antiquity. At the other end, the nineteenth century marked the apex of the baneful influence of modern foreign literatures: Spanish, English, and German, and even, toward the end, Scandinavian and Russian. As for the eighteenth or "French" century, it was irresponsibly depicted as having miraculously escaped any such contamination. The France of Louis XV was seen as having been the center of the civilized world or, at any rate of *l'Europe française*, the lawgiver in the universe of art and letters, and the arbiter of taste. French writers of the period were viewed as fully aware of the exceptional quality and variety of the masterworks of the Louis XIV era, and consequently were presented as contentedly and complacently engrossed in a self-satisfied contemplation of their navels. Such a childish view of literary history was especially prevalent among those critics of the early decades of the Third Republic who, because of their revulsion for the republican form of government, would nostalgically look back toward the great "French" century which ended with the monarchy when the Bastille fell. Their longing for the past merely reflected their political and social convictions. Among these nationalistic and conservative critics, some were brilliantly gifted; Jules Lemaître for instance, who, in an article written in 1884, characterized the French eighteenth century as " . . . the one century in our literature during which our strong and weak points were most freely emphasized, and least felt the influence of classical and foreign literatures."[1]

In the light of much serious scholarship[2] devoted to this question since these lines were heedlessly penned by Lemaître, we now tend to view the situation as having been quite radically different. The development of French literature strikes us on the contrary as being altogether unintelligible in the eighteenth century if we attempt to isolate it from other modern literatures, especially that of England. This is obviously true of all the idea-laden forms of literature cultivated by the *philosophes* and *idéologues*, on whom the influence of great English thinkers is openly acknowledged: Hobbes and Locke, Bacon and Newton, Berkeley and Shaftesbury, Bolingbroke, Toland, Hume, and many, many more. But it is equally true of prose drama influenced by Lillo and Moore, of poetry influenced by Pope and Ossian, by Thomson and Gray. And, of course, it is quite strikingly true, too, in the area of the novel, from Defoe and Swift to Ann Radcliffe and Lewis, and including the great quintet of Richardson, Fielding, Smollett, Goldsmith, and Sterne, not to forget many influential ladies of letters, starting with Aphra Behn, and going on quite uninterruptedly with Eliza Haywood, Charlotte Lennox, Sarah Fielding, and Fanny Burney, to name only the best remembered.

This is indeed a huge area, and a thoroughly fascinating subject, for nowhere else is a comparative approach more legitimate, indeed more necessary. But it is also an extremely difficult and complex problem, compounded by the facts that the Channel was no one-way street and that the French and the British novel never stopped cross-fertilizing each other throughout the eighteenth century . . . and forever after.

These are at least two good reasons why the following remarks will necessarily be very fragmentary, and also why there exists at this time no comprehensive and dependable treatment of the problem—although the

---

[1] Jules Lemaître, *Les Contemporains* (Paris, Boivin), II, 148. All French quotations have been translated into English by the author.

[2] Cf. Philippe van Tieghem, *Les Influences étrangères sur la littérature française* (1550–1880) (Paris, 1961), pp. 60–120.

bibliography of useful studies dealing with several aspects of it is indeed a large one.

The scholarly and helpful book published in 1949 by James R. Foster, under the partly misleading title of *History of the Pre-Romantic Novel in England*, fulfills part of the need. It studies the influence of French fiction in eighteenth-century England, at least so far as pre-romanticism is concerned. As Professor Foster puts it in his preface: "The aim of this book is to give an account of the pre-romantic narratives which appeared in England during the eighteenth century and to describe the French novels influencing them." [3]

Perhaps the most useful book available to scholars interested in investigating English influences on the French eighteenth-century novel is Harold Wade Streeter's study published in 1936 in New York: *The 18th Century English Novel in French Translation*. Although its subtitle designates it as *A Bibliographical Study*, it is much more than that. Streeter used the results of Daniel Mornet's research (published in 1910) in several hundred catalogues of eighteenth-century French private libraries, but went far beyond. His book quotes much eighteenth-century French criticism, culled especially from the periodicals of the time, and devotes a few short studies to such important individual writers as Mrs. Manley, Swift, Defoe, Smollett, Fielding, Richardson, Sterne, and a few adepts of the Gothic romance. Streeter's study, however, is bibliographical and does not eschew the fate of all bibliographies in that it is neither complete nor entirely accurate. Yet, for the 106 years 1700–1805, Streeter lists no fewer than 530 French translations of eighteenth-century English novels and offers statistical evidence showing clearly that the real invasion of English novels in translation started about 1750. [4]

One of the troubles with statistical evidence, however, when dealing with problems such as this, is that quantity only is measured, whereas surely what really means something in matters of influence is quality— no matter how relative this notion may appear *sub specie aeternitatis*. For instance the French translation of *Pamela*, published eight years before 1750, was, as we know, of unparalleled importance in this affair. Yet it counts only for one single unit in Streeter's statistical survey.

Another shortcoming of Streeter's study is that it considers only translations, without paying attention to those few French writers who could

---

[3] James R. Foster, *History of the Pre-Romantic Novel in England* (New York, 1949), p. vii.

[4] Harold Wade Streeter, *The Eighteenth Century English Novel in French Translation. A Bibliographical Study* (New York, 1936), p. 252.

and did read the original English. These were very rare, but here again quantity does not mean much. We recall, for instance, that Prévost, who translated *Clarissa* and *Grandison*, was fluent in English and most probably read in the original some of Defoe's novels which were not translated until much later. And we also know, through reading the letters Diderot wrote his mistress in the fall of 1762, that the future author of *Jacques le fataliste* was then reading the first volumes of Sterne's *Tristram Shandy*. This was five years before the last volume was to be published in England, and fourteen years before the publication of the first French translation.

This consideration is of particular significance not only for chronological reasons, but also because of the incredibly liberal views the eighteenth century took of the duties and prerogatives of translators. Several studies have been published on this subject.[5] Prévost, one of the leading professional translators of the era, made his views crystal-clear in 1755 in the following paragraph from his introduction to the translation of Richardson's *Sir Charles Grandison:*

Without changing in the least either the author's general design, or even for the most part his realization thereof, I gave a new face to his work by excising his languid excursions, his overworked descriptions, his unnecessary dialogues, his irrevelant reflexions. The chief reproach addressed by critics to Mr. Richardson is that he sometimes loses sight of the limits of his subject, and becomes wrapt up in details. I never stopped fighting this fault which weakens interest. Should some signs of it yet remain, I must acknowledge that they are not altogether avoidable in an epistolary narrative. I deleted or adapted to common European usage the manners of England when they are shocking to other nations. It seemed to me that these vestiges of erstwhile British coarseness, of which the English are unaware only because they shut their eyes to them, would disgrace a book in which politeness should go along with nobility and virtue. Lastly, in order to give a just notion

[5] Cf. Alfred Owen Aldridge, "Le problème de la traduction au XVIIIᵉ siècle et aujourd'hui," *Revue belge de philologie et d'histoire*, XXXIX (1961), 747–58; Henri Roddier, "L'Abbé Prévost et le problème de la traduction au XVIIIᵉ siècle," *Cahiers de l'Association Internationale des Etudes Françaises*, Vol. 8 (Juin, 1956), pp. 173–81; Constance West, "La Théorie de la traduction au XVIIIᵉ siècle," *Revue de littérature comparée*, XII (1932), 330–55; Frank Howard Wilcox, *Prévost's Translations of Richardson's Novels*, Vol. XII in *University of California Publications in Modern Philology* (Berkeley, Calif., 1925–26), pp. 341–411.

of my work, I merely have to call attention to the fact that the seven volumes of the English edition, which would add up to twenty-eight in the format of mine, are reduced here to eight.[6]

One more word of caution is in order before trying to assess influences. Mere popular success is not sufficient evidence; so that it has been convincingly argued that, in spite of the irrefutable popularity of Richardson's novels in French, they exerted little if any real literary influence. Indeed, there has been an international academic quarrel on this matter. The pioneering study of the French scholar Joseph Texte asserted in 1895[7] that the influence of Richardson's novels could be felt on just about all eighteenth-century French novels written after 1742. These exaggerated views brought about denials, some of which were just as extreme, for instance on the part of the Belgian scholar Servais Etienne[8] and especially of the British scholar Frederick Charles Green,[9] whose personal distaste for Richardson's novels will be made apparent below by a few quotations.

All these methodological prolegomena show some of the major obstacles which lie in the path of the dispassionate scholar who wishes to assess the impact of the English novel in France. Other difficult questions present themselves as well. Can the strong Anglomaniac wave which submerged mid-eighteenth-century France be equated with true literary influences? Obviously not, if we look at the strange fortune of Shakespeare in the Louis XV era: it is difficult to recognize the original *Hamlet* in the play by Ducis performed with this title in 1769. Were things very different with *Robinson Crusoe* or *Clarissa Harlowe*? When we read strongly worded excoriations of English novels printed in some French periodicals of the time, are we to believe that the critics who wrote them were reflecting public opinion? Most probably not, since the translated works were commercially profitable. Were these critics then speaking for the French novelists? Again probably not, when we look at the avalanche of pseudo-English novels penned by Mme Riccoboni, Baculard d'Arnaud,

---

[6] "Introduction" by Prévost to his *Nouvelles lettres anglaises, ou histoire du chevalier Grandison* (Amsterdam, 1776), I, vii–viii.

[7] Joseph Texte, *Jean-Jacques Rousseau et les origines du cosmopolitisme littéraire* (Paris, 1895). Cf. in particular Bk. II, Chs. iii and iv.

[8] Servais Etienne, *Le Genre romanesque en France depuis l'apparition de "la Nouvelle Héloïse" jusqu'aux approches de la révolution* (Bruxelles, 1922), *passim* and in particular pp. 55–58 and 110–27.

[9] Frederick Charles Green, *Minuet; A Critical Survey of French and English Literary Ideas in the Eighteenth Century* (London, 1935). Cf. esp. Chs. XIV and XV.

and a few other lesser-known figures.[10] Where then are we to look for dependable information on which to base a judgment?

Daniel Mornet's research in private library catalogues yields the first objective and meaningful data concerning, on the one hand, the relative popularity of English as compared with French fiction, and, on the other hand, the kind of English novels which sold best at the time. That time, for the sake of research convenience, was limited by Mornet to the two mid-eighteenth-century decades 1740–60. Only novels published during this period are taken into account. The nine most often represented English novels in the 392 post-1760 catalogues collated by Mornet account for 440 entries, whereas the nine most often represented French novels add up to 369 entries. Some of this surprising evidence must be interpreted. As it happened, the period 1740–60 was the one in which the masterpieces of Fielding and Richardson were published, whereas, in France, it was a most undistinguished period between the brilliant seventeen-thirties with Marivaux and Prévost, and the renaissance of the seventeen-sixties inaugurated in 1761 with the sensational publication of Rousseau's *La Nouvelle Héloïse*.

Nevertheless, once this is taken into account, the evidence still points, without any doubt whatsoever, toward an unprecedented and tremendous vogue of English fiction in France, and one not limited to only one or two authors. Here are the nine best-selling English novels, followed by figures representing the numbers of times they appear in the 392 catalogues:[11]

Richardson, *Pamela:* 78   Richardson, *Grandison:* 44
Fielding, *Tom Jones:* 77   Fielding, *Joseph Andrews:* 40
Richardson, *Clarissa:* 69   Sarah Fielding, *David Simple:* 35
Anonymous, *History of*   Eliza Haywood, *Betsy Thoughtless:* 26
   Charlotte Summers: 46   Aphra Behn, *Oroonoko:* 25

The preference of the French public, as reflected by these figures, closely parallels the attitude of the French professional critics and writers of the time as evidenced in their writings. And it should be noted that this convergence is not to be taken for granted in those days any more than in ours: Rousseau's *La Nouvelle Héloïse*, perhaps the top best seller of the

[10] Cf. Daniel Mornet's introductory volume to his edition of *La Nouvelle Héloïse* [Paris, 1925], I, 365–66), where French novels published between 1761 and 1780 are listed under the rubric "Romans moralisants et sentimentaux, prétendus 'traduits' ou 'imités' de l'anglais, 'Histoire anglaise,' etc."

[11] Daniel Mornet, "Les Enseignements des bibliothèques privées (1750–1780)," *Revue d'histoire littéraire de la France*, XVII (1910), 461.

century, was mercilessly panned at the time of its publication by nearly every critic who reviewed it.

But here again success does not necessarily mean influence. Success can to some extent be objectively, say scientifically, measured as in these statistics of Mornet's. Influence usually cannot. In order, however, to come to grips with the real problem, we need first to know what French novelists of the period admired and found new in these English novels. This in itself would be an extremely interesting and not too difficult problem to investigate. But it would take much time and patience. All I propose to try now is to examine one sample.

It is a remarkable and well-known document, the *Eloge de Richardson* by Diderot. Diderot dashed off this brief essay in a few hours in 1761, after reading the three novels, which he calls the "trois grands drames," in English and in French, and after long discussions of them with his friends, echoed in letters he wrote his mistress in 1760. The evidence both of these letters and of the essay focuses quite clearly on the causes of Diderot's enthusiasm. These are two in number, and to each corresponds a series of remarks. Both series are of equal importance and are tightly interwoven throughout the essay, so that the total effect is to give identical emphasis to each. As we begin reading the essay, the first theme, that of the moral effect of Richardson's novels, is presented:

> Until now the word novel (*roman*) has denoted a web of imaginary and frivolous events, the reading of which endangered the reader's taste and morals. I wish we could find another word for Richardson's works, which elevate the mind, move the soul, breathe the love of goodness, and which also go by the name of novels.

And, if we turn the page, we soon encounter the second theme, which has to do with the illusion of reality generated by Richardson's novels and with the fact that the reader imagines himself participating in their action:

> O Richardson! We assume in spite of ourselves a role in your works, we take part in the conversation, we approve, blame, become angry or indignant. How many times have I caught myself, like a child going for the first time to the theater, crying out: "Don't believe him, he is deceiving you . . . If you go there, you are lost."

And if we turn the page again and read on, we notice that the same two themes are resumed and developed:

> Richardson sows in the hearts the seeds of virtues, which first lie idle and quiet; they remain there secretly, until an occasion arises which sets them in motion and makes them germinate . . . .
>
> I can still remember the first time that Richardson's novels fell into my hands. I was in the country. How delightfully I was affected! At each moment I felt my happiness shortened by one page. Soon I experienced the feeling experienced by companionable men who have lived together for a long time and are about to be separated. At the end it seemed to me that I was suddenly left alone . . . .

And so on, page after page, until the end of the essay. These remarks by Diderot are particularly valuable, because they are the leitmotiv of most of the French critical comments expressed in his age. Depending on the critic, moralism or realism is more emphasized, but quite clearly these are the two poles of attraction, and, therefore, the two directions in which we ought to pursue our investigation.

There are several discernible reasons why the moralistic tone of Richardson's novels and the large volume of sermonizing they contain were well received in France. Perhaps the most effective was that the moral function which the novel was then suddenly assuming was likely to act as the most effective and the most urgently needed protection against the prejudices and attacks of the vast majority of critics. This becomes abundantly clear if we observe the chronology. At the time when the translation of Richardson's novels are published (*Pamela*, 1742; *Clarissa*, 1751; *Grandison*, 1755–56), the novel as a literary genre is held in France in very low esteem indeed. As I tried to show in a recent book,[12] the publication of novels in France was even completely banned for moral reasons by the Chancellor of France, the austere Daguesseau, in 1737. Now, Daguesseau was to retire from public life in 1750, at a time when novel-writing was still considered with the same suspicion or moral revulsion as, say, atheism or prostitution. Among the most violent attacks in the seventeen-forties and fifties, could be mentioned the published harangue of President de Caulet in 1744,[13] and a 400-page indictment published in 1755 by Abbé Jaquin.[14] As late as 1761, the virtuous Abbé

---

[12] Georges May, *Le Dilemme du roman au XVIIIᵉ siècle* (Paris and New Haven, 1963), Ch. III, "La Proscription des romans."

[13] In *Recueil de plusieurs pièces d'éloquence et de poésie présentées à l'Académie des Jeux Floraux ...* (Toulouse, 1745), pp. 251–65.

[14] Abbé Armand Pierre Jaquin, *Entretiens sur les romans ...* (Paris, 1755).

Irailh could still write that: "true writers will always consider novelists in the same way as great painters consider those who decorate fans and gift trinkets."[15]

But, if we make the effort to go on reading this sort of unprofitable remarks—not unlike those made in our own age concerning the cinema— we notice that even the fiercest enemies of the immoral novel gradually got into the habit of excepting Richardson's works from their condemnation. As early as 1742, only a few months after the publication of *Pamela* in France, the conservative Abbé Desfontaines[16] expressed the idea which Diderot resumed at the outset of his essay and which was to become a thoroughgoing critical cliché, after the publication of *La Nouvelle Héloïse:* namely, that all novels are horribly immoral and must be suppressed, especially Rousseau's, but not Richardson's because the latter's are not ordinary novels. Toward the end of the century, we could again hear the clear echo of this notion in the writings of such conservative critics as Marmontel[17] and La Harpe.[18]

However, if we take a closer look at Richardson's "trois grands drames," we cannot help but notice that while these novels never tire of actually preaching a strong conservative and conventional bourgeois code of ethics, they also seem to enjoy exciting those more carnal passions which Richardson probably tried in vain to suppress in himself. Pamela is more than once victim of attempted rape, and not infrequently beaten to boot; as for Clarissa, she is quite effectively raped and, to make things worse, in a house of ill fame; and Clementine suffers many like indignities through the many pages of *Grandison*. The British critic F. C. Green is quite sanguine on this point: "Richardson, thoroughly enjoying the vicarious sensations which he extracts from these descriptions [of Pamela's persecution] gives a long, circumstantial account of B.'s second and serious effort to violate Pamela . . . ."[19] We should note, however, that the translator was careful not to shock too deeply the habits of the French reading public: if he lightened the volume of moral preaching, he also took care to soften the strokes of the Englishman's realism. The end result is that the French version of *Pamela* was not as radically different as the

[15] Abbé Augustin Simon Irailh, *Querelles littéraires* (Paris, 1761), II, 353.

[16] *Observations sur les écrits modernes* (Paris, 1742), XXIX, 212.

[17] Jean François Marmontel, *Essai sur les romans considérés du côté moral* (1787), in *Oeuvres complètes* (Paris, 1819–20), III, 578–83.

[18] Jean François de La Harpe, "Les Romans." in *Lycée, ou cours de littérature ancienne et moderne* [Paris, Agasse], XIV (1799), 250–85.

[19] Green, *Minuet*, p. 371.

English original from some contemporary French novels, say *Le Doyen de Killerine* by Prévost (1735–40). As F. C. Green puts it in more colorful style:

> Very little of Richardson's realism, which was too low for French taste, survived the ordeal of translation, and, of course, it would have required a genius to imitate the homespun texture of his language in those parts where he is not trying to write "like a book." On the other hand, the French reader was spared the almost nauseous smell of Richardson's sanctimoniousness and sentimentality, both of which are deodorized and diluted. *Pamela*, though less ruthlessly "cut" than *Clarissa* or *Grandison* was, nevertheless, reduced very much in volume and in tone. To the Gallic reader of 1742, therefore, it was pre-eminently the sensational account of a squireen's clumsy and abortive attempts to violate an incredibly lettered and incredibly chaste serving-wench.[20]

As we can see from this brief examination of the question of moralism in the works of the very moralizing Richardson, the problem is inextricably bound up with that of realism. Yet, in spite of what F. C. Green seems to imply, Richardson's moralizing could in many ways be enjoyed by that segment of the French public which had just wept at the performances of Nivelle de la Chaussée's *comédies larmoyantes* and was just about to indulge in further handkerchief play in its admiration for Greuze, Gessner, Florian, and Bernardin de Saint-Pierre. On the other hand, as we will see now, some characteristic aspects of English realism were bound to run into harsh opposition on the other side of the Channel.

To be sure, the French reading public of the mid-eighteenth century had grown used to some forms of realism through reading the best French novels of the seventeen-thirties and forties, by Lesage, Prévost, Marivaux, Mouhy, Crébillon, or Duclos. English realistic fiction by Richardson and Fielding was not really more radical, except in what we might call social realism. By this I mean that the social origins of fictional heroes were likely to be considerably lower in the English than in the French novel of the period; one of the important consequences being that the manners described and the language used were likely to be substantially less refined in English than in French fiction. Hence the talk about "British coarseness," to which Prévost refers in his preface to his adaptation of *Grandison*. In other words, heroes of low social origins shocked much less per se (remember the shepherds and shepherdesses

[20] *Ibid.*, p. 368.

of the pastoral novel who, thanks to Gessner and Florian, were again to be in vogue toward the end of the eighteenth century) than they did because of the consequences, in terms of manners and language, which follow in realistic fiction. Of the seven English novels most often found by Mornet on the shelves of private mid-eighteenth-century French libraries, five feature protagonists of very low rank indeed: Pamela is a serving-maid, daughter of poor peasants; Tom Jones is a foundling; as for Charlotte Summers, she is a destitute orphan, a penniless parish girl; Joseph Andrews is none other than Pamela's brother; and David Simple's name alone is sufficiently representative of his station in life. It was, therefore, not because of this, but actually in spite of it that these novels were widely read in France. Nearly all the written comments made at the time in France about English novels, including the most favorable ones, express strict reservation about English vulgarity and brutality.

For, as the book referred to earlier attempts to show,[21] the French realistic novel of the seventeen-thirties, whose heroes and heroines were living in the lower strata of society, were quite different in this respect. Invariably their sojourn in the lower classes were presented as an episodic trial, to be followed by a quick exercise in social climbing; this is immediately obvious of Marianne and Jacob, the protagonists of Marivaux's two best novels; it is likely true of Jeannette, the *paysanne parvenue* of Mouhy, who eventually becomes *madame la marquise*. Whether or not this was due to the fact that the French upper classes had at the time a greater number of *parvenus* than the English aristocracy—although Pamela's and Tom Jones's ultimate fate leads us to doubt it—is a matter for further conjecture.

A yet more remarkable difference between French realistic fiction of the thirties and English realistic fiction of the forties and fifties is that French novelists displayed a much greater restraint and discretion than their British followers in their evocation of the customs, way of life, and speech characteristics of the underprivileged classes. The famous quarrel between the coachman and the linen merchant, in Marivaux's *Vie de Marianne*, is, in spite of all that was said about it at the time, quite tame and pale, or, say, refined and aristocratic, when compared with Pamela's tribulations, with some of the more unsavory adventures of Joseph Andrews and Parson Adams, or with some of the pitiful trials of the so-called "fortunate" parish girl, Charlotte Summers.

To quote one example not restricted to the lower classes, the French critic Fréron, who quite willingly discussed new English novels in the

---

[21] May, *Le Dilemme du roman au XVIIIᵉ siècle*, pp. 164–65.

pages of his periodical *L'Année littéraire* or in his *Lettres sur quelques écrits du temps*,[22] censored the way in which the anonymous author of the *History of Charlotte Summers* (a novel then erroneously attributed to Sarah Fielding) conducted a particularly picturesque episode. Lady Bountiful, Charlotte's rich and usually kind protectress, becomes quite incensed when her protégée refuses to marry old man Croft. She flatly refuses to believe that the old lecher has in fact tried to ravish Charlotte's honor. The Rev. Mr. Goodheart intercedes and tries to protect the innocent girl against her mistress' anger.

> This adventure brings about truly *English* scenes. The Rev. Goodheart, Chaplain of the castle, demands that Croft justify himself. Upon his refusal, the kind minister concludes to his guilt. Croft lays hold of a chair and throws it at his head. He then seizes a bottle and drenches the poor minister from head to toes. As for Margaret, milady's chambermaid, she pours forth a thousand insults at Croft. What say you, Sir, of such remarks, worthy of a history of fishmongers? Lady Bountiful herself indulges in manners of speech most indecent for a lady of her station and character. She rudely upbraids Charlotte for all the favors she has received from her, calls her a proud beggar, a rogue, a parish girl, because she refuses to marry Croft who has tried to steal her honor. With all due respect to the author, her lady is a bit extravagant.[23]

Remarks such as these could be collected in large numbers, especially when it comes to *Pamela*, *Tom Jones*, *Joseph Andrews*, not to mention Smollett's *Roderick Random*. As an enthusiastic admirer of *Pamela*, who deplored, however, the vulgarity and brutality of the novel, put it in 1742: "these, they say, are English manners—which excuses everything. It is an unanswerable argument."[24]

As we can readily see, all was not uniformly admired in English realism in mid-eighteenth-century France. We are led, therefore, to the following hypothesis. The kind of realism which the French were prepared to appreciate, admire, and imitate was the kind to which they had already grown accustomed through reading the novels of Richardson's

---

[22] Cf. Jean Bundy, "Fréron and the English Novel," *Revue de littérature comparée*, XXXVI (1962), 258–65.

[23] *Lettres sur quelques écrits du temps*, V, 27–29. Quoted by Streeter, *The Eighteenth Century English Novel in French Translation*, p. 87n.

[24] *Lettre sur Paméla* (London, 1742), p. 31.

French predecessors, especially Lesage, Prévost, and Marivaux. Indeed that kind of realism had been the chief new contribution of these novelists.

We may find a sort of indirect confirmation of this hypothesis as we recall the fortune of Defoe's novels in France. Aside from *Robinson Crusoe*, translated in 1720–21, soon after its publication in 1719, none of Defoe's novels were translated until long after his death. The first, and the only one translated during the eighteenth century, was *Moll Flanders*, published in 1721 and translated only forty years later. By that date, 1761, Defoe had been dead thirty years. As for the many other novels which remained untranslated—*Captain Singleton* (1720), *Colonel Jacque* (1722), *Lady Roxana* (1724)—they strike us nowadays as already presenting the two qualities which Diderot most admired in Richardson: attention to humble realistic detail, and strong moralizing intentions, owing to Defoe's own puritanical leanings as a commoner and a dissenter. If they remain untranslated and unnoticed in France at the time of their publication in the early seventeen-twenties was not the reason then that the French reading public was not prepared at the time to appreciate a form of realistic literary art which had not yet made its mark in the French novel? For surely the moralizing tone of Defoe, in spite of its strong Protestant flavor, would have been quite readily accepted, even if, admittedly, it was to become more palatable once France was engulfed in the wave of sentimentality. As a matter of fact, the best works of Swift, almost contemporary with these novels by Defoe, were quickly translated and widely read in France: a *Tale of a Tub* in 1721 and *Gulliver's Travels* in 1727. It seems quite clear, therefore, that the great success of this latter work in France is to be ascribed not only to Swift's talent but to the fact that the French public of 1727 was aesthetically as well as ideologically prepared to appreciate the book: Montesquieu and, before him, Bayle and Fontenelle had seen to it.

And so we are led to the tentative conclusion that the influence of the successful English novels which crossed the Channel in the middle of the eighteenth century cannot be effectively defined in terms of what the French most enjoyed in these novels. It was neither their moralism nor their realism which exerted the principal influence on the French novelists who admired them. Richardson's moralism, in French translation, greatly resembled Prévost's. As for realism—aside from the social kind against which French taste rebelled—it was already present in the works of Chasles, Lesage, and Marivaux.

We must, therefore, look in another direction. The principal innovation of the great English novelists—and this was especially the case with

Richardson, the most successful of them—was an original formula, an unprecedented recipe for combining two ingredients which, in the French tradition, had never mixed better than oil and water: namely, a conventional and middle-class sort of moralism and a virile realism devoid of prudishness. No French novelist had yet achieved a combination of these two ingredients which was nearly as successful as Richardson's. The French novel was either moral and unreal, in the *prècieux* tradition, or it was realistic and quite immoral in the popular acceptation of the word, in the *gaulois* tradition. And this was so, for all practical purposes, without any exception. In the history of French fiction realism had more or less behaved as though immoralism was inevitably to follow in its wake; as though, in the area of ethical values, cynicism corresponded to realism in that of aesthetic values. And then, all of a sudden, an unfamiliar sort of book, by an unknown Englishman, quietly and quite convincingly demonstrated that it was not so, and that a novelist, like a tragic poet, could have the loftiest moral purposes and yet feature detestable characters and describe the foulest crimes. *Pamela* squared the circle. And Diderot's essay, by virtue of its systematic insistence on the simultaneous presence of moralism and realism in Richardson's novels, evidenced as much lucidity as had Richardson himself. For, toward the end of *Pamela*, Richardson has his heroine say this about the fictional fare offered to the English public around 1740:

> There were very few novels and romances that my lady would permit me to read; and those I did, gave me no great pleasure; for either they dealt so much in the *marvellous* and *improbable*, or were so naturally *inflaming* to the *passions*, and so full of *love* and *intrigue*, that hardly any of them but seemed calculated to *fire* the imagination, rather than to *inform* the *judgment*.[25]

The new formula was almost immediately exploited, perhaps by Rousseau himself, surely by Baculard d'Arnaud, Marmontel, and several later novelists whose works testify to the influence of Rousseau and Prévost as much as to that of the English novelists: Restif de la Bretonne, for instance. The realism component of the new English formula could be immediately appreciated by a public whose taste had been educated by the French novelists of the seventeen-thirties. As for the moralism component, it, too, could be readily enjoyed by a public whose sensibility was at that precise time shifting toward sentimentality.

[25] Samuel Richardson, *Pamela*, letter CII, in ed. Leslie Stephen (3 vols.; London and Manchester, 1883), III, 402.

In other words again, the French novelists of the Richardsonian school were quite willing to stuff their novels with large doses of moralizing sermons, in order to indulge with impunity in realism. And the public was equally willing to shed pleasurable tears upon reading the melodramatic scenes which served as pretexts for subsequent moralizing. This particular effect of the English influence should probably be regretted, for it led to much bad novel-writing, and to the reactionary literary doctrines of late-eighteenth-century theorizers like Marmontel and of mediocre practitioners like Baculard d'Arnaud or Bernardin de Saint-Pierre. In this respect, we may to some extent agree with Servais Etienne's otherwise excessive assessment:

> It is to be deplored, and I shall never repeat it enough, that the English novel became known in France as early as the 18th century. Admittedly its true value was appreciated, but only its rough structure was borrowed. Its influence was a baleful one, because, while imitating the English, the French novelists forgot that they were French, and this spelled the end of the analytical novel. From then on, they will moralize, they will house young girls in brothels, they will have them die atrocious deaths, and they will believe they have written "great dramas" in the manner of Richardson.[26]

And, therefore, in order to identify the really favorable effect of the English novel on the advance of the French novel, we must, I believe, look in yet another direction.

The middle of the eighteenth-century was in France an age of Anglomania. Everywhere we look, we see English manners and customs, English ideas and institutions eulogized and admired in France. In this cultural environment, the fact that writers of such obvious talent and distinction as Fielding, Richardson, and Sterne chose to display their genius in a genre still held in France as inferior had an immense—though admittedly difficult to measure—role in promoting the entire genre of the novel to a rank of higher dignity and in encouraging, therefore, the best French writers to try their hands at it. And this was of huge and far-reaching importance for the future of the French novel.

Although I would agree, therefore, with those who believe that individual English novels had no discernible influence, save for inconsequential details, on such great French novels as *La Religieuse* or *La Nouvelle Héloïse*,

[26] Etienne, *Le Genre romanesque*, p. 102.

I would add that, on the other hand, the English novel in general played an essential role in their coming into being. The example of Richardson and Fielding, and later that of Sterne, was of decisive importance in the choice that Diderot and Rousseau then made of the novel medium. Both had, to start with, been scornful of this genre. Both, later on, admired the great English novels. Both, finally and at about the same time, wrote novels.

In other words, it is my belief that the most truly beneficial effect of the English novel in France was that it added its tremendous weight to the scale which was then only slowly tipping in favor of the novel genre. From this time on, a great writer, a consecrated one, no longer felt it beneath his dignity to write novels. Still later the time would even come when an aspiring writer felt it possible to earn a legitimate fame by writing a novel, instead of a verse tragedy in the manner of Racine or of Voltaire. The fact that the example of Rousseau's own great novel, published in 1761, had precisely the same effect, makes it almost impossible to distinguish in later years between the influence of the English novel and that of *La Nouvelle Héloïse*. But one thing is quite clear: from then on the novel, as a literary genre, is over the hump. The decisive battle has been won, and the English novelists have been the most effective allies of their French brothers.[27]

---

[27] It is ironical to note that, at the same time, France and England were fighting one of the longest and severest military conflicts of their history. And incidentally, one may well wonder whether French military defeats by the British did not contribute to the condescension with which some French critics looked at English literature and at the coarseness and brutality of "les manières anglaises."

The Tree of Knowledge and the Sin of Science: Vegetation Symbols in Goethe's Faust

BY HEINZ POLITZER

◄◄◄◄◄◄◄◄◄◄◄◄◄ ☼ ►►►►►►►►►►►►►

I

The fortunes of Faust have been manifold throughout the ages.[1] They definitely took a turn toward the fantastic when, in 1918, Oswald Spengler discovered the Faustian soul, "whose prime symbol is pure and limitless space."[2] Faust, the Magus of the North, Faust, the Renaissance Man, Faust, the contemporary of Luther, was turned into an exponent of modern technology. The figure that next to Don Juan, Don Quixote, Hamlet, and King Lear had done most to represent the imagination of the West was now singled out as the hallmark of its decline. While technology seemed to make rapid headway, things went from bad to worse for the unfortunate Faust. In a recent German production of Goethe's dramatic poem, for instance, the hero's study boasted, instead of its traditional Gothic arch, a "system of glass balls similar to the atomium shown at the Brussels World Fair."[3] During the same performance the

---

[1] E. M. Butler, *The Fortunes of Faust* (Cambridge, 1952).

[2] Oswald Spengler, *The Decline of the West* [abridged edition by Helmut Werner, trans. Charles Francis Atkinson] (New York, 1962), p. 97.

[3] Siegfried Melchinger, "Faust für uns," in Gründgens, *Faust* (Frankfort-on-Main, 1961), p. 14.

Witches' Sabbath of the first Walpurgis Night was ushered in by a most contemporary explosion: "Sudden darkness, a veil, onto which the mushroom shape of an atomic cloud is projected, then a glaring light across the raging, bubbling, whirling mass, rock 'n roll [sic], a few Martians inbetween [sic], Faust and Mephistopheles immersed in this eddy. . . ."[4]

What might have been dismissed as the stage stunts of Gustav Gründgens, a director known for his theatrical antics, has been supported by one of the most perspicacious critics in the field of Germanics today. In a series of lectures first broadcast over the third program of the BBC and subsequently reprinted in *The Listener*, Erich Heller, pronouncing on "Faust's Damnation" and "The Morality of Knowledge," traces the history of the Faust figure from Goethe's eighteenth century back to the sixteenth of Johann Spiess' first chapbook and sees in this rather primitive document one of the sources of the moral crisis that has befallen our civilization. To be sure, the time of the chapbook Faust was a time of discovery and excitement. A superman in the garb of a sixteenth-century magician, Doctor Faustus rebelled against the instructions of his church and set out to probe the forbidden depths of science. Symbolically, he concluded a pact with the devil, the roaring lion. Heller concludes:

> That time has passed, the mind has won its freedom, and the beast has not yet devoured us. Only that after centuries of free thought, free science, free testing, and free dare-devilling, there stood a doctor of nuclear physics in an American desert, watching the first experimental explosion of the atomic bomb, and saying that for the first time in his life he knew what sin was. The story published by Johann Spiess has indeed proved its power to stay.[5]

Viewing the figure and the legend of Faust from the vantage point of an atomic apocalypse, Heller is thoroughly consistent with his own pessimistic views when he rejects Goethe's hero as well as Goethe's God.

---

[4] Melchinger, "Faust für uns," pp. 18–19.

[5] Erich Heller, "Faust's Damnation: The Morality of Knowledge," *The Listener*, January 11, 1962, p. 60. Heller's critical stance has been termed "theological aesthetics" (William H. Rey, "Theological Aesthetics?," *The Germanic Review*, XXXV [1960], 243–61). As a matter of fact, he seems deeply convinced that our time represents "the last days of mankind." His teacher, the great Viennese critic and satirist Karl Kraus, wrote a play with this title, a monumental drama ending with God repeating the words attributed to Emperor Wilhelm II of Germany at the outbreak of World War I: "I did not want it" ("Ich habe es nicht gewollt") (Karl Kraus, *Die letzten Tage der Menschheit* [Munich, 1957], p. 770).

"The complexities of Faust's moral character," Heller says, "are unre-
solvable. He is an ungovernable theological problem-child, presenting no
simple alternative of good or evil to the Goethean God who, far from
being the God of the philosophers, does not even seem to know his own
mind. . . ." [6]
Heller measures Goethe by the standards of modern moral theology
(which, whatever else they may be, are not the standards the poet had in
mind when his *Faust* was taking shape). I propose, instead, to put the
poem back into the context of the eighteenth century, and of literature.
Although the complexities of Faust's character may defy resolution, the
poetic richness of the figure will at least stand out against the warp and
woof of the classical and romantic tendencies which constitute the very
fabric of Goethe's work as well as of much of eighteenth-century literature.
I shall suggest that *Faust*, far from being meant to set a moral example,
forms a poetic parable. Considering it as such, we shall find Goethe's play
as paradoxical and as open to a variety of interpretations as the human
condition of which it treats. The moral ambiguity for which his hero has
been blamed may then appear as irony; the irony of resignation and
reconciliation which distinguishes Goethe's later writings.

II

At first glance, the God in Goethe's "Prologue in Heaven" seems out of
date. He may not be the God of the philosophers, but he certainly presides
over the best of all possible worlds. As if it were composed by Wolfgang
Amadeus Mozart, the song of His archangels resounds with the harmonies
of the spheres. The work of His hands is admittedly incomprehensible but
still as gloriously palpable as it was on the first day of creation. There is,
of course, the inevitable change from paradisaical light to deep and
horrifying darkness, from smooth to stormy sea, from diurnal calm to
nocturnal lightning. Yet, in the final analysis, the thunder is nothing but a
release of cosmic tensions: the bolt mentioned by Michael in the third
stanza had already been integrated into a harmonious universe by
Raphael in the first. This thunder is the sound produced on his journey
by the sun, the harbinger and guarantor of God's bright day.

[6] Heller, *The Listener*, January 18, 1962, p. 122.

Even the devil is stripped of his demoniac powers here: he is a wit, a *Schalk* (339),[7] a rationalist, paradoxically complaining that man's reason is the sole reason for his lowering himself beneath the level of the beasts. Mephistopheles is distinguished from the angels, the genuine sons of the gods (344), primarily by being not an entity but a part, a stimulus, a necessary mechanistic device to keep the creation, and man, going. God, benevolent but still a despot, does not seem to feel any pangs of His divine conscience when He allows His adversary the audacity to propose a wager.

If it is the devil who suggests the wager, it is, however, the Lord himself who introduces Faust, the doctor, as a pawn in this cosmic game. The devil responds as if God could not have picked a better man. Mephistopheles' description of Faust is in blatant contradiction to all he had previously been blaming mankind for: the doctor, he says, is not at all possessed by reason but obsessed by madness. What is worse, he is only half conscious of the frenzy which compels him to ask the heavens for the fairest stars and the earth for whatever supreme lust it has to offer. In any case, it is in the words of a most enlightened devil that the image of a most romantic man is introduced into a highly neoclassical heaven.

By conjuring up such an image of man, cursed like Cain, bedeviled like Satan himself, Mephisto indeed threatens to endanger the harmony of the universe. The Lord immediately counteracts the threat by pointing to the fact that even in his present confused state, Faust is still serving a higher purpose and pursuing an aim that will become evident as soon as the Almighty has decided to reveal His plan:

> Wenn er mir jetzt auch nur verworren dient,
> So werd' ich ihn bald in die Klarheit führen.   (308–9)

Ostensibly to complement and exemplify this maxim, the Lord now uses a simile which seems to be crucial to our understanding of the poem as a whole and to our consideration of it as a model of German eighteenth-century literature.

---

[7] In numbering the verses and spelling the quotations I have followed the *Sophien-Ausgabe* of Goethe's Works, Vols. 14 and 15 (Weimar, 1887 and 1888). For the translation of the quoted passages I am indebted to Walter Kaufmann, *Goethe's Faust* (Garden City, N.J., 1962) and Peter Salm, *Johann Wolfgang von Goethe, Faust: First Part* (New York, 1962). The responsibility for the final form of the paraphrases is, however, mine.

Comparing Himself to a gardener, the Lord expresses His belief in the
organic processes of His creation. The green sapling, he affirms, heralds
the blossom and the fruit, the harvest of the years to come:

> Weiss doch der Gärtner, wenn das Bäumchen grünt,
> Dass Blüth' und Frucht die künft'gen Jahre zieren.   (310–11)

For the world of the "Prologue in Heaven" is orderly and predictable.
The first faint green that adorns the branches also guarantees the wealth
to be reaped in the fall. God is concerned with each single plant; one can
visualize Him bending His magnificent old man's head over each sprig
and shoot, enjoying its beauty as much as He enjoys the order of His
universe at large. He might in this respect be said to resemble the gardener
of whom an anonymous author demands, in the *Théorie et pratique du
jardinage* (published in France in 1709), that he

> be something of a geometrician, must understand architecture,
> must be able to draw well, must know the character and effect of
> every plant he makes use of for fine gardens, and must also know
> the art of ornament. He must be inventive, and above all in-
> telligent; he must have a natural good taste cultivated by the
> sight of beautiful objects and the rejection of ugly ones, and must
> also have an all-round interest and insight in these matters. [8]

In stanzas of balanced grandeur the archangels in the "Prologue in
Heaven" have just praised the ordering of the chaos and its organization
as though it were a kind of Sans-Souci, a carefree retreat like the one
Frederick the Great began to build in Potsdam in 1744. And like Frederick's friend, Voltaire, the God in Goethe's "Prologue" seems to feel
that it is necessary only to cultivate one's garden.

   This God whom Goethe created exactly in the year 1800 must have
seemed a late comer, a relic from a previous era rather than the rightful
ruler of a new century to a historian of ideas like Arthur O. Lovejoy. For,
in *The Great Chain of Being*, Lovejoy states:

> The God of the seventeenth century, like its gardeners, always
> geometrized; the God of Romanticism was one in whose universe
> things grew wild and without trimming and in all the rich diversity
> of their natural shapes. The preference for irregularity, the

[8] Quoted from Marie Luise Gothein, *A History of Garden Art*, trans. Mrs. Archer-
Hind (London, 1928), II, 111.

aversion from that which is wholly intellectualized, the yearning for échappées into misty distances—these, which were eventually to invade the intellectual life of Europe at all points, made their first modern appearance on a grand scale early in the eighteenth century in the form of the new fashion in pleasure-gardens. . . . [9]

Lovejoy calls these pleasure-gardens by their German name, *englische Gärten*—an oddity which has been noted before. [10] One does not have to be a Freudian to suspect that the German term slipped into Professor Lovejoy's vocabulary because the *englische Garten* corresponded so well with the very idea of German romanticism and with its most significant exponent, Goethe's *Faust*.

III

The influence romanticism had especially on the first part of Goethe's tragedy is undeniable. Take, for instance, the dialogue between man and devil, leading up to Faust's signing the pact. The scene is the scholar's study and Mephistopheles has been exhorting Faust to stop playing with his sorrow, "which, like a vulture, feeds upon your life" (1636); thereby, incidentally, conjuring up the image of Prometheus, fettered to the rocks of Mount Caucasus while a bird of prey feeds upon his intestines—the *Urfaust* to precede all *Urfausts*. Goethe's Faust continues to disparage Mephistopheles. Haughtily he wonders whether the devil is at all capable to understand the noble ambitions of man. The importance of this question does not lie in its obvious answer. Its significance stems from the part it plays in the organic development, the planned growth of the *Faust* poem as such. Here a correspondence between the two agreement or pact scenes (the one in heaven between the Lord and the devil and the other on earth between Faust and Mephistopheles) is already being established. For the Lord had, in *His* turn, assured Mephistopheles that "a good man in his dark striving is well aware of his right way" (328–29), words which, in all their commonplace simplicity, give the devil fair warning of the predestined outcome of his bargain and are almost literally repeated by Faust when he asks his tempter: "Was ever a man's spirit in its highest

[9] Arthur O. Lovejoy, *The Great Chain of Being* (New York, 1960), p. 16.
[10] Raymond Immerwahr, "The First Romantic Aesthetics," *Modern Language Quarterly*, XXI (1960), 3. Here and below I am indebted to Raymond Immerwahr for many valuable references.

striving grasped by your like?" (1676–77). At the same time this correspondence tends to enforce the contrast between the self-assured calm of the Heavenly Gardener and the Promethean impetus of the doctor, His "servant" (299) and creature, and between man's *dark* striving which the Lord included in His design as a matter of course and the *highest* striving professed by one who, ironically enough, has to serve as a pawn in the cosmic game.

Then Faust continues: What, if anything, will the devil be able to offer him? Can he provide him with food which does not satisfy, red gold which runs through one's fingers like mercury, games in which no man can ever win, a girl who, lying in one's arms, already ogles the next fellow, or honor which vanishes like a meteor? Thus far, the answer to this tortured litany of questions is undoubtedly yes. Mephistopheles will easily be able to accommodate the insatiable Faust by providing him with further dissatisfactions. (Neither he nor Faust can, at this point, foresee the unshakeable loyalty of Gretchen, which in the end will be used subtly but unmistakably by God, the rationalist, to justify the victory which he would have won anyway.) These demands on the part of Faust do not pose a problem or a challenge to the devil at all. Yet they are far more than a mere "contemptuous enumeration of a long series of sensuous pleasures and little jugglers' tricks which were bound to result in disappointment and empty delusion."[11] They are a statement, in the noncommittal form of questions, of man's general predicament. They justify his higher ambitions as attempts to abandon the dungeon of reality and break out of his earthly bondage by boldly transcending it. The poetic form may be highly romantic, but the existential content is as old as the human condition itself.

From here, however, Faust proceeds to demand the truly absurd, the completely paradoxical, the genuinely Faustian squaring of the circle. Just as in the "Prologue" the image of a garden appears immediately before Mephistopheles suggests his wager to the Lord, so Faust himself produces a garden image, or at least a vegetation symbol, just before he offers *his* bet to the devil. He demands no more nor less than the suspension of the natural sequence of the seasons. He asks for the reversal of the growth processes of the creation. With a titanic gesture he clamors for the disordering of the cosmos which God had cultivated so carefully in the "Prologue in Heaven." And it is not chance but a direct answer and challenge to the Lord's image of Himself as a gardener when Faust, too,

[11] Hermann J. Weigand, "Wetten und Pakt in Goethe's 'Faust,'" *Monatshefte*, LIII (1961), 326.

introduces a vegetation symbol. He wants to see the fruit that rots before it is broken from the branches, that is, before it has ripened, and the tree whose foliage turns green anew day after day:

> Zeig' mir die Frucht, die fault, eh' man sie bricht,
> Und Bäume, die sich täglich neu begrünen!   (1686–87)

This demand is obviously one which the devil is unable to fulfill. It is the sheer grasp for the impossible. Nor is this condition meant by Faust ever to be fulfilled. Wherever his path is going to turn, his ultimate destination is assured from the beginning. The devil will be left to whistle for his prey.

This agreement between creature and creator, between man's growing and striving on the one hand and a divine gardener's cultivation of his garden on the other, has been termed Goethe's "avoidance of tragedy." Goethe, Erich Heller stated upon an earlier occasion, "may have succeeded in creating a new genre: sentimental tragedy, or the tragedy of human *feelings*. . . ." And he continues: "what he could not write was the tragedy of the human *spirit*. It is here that the tragedy of Faust fails and becomes illegitimately ambiguous, because there is for Goethe in the last analysis no specifically human spirit."[12] This is certainly true but also profoundly false. It may not have been an intellectual, and certainly was not a moral, concept to see human growth, both physical and spiritual, in the image of a plant, a flower, or a tree, but it was poetically legitimate and convincing. It instilled Goethe with that kind of optimism which was based on and encouraged by his recognition of the organic growth of living beings. Thus even a dramatic structure like his *Faust*, with all its correspondences, parallels, self-quotations, and hidden parodies, was allowed to develop in a most natural fashion.[13] Here, too, Goethe followed the almost biological demands of his creative imagina-

---

[12] Erich Heller, *The Disinherited Mind* (Cambridge, 1952), p. 43. The emphasis is Heller's.

[13] Basically, Goethe respected the law of the nature from the very beginning: In his early essay "Of German Architecture" ("Von deutscher Baukunst") of 1772 he exclaimed with regard to the Strasbourg Minster and its builder, Erwin von Steinbach: "Diversify the immense wall which you are supposed to extend heavenward so that it may rise like a sublime and widespread tree of God, with a thousand boughs, millions of branches, and leaves like the sand on the sea announcing to the land around the majesty of the Lord, its master." ("Vermannigfaltige die ungeheure Mauer, die du gen Himmel führen sollst, dass sie aufsteige gleich einem hocherhabenen, weitverbreiteten Baume Gottes, der mit tausend Ästen, Millionen Zweigen und Blättern wie Sand am Meer ringsum der Gegend verkündet die Herrlichkeit des Herrn, seines Meisters.") *Goethes Schriften*, XXX (Stuttgart, n.d.), XVI, 15. I owe this reference to my colleague, Professor Marianne Bonwit.

tion. What had begun as a tragedy of human feelings ripened into a human parable of resplendent spirituality.

The strictures expressed by Heller are closely related to, if not identical with, the attitude of Schiller, projected from classical idealism into an existential argument. Goethe himself has told of his first meeting with Schiller: how both of them attended a meeting of a natural research association, the *Naturforschende Gesellschaft*, in Jena in 1794; how on the way home a conversation developed between them; and how the two of them became engrossed in their subject, which, again not by chance as far as Goethe was concerned, dealt with botanical problems. Goethe himself reports:

> By then we reached his house, and the conversation tempted me to enter. I set forth in a lively manner the metamorphosis of plants and, with some characteristic strokes of the pen, caused a symbolic plant to arise before his eyes. He perceived and observed it all with great interest, with a decided power of comprehension. But when I finished he shook his head and said, "This is no experience, this is an idea." I was startled, chagrined in a certain measure; for the point which separated us was by this expression most palpably indicated. . . . The old grudge was about to flare up in me again. I controlled myself, however, and answered, "It can be anything but disagreeable to me to have ideas without knowing it, and even to see them with my own eyes." [14]

His *Faust* was such an idea, for him and posterity to behold with their own eyes. So are the tree images and vegetation symbols that thrive throughout this poem as they do through the rest of his works. He was less than twenty years old when he painted the immortal picture of the birch trees spreading clouds of sweet incense before the path of the rising moon:

> Luna bricht durch Busch und Eichen,
> Zephyr meldet ihren Lauf,
> Und die Birken streun mit Neigen
> Ihr den süssten Weihrauch auf. [15]

[14] *Goethes poetische Werke* (Stuttgart, n.d.), VIII, 1402–3. The translation is adapted from the version in *Goethe's World*, ed. Berthold Biermann (New York, 1949), pp. 204–5. In connection with our subject it is interesting to note a distinction made in 1903 by Hugo von Hofmannsthal: "Goethe and Schiller relate to one another like the gardener and the seafarer. In extraordinary nights the calm gardener held his hands up to the stars and conversed with them as he did with the flowers in his garden, whereas the seafarer had nothing but his courageous heart and his storm-tossed boat" ("Schiller," *Prosa II* [Frankfort-on-Main, 1951], p. 176).
[15] "Die schöne Nacht," *Goethes poetische Werke*, I, 38.

He was seventy-three when he sketched, as if with a Chinese brush, the branches of slender willow trees merrily reflected in the mirror of a nearby lake and performed the poetic miracle of calling these branches "hair," neither co-ordinating them nor comparing the one with the other, neither saying "branches and hair" nor "branches like hair," but forging them into one new vision, one new word, which will remain descriptive of willow trees as long as there is a German language:

> Schlanker Weiden Haargezweige
> Scherzen auf der nächsten Flut. [16]

Is this an anthropomorphism? Is it a new myth which changes human hair into foliage? Is it a mirage produced by artistic perfection? Whatever it is, these "Haargezweige," too, are a genuine Goethean vegetation image in that they represent an idea so that it can be seen, and even touched.

Not only was Goethe's God a gardener, the poet himself was one, interested in garden lore and in the theory of gardening. He had been favorably impressed by the first great English garden in Germany, which Franz von Anhalt-Dessau had created in Woerlitz near Dessau, 1775–80. He knew the five volumes of Christian Cajus Lorenz Hirschfeld's strongly romanticizing *Theorie der Gartenkunst* (1779–85). In an essay he drafted in 1822 to describe the botanical undertakings in the duchy of Weimar, he maintained that "the inclination to lay out aesthetic gardens was quite generally greatly enhanced by Hirschfeld." [17] During his earlier years in Weimar Goethe seems to have been in hearty sympathy with Hirschfeld's ideas. He took an active part in the redesigning of the ducal park, changing it into a sentimental landscape. [18] In his charming little essay of 1778, "Das Luisenfest," he described the dedication of a hermitage in this park to the Grand Duchess Louise. As we shall see, Goethe grew cooler and cooler toward the wild and demoniac side of the *englische Garten* the older he grew. One could even interpret the landscape which is the background and perhaps the hidden hero of his novel, *The Elective Affinities*, of 1808 and

---

[16] "Dämmrung senkte sich von oben . . . ," *Ibid.*, I, 870.

[17] "Schema zu einem Aufsatze, die Pflanzenkultur im Grossherzogtum Weimar darzustellen," *Goethes sämtliche Werke* (*Jubiläumsausgabe*) (Stuttgart, 1902ff.), XXXIX, 338; Immerwahr, "The First Romantic Aesthetics," p. 6.

[18] *Goethes poetische Werke*, VIII, 1389–96; Gothein, *A History of Garden Art*, p. 304; Immerwahr, p. 6. See also: Eva Maria Neumeyer, "The Landscape Garden as a Symbol in Rousseau, Goethe and Flaubert," *Journal of the History of Ideas*, VIII (1947), 198.

1809, as a symptom of the poet's gradual withdrawal from both the French park and the *englische Garten* and a move toward a more symbolic representation of an inner world. "The limits of the natural are extended into uncertainty," says Emil Staiger.[19]

Yet Goethe remained fond of his garden. Much of his later work is associated with one of the two summer houses or *Gartenhäuschen* in the back corners of his Weimar residence.[20] He loved to stroll there, and perhaps the most impressive likeness of his appearance in his old age was rendered by Franz Grillparzer when he saw him, in 1826, "walking up and down in his little garden." And Grillparzer continued in his *Autobiography*:

> The cause of his stiff bearing before strangers now became clear to me. The years had not passed without leaving some traces. As he walked about in the garden, one could see that the upper part of his body, his head and shoulders, were bent slightly forward. This he wished to hide from strangers, and hence that forced straightening-up produced an unpleasant impression. The sight of him in his unaffected carriage, wearing a long dressing-gown, a small skull-cap on his white hair, had something infinitely touching about it. He looked like a king, and again like a father.[21]

And, we are tempted to add, like the Divine Gardener whom he had drawn, twenty-six years earlier, in his "Prologue in Heaven," and with whom, mythologically speaking, he may have confused himself occasionally during his old age.

Once he had written this "Prologue," however, the problem of the tragedy of *Faust* and its avoidance cannot have bothered him greatly any longer. To be sure, he had given the poem the name of "tragedy," and clung to this term in order to mystify his contemporaries, or out of sheer habit. But the older he grew, the more clarity he gained about the ultimate outcome of the plot—which was, of course, Faust's *salvation*—and the more serene he became in his attitude toward it. Thus, in 1820 he wrote from Jena to the aesthetician Karl Ernst Schubarth: "Mephistopheles may only win half of the wager, and when half of the guilt keeps burdening Faust, then the right of the old gentleman to acquit the sinner comes into force immediately, and concludes the whole in the happiest mood"

---

[19] Emil Staiger, *Goethe 1786–1814* (Zurich, 1956), p. 428.
[20] Gothein, *A History of Garden Art*, p. 498.
[21] *Grillparzers sämtliche Werke*, ed. August Sayer (Stuttgart, 1892ff.), XIX, 137. Translation adapted from Alfred Remy's version in *Goethe's World*, ed. Berthold Biermann, pp. 364–365.

("... so tritt das Begnadigungsrecht des alten Herrn sogleich herein, zum heitersten Schluss des Ganzen" [22]). This idea saved him from imbuing his poem with the pathos of tragedy as well as from misusing the power of persuasion inherent in a morality play. Instead, he bestowed upon it the irony of a man grown old and wise, and the unfathomable depth of a parable dealing with the multifariousness of human life.

If, on the other hand, Faust's poetic character reveals so many layers, is not the romantic drive that compels him to enter upon his pact with the devil identical with man's hunger for the forbidden fruit? Is not the tree whose image is conjured up by both the Lord and Faust the tree of knowledge, even if we do not consider the play in the light of theology? Is Erich Heller not right when he equates Faust's desire to penetrate the inmost fabric of the world and to discern its will and fount—

> ... Dass ich erkenne was die Welt
> Im Innersten zusammenhält,
> Schau' alle Wirkenskraft und Samen ...—   (382–84)

with a modern scientist's will to grasp the character of energy ("Wirkenskraft") and the atom ("Samen")?

One of the personages in the drama seems indeed to think so. It is Mephistopheles, the devil. In the "Prologue" he mentions his "female cousin, the illustrious snake" (335) only fifteen lines after the Divine Gardener has spoken of His little tree. In its branches the serpent seems to lie in wait for all who are greedy for the fruit of knowledge. Will they not, by breaking the fruit from the tree of knowledge, commit the sin of science?

A similarly revealing combination of tree, knowledge, and serpent recurs after the successful conclusion of the pact with Faust when Mephistopheles grants an interview to the Student, who is both a parody of the old doctor and the chrysalis out of which a new one will slip forth. Here the devil goes romantic and sounds like the proponent of what Professor Lovejoy would have called the *englische Garten* when he coins what, in spite of its deeply self-contradictory character, has become one of the most humdrum quotations from Goethe's poem. "Gray, my dear friend, is every theory," he advises the young initiate, "and green the golden tree of life" (2038–39). The golden tree, a *topos* dating back to the *trionfi* of the Renaissance and beyond them to the golden apples of the Hesperides,

---

[22] Hans Gerhard Gräf (ed.), *Goethe über seine Dichtungen* (Frankfort-on-Main, 1904), II, 2, 272.

is suddenly seen sprouting with the green foliage of life. But of what life? The life of knowledge, of philosophy, of law and medicine, which the devil had derided so eloquently just before? Do these pursuits lead to the sin of science which the neophyte is to commit henceforth? Far from it! The devil speaks of the life of the senses, prescribing to the freshman the same recipe with which he will bait the old professor, first by introducing him to the witch's kitchen and then by procuring Gretchen. The theory of which he speaks is the art of curing all the woes of womanhood by one approach, and one only. The serpent that raises its head here is certainly not the sin of atomic science. It is sex, gray *in abstracto*, but green and golden, when it is practiced. Then the little disciple asks Mephisto for an autograph to take home in his album, and the devil promptly writes the oracular prediction that divine omniscience and an almost Nietzschean stance beyond good and evil are in store for the human race. But we know because he plays the part of pimp in the Gretchen episode that he means nothing here but the lust of the senses when he calls after the departing apprentice: "Just follow my advice and my cousin, the snake, and sooner or later you will certainly shudder at your similarity with God!"

Folg' nur dem alten Spruch und meiner Muhme der Schlange,
Dir wird gewiss einmal bei deiner Gottähnlichkeit bange! (2049–50)

The emblem of Faust's fate is indeed the tree of knowledge. Yet throughout the second half of the first part of the poem—and especially its most dramatic (and probably oldest) portion, the Gretchen episode—knowledge is, as Mephistopheles and the Hebrew in the Book of Genesis would have it, synonymous with the possession of woman by man. This is precisely the misunderstanding to which the devil falls victim; he, Mephistopheles, who is as literal as only very one-sidedly intelligent people can be. He mistakes Faust for a new Adam and offers him in Gretchen a new Eve. He even goes a step further by introducing Faust to Eve's predecessor, Lilith, "the first of Adam's wives" (4119). Clad only in her beauteous hair, Lilith passes through the swirl and jostle of the romantic Walpurgis Night. She is followed by a couple of witches, an old one and a young one. The quartet which now develops between these two witches, Faust, and Mephistopheles leaves nothing to be desired as far as the obscene connotations of apple and tree imagery are concerned (4128–43). In grim parody the paradisaic tree of knowledge bears no fruit but lust.

But Faust's thirst for knowledge cannot so easily be quenched, as he had clearly foreseen—and given the devil fair warning—in his stipulation of the terms of the pact. For him, knowledge does indeed mean magic, although he will curse this magic in the end. Paradoxically, Goethe's devil cannot help him here beyond rejuvenating him and initiating him into knowledge (of womanhood) as he understands it. The sin he holds in store is a sin of the senses, and not of science.

The scene in which Faust comes closest to succumbing to his seducer (and, in true Faustian fashion, threatens to plunge himself and his beloved into the abyss of utter ruin) is most appropriately called "Forest and Cave." Its origins date back to the days of the *Urfaust*. But only in the period of Goethe's maturation, 1787–90, was its setting moved from the street in front of Gretchen's house to a landscape displaying all the "échappées into misty distances" which Lovejoy would have seen in one of his *englische Gärten*. Goethe speaks of the storm roaring in woods and creeks, of giant spruce trees falling, hitting, and smashing the neighboring branches and trunks; of hollow thunder over shaking hills, and sheltered caves in which to hide from the fury of the elements (3228–32); of rocky cliffs and fissured rocks and soggy moss and dripping stones (3272–74); of cataracts foaming from crag to crag and racing madly toward the depths (3350–51). Faust even goes so far in his romanticizing as to transplant the image of his beloved from her petty bourgeois and narrow surroundings to a little cabin on an alpine meadow, a setting which is thoroughly alien to her (3353).[23] This is true romantic scenery in the style of Caspar David Friedrich, and a proper background for Faust's desire to uproot the tree of knowledge and to "take back" God's cosmic order, replacing it with a chaos of extravagant irregularity and surprising boldness.

Instead of uprooting the tree of knowledge, however, Faust merely bends its branches with the weight of his archromantic imagery. Here, if anywhere in Goethe's poem, he is the poet, the romantic poet, the *poète maudit*. To be sure, he speaks even now of his dominion over the world

---

[23] How deeply rooted Goethe's romantic scenery is in the general *Naturgefühl* of the late eighteenth century can be seen from a comparison of the "Forest and Cave" scene with a passage from Hirschfeld's *Theorie der Gartenkunst*. The aesthetician speaks of the romantic character per se. Art, he says, can influence it only little, since it is completely a work of nature. And nature, he continues, "creates it not merely by means of mountainous regions, rocks, peaks, grottoes, waterfalls, cataracts and strange positions and configurations of these objects, but also by unusual combinations and juxtapositions, by an extravagant irregularity of arrangement, and by a surprising boldness of contrasts." This romantic landscape is not complete without at least a hint of Faust's alpine range in the background. Hirschfeld, too, mentions the "mountains grown over with spruce trees, the green tops of which are surmounted by peaks covered with eternal snow, as it happens in many regions of Switzerland" ([Leipzig, 1782], IV, 90, 91). Translation by Raymond Immerwahr, "The First Romantic Aesthetics," p. 6.

(3220). But his vision is directed toward a poetic, not a philosophic, and least of all not a scientific regimen. What he accepts as a gift from the spirit is a kingdom of the soul, the inner empire of creation. To be sure, the serpent has wormed its way also into this realm and appears in the person of Mephistopheles, whom Faust here actually twice calls "Snake!" (3324). And this time, on the serpent's bidding, Faust does break the fruit from the tree. The fruit, however, is carnal and concrete, the green and golden apple of sexual satisfaction. Gretchen surrenders. Yet Faust's passion proves the laws of nature, instead of suspending them, as he had demanded. This fruit carries in itself the decay caused by ennui and dissatisfaction. Faust being Faust, his love for Gretchen is doomed to end, come what may. If the Gretchen episode is a tragedy—with the possible exception of Faust's death the only truly tragic part of the whole poem— it is also distinguished by the inevitability of a natural process. It shows the rhythm of ebb and flood, the inexorability of the seasons. The fruit "that rots before it is broken from the branches" is still denied to Faust.

IV

When the curtain rings down on Part One, we leave Gretchen alone in a medieval dungeon on the morning of her execution. At the opening of Part Two, we are set down in an ideal and timeless landscape. Night falls and changes to morning again. We find Faust unconscious—sleep is to heal him from the wounds which he had inflicted upon his beloved. The country is pleasant; the waterfall, far from being an unbridled cataract, resembles a Roman fountain, streaming forth mightily from rock to rock. The destructive forces of nature have been tamed, and the time-hallowed image of reconciliation, the rainbow, embraces all the changes in the flowing and foaming streams of water. If this garden is not French in the style of a Poussin painting, it certainly is neoclassical; Ariel chants, accompanied by Aeolian harps. This stage direction, which sets the tone of the scene before the first word has been spoken, points back to Shakespeare's *Tempest* in its finality and valedictory wisdom as well as reminding us of Greek Antiquity and its revival in the idyls of the rococo.

Yet according to the organic logic which determines Goethe's poem, this Ariel is more than Shakespeare's light-winged sprite. He is a close relative of the archangels who opened the "Prologue in Heaven" with their measured song. As they greeted the rising of the light, so does Ariel when across the sky, as Goethe says in another stage direction, "a colossal uproar heralds the approach of the sun." Very much like the archangels before him, Ariel tries to translate the vision of light into the acoustics of the word. The immensity of the apparition is compared to thunder, to the rattling of rock portals opening and to the crackling produced by the wheels of the sun's chariot. Undoubtedly the corresponding imagery is intended to produce a sort of unity between the opening scenes of Parts One and Two.

Goethe's *Faust* not only grew like a tree during the better part of his life but is also a very symmetrical composition. Thus the beginning of the second part does not only correspond to the "Prologue in Heaven," it serves in addition to span the distance to the epilogue in heaven, the last scene of the poem. Light imagery enlivens the three corner scenes. To the archangels in the "Prologue," light is a reality, incomprehensible like the rest of the creation to be sure, but overwhelming nevertheless in its physical presence. Ariel, however, describes the light quite differently: "The unheard-of cannot be heard," he says ("Unerhörtes hört sich nicht" [4674]). Here we have already reached that region beyond the effability of the effable, of which the end of Goethe's poem will say that it is "the indescribable" (12109). We have left the realm of tragedy which is determined by the stark realities of space and time. Beckoned by Ariel, we have entered the regions of symbolic representation, the sphere of the parable. Faust himself is the first to notice it when he wakes up from the healing slumber. Although he is still not able to expose his naked eye to the source of all life, the sun, he allows himself a moment of leisure to contemplate its many-hued reflection in the waterfall. He is now able to comprehend the essence of all existence in the rainbow mirroring human love and strife:

Am farbigen Abglanz haben wir das Leben.   (4727)

The opening scene of Part Two was written very late in Goethe's life, between 1826 and 1828. Mephistopheles is conspicuously absent, and so are any traces of the demoniac landscape that inspired a scene like "Forest and Cave." Quite obviously, Goethe's taste had changed, in staging as well as in gardening. In 1825 he had delivered himself of what amounted to a downright condemnation of the *englische Garten*. On June 15, on a ride with the Chancellor von Müller that led the two men to the palace of the Grand Duke, he commended the way French gardens were laid out, at any rate in the neighborhood of great castles. "The spacious arbors and bowers," he said on this occasion, "the Quinconx, allow a large party to come and go in a decorous way, whereas in our English places (which I might call Nature's little jokes) we keep knocking against one another, and either get boxed in or quite lost." ("Die geräumigen Laubdächer, Berceaux, Quinconces, lassen doch eine zahlreiche Gesellschaft sich anständig entwickeln und vereinen, während man in unsern englischen Anlagen, die ich naturspässige nennen möchte, allerwärts aneinander stösst, sich hemmt oder verliert."[24]) After all, Goethe never followed personally the example he had set in the park at Weimar and failed to treat the garden at his own town house in the new picturesque style.[25] As evidenced by the drawings from his own hand, he continued to prefer to be surrounded by a certain classical order in the old fashion.

Since he considered his *Faust* to be part and parcel of the confession of his life, are we not justified in assuming that he returned to the geometrizing God of the seventeenth century when, toward the end of his life, he finished what he had come to call his "main business" ("das Hauptgeschäft"),[26] the Faust poem? Did the French garden, cultivated by enlightened taste, eventually win out over the Faustian romanticism of the *englische Garten?* Was the happy ending he accordingly held in store for the superhuman doctor nothing but a salvation *de convenance?* Did he betray romantic agony by exchanging it for the stolid avoidance of the tragic spirit, as certain members of the Young Germany movement, especially Ludwig Börne, had already charged he was doing? Or was he so lost in ambiguities and self-contradictions that Faust, in the last analysis, stops being Faust? A modern German critic of the stature of Siegfried Melchinger seems to think so when he exclaims: "The identification of Goethe's Faust with the Faustian man has become more than questionable."[27]

To answer these questions, let us return once more to the image of the tree. Early in the second part the poem reaches a point where Faust's demand to see a tree the foliage of which turns green anew day after day comes close to being fulfilled. The doctor, transported to the court of a Renaissance emperor, participates in a masquerade. The first group to enter on the stage is a bevy of young girl gardeners. They come from sixteenth-century Florence and offer artificial flowers which in their splendor continue to blossom all year round:

---

[24] Flodoard von Biedermann, *Goethes Gespräche: Gesamtausgabe* (Leipzig, 1910), III, 212. Translation by Gothein, *A History of Garden Art*, p. 318.

[25] Gothein, *ibid.*

[26] *Tagebücher*, July 22, 1831, *passim. Goethes Schriften* (Stuttgart, n.d.), XIII, 954.

[27] Melchinger, "Faust für uns," p. 9. Also Wilhelm Böhm, *Faust, der Nichtfaustische* (Halle, 1933).

Unsere Blumen, glänzend künstlich,
Blühen fort das ganze Jahr.   (5098–99)

They are followed by vegetation symbols which are more natural: olive branches with olive fruit, ears of corn forming a garland, and rose buds. In his study of the imagery in *Faust Part Two*, Wilhelm Emrich has argued that Goethe discusses here the truth of art versus the truth of nature,[28] a subject that gave him and eighteenth-century aestheticians much to think about and that also underlies the controversy over the French park against the *englische Garten*. But Emrich overlooks the fact that these likenesses of nature are but artful illusions which could never satisfy a man striving for the innate authenticity of existence proper. Eventually the evergreen flowers, like the emperor's beard and the rest of the masquerade, seem to be consumed by fire. As far as the plot is concerned, they are not introduced to satisfy Faust but to amuse an easygoing and slightly corrupt monarch. Their function in the poem as a whole is to serve as allegories of the beautiful illusion, the *schöne Schein*, in contradistinction to the symbol of the rainbow, which had appeared to Faust as the reflection of life. This reflection, this resplendence ("Abglanz") of light in the spraying waters points beyond itself to the absolutes of truth and divinity; it is multifaceted, and has as many meanings as it finds spectators. In other words, it is a genuine symbol.

Goethe was apparently the first to draw a clear line of distinction between symbol and allegory.[29] In the posthumously published part of his *Maxims and Reflexions* he gave the now well-known definition according to which

> allegory transforms the phenomenon into a concept, the concept into an image, yet [only] in such a manner that the concept continues to be in the image and can be had and held completely and within its given limits and is able to be fully expressed in terms of the image.—The symbol, on the other hand, transforms the phenomenon into an idea, the idea into an image, and this in such a fashion that the idea continues to remain infinitely effective and inaccessible within the image and would remain inexpressible, even if it were expressed in all languages.
>
> ("Die Allegorie verwandelt die Erscheinung in einen Begriff, dem Begriff in ein Bild, doch so, dass der Begriff im Bilde immer

---

[28] Wilhelm Emrich, *Die Symbolik von Faust II* (Bonn, 1957), p. 143 *passim*.
[29] René Wellek, "The Concept of 'Romanticism' in Literary History," II, *Comparative Literature*, I (1949), 148.

noch begrenzt und vollständig zu halten und zu haben und an demselben auszusprechen sei.—Die Symbolik verwandelt die Erscheinung in Idee, die Idee in ein Bild, und so, dass die Idee im Bild immer unendlich wirksam und unerreichbar bleibt und, selbst in allen Sprachen ausgesprochen, doch unaussprechlich bliebe.") [30]

After all we have said about the organic structure of the *Faust* poem, we should not be surprised to find the allegory of the everblooming flowers at the beginning of Part Two balanced by a genuine tree symbol at its very end.

Linden trees spread their dark foliage through the first line of the fifth act (11043), the last scene, which Goethe composed during the year preceding his death. An anonymous wanderer greets these trees, which, in the vigor of their old age, are the first and supreme welcome he receives on his return from a stormy voyage. It is, of course, true that Goethe found these linden trees in the eighth book of Ovid's *Metamorphoses*, together with the names of the oldsters, Philemon and Baucis, who live in their shadow. [31] But in a conversation with Eckermann he disclaimed the ancestry of the Roman poet, at least for the two old people: "My Philemon and Baucis have nothing to do with that famous couple from classical antiquity. I just gave them these names to throw them into bolder relief." [32] What is valid for the human beings is certainly good for the trees as well. Linden trees are, in German folklore and folk song alike, the epitome of man's intimate at-homeness in the world. They may not represent the demoniac forces conjured up by literary romanticism, as did the spruce trees in the "Forest and Cave" scene, but they are surrounded by the sweeter aura of popular romanticism, in which, for instance, Franz Schubert had enveloped them in his song from the *Winterreise* cycle.

Their very name, *Linde*, connotes gentleness in German, and so these calm and calming trees are set in sharp contrapuntal relationship to Faust himself. Like them, the hero has grown old; like them, he has remained vigorous; yet he has developed into a tyrant who, still aided and abetted by Mephistopheles, now loathes the magical powers on which he has relied for so long. The region in which the linden trees grow and Philemon and Baucis live is described as "open," whereas the tower of the one-hundred-year-old ruler rises over a spacious garden, its decorative

---

[30] *Goethes poetische Werke*, II, 813.
[31] Ovid, *Metamorphoses*, Loeb Classical Library (Cambridge, 1946), I, 448ff.
[32] Johann Peter Eckermann, *Gespräche mit Goethe* (Wiesbaden, 1955), pp. 470–71.

planting divided symmetrically by a straight, wide canal. Thus, the contrast between French park and *englischer Garten*, that is, the dichotomy of classicism and romanticism, accompanies Faust to the very end of his days. Moreover, the natural beauty of Philemon and Baucis' linden trees produces the last acute conflict in the life of Faust, who seems to be both the master and the prisoner of his geometrized landscape.

Faust is obsessed with the idea of acquiring these linden trees, of doing away with them, and of incorporating the narrow strip of land that bears them into his fief. At the root of his obsession we can observe distinctly anti-Christian aggressions: There is a chapel next to the trees, and its bell keeps reminding Faust of the dreary fact that the work of colonization which he has been undertaking with the help of Mephistopheles is incomplete as long as church and hut and linden trees are not his (Faust's) own. The bell may also warn his conscience that his pioneering work is, and remains, devil's work. At the same time the fragrance of the trees conspires with the "accursed tolling" (11151) of the little bell to announce his death:

> Des Glöckchens Klang, der Linden Duft
> Umfängt mich wie in Kirch' und Gruft.   (11253–54)

These linden trees are the last image of the natural order of things against which Faust has been rebelling all his life. Goethe is thoroughly consistent in the choice of his imagery when he singles them out for Faust to destroy. This time the magician succeeds, after a fashion. Mephistopheles has promised to resettle Philemon and Baucis, but his reference to Naboth's vineyard does not bode well for the old couple (11287). The devil has chosen his simile appropriately; just as, in Kings I:21, Naboth has to die for the sake of his grapes, so Philemon and Baucis must die for the sake of their linden trees. Their guest, the Wanderer, who dared resist the devil and his accomplices, is murdered. Like the evergreen flowers before, so now the linden trees go up in flames, together with the oldsters' hut and chapel. And sure enough, even the serpent raises its head again, if only metaphorically. From his tower platform Lynceus the watchman observes first the sparks flying through the "double night of the linden trees" (11308–9) and then the sharp flames, *like serpents* licking at the tree tops until the little chapel below is crushed by falling branches:

> Das Capellchen bricht zusammen
> Von der Äste Sturz und Last.
> *Schlängelnd* sind, mit spitzen Flammen
> Schon die Gipfel angefasst.
>
> (11330–33—my italics)

But can these trees, these age-old, protective, and homey linden trees, be exalted to anybody's idea of the tree of knowledge? True, they tempt Faust, and he succumbs to the temptation. Yet the sin which he commits is neither the sin of the flesh, as it was in Part One, nor the sin of magic and of science. Half sinning and half sinned against by Mephistopheles, he infringes upon the simplest law of humanity: he disregards the respect one human being is meant to pay to another. His "I," this superhuman Ego of Faust, trespasses against the "Thou" of Philemon, Baucis, and the Wanderer. Moreover, with the murder of the Wanderer, the time-hallowed law of hospitality is also broken. What happens between Faust and his victims does not happen between the ruler and the ruled, the tyrant and the meek, the magician and the laymen, the devil's disciple and the pious bystanders. It happens between man and man. The law of pure humanity proclaimed by Iphigenie in Goethe's so-called classical period is blatantly violated by the Faust of his old age. And the offender perishes, blind and yet seeing, like Oedipus.

What blind Faust sees in his last vision is the conquest of the sea by the land, a "change of natural events,"[32a] not unlike the one he had once demanded from Mephistopheles prior to the concluding of their pact. Listening to the noise of the shovels and spades at work, he seems at long last to have attained what he was striving for, the Faustian *non plus ultra,* a metamorphosis of the elements. What he actually hears, however, is the digging "not of a ditch but of his grave," as the devil, rubbing his hands, informs the spectators (11558). As Prometheus stole the fire from heaven, so does Faust intend to open new land for the sake of mankind. But his Promethean stance remains self-deceiving. To his very end he fails to upset the order maintained by the Divine Gardener. And to his very end he persists in trying.

But Faust is saved. Ostensibly, he is redeemed in the epilogue when angels chanting a moralistic doggerel carry his immortal soul upward. Yet his fate as a parabolical figure is most clearly revealed at the moment of his last, worst crime. While he reluctantly condones the crime against Philemon and Baucis, he is dreaming of a lookout from which to gaze into infinity, a sentinel's post where he can watch both the natural and the supernatural worlds. This tower is to rise from the spot where the half-charred linden trunks stand:

> Doch sei der Lindenwuchs vernichtet
> Zu halbverkohlter Stämme Graun,
> Ein Luginsland ist bald errichtet,
> Um ins Unendliche zu schaun.   (11341–45)

[32a] Heinrich Rickert, *Goethes Faust* (Tübingen, 1932), p. 401.

This "Unendliche" is a space beyond all spaces. Faust remains his restless self until the end. His ultimate guilt is his supreme triumph; his last triumph over reality is his deepest disgrace as a human being. He is always to be saved, and never.

There is a German adage which says that God sees to it that trees do not grow into heaven. Goethe saw to it that Faust's burned-down linden trees grew into infinity. Thereby they assumed the quality of the ineffable which the poet was so fond of ascribing to the genuine symbol. These linden trees are images neither of knowledge nor of innocence, neither of sin nor of grace, but of Faust's fate as such. As Goethean symbols they are "infinitely effective" and "would remain inexpressible" even if they were "expressed in all languages." What they seem to be communicating to us is that they are no longer correlatives "of objects one is able to know but, by their very existence, representations of a presence inseparable from the expression they have found, as if they were the second surface of the same reality."[33] This second surface shows Faust, shows Everyman, as simultaneously guilty and innocent. Sin and grace are inseparably interwoven. Proceeding from this paradox, Goethe turned the tragic legend into a parable which, but for the love of God—"die Liebe *gar*" (11938—my italics)—would end in a minor key.

But does this parable end at all? On the stage Faust is not *really* saved but shown in an infinite upward movement. No doubt he approaches his goal: but within the verbal context of Goethe's poem he fails to arrive. Or, to use Barker Fairley's admirable phrase: "If we have to admit that the poem stops, we can at least point out that it does its best not to stop. The text stops, but Faust goes on."[34] Nor does the Lord of the "Prologue" reappear to welcome His *enfant terrible*, His *enfant prodigue*. Is He, the omniscient and omnipotent one, too magnanimous to put the devil to shame? Or is He ashamed of Himself because of the preordained ease with which He has won the game? Rather than apply psychology to the Lord, I would resort to aesthetic considerations. If God had reappeared, the poem would inevitably have turned into a comedy, though perhaps a divine one. Yet, essentially it was meant to be neither a comedy nor a tragedy but a highly symbolic simile, a statement, open to infinity, of the condition of man.

Only with the help of such a statement could Goethe hope to reconcile the schism that sundered both the age and its art. On September 23, 1827, he sent a letter to the writer, Karl Ludwig Iken, discussing the

---

[33] Maurice Marache, *Le Symbole dans la pensée et l'oeuvre de Goethe* (Paris, 1960), p. 17.
[34] Barker Fairley, *Goethe's Faust* (Oxford, 1953), p. 43.

third act of Part Two. This act, the Helena episode, had been published the same year, with the revealing subtitle, "a classico-romantic phantasmagory." About it Goethe wrote: "I have never doubted that the readers whom I really had in mind would immediately grasp the principal meaning of my presentation. The time has come," he continued, "when the passionate conflict between classical and romantic writers should finally be reconciled." ("Es ist Zeit, dass der leidenschaftliche Zwiespalt zwischen Classikern und Romantikern sich endlich versöhne.")[35] This conflict, which I chose to exemplify by dwelling on the vegetation imagery in *Faust*, was mitigated, if not settled, by means of Goethe's poem. If René Wellek was able to recognize "a fundamental unity in the whole of German literature from roughly the middle of the eighteenth century to the death of Goethe," I feel tempted to add that it was Goethe who was born in the middle of this century and that is was he who served both as its unifying factor and its catalyst. Wellek seems to be speaking of Goethe's *Faust* in particular when he characterizes the development of eighteenth-century German literature in general by stating that it represents

> an attempt to create a new art different from that of the French seventeenth century; it is an attempt at a new philosophy which is neither orthodox Christianity nor the Enlightenment of the eighteenth century. This new view emphasizes the totality of man's forces, not reason alone, nor sentiment alone, but rather intuition, "intellectual intuition," imagination.[36]

Only insofar as this mobilization of the totality of man's forces—the liberation of man's intellectual intuition—is concerned am I prepared to see a modern hero in Goethe's parabolical Faust.

Goethe towered high enough over his age to feel the cold and urgent pressures of things to come. He sensed them, disliked them intensely and turned away to cultivate his garden. Five days before his death, on March 17, 1832, he wrote to Wilhelm von Humboldt. Again he came back to his *Faust*, speaking of the poem at this occasion as "these very serious jokes" ("diese sehr ernsten Scherze"). Then he went on to say:

> But truly, the day is so absurd and confused that I am persuaded that the pains I took for such a long time and so honestly with this strange construct of mine would be badly rewarded. It will

[35] Gräf, *Goethe über seine Dichtungen*, p. 412.
[36] Wellek, " 'Romanticism' in Literary History," p. 150.

be driven to the shore and lie there like a wreck in shambles and, to begin with, be covered with the rubble and the sand of the present. Perplexing teachings leading to perplexed actions hold their sway over the world, and I am most of all concerned with increasing, if at all possible, all that is about me and has remained with me, and to cohobate my characteristics. . . .

("Der Tag aber ist wirklich so absurd und confus, dass ich mich überzeuge, meine redlichen, lange verfolgten Bemühungen um dieses seltsame Gebäu würden schlecht belohnt und an den Strand getrieben, wie ein Wrack in Trümmern daliegen und von dem Dünenschutt der Stunden zunächst überschüttet werden. Verwirrende Lehre zu verwirrtem Handel waltet äber die Welt, und ich habe nichts angelegentlicher zu thun, als dasjenige, was an mir ist und geblieben ist, wo möglich zu steigern und meine Eigenthümlichkeiten zu cohobiren. . . .") [37]

He used the word "cohobate," which is taken from the Faustian world of an alchemist's kitchen and means to subject a thing to change by repeatedly distilling it. The old gardener could have used the word "change by growth" instead. It meant the same to him. For the "strange construct," this *Faust*, "the moulded form which develops while it lives" (this "gepragte Form, die lebend sich entwickelt") [38] is also a grown organism, a symbol not only of magic, knowledge, or science but of total human existence. [39]

---

[37] Graf, *Goethe über seine Dichtungen*, pp. 607–8.

[38] *Goethes poetische Werke*, I, 541.

[39] While reading the proofs of this article, the author had his first chance to acquaint himself with Helmut Rehder's paper, "Studies in Goethe's Poetic Imagery, II: The Garden and the Wilderness," *The University of Texas Studies in Literature and Language*, VI (1964), 334–45. With immense learning and profound wisdom Rehder asks questions not altogether unrelated to those raised in this paper. When he suggests, in conclusion, that the reader "may discover that Goethe's own poetic practice reveals a preference for the image of wilderness over that of the garden," he seems to have scanned Goethe's poetic language from the modern point of view rather than from the context of the eighteenth century, into which this paper had attempted to re-integrate Goethe's symbolism. Different points of departure seem to have led to incongruous answers. Perhaps, however, it is the questions that count. In this respect the author confesses to have derived a high degree of comfort and support from Rehder's realization "that the end of knowledge by intuition or induction is but the beginning of an endless process of tracing and comparing the preverbal image—the image as the spark of the unspeakable."

The Enlightenment

and the French Revolution

BY ALFRED COBBAN

◄◄◄◄◄◄◄◄◄◄◄◄◄◄ ☼ ►►►►►►►►►►►►►

The debate over the problem of the relation between the ideas of eighteenth-century France and the Revolution is not new. I have been aware of it ever since reading, as a schoolboy, what then seemed to me, and must still seem to many, the convincing explanation of Taine. "When," he wrote, "we see a man . . . apparently sound and of peaceful habits, drink eagerly of a new liquor, then suddenly fall to the ground, foaming at the mouth, . . . we have no hesitation in supposing that in the pleasant draught there was some dangerous ingredient."[1] The man, of course, was France, the liquor the Enlightenment, and the fit that overtook the unwise imbiber was the French Revolution. Similies are the camouflage of bad history, but Taine also puts it more succinctly. "Millions of savages," he says, "were launched into action by a few thousand babblers."[2]

Does anyone read Taine now? Some sixty years ago Aulard said that at the Sorbonne a candidate for the diploma in historical studies or the doctorate would disqualify himself if he quoted Taine as an authority on any historical question.[3] Curiously enough, on the basic aspects of the problem under discussion here, Taine and his critic were in fundamental agreement. They both believed that a historian should be interested

[1] Hippolyte Taine, *Les Origines de la France contemporaine: L'Ancien régime* ([1875] 14th ed.; Paris, 1885), pp. 221–22.
[2] *Ibid.*, p. 521.
[3] A. Aulard, *Taine, historien de la révolution française* (Paris, 1907), p. viii.

in causes, not as yet having learned from philosophers of history the impossibility of getting from one set of facts to another set of facts except by the interposition of a third set of facts, and so on ad infinitum; and they believed that ideas were the essential motive force in history. We should not be too critical of their interpretation of the relationship between the Enlightenment and the Revolution. The belief that the Revolution was caused by the spread of enlightened ideas is natural enough. It was put forward at the time by Burke and schematized by the Abbé Barruel in the form of a triple conspiracy—conspiracy being the easiest way of accounting for any great calamity of which one does not understand the origins. The three prongs of the conspiracy, as Barruel saw it, were (1) an anti-Christian conspiracy by the philosophers; (2) these sophists of impiety were joined by the sophists of rebellion in the occult lodges of the Freemasons; (3) impiety and anarchy became fused into a conspiracy against all religion, government, and property in the sect of the *Illuminés*. The heads of the conspiracy were Voltaire, d'Alembert, Frederick II, and Diderot, its chief weapon the *Encyclopédie*, and its active agent the club of the Jacobins. [4]

The historians of the nineteenth century continued the same basic assumption, except that instead of regarding the Revolution as a disaster, they began to regard it as a good thing, and hence not the work of conspirators spreading dangerous ideas but of the people inspired by noble ones. Thus, for Lamartine the Revolution came into existence the day when printing was invented, for this made public opinion possible: eighteenth-century philosophy was the code of civil and religious liberty put into action in the Revolution by the people. [5] Michelet is more specific. He says, "When these two men [Voltaire and Rousseau] had formed their ideas, the Revolution was accomplished in the high realm of the mind." [6] But this was only because they expressed the thought of the masses, "the chief author was the people." [7] Of course, the eighteenth century could not have seen the Revolution as the revolt of the masses, since the masses did not exist before the great growth of population and urbanization that characterized the nineteenth century. The eighteenth-century belief in the primacy of ideas, however, persisted, even when the newer conditions of the nineteenth century had brought economic motivation to the fore, as it was in the history of Louis Blanc. Writing, like Karl Marx, in that

[4] A. de Barruel, *Mémoires pour servir à l'histoire du jacobinisme* (Hambourg, 1803).
[5] A. de Lamartine, *Histoire des constituants* (Paris, 1855).
[6] Michelet, *Histoire de la révolution française* (Paris, 1877), I, 59–60.
[7] *Ibid.*, p. xliv. Preface of 1847.

great incubator of revolutionary thought the British Museum, Louis Blanc used the Croker collection of pamphlets, from which, aided by his own experience of France under the July Monarchy, he discovered the contempt of the revolutionary bourgeois for the people and the hatred of the people for the bourgeois.[8] This, added to the struggle of the *Tiers Etat* against the privileged orders, could have been interpreted in terms of a class struggle and conflict of economic interests, but Louis Blanc, for all his socialist ideology, still puts the revolutionary struggle as one of conflicting principles—authority, individualism, and fraternity, corresponding respectively to noblesse, bourgeoisie, and people. There were few students of the revolutionary period who, like de Tocqueville, saw social and political factors as more powerful than ideas.[9] Even socialist historians, such as Jaurès, Mathiez, Lefebvre and Labrousse, for all their awareness of economic factors, still seem to interpret the Revolution as basically a conflict of principles, a struggle for the hearts of men. "All historians agree on the influence of *lumières* on the Revolution," wrote Professor Jacques Godechot recently, "but disagree whether their influence is essential, or secondary to economic factors."[10]

The problem adumbrated here is not one which is peculiar to the French Revolution. The degree of influence to be attributed to ideas is an unresolved question in respect of all great historical movements—Renaissance and Reformation, Industrial Revolution, benevolent despotism, as well as French Revolution. The attempt to dispose of this difficulty by treating ideas as merely the ideologies of social classes underestimates the elasticity of principles, what Whitehead called the "adventures of ideas."[11] They cannot be identified with social forces; for once an idea has been let loose on the world, no one knows where it will settle or what new movement it will start. This is not a reason for abandoning the attempt to establish connections between changes in ideas and political and social developments, but it does suggest that these connections need to be examined with as much care and criticism of the evidence as would be applied to any other historical problem. Although contemporaries and historians have agreed on the causal relation between the thought of the eighteenth century, or more specifically the Enlightenment, and the Revolution, it has usually been on the basis of assumptions about both that have hardly survived more recent historical analysis.

[8] Louis Blanc, *Histoire de la révolution française* (Paris, 1847), I, 9.
[9] A. de Tocqueville, *L'Ancien régime et la révolution* (Paris, 1856).
[10] J. Godechot, *Les Révolutions* (1770–1777) (Paris, 1963), p. 284.
[11] A. N. Whitehead, *Adventures of Ideas* (New York, 1933).

What do we now understand by the Enlightenment? Its enemies, from the time of Burke and the Abbé Barruel, have condemned it for dealing in abstractions, to which the real interests of actual men and women are sacrificed. It can hardly be denied that the Enlightenment, though scientific and empirical on the one hand, was also a system of abstract, generalizing thought which tried to substitute impersonal for personal forces over a large range of human life: indeed the measure to which it succeeded in doing this is the measure of its success in changing much of the social ethic of Western civilization. If we look for rational, physical causes of misfortunes instead of attributing them to witchcraft, if we accept the impersonal wage system in place of personal slavery, if we reject the torture of individuals as a means of eliciting the truth and use instead the impersonal rules of the law, if we do not regard personal salvation as so important that we are prepared to burn people in order to achieve it for them as well as for ourselves, if we do not believe that the stars are concerned with our individual fortunes, and so on, we are tacitly acknowledging the influence of the Enlightenment over our assumptions and actions; for the opposite was in each case the normal view before what has so often been condemned as the abstract thought of the Enlightenment extended the scientific, generalizing approach from physical nature to human actions. The Enlightenment was the end of a spiritual world ruled by angels and demons, cherubim and seraphim, Beelzebub and Satan. "Farewell rewards and fairies." In religion, the Enlightenment substituted the impersonal god of deism for a personal deity, and skepticism about the dogmas of revealed religion was followed by toleration. Systems of ethics based on religious authority and sanctions were replaced by ideas of utilitarianism and humanitarianism and the search for a new ethic. There is a paradox by which the ages most condemned at the time for immorality are in fact those most concerned with morality. Such were fifth-century Athens and eighteenth-century Western Europe.

It is not my purpose, nor is it necessary here, to provide a detailed survey of the ideas of the Enlightenment; but any account, however brief, cannot fail to point out that one element is the strong current of political liberalism that runs through it. This is particularly important for the present argument, in that the Revolution, whatever else it may have been, was also a struggle for political power. In the course of this were revived many of the political concepts employed by the political writers of seventeenth-century England to justify the revolutions of that century. Locke's political ideas, in particular, were introduced into eighteenth-century France in the translations and commentaries of Burlamaqui and

Barbeyrac. They were reproduced by the chevalier de Jaucourt in his contribution to the *Encyclopédie*. They appear in a modified form in the writings of Montesquieu, Rousseau, d'Holbach, or Mably, and are not absent from those of Voltaire and Diderot. However, the political content of the French Enlightenment must not be exaggerated. If we exclude Montesquieu and Rousseau, we are left for the most part with general sentiments about the desirability of liberty and the undesirability of despotism, with especial reference to freedom of thought and religion. The influence of Montesquieu's emphasis on the virtues of the English constitution did not outlast the third quarter of the century, and his famous *Esprit des lois* was often, though not quite correctly, interpreted merely as a defense of the claims of the French parliaments.[12] Rousseau's *Contrat social* had no ascertainable influence before the Revolution and only a very debatable one during its course.[13] True, there is the oft-repeated story of Marat reading it to enthralled crowds at street corners,[14] but anyone who could believe this could believe anything.

Alternatively, there has been the suggestion that the *philosophes* were the theorists of benevolent despotism. This view has been too effectively dealt with elsewhere to require any further demolition here.[15] In so far as it ever appeared to have any plausibility was due to the confusion of the *philosophes* with the small group of Physiocrats, and only with the first generation even of these.

It must be recognized that the French Enlightenment was on the whole lacking in systematic political theory; it was hardly to be expected in a country which had no active politics. Since the French Revolution was primarily a political revolution, this must cast doubt upon its supposed causal relationship with the Enlightenment. But we are left with the need to ask, if they did not come from the Enlightenment, what were the sources of the political theories of the Revolution, which if they did not cause it—and this would be difficult to prove in any case—at least were used to justify it. Framed in these terms, however, this is a problem that is not susceptible of a single answer. There is now general agreement that the

[12] Cf. E. Carcassonne, *Montesquieu et le problème de la constitution française au XVIIIᵉ siècle* (Paris, 1927).

[13] This is discussed by Dr. Joan Macdonald in her book, *Rousseau and the French Revolution, 1762–1791* (London, 1965); cf. Alfred Cobban, *Rousseau and the Modern State* (2nd ed.; London, 1964), pp. 280–82.

[14] Mallet du Pan, *Mémoires* (Paris, 1851), 126n.

[15] E.g. Peter Gay, *The Party of Humanity* (New York, 1964); Arthur Wilson, "The Development and Scope of Diderot's Political Thought," *Studies on Voltaire and the Eighteenth Century*, Vol. XXVII, ed. T. Besterman (Geneva, 1963).

picture of the French Revolution as a bloc with one inspiration, though used in the propaganda both of supporters and opponents of "the Revolution," is invalid. The historic reality is a series of revolutions, very different in their aims and therefore in any theoretical affiliations they may have had.

The revolutionary period opened, in 1787, with what has been termed the *révolte nobiliaire*. This was in effect an attempt on the part of sections of the privileged classes to take over the government of France. It was an aristocratic movement, using the term in its strictly political sense of government by those who believed in rule of an aristocracy. Thus one could have a "bourgeois aristocrat" or even a "peasant aristocrat," and on the other hand a patriot noble.[16] The theoretical justification for such a polity evidently cannot be sought in the Enlightenment. There is an obvious ancestry—without venturing into any speculations about causal connections—in the political literature of the Fronde and of the so-called faction of the duke of Burgundy under Louis XIV.

A second revolution, the peasant revolt of 1789, which has been correctly singled out by Lefebvre as a separate and autonomous movement, was a practical revolt against practical grievances. It could have occurred at any time when circumstances were favorable, and no theory was needed to instigate or justify it. There had been a paper attack on "feudalism," it is true, running through the century,[17] but this bore remarkably little relationship to the ills of the peasantry, and when it was employed on the famous night of the Fourth of August, it was used in an attempt to save what could be saved of the seigneurial rights and dues by limiting the definition of "feudal" rather than to promote the rising against them.[18]

What made the peasant revolt possible, however, had been a third revolutionary movement, that of the *Tiers Etat*, which followed on the *révolte nobiliaire*. Here we certainly meet with political ideas in abundance, at least of expression. This is not the place for a detailed analysis of the ideology of the *Tiers Etat*. It can hardly be questioned, however, that its central theme was the idea of popular sovereignty, which was given its fullest expression by the Abbé Sieyes in the most famous pamphlet of the Revolution, which, because it embodied the wishes of the Third

[16] Alfred Cobban, *The Social Interpretation of the French Revolution* (Cambridge, 1964), pp. 82–83.

[17] Dr. J. Q. C. Mackrell has studied this in his London Ph.D. thesis and forthcoming book, "The Attack on 'Feudalism' in Eighteenth-Century France."

[18] Cobban, *Social Interpretation*, pp. 39–40.

Estate, obtained unprecedented circulation. In *Qu'est-ce que le tiers état?* Sieyes stated the new political ideology in uncompromising form. "The nation," he wrote, "is prior to everything. It is the source of everything. Its will is always legal. The manner in which a nation exercises its will does not matter; the point is that it does exercise it; any procedure is adequate, and its will is always the supreme law."[19] The logical consequence of this extreme assertion of popular or national sovereignty, as I have suggested elsewhere, is to identify the people with the government, the rulers with the ruled.[20] The result of apparently removing the need for any check on government must be something very like what Professor Talmon has called totalitarian democracy. It should be noted in qualification that the application of this idea in the French Revolution was nothing like as extreme as it has been subsequently, and that totalitarianism, even in an embryonic form, is more easily associated with the Napoleonic dictatorship than with the revolutionary assemblies.

For our present purpose, however, the problem is whether, or how far, the revolutionary idea of popular sovereignty can be derived from the thought of the Enlightenment; and the answer must be that it is not easily to be found in the writings of the *philosophes* or of their seventeenth-century predecessors. Locke, who summed up the political thinking of the seventeenth century and passed it on to the eighteenth, directed his whole argument to limiting sovereignty of any kind. The same can be said of Montesquieu, de Jaucourt, Voltaire, and d'Holbach. To Rousseau alone is it even plausible to attribute any conception of the sovereignty of the people; and it is not difficult to see that even in his case the attribution rests upon an elementary, though common, misunderstanding of his thought. Sovereignty for Rousseau resides in the General Will, and the General Will is an ideal will—what would be willed by the people if it were willing only in the common interest, enlightened and disinterested. Even so the General Will is restricted by him to the function of making general laws. Government, involving individual acts, does not enter into its scope.[21]

Indeed any theory of absolute sovereignty is incompatible with the political liberalism of the Enlightenment. The supremacy of the interests of the people is another matter, and this indeed can be attributed to the thinkers of the Enlightenment, who were all more or less explicitly utili-

[19] *What Is the Third Estate?*, ed. S. E. Finer (London, 1963), pp. 124, 128.
[20] Alfred Cobban, "An Age of Revolutionary Wars: An Historical Parallel," *Review of Politics*, XIII (1951), 131–41.
[21] Cobban, *Rousseau and the Modern State*, pp. 71–81.

tarian in their social philosophy. The revolutionary theory of popular sovereignty only appeared when the belief that government should be in the interests of the people was fused with the principle of sovereignty, deriving from quite a different source. Eighteenth-century France learned the idea and the practice of sovereignty from the absolute monarchy. It was not difficult, when the leaders of the *Tiers Etat* made their bid for power, to envisage their aim as the transference of the sovereignty from the monarchy to the people. That this was so was tacitly acknowledged when they substituted *lèze-nation* for *lèze-majesté*.

The Revolution, thus, was inaugurated not by the application of an old political idea but by the invention of a new one. Even this might not have been so decisive if it had not been applied also in a new political and social situation, for in the last quarter of the eighteenth century romanticism and the religious revival were creating new political conditions. They gave emotional content and organic unity to the idea of the people, and so made possible the rise of what might loosely be called totalitarian thought. It is significant that even in the contemporary world, totalitarian regimes have only been successfully established in countries with strong religious orthodoxies, such as Italy, Germany, and Russia.

The end of the eighteenth century may truly be said to have witnessed a partial transition from an individualist to a collectivist view of society; but this was not a continuation of, but a break away from, the ideas of the Enlightenment. For Locke and his followers a state had been a society of individuals associated together by voluntary choice for the pursuit of common interests and ideals. Rousseau's people was a *corps moral*, that is to say an artificial body, a collection of individuals.[22] With the romantic movement the idea of the people gained historic dimensions and organic unity. It became the nation. In Lockian and enlightened thought the state had existed for the sake of the individual. Now the view began to grow that the individual existed for the sake of the nation. It was a sign of the new age when, in the first revolutionary constitution, the king of France became the *roi des Français*. The Revolution ends the age of individualism and opens that of nationalism. At the same time, politics became more emotional, now that it had to appeal to large numbers. Journalism assumed its modern role of whipping up popular passions and lowering the level of political discussion. Wars became national and therefore much more bitter. In all this can be seen not the fulfillment but the frustration of the Enlightenment. It has always been

[22] *Ibid.*, p. 69; cf. R. Derathé, *J.-J. Rousseau et la science politique de son temps* (Paris, 1950), pp. 238, 369; Appendix III, pp. 410–13.

difficult to believe that the liberal political ideas of the Enlightenment were the source of revolutionary terrorism, oligarchy, and military dictatorship. It ceases to be a problem if we realize that such developments were indeed not the result of the Enlightenment but of the new social and political trends that appeared in the last quarter of the eighteenth century.

The revolutionary period, which in the past has been most often linked with the Enlightenment, cannot be understood unless we realize that it was also the period of the romantic and conservative reaction. In the Revolution itself, historians have in recent years discovered the presence of conservative and even reactionary trends, and this has involved much rethinking and rewriting of its history. Now, being invited to think in new ways about subjects which one had thought were safely docketed and pigeonholed can be very distressing, as is shown in an article by Mr. Franklin L. Ford.[23] A lecture I gave some ten years ago suggesting the need for revisionism in revolutionary history seemed to him to cast doubt on the fundamental reality of the Revolution, and in his article Mr. Ford set out to reassert that there *was* a revolutionary age. The article is hardly likely to have a major influence on historical thought, and I would not have troubled with it if it did not also illustrate a common form of confusion which is relevant to the present discussion. To prove that there really was a French Revolution that effected revolutionary changes throughout the whole gamut of European society, Mr. Ford lists the developments of the turn of the century in literature, music, the visual arts, administration and institutions, social structure, the strategy of war, and so on. That there were these and many more changes is undeniable: they can be found in any textbook. But Mr. Ford's anxiety to rehabilitate the French Revolution led him into making the assumption that all these changes—revolutionary, counterrevolutionary, non-revolutionary—were identified with, or resulted from, the French Revolution. Therefore, the conclusion is, "In 1789, after long, confused preliminaries, the old Europe began a transformation, convulsive, bewildering, to some of the participants wildly exhilarating, to others bitterly tragic."[24]

The history of a period that is full of such a variety of currents and cross-currents is more complicated and requires a more sophisticated analysis than this simple approach allows for. For the same reason, any attempt to link the Revolution—or to be more exact any of the successive revolutions—with the Enlightenment, as a single case of cause and effect,

[23] F. L. Ford, "The Revolutionary-Napoleonic Era: How Much of a Watershed?," *American Historical Review*, LXIX (1963), 18–29.
[24] *Ibid.*, p. 29.

is unacceptable. To do this would be to distort the ideas of the Enlightenment and to reduce the history of the Revolution to a myth. It does not follow from this that we must write off the Enlightenment completely as an influence in the Revolution. Agreed that the Enlightenment had no identifiable part in causing any of the successive revolutions between 1787 and 1795, and that the revolutionary ideology of popular sovereignty ran counter to its basic political ideas, even so there was a great deal more in the Revolution than this.

To see only the principle of sovereignty in the political ideology of the revolutionaries is to ignore the strong elements of liberalism, derived from the Lockian tradition of the Enlightenment, in it. It would also be a willful disregard of patent facts to pretend that when the members of the *Etats Généraux* and the subsequent revolutionary assemblies came to Versailles, they did not bring along the effects of their education and their reading in the literature of the eighteenth century. They were inevitably the children of the Enlightenment, and if, as I have suggested, they could get little in the way of specific political theory from the *philosophes*, they could get much in the way of humanitarian ideas and legal reform. Thus, torture as an element in judicial procedure, which reached its height between the fifteenth and seventeenth centuries, was eliminated from the law and very largely from practice. Despite the opposition of powerful vested interests, the Revolution saw the inauguration of a campaign for the abolition of both slavery and the slave trade, though it only achieved success in France in 1848. Religious toleration and the extension of civic rights to non-Catholics had made some progress before the Revolution: it was carried through to completion in the course of the revolutionary secularization of the state. The codification of the laws, which the revolutionary assemblies set in hand and Napoleon completed, represents the fulfillment of an ideal of Voltaire. And, not to go into further detail, the positive creed of the Enlightenment, the search for happiness (*bonheur*) was also one end of the Revolution. "Un peuple," declared St. Just on November 29, 1792, "qui n'est pas heureux, n'a pas de patrie."

But in reaching this utilitarian ideal we have also reached the point at which the Revolution broke away from the Enlightenment. Here, Bentham and utilitarianism carried forward its true inheritance. The Revolution, meanwhile, strayed from the primrose path of enlightened happiness to the strait and narrow road of Jacobin virtue, from the principle of representative and constitutional government to the rule of an authoritarian élite, from the *philosophes'* ideal of peace to the revolutionaries' crusading war and the Napoleonic dream of conquest. Nothing could have been more alien to the Enlightenment than this transition from the ideals of democracy and peace to a policy of dictatorship and war. It has been said that the principles of the *lumières* light up the Revolution intermittently, like the beam of a lighthouse swinging round brilliantly and then disappearing. The influence of the Enlightenment cannot be disregarded in any history of the French Revolution; but the revolutionaries did not set their course by its light in the beginning, nor did they steer the ship of state into the haven of the Enlightenment in the end.

Where The Statue Stood:

Divergent Loyalties to Newton

in the Eighteenth Century

BY HENRY GUERLAC

◄◄◄◄◄◄◄◄◄◄◄◄◄ ☼ ►►►►►►►►►►►►►

I

Since I shall be speaking about Isaac Newton and shall have something to say about the interpretations placed upon his work by some scientific thinkers of the eighteenth century, I shall take my text from Voltaire, his great popularizer in France. In April, 1735, Voltaire wrote to his friend Cideville:

> Verses are hardly fashionable any longer in Paris. Everyone begins to play the mathematician and the physicist. Everyone wants to reason. Sentiment, imagination and charm are banished. I am not vexed that philosophy is cultivated, but I should not want it to become a tyrant to exclude everything else. [1]

When Voltaire wrote, science was indeed flourishing in France as never before and was rapidly becoming fashionable among men of letters. The reign of "philosophie," and of that divinization of nature Carl Becker wrote of, was presaged by this cult of natural science. More

[1] *Voltaire's Correspondence*, ed. Theodore Besterman (Geneva, 1954), Vol. 4, pp. 48–49, No. 838.

particularly, this decade marks the beginning of Newton's ascendancy over the mind of the Enlightenment. His doctrines were at last finding favor in the Academy of Sciences, hitherto wedded to the physics of Descartes and Malebranche; and by Voltaire's efforts—in his *English Letters* of 1734 and in his *Elements of the Newtonian Philosophy*, published four years later—the gospel was brought to a wider audience. Indeed, during the late thirties and the forties the French scientific community was deeply divided by the contest that raged between the partisans of Descartes and Malebranche and the young defenders of Newton's System of the World, men like Maupertuis, Clairaut, and d'Alembert. But the Newtonians soon gained the upper hand; as early as 1743 d'Alembert could call the Cartesians "a sect that in truth as much weakened today." While fifteen years later, in the second edition of his *Traité de dynamique*, he altered this phrase to read "a sect that in truth *hardly exists* today." And this more than anything indicates how swift—after a half century of neglect—was Newton's conquest of France.[2]

For this victory Voltaire—with typical exaggeration—was later to claim the principal credit.[3] In advancing this claim, Voltaire is less than fair to Maupertuis, from whom in fact he learned a good deal, and who, as early as 1732, had published an admirably clear and readable popular account of Newton's System of the World and the theory of universal gravitation.[4]

Yet Voltaire did prepare the principate of Newton, for he was one of the earliest to perceive, or to stress, the vast ideological import of Newton's scheme, and more especially of Newton's method. At the hands of the *philosophes*, when generalized and extended to other spheres, this method served as a critical instrument for the exposure of humbug, prejudice, and intellectual pretension. This "method of analysis," as it was called, was taken to be the necessary and indispensable instrument for all kinds of thinking. "Philosophy," Voltaire wrote, "consists in stopping where the torch of physical science fails us."[5]

[2] D'Alembert, *Traité de dynamique* (1st ed.; Paris, 1748), "Préface," p. v; and 2nd ed. (Paris, 1758), "Discours préliminaire," pp. v-vi. My italics.

[3] See, for example, the letter to Horace Walpole (July 15, 1768). Besterman, No. 14179.

[4] Maupertuis, *Discours sur les différentes figures des astres avec une exposition des systèmes de MM. Descartes et Newton* (Paris, 1732). For Maupertuis' assistance to Voltaire see Pierre Brunet, *Maupertuis* (2 vols.; Paris, 1929), I, 22–26; E. Sonet, *Voltaire et l'influence anglaise* (Rennes, 1926), pp. 117–18.

[5] *The Portable Voltaire*, ed. Ben Ray Redman (New York, 1949), p. 228. Cf. the passage in Voltaire's *Traité de métaphysique* cited by Cassirer: "When we cannot utilize the compass of mathematics or the torch of experience and physics, it is certain that we cannot take a single step forward." *The Philosophy of the Enlightenment*, trans. Fritz C. A. Koelln and James P. Pettegrove (Princeton, N.J., 1951), p. 12.

All this is by way of introduction. I do not propose to discuss the place of Newtonianism in the philosophy of the Enlightenment, nor ask how well the men who marched under Newton's banner actually understood him. For this you may consult the books of Carl Becker, Preserved Smith, and Ernst Cassirer, where, in the order I have named them, you will find examples of what J. A. Passmore has recently distinguished as the "polemical," the "cultural," and the "problematic" approaches to intellectual history.

Instead I propose to ask, and try to answer, questions of a different sort. What, in fact, was Newton's method, and what was his idea of science? Have we really understood it? How well did scientists of the eighteenth century understand it?

II

At the start, let me examine a familiar proposition. We usually think of modern physical science as somehow dating from the massive achievement of Newton, especially from the appearance in 1687 of his great work, the *Mathematical Principles of Natural Philosophy*. And we are accustomed to think of the eighteenth century as an age richly ornamented with men of scientific genius who were worthy of following in Newton's footsteps. Their task was to fill out and correct the details of his *System of the World*, and to extend his method and spirit to illuminate the darker corners of nature.

Not everyone agrees with this interpretation. A short time ago I read—I confess for the first time—that strange book, *La Formation de l'esprit scientifique* by the late Gaston Bachelard. I was puzzled to find him relegating the eighteenth century to what he called "the pre-scientific age." His condemnation, I discovered, was sweeping: according to Bachelard, the scientists of that age generalized too readily; their explanatory concepts were hasty and vague; their aim was too often to entertain, astound, or edify. When they experimented—like the Abbé Nollet in his famous *expériences de gala*—showmanship took over. Their writings, too, are either stuffed with irrelevant erudition, or they are chatty conversations between the "savant" and the "curieux."

Bachelard may have been a respected philosopher, yet he was certainly a bad historian. To be sure, he gives us many absurd examples of the "pre-scientific mentality" at work among eighteenth-century scientists, but these examples are taken from some of the cruder popular books, from the works of unregenerate conservatives like Father Castel, from the writings of cranks like the future "Ami du Peuple," J. P. Marat, or of curious, minor figures like the Abbé Bertholon or the Baron de Marivetz. That some of these names are unfamiliar helps me make my point. One would never know from reading Bachelard that in the company of these men there flourished physicists like d'Alembert, Coulomb, or Lagrange; astronomers like Bradley and Herschel; chemists like Joseph Black and Lavoisier; naturalists like Linnaeus and Buffon; or electrical discoverers like Benjamin Franklin. Poor Franklin is mentioned only once, and in a tone of solemn reproof, for the famous "electrical banquet" where, on the banks of the Schuylkill River "a turkey is to be killed for our dinner by the *electrical shock*, and roasted by the *electrical jack*, before a fire kindled by the *electrified bottle:* when the healths of all the famous electricians in *England, Holland, France* and *Germany* are to be drunk in *electrified bumpers*, under the discharge of guns from the *electrical battery*."[6] Bachelard is electrically shocked by this bit of whimsy.

Yet there is something in all this to give us pause. The scientific effort of the eighteenth century was incredibly diverse in character and very uneven in quality. All this, I suppose, was the price paid for the often amateur character of science, for democratizing it and making it an instrument of enlightenment.

But the leaders of French science could be as censorious as Bachelard. They did their best to distinguish between cloth of gold and fustian. They snubbed Marat (to their peril, as it turned out) and studiously ignored most of the men in Bachelard's rogues' gallery. Even Buffon was castigated by his fellow Academicians for seeking public applause, departing from scientific rigor, and mingling science with rhetoric.

The Academy of Sciences at Paris, throughout the century, it is generally agreed, represented science at its best; the ablest scientific men in France were its members or at least its correspondents. And just as the Académie Française was supposed to preserve the purity of the French language, so the Royal Academy of Sciences recognized as its prime function to set standards for what was a relatively new kind of intellectual activity.[7]

After about 1750, it was Newton's example and method which set the standard, just as earlier it had been the methodological principles of Descartes and Malebranche. The prolonged resistance to Newton during the first half of the century, and the ensuing debate between the partisans

---

[6] *Benjamin Franklin's Experiments*, ed. I. B. Cohen (Cambridge, Mass., 1941), p. 200.

[7] See, for example, *Oeuvres de Condorcet*, eds. A. Condorcet O'Connor and F. Arago, Vol. 7 (1847), pp. 295–306, esp. pp. 298–99.

of Descartes and Newton, should perhaps be viewed not so much as a contest between rival theories as a confrontation of two rival standard-bearers, of two different conceptions of science and its proper method.

The delay in accepting Newton's discoveries is otherwise inexplicable, for it was astonishingly long. Some forty years elapsed after Newton published (in 1672) his first experiments on light and color before they were accepted in France. And not until almost sixty years after the appearance of Newton's *Principia* did any scientist in France see in it much more than a display of geometrical ingenuity. These men simply did not understand what Newton was driving at.

The gulf that separated Newton from his contemporaries on the Continent— even from a man of the repute and sagacity of Christian Huygens—was far deeper, and more difficult to bridge, than we usually realize. Our usual angle of vision is principally at fault. We have the habit of thinking of Newton as the last and greatest of the Mechanical Philosophers, as one who synthesized the various ingredients prepared by his predecessors. Instead we ought to think of him as a rebel and bold innovator, as one who was nurtured by the mechanical philosophy of the seventeenth century but who was able to transcend it. A close comparison of the contrasting viewpoints is well worth making.

III

The scientific revolution of the seventeenth century, we all know, found expression in two divergent ways of understanding the natural world. One approach—essentially critical, at least at the start, and suspicious of theory—stemmed from Francis Bacon. His disciples of the New Experimental Philosophy urged a continued devotion to observation and experiment: they hoped that by exploring nature the way Bacon had proposed, they might find the "axioms" or "principles" of a new philosophy of nature. Just how this was to be done, nobody was quite sure; meanwhile they observed, experimented, and compiled "histories."

Yet a certain disenchantment with this approach is evident even among the early Fellows of the Royal Society, a body that tirelessly conjured with the name of Verulamus. In 1667 Joseph Glanvill wrote to Lady Margaret of Newcastle: "We have yet no certain theory of nature, and in good earnest, madam, all that we can hope for, as yet, is but the history of things as they are; to raise general axioms, and to make hypotheses must, I think, be the happy privilege of succeeding generations." [8]

In contrast, the Mechanical Philosophers were less circumspect. By inventing new systems of largely speculative physics, they hastened to fill the vast emptiness left by the collapse of Aristotle's imposing world scheme. Such in essence were the great "hypothetical" systems of René Descartes, of Thomas Hobbes, and Pierre Gassendi which dominated men's thinking during the whole second half of the seventeenth century. These men are spoken of as "Mechanical Philosophers" because they shared the conviction that the real world consists only of material particles, whose motions and combinations could somehow account for the properties, the qualities, of visible things.

To the late seventeenth century this was physics. It was indeed the principal function of the natural philosopher, of the physicist, to suggest plausible mechanisms, or mechanical models as we should now call them, of the "secret motions of things." Such systems need not be, indeed could not be, true in any real or absolute sense. The Mechanical Philosophers themselves were explicit about this. Descartes wrote that God has "an infinity of diverse methods" to make things appear as they do. The human mind, he added, cannot really know what method God has employed. Descartes would not have been horrified to learn of Poincaré's proof that if it is possible to represent a phenomenon by a mechanical model, then an infinity of such models is possible.

Hobbes was equally candid. The greatest part of natural philosophy, he wrote, is made up of "things that are not demonstrable" and the most that man can attain to "is to have such opinions as no certayne experience can confute, and from which can be deduced by lawful argumentation no absurdity." [9] Locke advanced similar opinions in his *An Essay Concerning Human Understanding*. Natural philosophy cannot lead to certitude, cannot really be a science, for it cannot be demonstrative. And he warns us not to adopt any hypothesis too hastily, or "take doubtful systems for complete sciences." Beware of receiving for unquestionable truths what are really but doubtful conjectures, "such [he adds] as are most (I had almost said all) of the hypotheses in natural philosophy." [10]

---

[8] Cited by Douglas Grant, *Margaret the First, A Biography of Margaret Cavendish,* 1623–1673 (London, 1957), p. 209.

[9] *Portland Manuscripts*, II, 128; Hobbes to Newcastle, July, 1636. This passage, like the previous one from Glanvill, I owe to my student, Mr. Robert Kargon, whose unpublished doctoral dissertation "Atomism from Hariot to Newton" (Ithaca, 1964) has thrown new light on the mechanical philosophers of the seventeenth century.

[10] John Locke, *An Essay Concerning Human Understanding*, Ch. IV, § 12, pp. 12–13 and Ch. IV, § 3, p. 26.

Many men in England, like Joseph Glanvill as we have seen, were despairing enough to fall back upon a crude Baconian empiricism. But others, notably Robert Boyle, sought to combine the experimental and the mechanical philosophies. Boyle, in effect, called upon Bacon, that is upon experiment, to legitimatize Descartes and Gassendi. In his long career as an investigator he was guided by a single purpose: to illustrate by physical and chemical experiments the plausibility of the corpuscular hypotheses; to use the corpuscular theories in elucidating the rare and the dense, the elasticity of air, the nature of color, and much else. Yet it is difficult to agree with Boyle's admiring *confrères* of the early Royal Society that he was really successful. His method, too, was in some respects "hypothetical."[11]

IV

It was left to Isaac Newton to discover a path to a higher certitude. At the very start of his career, while still a student at Cambridge, he hit upon the method he was to follow all his life. As his early notebooks of this period show, he had been exposed to the works of Descartes and had studied the *Physiologia* of Walter Charleton, a book that seems to have introduced him (and others in England) to the atomistic hypotheses of Gassendi. This latter brand of the mechanical philosophy had a great influence on Newton, but as far as method was concerned he resisted its blandishments. He struck out for himself, narrowed and bridled his speculative ambitions, discarded the hypothetical route, and adopted what he once called his "mathematical way." Though he may have been unaware of the fact, this was the way Galileo had followed when he insisted upon the importance of "geometrical demonstrations founded upon sense experience and very exact observations," upon the necessity of combining "manifest experiences and necessary proofs."[12]

The most often quoted of Newton's scattered statements about his method and his "mathematical way" are to be found in his later writings,

[11] That Boyle shared, and perhaps inspired, Locke's doubts concerning the degree of certainty attainable in natural philosophy is argued by James Gibson, *Locke's Theory of Knowledge and Its Historical Relations* (Cambridge, 1917), pp. 257 and 260–65.

[12] *Discoveries and Opinions of Galileo*, translated with an Introduction and notes by Stillman Drake (Garden City, N.J., 1957), p. 179. Professor Strong has written: "Newton's 'mathematical way' encompassed both experimental investigation and demonstration from principles, that is, from laws or theorems established through investigation." E. W. Strong, "Newton's Mathematical Way," *Journal of the History of Ideas*, XII (1951), 90–110.

in the appendages and asides of his major works: the "Queries" of his *Opticks*, the "Rules of Reasoning" and the "General Scholium" of the later editions of the *Principia*. He describes his method as that of "analysis and composition." Analysis, the upward route, with which one must begin, "consists in making Experiments and Observations, and in drawing conclusions from them by induction." These may serve as "causes" or "principles" or "laws." Composition—the downward synthetic route—consists in drawing out the consequences of these "principles" or "laws" by deductive inference. [13]

There was nothing original about this dual method. Indeed it was formulated as far back as the thirteenth century, if not before; in the sixteenth century it was expounded at great length by Paduan methodologists like Zabarella, and it is echoed in the writings of Galileo. Even the terms in which Newton describes his method are the ancient ones. What is important is the degree of emphasis to be placed on experiment and induction; what is new is the language in which the operations are exclusively to be expressed, the language of mathematics.

"Hypotheses," Newton wrote in the *Opticks*, "are not to be regarded in experimental philosophy." And this is elaborated in the "General Scholium" of the *Principia* in these famous words:

> I frame no hypotheses; for whatever is not deduced from the phenomena is to be called an hypothesis; and hypotheses, whether metaphysical or physical, whether of occult qualities or mechanical, have no place in experimental philosophy. [14]

But how does one arrive, by induction from observations and experiments, at "axioms," "causes," or "principles" which are more reliable than the "hypotheses" of the Mechanical Philosophers? The answer lies for Newton in his confidence in the simplicity and order of the universe. Nature, he wrote, "is wont to be simple, and always consonant to itself"; the universe is ordered by laws at once uniform and unvarying. We may therefore invoke what writers in the eighteenth century were to call "analogy," and draw forth laws of general applicability by generalizing our observations and the results of even a single well-conducted experiment. This we do with most assurance if we use the language of mathematics, for, as

[13] Sir Isaac Newton, *Opticks, or a treatise of the Reflections, Refractions, Inflections and Colors of Light, Reprinted from the Fourth Edition* (London, 1931), p. 404.

[14] Sir Isaac Newton, *Mathematical Principles of Natural Philosophy*, ed. Florian Cajori (Berkeley, Calif., 1934), p. 547.

Newton's teacher, Isaac Barrow, said in a lecture Newton probably heard, "Magnitude is the common Affection of all physical things, it is inter-woven in the Nature of Bodies, blended with all corporeal Accidents, and well nigh bears the Principal Part in the Production of every natural Effect."[15] The language of mathematics is therefore the language in which experimental results are to be set down, observations recorded, and the laws of nature best expressed. And once the laws are determined, inferences from them can be drawn, not in the fluid, imprecise language of common speech, but by using the compact symbols and the tested rules of mathematical reasoning. The way followed, therefore, in both analysis and composition is the "mathematical way," and from this the method gained its precision and power. If arguing from experiments and observations be only, as Newton put it, "the best way of arguing which the Nature of Things admits of," yet if done in the mathematical way it gains a degree of clarity and certitude which verbal discourse cannot supply.

V

Newton's method, "exact, profound, luminous and new"—the words are d'Alembert's—had of course its most dramatic application, and first demonstrated its range and power, in that noble work significantly entitled the *Mathematical Principles of Natural Philosophy*, published when Newton was in the prime of life. But it is not often remembered that all the essentials of that method were embodied in his earliest scientific contribution: the paper on light and color, read on his behalf at the Royal Society in 1672, when Newton was twenty-nine years old. The unfavorable reception accorded this classic paper reveals, as well as anything can, how strange his procedure appeared to contemporaries.

I need only remind you of the following well-known experiments. Newton set up a prism in a darkened room. A beam of sunlight from a small hole in the window shutter passed through the prism and displayed on a screen the "celebrated phenomena of colours," i.e., a solar spectrum. This well-known effect was commonly explained, in Newton's day, by assuming that some sort of essential change, a "modification" or "qualifi-cation" of the sun's white light, was produced by passage through the transparent refracting medium. But a striking quantitative disparity led

[15] Isaac Barrow, *Mathematical Lectures*, trans. John Kirkley (London, 1734), p. 21.

Newton to examine the matter closely: the colored spectrum he obtained formed a band about five times longer than it was wide. This seemed to Newton an "extravagant disproportion" that could not be explained by the well-known law of the bending or refraction of light (Snell's Law). After excluding certain disturbing factors, Newton concluded that the effect was real, and a possible explanation occurred to him. To test it, using a second prism, he carried out what he called his "experimentum crucis."

Close to and beyond the first prism, he placed a board pierced by a small hole. By rotating the first prism he could make the successive colors of the spectrum pass through the hole, to be refracted again by a second prism, and observe the result projected on a wall or screen. The rays of each given color passed through the second prism with their colors unaltered, and were refracted or bent to the same extent as before. To each colored ray, therefore, a number could be assigned: its characteristic refrangibility. And Newton wrote: "To the same degree of Refrangibility ever belongs the same colour, and to the same colour ever belongs the same degree of Refrangibility."[16] Since the rays were unaltered by the second prism he concluded that colors are not "modifications" of white light, but that solar light consists of a bundle or mixture of rays that are differently refrangible. These rays, each of which produced a characteristic sensation of color, are merely separated out by the prism. As a confirmation, he passed the rays of a complete spectrum through a biconcave lens and showed that as they are brought to a common focus, the colors fade and whiteness is produced.

Newton's paper produced a controversy that filled the pages of the *Philosophical Transactions* for successive issues. His results were criticized by Robert Hooke; by a young French Jesuit, Father Gaston Pardies; and by the greatest scientist of the day, Christian Huygens. Now all three of these critics held to some form of the "modification theory" of the cause of color; and all of them believed that light was a wave motion, or pulse, in an invisible, all-pervading ether. For this reason, modern historians have sometimes described this episode as a dispute between supporters of a wave theory and Newton, the defender of the theory that light is particulate or corpuscular in nature. This is not correct, for Newton did not explicitly defend the corpuscularity of light (he merely hinted at it

---

[16] *Isaac Newton's Papers & Letters on Natural Philosophy*, ed. I. B. Cohen (Cambridge, Mass., 1958), p. 53.

as a possibility), nor did he attempt to explain color in terms of it. The dispute turned on something far more fundamental, as we shall now see.[17]

Both Pardies and Hooke spoke of Newton's explanation of prismatic colors as his "hypothesis," a word which had many different meanings in the seventeenth century, but which Newton understood in a pejorative sense. To him it already meant a gratuitous or *a priori* assumption not scrupulously inferred from experience. This is clear from his reply to Pardies:

> In answer to this, it is to be observed that the doctrine which I explained concerning refraction and colours, consists only in certain properties of light, without regarding any hypotheses, by which those properties might be explained. For the best and safest method of philosophizing seems to be, first to inquire diligently into the properties of things, and establishing those properties by experiments and then to proceed more slowly to hypotheses for the explanation of them. For hypotheses should be subservient only in explaining the properties of things, but not assumed in determining them; unless so far as they may furnish experiments. For if the possibility of hypotheses is to be the test of the truth and reality of things, I see not how certainty can be obtained in any science; since numerous hypotheses may be devised, which shall seem to overcome new difficulties.[18]

Huygens' reaction is notably illuminating. At first he commented that Newton's theory was "very ingenious," but perhaps not convincingly supported by experiment. Later he remarked that even if the experiments could be trusted, there yet remained the great difficulty "of explaining by *mechanical* physics what causes the colors of the rays." He was unimpressed by Newton's remarkable results precisely because Newton did *not* advance a mechanical hypothesis: "He hath not taught us, what it is wherein consists the nature and difference of Colours, but only this accident (which certainly is very considerable) of their *different refrangibility*."[19]

[17] That the debate over Newton's paper was not a conflict between the corpuscular and undulatory theories of light has been pointed out by Richard Westfall in his suggestive paper "Newton and His Critics on the Nature of Colors," *Archives internationales d'histoire des sciences*, Vol. 15 (1962), pp. 47–58. I cannot, however, accept Professor Westfall's interpretation that the debate turned on the nature of qualities, on mechanical versus peripatetic language, or that Newton's first paper "was interpreted by the champions of the mechanical philosophy as a reversion to conceptions associated with the rejected philosophy."

[18] *Isaac Newton's Papers and Letters*, p. 106.

[19] *Ibid.*, p. 136. By "accident" Huygens of course means "property." Newton was by no means alone in having recourse to the old scholastic vocabulary.

Newton's point of view was obviously quite strange, and in a manner suspect, to all three men, Hooke, Pardies, and Huygens. He wished only, he insisted, to "speak of light in *general terms*, considering it abstractly" as "*something or other* propagated every way in streight lines from luminous bodies without determining what that thing is." [20] By dealing only with that ancient Greek abstraction, that mathematical entity, the light ray, he was striving for a higher certitude by considering only what he could measure and describe in the language of mathematics. It is apparent that in this early paper he had already imposed a rigid discipline upon himself and adopted the cautionary rule that hasty, gratuitous "explications" can actually block the way to scientific discovery.

The full power of Newton's "mathematical way" could scarcely reveal itself in this brilliant, but restricted, paper on light and color. He had effectively disposed of the "modification theory" of color, though he had done little else of theoretical import. It was a clever performance; but, as Huygens saw it, this was hardly the kind of approach that could lead to an understanding of the System of the World.

Yet this was precisely what Newton was later to achieve in the *Principia*, though once again his goal and his method were misunderstood. In the *Principia*, Newton showed how inadequate was Descartes' physical picture of the planets whirled about in a great solar vortex. This "hypothesis," in Newton's sense of the term, simply could not account mathematically for the elliptical orbits of planets, or for the two other laws of Kepler. On the other hand, Newton's own "mathematical way," after a display of mathematical ingenuity, led him to the observed motions, and yielded a remarkably accurate—although abstract and schematic—account of the System of the World.

But just as in his study of light and color, the underlying mechanism remained hidden. To Newton's universe, the favorite image of a great clockwork mechanism, applicable though it is to Descartes' world, is singularly inappropriate. The springs and wheels operating it are left undescribed. It was enough that mysterious forces like universal gravitation or attraction were shown by his investigations to work their wonders. To accept their reality, they need not be explained: "What I call Attraction may be perform'd by impulse, or by some other means unknown to me. I use that word here to signify only in general any Force by which

---

[20] *Ibid.*, p. 119. See also p. 106 where, in his reply to Pardies, Newton explains that by "rays of light I understand its least or indefinitely small parts, which are independent of each other; such as are all those rays which lucid bodies emit in right lines, either successively or all together."

Bodies tend towards one another, whatsoever the Cause."[21] It was enough for Newton that such forces could be measured and the laws of their action determined, just as he had been content to describe the behavior of colored rays without seeking the cause of their different colors: "For we must learn from the Phaenomena of Nature what Bodies attract one another, and what are the Laws and Properties of the Attraction, before we enquire the Cause by which the Attraction is performed."[22]

Once again, content to set forth the quantitative laws of motion and their consequences, Newton was offering an abstract mathematical description in place of the pictorial type of "explication" favored by the Mechanical Philosophers. This explains why the first criticism elicited by the *Principia*, when it became known on the Continent, was that it was a brilliant display of mathematics, but that it was not *physics* at all. This was the reaction of Christian Huygens and of the anonymous reviewer of Newton's book in the *Journal des sçavans*. As physics was then understood, these men were perfectly right. Precisely as the title of his book proclaimed, Newton was setting forth the *mathematical principles* of natural philosophy, not a natural philosophy in the accepted sense.

Newton's use of his "mathematical way" led, therefore, to a peculiar outcome of which he was quite well aware. At the base of his whole system were forces, laws, or principles—chief among them, a universal attraction—the underlying causes of which he did not, perhaps could not, visualize, and about which he was reluctant to speculate in print. Huygens —who understood Newton better than most—had merely chided him for not going far enough. Others felt he had gone too far, perhaps too far backward. They accused him of basing his whole System of the World upon something that was either an absurdity or a mystery; upon the philosophically repellant notion of action-at-a-distance; or upon an occult quality, like those Aristotelian notions that reputable physics had abandoned.

Newton, we know, was doing nothing of the kind. He was not postulating "hypothetically" his Law of Gravitation. Uncomfortable though it

---

[21] *Opticks*, p. 376.

[22] *Ibid.* Cf. *Principia*, Definition VIII, pp. 5–6, where he writes: "I . . . use the words attraction, impulse, or propensity of any sort towards a centre, promiscuously, and indifferently, one for another; considering those forces not physically, but mathematically: wherefore the reader is not to imagine by those words I anywhere take upon me to define the kind, or the manner of any action, the causes or the physical reason thereof . . . ." See also Bk. I, sec. XI, p. 164: "But these Propositions are to be considered as purely mathematical; and therefore, laying aside all physical considerations, I make use of a familiar way of speaking, to make myself the more easily understood by a mathematical reader."

was, he had inferred it from phenomena, and he had shown with what simplicity and precision it explained the observed motions of bodies. Such non-visualizable entities—if I may call them that—entities at best or only representable in equations, are a commonplace to the physicist of today. He is, for the most part, quite happy with them. What—to take an example—is entropy? What, for that matter, is an electron or a photon, entities that display both particle-like and wavelike properties. The modern physicist, being human, may sometimes wonder; but his, too, is the "mathematical way." His trust in it, his reliance upon it, is all but universal. And this reliance dates from the delayed acceptance of Newton's *Principia* and from the stormy burial of the old "hypothetical way" in the third and fourth decades of the eighteenth century. For then, by a typical group of French scientists, a mathematical positivism came to be accepted as the most secure road to the knowledge of physical nature. What Newton had carefully described as the *mathematical principles* of natural philosophy, of physics, became for many—though Newton could hardly have agreed—the ideal of physics itself.

We can illustrate this interpretation from the words of d'Alembert, one of the earliest of Newton's disciples in France. He set forth his views, about the middle of the eighteenth century, in his *Traité de dynamique* and in his widely read *Preliminary Discourse* to the *Encyclopédie*. Nature, he wrote,

> is a vast machine whose inner springs are hidden from us; we see this machine only through a veil which hides the workings of its more delicate parts from our view. . . . Doomed as we are to be ignorant of the essence and inner contexture of bodies, the only resource remaining for our sagacity is to try at least to grasp the analogy of phenomena, and to reduce them all to a small number of primitive and fundamental facts. Thus Newton, without assigning the cause of universal gravitation, nevertheless demonstrated that the system of the world is uniquely grounded on the laws of this gravitation. [23]

As Newton has shown us we can do, we extend our investigations even to those motions produced by hidden forces and causes, provided that the laws and relationships according to which these causes operate are known to us: "The knowledge or the discovery of these relationships is almost always the only goal we are allowed to reach, and consequently the only

[23] D'Alembert, *Mélanges de littérature, d'histoire et de philosophie* (4th ed.; Amsterdam, 1767), IV, 258–59.

one we should have in view." [24] By the application of mathematical calculations to experience, deducing sometimes a great number of consequences from a single observation, one can arrive at truths which closely approximate the certitude of geometrical demonstrations. For contrary to popular belief, d'Alembert reminds his reader, "The most abstract notions, those that ordinary men regard as most inaccessible, are often those that shed the brightest light." [25]

D'Alembert's message is that the frail, imperfect human mind cannot penetrate the reality of nature and is equipped only to observe, compare, and measure. It is also the message of that curious little philosophical tale of Voltaire's entitled *Micromégas*. Perhaps you remember the story. Micromégas, a giant eight leagues high, is a resident of a planet revolving around the bright star Sirius. Banished by the mufti of his planet for scientific heterodoxy, he becomes the first spaceman. Applying his knowledge of the laws of gravitation and hitchhiking on a convenient comet, he makes his way to our solar system. Here he picks up a companion, a resident of Saturn, a mere dwarf some thousand fathoms tall. Together they navigate to the earth. At first sight this ridiculous planet seems uninhabited, but at last they discern a tiny object, a ship in the Baltic sea transporting a group of philosophers and mathematicians. Struck by the ignorance these tiny insects reveal about metaphysical matters, and their lack of agreement among themselves, the two visitors pursue the conversation as follows:

> The traveller was moved to pity for the tiny human race, in which he discovered such astonishing contrasts. "Since you are of the small number of wise men," he said to these gentlemen, tell me, I pray, what you are interested in."
> "We dissect flies," said the philosopher, "we measure lines, we gather mathematical data. We are agreed on two or three points we understand, and we argue about two or three thousand we do not."
> A fancy forthwith struck the Sirian and the Saturnian to question these thinking atoms, to find out the things on which they were agreed. "What do you reckon to be the distance," asked the Saturnian, "between the Dog-star and the bright star of Gemini?"
> "Thirty-two and a half degrees," they all replied at once.
> "And what is the distance from here to the moon?"

---

[24] D'Alembert, *Discours préliminaire de l'Encyclopédie*, ed. Louis Ducros (Paris, 1893), p. 40.

[25] D'Alembert, *Discours préliminaire*, p. 45. Cf. the *Traité de dynamique* (ed. 1758), p. ii, and *Mélanges*, IV, 182–83.

"In round numbers, sixty semi-diameters of the earth."

"How much does your air weigh?" he continued, thinking to startle them. But they all told him that air weighs about nine hundred times less than an equal volume of the lightest water and nineteen thousand times less than ducat gold. The little dwarf from Saturn, astounded at their replies, was tempted to take for sorcerers these same people to whom a quarter of an hour before he had refused a soul.[26]

The positivistic view set forth by d'Alembert, and advanced in this playful fashion by Voltaire—that physical science at its best can only be a mathematical description of the interconnecting laws of nature—was widely held in eighteenth-century France. Condillac, in some ways the most respected thinker of the age and one whom the scientists were pleased to quote, held a similar opinion. The study of nature, he once wrote, should be limited to discovering the relations (*rapports*) that obtain among the objects of our experience. We cannot construct true systems of nature, for we know nothing of the elements of things, nothing, that is, of nature's underlying mechanism; we can only observe the remote effects. The best causes (*principes*) a physicist can invoke are those phenomena which, like attraction, explain other phenomena, but which themselves depend upon causes that we do not, and perhaps cannot, know.[27]

But was this Newton's own view? Would he have agreed with d'Alembert and Condillac? Was he satisfied with his abstract framework of laws and relations as the only knowledge open to the inquiring mind? I really do not think so. Behind his mathematical demonstrations and his experiments we discern the basic conceptual model of the seventeenth-century thinkers: that the underlying realities in nature are material particles in motion. In all his investigations he was guided by an atomistic philosophy of nature derived from Gassendi and Charleton; it served him invaluably as a psychological prop and a heuristic aid. We may be certain that he believed in it, though he could not demonstrate it. Yet with astonishing consistency and self-discipline he kept those beliefs from obtruding on his "scientificall" demonstrations. These beliefs are set forth for what they

[26] My translation is from Ira O. Wade, *Voltaire's "Micromégas," A Story in the Fusion of Science, Myth and Art* (Princeton, 1950), pp. 141–42. For other expressions by Voltaire of this view of science, see my article "Three Eighteenth-Century Social Philosophers," in Gerald Holton (ed.), *Science and the Modern Mind* (Boston, 1958), pp. 17–18, notes 17 and 18.

[27] *Oeuvres philosophiques de Condillac*, ed. Georges Le Roy, I (1947), 207; III (1951), 439.

were—guesses, probabilities—in the asides and discursive appendices of his serious work. We read them in the *scholia* of the *Principia*, in the famous Queries of the *Opticks*, in some letters and unpublished papers. In short, as far as was humanly possible, Newton kept his science (as we would call it) wholly separate from his speculative natural philosophy. [28]

What, then, did Newton think he was doing, if he did not believe that his "mathematical way" was giving birth to a new physics? I should like to urge a new and perhaps radical interpretation. I suggest that he was preparing the way for, setting the stage for, a new natural philosophy, not wholly unlike those he had attacked. With his abstract, mathematical scheme of laws he believed himself to be marking the boundary conditions for this new natural philosophy, supplying a frame or scaffolding which later generations would fill in and to which they would give substance. The title of Newton's great book, to refer to it once again, is eminently revealing: what he is setting forth are only the *mathematical principles* of natural philosophy. But that philosophy itself is still to come, the work of other hands, though here and there Newton offers hints and suggestions as to what it may contain. This, I believe, is what the famous Queries of the *Opticks* are all about. The speculations and guesses we find there were intended to be so many signposts for later workers. By contrast, what he gave the world in the body of his scientific work was like the steel frame of some great building. The mathematical laws of optics and celestial mechanics are the girders and supporting members; other men will come with the bricks, the mortar, and the cut stone to fill in the walls and lay out the partitions. According to what rules did he feel this should be done? Surely, we must imagine, by following the methodological precepts of "experimental philosophy" as he is at pains to set them forth at the end of the 31st Query. But one thing at least seems certain. The new building, the new Temple of Natural Philosophy, must be erected here, within his framework, inside the boundaries he had marked out by his mathematical laws, and not elsewhere, at some point far afield among the infinite possibilities of which Descartes had written.

We should not be surprised, therefore, that Newton's achievement received various and conflicting interpretations in the course of the eighteenth century, that it was called upon to support quite different methodological and epistemological principles. Cassirer, it seems to me, is much too sweeping when he writes that the ideal of a mechanical philosophy of

[28] D'Alembert was fully aware of the speculative dimension of Newton's thought, an aspect which Newton "abstained almost completely from speaking of in his best known writings" (*Discours préliminaire*, p. 107).

nature "was gradually superseded until it was finally abandoned entirely by the epistemologists of modern physics."[29] By no means every thinker of the age felt that the physicist "must finally give up trying to explain the mechanism of the universe" and that "he has done enough if he succeeds in establishing definite general relations in nature." Certain men—like some of the odd persons Bachelard mentions in his book, or like the Baron d'Holbach in his *System of Nature*—understood Newton not at all, though they sometimes invoked his name. Others, for example the Dutch methodologists and such English and American scientists as Stephen Hales, Joseph Black, Joseph Priestley, and Benjamin Franklin, saw in Newton the advocate of an experimental philosophy by which men can, with some speculative license, penetrate into the inner workings of material nature. It is this tradition, we might well recall, that culminates, soon after the century's close, in John Dalton's atomic theory. For such men, the hints in the Queries were so many delphic utterances, so many clues to be patiently pursued. Indeed, they seem to have read Newton's program more truly than those we think of as the rigorous Newtonians, than d'Alembert and the other advocates of a positivistic view of science that Newton almost certainly never envisaged.

[29] Cassirer, *Philosophy of the Enlightenment*, pp. 53–54.

Index